THE SANCTITY OF LIFE AND THE CRIMINAL LAW

Described by the *New York Times* as 'Britain's foremost scholar of criminal law', Professor Glanville Williams was one of the greatest academic lawyers of the twentieth century. To mark the centenary of his birth in 2011, leading criminal law theorists and medical law ethicists from around the world were invited to contribute essays discussing the sanctity of life and criminal law while engaging with Williams' many contributions to these fields. In re-examining his work, the contributors have produced a provocative set of original essays that make a significant contribution to the current debate in these areas.

DENNIS J. BAKER is a lecturer in law at King's College London.

JEREMY HORDER is Edmund-Davies Professor of Criminal Law at King's College London.

THE SANCTITY OF LIFE AND THE CRIMINAL LAW

The Legacy of Glanville Williams

Edited by

DENNIS J. BAKER

and

JEREMY HORDER

CAMBRIDGE
UNIVERSITY PRESS

CAMBRIDGE
UNIVERSITY PRESS

University Printing House, Cambridge CB2 8BS, United Kingdom

Cambridge University Press is part of the University of Cambridge.

It furthers the University's mission by disseminating knowledge in the pursuit of
education, learning and research at the highest international levels of excellence.

www.cambridge.org
Information on this title: www.cambridge.org/9781107536241

© Cambridge University Press 2013

First published 2013
First paperback edition 2015

A catalogue record for this publication is available from the British Library

Library of Congress Cataloguing in Publication data
The legacy of Glanville Williams, criminal law and the sanctity of life / edited by
Dennis J. Baker and Jeremy Horder.
pages cm
Includes index.
ISBN 978-1-107-02047-4
1. Williams, Glanville Llewelyn, 1911– 2. Criminal law – Philosophy. 3. Law and
ethics. 4. Criminal law – Great Britain – Philosophy. 5. Law teachers – England –
Biography. I. Baker, Dennis J., editor of compilation II. Horder, Jeremy, editor of
compilation III. Williams, Glanville Llewelyn, 1911– honoree.
KD632.W55L44 2013
345.410092–dc23
2012029785

ISBN 978-1-107-02047-4 Hardback
ISBN 978-1-107-53624-1 Paperback

CONTENTS

CONTRIBUTORS

ANDREW ASHWORTH
QC, DCL, FBA, Vinerian Professor of English Law, All Souls College, University of Oxford.

JOSHUA DRESSLER
Frank R. Strong Chair in Law, Moritz College of Law, Ohio State University.

ANTJE DU BOIS-PEDAIN
Senior Lecturer, Faculty of Law, University of Cambridge.

ANTONY DUFF
FBA, FRSE, Professor of Philosophy, Department of Philosophy, University of Minnesota.

GEORGE P. FLETCHER
Cardozo Professor of Jurisprudence, Law School, Columbia University.

PETER GLAZEBROOK
Fellow emeritus, Jesus College, University of Cambridge.

JOHN KEOWN
Rose F. Kennedy Professor in Christian Ethics, Georgetown University.

PENNEY LEWIS
Professor of Law, School of Law, King's College London.

MICHAEL S. MOORE
Charles R. Walgreen, Jr. Chair, Professor of Law, Professor of Philosophy, Professor in the Center for Advanced Study, Co-Director

of the Program in Law and Philosophy, College of Law, University of Illinois.

PAUL H. ROBINSON
Colin S. Diver Professor of Law, Law School, University of Pennsylvania.

A. P. SIMESTER
Professor of Law, National University of Singapore and Senior Research Fellow, Institute of Criminology, University of Cambridge.

A. T. H. SMITH
Professor of Law, Pro Vice-Chancellor and Dean of Law, Victoria University, New Zealand.

JOHN STANTON-IFE
Senior Lecturer in Law, School of Law, King's College London.

SIR ROGER TOULSON
Lord Justice, Court of Appeal, England and Wales.

PREFACE

This Festschrift marks the 100th anniversary of the birth of Glanville Williams, QC, LLD, FBA in 2011. The chapters herein were presented at a conference hosted by King's College London in 2011. The conference was initiated to celebrate the legacy of Williams, which is as significant as that left by giants such as Sir Edward Coke, Sir Matthew Hale and Sir James Fitzjames Stephen. In the twenty-first century Williams continues to collect citations in court reports and law reviews at a pace that many living academics can only envy. The Supreme Court of the United States, the Federal Circuit Courts in the United States, the Supreme Court of the United Kingdom, the Supreme Court of Canada, the High Court of Australia, the Supreme Court of New Zealand and numerous provincial and state appellate courts in those jurisdictions continue to draw on his ideas. (A rough citation count in the leading legal databases shows that he has thousands of citations – and plenty of those have a 2012 date.) His influence was as good as it gets for a legal academic.

An amusing story not covered by Peter Glazebrook in his biographical note, is that of the Australian comedian (Campbell McComas) who impersonated Glanville Williams in 1976. McComas dressed up as Williams and gave a hoax lecture at Monash University in Melbourne. Legend has it that approximately 450 academics and students attended the hoax lecture. Many of those attending were convinced that McComas was Williams, until McComas ended the lecture with the words: 'thank you for having me, but you have been had'.

This volume focuses on Williams' work in criminal law and medical law ethics. It is worth noting in passing that he also made significant contributions in the law of tort and in general jurisprudence. As his work and expertise in criminal law dominated his career, this book contains more chapters on criminal law than it does on medical law. Criminal law may have dominated his work, but his most controversial work was in medical ethics. In 1997, the *New York Times* reported of his *Sanctity of Life* that: 'It analyses laws against abortion, contraception, artificial insemination, euthanasia and other practices. One reviewer wrote, "His viewpoint, based on reason and human need rather than tradition and eschatology, is unfailingly convincing."'

The book contains original chapters from leading criminal law theorists and medical law ethicists from a number of countries. The contributors discuss central topics in contemporary criminal law and medical law while engaging with Williams' many contributions to those fields. By bringing together contributors from both the criminal law and medical law fields, this collection seeks to make a significant contribution to the current state of theoretical debate in those fields.

The chapters

Given the number of chapters, and bearing in mind the need to keep the volume within certain space bounds, we have resisted the temptation to write an introductory chapter. Instead, we provide a précis of the collection here. All the chapters are stand-alone contributions in that they contain introductions, conclusions and independent theses, so we will keep our comments as brief as possible. Chapter 1 is a biographical note from Peter Glazebrook, which sheds some light on Williams' personality and personal life. Glazebrook also draws attention to Williams' most significant achievements and some of the significant legal debates in which Glanville Williams was involved. In a similar vein, George Fletcher reflects on the core legal debates in criminal law during the Williams era. Fletcher revisits topics such as consent and *mens rea*, acts and omissions, and justification/excuse among others. Chapter 2 encapsulates the legal thinking of the time and draws together the past, present and potential future debates in the criminal law with reference to Williams' thinking on these topics. From Fletcher's chapter it is easy to get a very good historical sense of how a number of current debates evolved and how things might change in the future. In Chapter 3, Andrew Ashworth analyses the justice of preventive orders by re-examining Williams' classic 1953 paper on bind-over powers. Ashworth argues that Williams' critique of bind-over powers has had an enduring effect.

Following Ashworth's contribution are two chapters that, at the margins, touch on some common themes: the first is by Michael Moore and the second is by Paul Robinson. In Chapter 4, Moore considers the distinctions between the general and special parts of the criminal law, and asks how those distinctions should be conceived. Moore tries to ascertain whether anything can be gained by identifying a fruitful distinction between these parts of the criminal law. He also outlines the potential content of the general part. Meanwhile, in Chapter 5 Robinson argues that Glanville Williams, while a pioneer in his time, adopted a fairly traditional approach when it came to the structure for organising criminal law doctrines. For instance, even though Williams was aware of the justification–excuse distinction, he rejected it as an organising principle because he did not regard it as having practical value. Robinson aims to demonstrate that there are meaningful practical benefits that can flow from recognising such distinctions. Paul Robinson draws attention to four core distinctions that Williams did not make to show that there is great practical value in investigating the interrelation among doctrines.

In Chapter 6, Joshua Dressler examines the defence of necessity with reference to the famous case *The Queen* v. *Dudley and Stephens*. Dressler considers this case in terms of the justification–excuse distinction (considered by Robinson in Chapter 5), a distinction in terms which Williams never considered. Dressler analyses the case with a view to drawing a distinction between the question of whether extreme circumstances can justify a purposeful killing of an innocent person, and the arguably separate question of whether an unjustifiable purposeful killing might nonetheless be excusable. Dressler submits that the failure to recognise this type of killing as excusable mis-shaped the law of necessity and duress. He takes the view that if Williams had recognised some forms of unjustifiable killing as excusable, he might have been able to influence appropriate law reform.

Following Dressler's chapter there are two chapters on the fault element. The first, Chapter 7, is by Antony Duff. Duff considers intention in the wider sense, including what is termed as oblique intention, and argues that it should not be assumed that we can provide a clear, coherent set of criteria for the application of intention that precedes, and is independent of, any normative conception of criminal responsibility and liability. Rather, it should be recognised that intention functions, especially when so-called oblique intention is in issue, as a 'thick' normative concept. Consequently, disagreements and doubts are to be expected when we argue about the proper applications of such concepts. The second chapter on culpability is by Andrew Simester. Chapter 8 examines the role of culpability in establishing criminal liability. He observes that the conventional view is that criminal liability must rest upon a finding of fault, and he seeks to defend that view. Simester aims to shed light on the role that the fault elements play in establishing liability.

Following these two chapters we have two chapters on unrelated issues. Chapter 9, by John Stanton-Ife, examines the theoretical and doctrinal limits of consent in sexual relations involving mentally disordered participants. Stanton-Ife takes the view that a mentally disordered person's consent to sexual activity should be treated as valid (as long as he or she is not being exploited) where it is based on innate human desire and sexual need. Meanwhile, in Chapter 10 Sir Roger Toulson explores a number of core problems in the law of joint enterprise complicity in the twenty-first century. Sir Roger provides a good historical account of how the law evolved. A core argument put forward is that this form of complicity is based on a broad theory of causation. Sir Roger also discusses the law governing whether, and if so when, a participant in a joint enterprise might be liable for manslaughter rather than murder. He observes that the law used to allow for a manslaughter verdict whether or not V's death was foreseen by D. However, D would have been guilty of murder if, but only if, he had the *mens rea* for murder. But the law changed with the decisions of the Privy Council in *Chan Wing-Sui* and of the House of Lords in *Powell and English*. Under the current law D could be liable for murder as long as he foresaw that the perpetrator might kill or cause serious injury to V. D might be able to show that he had no such foresight if it can be demonstrated that 'P's act in killing the victim was fundamentally different from anything foreseen by D'. If foresight of P's actions and their consequences is not established, D will not be guilty of either murder or manslaughter even though he took part in an attack, which carried a risk that someone might be killed that a reasonable person would have found to be patently obvious. Sir Roger is critical of this development as it allows the participant to go completely unpunished where some censure seems appropriate.

In the final part of the volume we have a collection of chapters on the sanctity of life. These start with Chapter 11 by John Keown. Keown revisits the classic debate on euthanasia between Williams and Kamisar. Keown argues that the Williams versus Kamisar debate has served to frame the public policy debate on euthanasia to this day. Kamisar also criticises Williams' argument that voluntary euthanasia can be effectively policed by the law. The core problem is that Williams' proposed legislative reforms would have resulted in the system relying too heavily on the 'good sense' of a doctor. Keown argues that this would not have provided a sufficient safeguard. Meanwhile, in Chapter 12 Penney Lewis examines whether the defence of necessity has brought about legal change on assisted dying in the common law world. Lewis concludes that Glanville Williams' proposal to use the defence of necessity as a means for defending homicide charges in euthanasia cases has not been taken up. Chapter 13 by Antje du Bois-Pedain focuses on the duty to preserve life and its limits in English criminal law. Du Bois-Pedain provides a philosophical re-thinking of that duty. The final chapter is by A. T. H. Smith. Tony Smith worked very closely with Glanville Williams in Cambridge, so it seems fitting to end the collection with his chapter. Chapter 14 gives us further insight into Williams and the state of debate in criminal law before and during the period in which he worked as a scholar. He also provides some valuable insights into the vocation of professing law.

Dennis J. Baker
Jeremy Horder

Glanville Llewelyn Williams 1911–1997: a biographical note*

PETER GLAZEBROOK

When, in 1957, at the age of 46, Glanville Williams was elected a Fellow of the Academy, his name had long been a byword among both practising and academic lawyers throughout the English-speaking world as that of its sharpest, most radically critical and most prolific living jurist. He had published three monographs on complex and detective aspects of the common law of obligations, whose originality, sophistication, penetration, breadth of reference, historical acuity, and analytical and critical clarity had set new standards for legal writing in this area. He had been the first to demonstrate how the techniques of linguistic analysis could be used to expose the emptiness of much jurisprudential debate and the irrationality of many a legal distinction. And he had capped all this with (what in its second edition was) a 900-page treatise on the general principles underlying the criminal law, which not only marked a fundamental change of direction in his own work, but also transformed the study of that subject, setting the agenda in it for several decades, and had led to his appointment as the only foreign Special Consultant for the American Law Institute's great project for a Model Penal Code. He had gone on, following paths first trodden by Jeremy Bentham, to appraise, and find wanting, many of the sacred cows of the English way of administering criminal justice, equalling his mentor in critical rigour and in the disdain shown for 'Judge & Co.', but writing infinitely more readable prose that re-ignited debates which still continue. He had also made a pioneering and outspoken study of the lengths to which Anglo-American law went to protect human life that would be seen as a seminal text when, nearly two decades later, medical law and ethics began to attract the attention of English law faculties. There had, moreover, been

* Reprinted from *Proceedings of the British Academy: Biographical Memoirs of Fellows*, I.

very few years in which he had not published half a dozen or more papers unravelling doctrinal complexities or critically analysing, often with iconoclastic zeal, judicial decisions and parliamentary legislation. And he had written a best-selling guide for aspiring law students which for half a century was for almost all of them to be their first introduction to their chosen profession. On top of all this, he had been active in the cause of law reform as polemicist, committee member and draftsman.

His election to the Academy could not, therefore, be said to have been premature. He was then a Fellow, and Director of Studies in Law, of Jesus College, Cambridge and Reader in English Law in the university. But he had already held two chairs in the University of London (the first at the London School of Economics, the second at the age of 39 its senior law chair, that of the Quain Professor of Jurisprudence at University College), and he was to hold two more at Cambridge (initially one of the university's first 'personal' chairs, and then the Rouse Ball Professorship of English Law). On reaching retirement age – he never, of course, really retired – he was rightly acclaimed by another member of the Academy, Sir Rupert Cross, Vinerian Professor at Oxford, as 'without doubt the greatest English criminal lawyer since Stephen'.[1]

I

Born on 15 February 1911, Glanville Williams was the son of Benjamin Elwy Williams of Bridgend, Glamorgan, and his wife Gwladys, daughter of David Llewelyn of Pontypridd. His father, who came from a long line of modest, chapel-going, Carmarthenshire and Cardiganshire farmers, was then a partner in a local firm of tailors. His mother had been a primary school teacher.

The infant was precocious. There was no stage of baby language. On his first visit, aged three, to the dentist, hearing that a milk tooth was to be extracted, he looked up in alarm and asked 'Is it imperative?' An only child, with poor health, sometimes confined to bed, who was uncomfortable in large groups, preferring the companionship of a few close friends,

---

[1] 'The Reports of the Criminal Law Commissioners (1833–1849) and the Abortive Bills of 1853', in P. R. Glazebrook, *Reshaping the Criminal Law* (London: Sweet & Maxwell, 1978), pp. 5, 20. The reference is to Sir James Fitzjames Stephen (1829–1894), author of *A General View of the Criminal Law of England* (London: Macmillan, 1863), *A History of the Criminal Law*, 3 vols (1883) and *A Digest of the Criminal Law* (London: Macmillan, 1877), who drafted a Criminal Code, which, though it received the blessing of a Royal Commission, was not enacted in England, but was adopted elsewhere in the Empire.

he developed his own interests and games. He built an elaborate model theatre, with performing puppets, and became a sufficiently competent conjuror to perform at school entertainments. Family holidays were often spent on the beautiful Glamorgan coast at Ogmore, where a neighbouring cottage was occupied by the young family of the Reverend William Evans, who (as Wil Ifan) was to be crowned bard at the National Eisteddfod. During the day, the children played on the long empty stretches of sand, exploring the rock pools and caves; in the evenings the two families read verse and prose to one another. These holidays left lasting impressions and life-long loves both of the country-side and of the classical poets, novelists and essayists of these islands.

At twelve, he went, with a scholarship, to Cowbridge Grammar School as a boarder. Dogged by a weak chest, he spent almost as much time in the school sanatorium as he did in the classroom, he nonetheless won a classical scholarship to the University College of Wales at Aberystwyth, to which he went aged 16, in 1927, living (in view of his age and frail health) at the home of his uncle Sir William Llewelyn Davis, Librarian of the National Library of Wales, a Celtic scholar and author of two Welsh grammars. His uncle's efforts to make him a Welsh speaker – his father, as a Carmarthen man, was bilingual but his mother was not – were, however, unavailing. Throughout his life Glanville remained unmoved by the claims of either Welsh nationalism or the Welsh language.

His four years at Aberystwyth were formative ones. (The first, before he turned to Law, was spent on Latin, English, Philosophy and History.) The Law Department, under the charismatic Professor T. A. Levi was, in that interwar period, a remarkable legal nursery. Among the students were a future lord chancellor, two law lords, a bevy of other judges and more than half-a-dozen professors of law, while several of the lecturers were also to have distinguished careers elsewhere. A First, and a scholar-ship, was to take him as an affiliated (i.e., graduate) student to St John's College, Cambridge, where the Law Fellows were Stanley Bailey (who had lectured at Aberystwyth) and Sir Percy Winfield. Winfield was to supervise his PhD research – after another First (Division 1), with an outstanding paper in Legal History, in the Law Tripos in 1933 – and to secure his election as a Research Fellow of the college in 1936.

While at Aberystwyth the law student had invented an alphabetical shorthand system for taking lecture notes. He patented it (as 'Speedhand') and compiled a manual,[2] and it was long taught in

---

[2] 1st edn, 1952, 8th edn, 1980.

secretarial schools in Britain and South Africa. He also learnt to play golf on the finely sited course at Harlech and (under the tutelage of members of his uncle's staff) to bind books. Both hobbies were pursued for many years. More significantly, he was active in the university's vibrant pacifist movement, becoming President of the University of Wales branch of the League of Nations Society and representing it at a League conference in the United States in 1931.

II

For all lawyers, whatever their specialism, Glanville's name (and for many, even beyond the circle of friends and colleagues, this was both a sufficient and the customary appellation) is now inseparable from the criminal law. But it was the law of civil obligations, and particularly the law of torts – which governs the payment of compensation for injuries to a person, property, business interests and reputation – on which he cut his scholarly teeth, and established his formidable reputation.[3] Torts lawyers long mourned his desertion of their subject. His PhD dissertation was on 'The History of Tortious Liability for Animals'. It was completed in little more than two and a half years, during which time he also sat the Bar exams. Its examiners (Sir William Holdsworth and Winfield) not only recommended that 'in view of its exceptional merit' the oral examination should be dispensed with, but each also went on to say that if only the dissertation had been in print and its author of sufficient standing, they would have recommended the award of the LLD. 'The minute study of the authorities, of all periods, printed and manuscript', reported Holdsworth, 'the grasp of principle which he has shown, and his power to criticise the rules and principles which he has expounded, make his thesis an admirable example of the manner in which legal history ought to be studied and applied. It is obvious that it is only a lawyer of very remarkable ability who could turn out a piece of this kind.'[4] The examiners' sole complaint was of the severity of the candidate's criticisms of the illogical reasons offered by judges for decisions that produced practically convenient results. They were, however, mistaken in thinking that increasing age would remedy this trait.

---

[3] See generally, B. A. Hepple, 'Glanville Williams 1911–1997: Civil Obligations', *Cambridge Law Journal*, 56 (1997), 440–5.
[4] Cambridge University archives.

The dissertation was expanded to become *Liability for Animals. An account of the development and present law of tortious liability for animals, distress damage feasant and the duty to fence in Great Britain, Northern Ireland and the common-law Dominions,* published by Cambridge University Press in 1939[5] and greeted as 'one of the best legal treatises' to be published 'in England'.[6] The subject is fascinating and complex, presenting problems which go to the heart of notions of legal responsibility and have demanded solutions ever since the human race began to keep animals for its own purposes and to look to tribunals for the settlement of its disputes. For it is the animals, not the humans, who do the damage, and they have wills of their own. Yet taking it out on them, though it has in various societies and at various times been done, affords those whom they have harmed rather limited satisfaction. And the arrival on the scene of motor vehicles had added one more problem: hitherto there had been no reason why animals and humans should not share the highways on more or less equal terms. Although a modern law, the author argued, ought to be based on negligence, penetrating historical analysis[7] explained how and why so much liability without fault had survived.

Someone who could, in his mid-twenties, handle such a wide-ranging topic in so masterly a fashion was clearly going to be a jurist to be reckoned with, as a 1938 paper on the 'Foundations of Tortious Liability'[8] had also signalled. Two generations of grand old men (including his own research supervisor) had, he argued, all got it wrong. The law of torts was neither founded on a single general principle that was subject to exceptions, as some of them had concluded, nor was it, as others said, simply a host of single instances. Rather there were several general rules of, and also several general exceptions to, liability, together with stretches of disputed territory. A further sixty years of hard-fought debate, judicial and academic, has confirmed the accuracy of this analysis.

Plans for a year at the Harvard Law School were frustrated by the onset of war in 1939. He registered as a Conscientious Objector and, being (in

---

[5] The Syndics (of Cambridge University Press), having noted the receipt of several grants in aid of publication (and gravely underestimated sales) magnanimously agreed to bear the 'remaining losses'.

[6] Dean Cecil Wright of Toronto, *Canadian Bar Review,* 17 (1939), 613, 615.

[7] Which 'represents an important stage in the development of our knowledge' of the emergence of the action on the case: M. J. Prichard, '*Scott* v. *Shepard* (1773) and the Emergence of the Tort of Negligence', Selden Society Lecture (1976), p. 35.

[8] *Cambridge Law Journal,* 7 (1939), 111.

the event unnecessarily) well-stocked with arguments for his interview
with the tribunal, was without ado allotted to civil defence work and
encouraged to continue teaching law, which he was to do in the company
of a handful of the elderly, the medically unfit and of refugees from
Germany. His jurisprudence lectures are remembered by its briefly
sojourning students (and those of the evacuated LSE) as a bright spot in
a muted Cambridge. He continued, too, to act as a 'Poor Man's Lawyer'
(Legal Aid still lay in the future), and to help with the Society of Friends'
club for refugees. No new university appointments were being made and
when his Research Fellowship and University Assistant Lectureship
expired in 1941, he combined practice at the Bar[9] – for the rest of his
life he was to marvel at how little law many very successful barristers knew,
and even then how often they got that little wrong – with *ad hoc* law
teaching and, during the long vacations, work on a fruit farm.

Among the many legal problems exposed by the outbreak of war
was the unsatisfactory state of the law governing contracts whose performance had for that or any other reason become impossible. It
remained as the litigation engendered by the First World War had left
it. Glanville edited, and added to, a monograph[10] written by one of his
contemporaries as a research student who had returned to New Zealand
to practise law there. And when the *Law Reform (Frustrated Contracts)
Act 1943* was enacted he wrote a Commentary on it,[11] which said,
elegantly, almost all that has ever needed saying. As H. C. Gutteridge
noted:

> No one who consults this commentary can fail to be impressed by the
> depth of [the author's] learning and by the amazing versatility which he
> displays. Nothing seems to have escaped his attention. In fact [he] has at
> times allowed his flair for incisive criticism to get the upper hand of him
> so that it becomes a little difficult to distinguish between his expository
> conclusions and his views as to what Parliament ought to have done or
> the draftsman should have said.[12]

Having shown his paces as both lawyer and legal historian, Glanville
was next to demonstrate his skill as a legal philosopher. A five-part

---

[9] In Walter Raeburn KC's chambers in King's Bench Walk.
[10] R. G. McElroy, *Impossibility of Performance: a Treatise on the Law of Supervening
     Impossibility of Performance of Contract, Failure of Consideration and Frustration*, ed.
     with additional chapters by G.I.W. (Cambridge University Press, 1971).
[11] *The Law Reform (Frustrated Contracts) Act 1943* (1944) and (1943), *Modern Law
     Review*, 7 (1944), 66.
[12] *Law Quarterly Review*, 61 (1945), 97.

article, 'Language and the Law',[13] and a paper, 'International Law and the Controversy concerning the word "Law"',[14] which, but for wartime publishing difficulties, might well have appeared together as a monograph, were the first serious attempt to apply the philosophical technique of linguistic analysis to law and jurisprudence. In the paper on international law, he sharply attacked the many jurists and international lawyers who had debated whether international law was 'really' law. They had been wasting everyone's time, for the question was not a factual one, the many differences between municipal and international law being undeniable, but was simply one of conventional verbal usage, about which individual theorists could please themselves, but had no right to dictate to others. This approach was to be refined and developed by H. L. A. Hart in the last chapter of *The Concept of Law* (1961), which showed how the use in respect of different social phenomena of an abstract word like 'law' reflected the fact that these phenomena each shared, without necessarily all possessing in common, some distinctive features. Glanville had himself said as much when editing a student text on jurisprudence,[15] and he had adopted essentially the same approach to 'The Definition of Crime'.[16]

In 'Language and the Law', he ranged more widely, taking as his starting point C. K. Ogden's and I. A. Richards' *The Meaning of Meaning* (1923). He showed, with examples from a vast variety of legal rules and decisions, and references to a host of juristic debates, that the resolution of legal and jurisprudential questions called for careful attention not just to the different meanings and uncertainties attaching to almost all words, but to (at least six) different sorts of meaning, behind which value judgments almost always lie concealed. It was with these, rather than verbal distinctions and semantic issues, that the jurist should be primarily concerned. The mistakes of supposing, for instance, that abstract concepts could usefully be discussed otherwise than in regard to 'concrete referents', that law had an existence other than as a 'collection of symbols capable of evoking ideas and emotions, together with the ideas and emotions so evoked', that uncertainties in the meaning of words could be eliminated by technical legal definitions, that there were any 'single' facts to which single terms could be applied, and that

---

[13] *Law Quarterly Review*, 61 (1945), 71–86, 179–95, 293–303, 384–406; *Law Quarterly Review*, 62 (1946), 387–406; supplemented by 'A Lawyer's Alice', *Cambridge Law Journal*, 9 (1946), 171–84.

[14] *British Yearbook of International Law*, 22 (1945), 146–63.

[15] Sir John Salmond, *Jurisprudence*, 10th edn (London: Sweet & Maxwell, 1947), p. 33.

[16] *Current Legal Problems*, (1955), 107–30.

distinguishing between the 'substance' and the 'quality' of a thing, or between a person's 'identity' and 'attributes' could resolve legal problems,[17] were all ruthlessly exposed, as was the claim of the extreme logical positivists that ethical, and therefore legal, statements were meaningless. As Hart said, 'these articles not only sweep away much rubbish, but also contribute much to the understanding of legal reasoning'.[18]

Many of their arguments were incorporated and developed in an edition of Sir John Salmond's classic student textbook on *Jurisprudence*,[19] many pages of which were extensively revised or rewritten, marking out ground which others were later to till. A key theme (sections IV–VI) of Hart's influential lecture 'Definition and Theory in Jurisprudence' (1953) was foreshadowed in the treatment of the juristic controversy as to whether legal corporations were to be regarded as 'real' or 'fictitious' persons.[20] Glanville's concentration on legal rules and rulings did, however, lead him to exaggerate the arbitrariness of ordinary linguistic usage, and so to underestimate the connections that underlie it, with the result that these writings had more influence among lawyers than philosophers.[21]

In 1945, his wartime connection with the LSE solidified with his appointment as Reader in English Law there. He became Professor of Public Law the following year. He did his duty by the title of his chair[22] with (among several other papers) a scathing denunciation of the shabby reasoning offered by the law lords for holding that William Joyce ('Lord Haw-Haw'), a US citizen of Irish birth, owed allegiance to the British Crown, and so had committed treason when he broadcast for the Germans during the war.[23] And he wrote another elegant commentary on another

---

[17] Elaborated on in a classic article: 'Mistake as to Party in the Law of Contract', *Canadian Bar Review*, 23 (1945), 271–92, 380–416. Later examples of this genre are 'Forgery and Falsity', *Criminal Law Review* (1974), 71 (demonstrating the fatuity of a general defence of forgery) and 'The Logic of "Exceptions"', *Cambridge Law Journal*, 47 (1988), 261.

[18] 'Philosophy of Law and Jurisprudence in Britain (1945–52)', *American Journal of Comparative Law*, 2 (1953), 354, at p. 361.

[19] See above n. 15. The editor's alterations and rewriting are listed in Appendix V.

[20] At p. 330.

[21] Cf. J. Wisdom, *Philosophy: Metaphysics and Psycho-Analysis* (Oxford: Blackwell, 1953), pp. 249–54, which shows that Wisdom had not read the papers of which he was so critical with any care.

[22] S. A. de Smith's classic, *Judicial Review of Administrative Action*, 1st edn (London: Stevens, 1959), 5th edn (London: Sweet & Maxwell, 1999), began as a PhD dissertation under his supervision.

[23] 'The Correlation of Allegiance and Protection', *Cambridge Law Journal*, 10 (1948), 54–76.

reforming statute, the Crown Proceedings Act 1947,[24] in which Parliament had at last recognised both that the immunity of the Crown (i.e., government departments) from civil suit could no longer be justified, and that legal fictions were not the right way to the outcomes which justice required. His principal interest still lay, however, in the darkest areas of private law. The immensely obscure and (as he demonstrated) gravely defective rules governing cases where a legal obligation is owed, or harm has been caused, by more than one person, were made the subject of two complementary treatises[25] totalling over 700 pages, which half a century later had not been replaced. The 'great analytical and dialectical ability'[26] displayed in them was admired by judge[27] and jurist alike.[28]

It was not until the early 1960s that Glanville, then in his fifties, decided to devote himself single-mindedly to the criminal law. But it is in what Professor B. A. Hepple has described as his 'astounding' Inaugural Lecture as Quain Professor in 1951 on 'The Aims of the Law of Tort'[29] that his work in private law may be seen to culminate.

> This has never been bettered as an account of the social function or *raison d'être* of the law of tort, in particular the action for damages ... He concluded that there was a lack of coherence with the law ... trying to serve a multiplicity of purposes but succeeding in none ...[30] The future student of the intellectual history of this branch of the law may place him at the end of one period of legal scholarship and the beginning of another. He brought the 'scientific' positivism of early twentieth-century scholars, such as Salmond and Winfield, to its apotheosis, but his utilitarian concerns with the wider purposes and policies of the law were a harbinger of the socio-legal revolution in legal scholarship which began in the late 1960s.[31]

III

Criminal Law: The General Part, first published in 1953, with a second edition in 1961, stands high in the list of great books written about English

---

[24] *Ibid.*
[25] *Joint Obligations: A Treatise on Joint and Joint and Several Liability in Contract, Quasi-contract and Trusts* (1949) and *Joint Torts and Contributory Negligence: A Study of Concurrent Fault in Great Britain, Ireland and the Common Law Dominions* (1951).
[26] Lord Wright, *Law Quarterly Review*, 66 (1951), 528.
[27] Lord Justice Denning, *Law Quarterly Review*, 65 (1950), 253.
[28] L. C. B. Gower, *Modern Law Review*, 13 (1950), 400.
[29] *Current Legal Problems*, 4 (1951), 137.
[30] *Cambridge Law Journal*, 56 (1997), 444-5.   [31] *Ibid.*, p. 441.

law in the twentieth century.[32] It was another astonishing achievement, transforming scholarly and (rather more slowly) professional attitudes to its subject. The mapping of the territory was so comprehensive, the analysis so penetrating, the critique so trenchant and the prose, enriched with echoes of the Bible and the English classics, so lucid and so elegant. In over (in its second edition) 900 pages there is not a sentence that is obscure, or ambiguous or superfluous. It has provided a programme for debate and further research which is only now being travelled beyond. Much of his own subsequent writing on the criminal law, including the innovatory *Textbook* (1st edition 1978, 2nd edition 1983), was devoted to developing, elaborating and defending the principles propounded in *The General Part*, to which he adhered with remarkable consistency and, in almost all instances, well-warranted tenacity.

It is, first and foremost, its creativity and vision, its breaking out of the straitjacket of traditional legal categories, that makes *The General Part* such a great book. The masterly survey and description of the case and statute law, for which the rest of the common law world was scoured to supplement the rather sparse English material, was there to serve a higher purpose. For 'unfortunately, as has appeared only too plainly from these pages, there is no unanimity about anything in criminal law; scarcely a single important principle but has been denied by some judicial decision or by some legislation'.[33] Nor was the author much concerned to predict how future courts would respond to particular issues, for he took a dim view of the rough and unthinking ways in which 'the charmed circle of the judiciary' frequently resolved questions of criminal liability. Placing few bets he felt no need to hedge them. Rather, he set out to persuade his readers not that England had, but that it was possible for a common law jurisdiction like it to have, a criminal law that was fair and just because principled, internally con- sistent and rational (the criteria were professedly utilitarian which was why he thought a general 'lesser of two evils' – he called it a necessity – defence so important).[34] The discretions conceded to judges and juries (he profoundly distrusted both) had, therefore, to be kept to the

---

[32] It was awarded the Ames Prize by Harvard University.

[33] *Criminal Law: The General Part* (London: Stevens, 1953), at p. 435; cf. also p. 130. All further page references are, unless otherwise indicated, to this (1st) edition. For a fuller discussion, see P. R. Glazebrook, 'Glanville Williams: 1911–1997: Criminal Law', *Cambridge Law Journal*, 56 (1997), 445–55.

[34] At pp. 567–87; 'The Defence of Necessity', *Current Legal Problems*, (1953), 216; *Sanctity of Life*, at pp. 286–7; 'A Commentary on *R v. Dudley and Stephens*', *Cambrian Law*

minimum. The cases and statutes that stand in the way are identified, and the arguments for and against them deployed for the benefit of counsel, judges and Parliament. The statutory reforms that are needed are then clearly indicated. The Benthamite Criminal Law Commissioners of 1833 and 1845, with their master himself (whose fondness for neo-logisms he shared) are, it is evident,[35] men after the author's own mind and heart.

Heart as well as mind. The aim was not intellectual tidiness for its own sake – though intellectual untidiness and the logical fallacy was always very shocking – but a criminal law that would operate less heavy-handedly, less discriminatorily, and be less susceptible to the gales of vindictive passion and emotion.[36] Legal argument was, of course, rel-ished. But what lay behind the missionary zeal evident in all his writing about English criminal justice was his belief (for which *The Sanctity of Life and the Criminal Law* (1956) provides further extensive evidence) that, being entangled with the 'mystical' concept of retribution,[37] it was quite unnecessarily punitive. Far too often its enforcement did more harm – caused more avoidable human suffering – than it prevented, and to this the form of the substantive criminal law significantly contributed.

Judges were distrusted not just because they were frequently guilty of 'astonishing assumptions of legislative power',[38] but because they appeared 'convinced of the efficacy of punishment as medicine for all social divergences'[39] and adopted 'a crude retaliation theory, where the degree of punishment is linked rather to the amount of damage done than to the intention of the actor'.[40] So he always opposed the extension of the criminal law, either analogically or legislatively, to omissions to prevent harm.[41] The courts and the prisons were already overburdened with those who caused the harm; the need for them to deal also with those who failed to prevent it had never been demonstrated. And juries, those fig leaves for which judges reach when embarrassed by the

Review, (1977), 94; 'Necessity', *Criminal Law Review*, (1978), 128. Its introduction, at his urging, into the Model Penal Code (Art. 3) has been said to represent 'a revolution in [legal] thinking': G. P. Fletcher, *Basic Concepts of Criminal Law* (New York: Oxford University Press, 1998), p. 142.

[35] For example, at pp. 28, 54, 65–6, 108, 230, 242.   [36] At p. 463.   [37] At p. 458.

[38] At p. 125: 'Statute Interpretation, Prostitution and the Rule of Law', in C. F. H. Tapper (ed.), *Crime, Proof and Punishment* (London: Butterworth, 1981), p. 71.

[39] *Ibid.*   [40] At p. 109.

[41] For example, *ibid.*, at pp. 3–7, 477. See also, Glanville Williams, 'What Should the Code do about Omissions?' *Legal Studies*, 7 (1983), 92; 'Letting Offences Happen', *Criminal Law Review*, (1990), 780; 'Criminal Omissions: The Conventional View', *Law Quarterly Review*, 107 (1991), 86.

nakedness of their own reasoning, were not to be trusted to determine the limits of criminal liability since 'to entrust the defendant's liberty to a jury on these terms is not democracy; it is certainly not aristocracy; it is the despotism of small, nameless, untrained, ephemeral groups, responsible to no one and not even giving reasons for their opinion'.[42]

The aim, therefore, was law that was as clear and certain as the best lawyers could make it, with the minimum of offences and these narrowly, rather than broadly, defined. And among *The General Part*'s many strengths, and an important factor in its persuasiveness, is its repeated demonstration, as the author confronts one question after another, that adherence to a few simple principles and to a consistent terminology reflecting them, would do a great deal to reduce the criminal law's unfairness, harshness, uncertainty and irrationality.

The principles found (and recommended) are these. The description of the prohibited occurrence must be seen as including all the legal rules relating to the offence save those concerning the defendant's fault.[43] For all offences that merit the name of crimes, including those where Parliament had been silent on the point, proof that the defendant intended or knew that he was or, at the very least might be, bringing about that occurrence so described should be required.[44] That an ordinary reasonable person in the defendant's position would have realised that he was or might well be doing so supports an inference, but no more than an inference, that the defendant himself realised that. Such inferences are rebuttable by the defendant.[45] For those offences where there are good reasons for departing from the last two principles there should be liability only where the defendant is proved to be negligent.[46] Further, it is rarely, if ever, practicable for the criminal law to distinguish between the defendant who intended the occurrence that was prohibited and the defendant who knew that it was virtually certain that he would bring it about.[47] It is, on the other hand, often desirable to distinguish between such a defendant and one whose fault lies in knowingly taking an unreasonable risk of doing so, this (advert recklessness) being a

---

[42] 'Conspiring to Corrupt', in R. E. Megarry (ed.), *Law in Action* (London: Stevens, 1965), pp. 71–6; 'Law and Fact', *Criminal Law Review*, (1976), 472, 532; 'The Standard of Honesty', *New Law Journal*, (1983), 636.
[43] At pp. 15, 16, 19.   [44] At pp. 21, 59, 138.   [45] At pp. 49, 51, 77, 81.
[46] At pp. 29, 87–8; *The Mental Element in Crime* (Jerusalem: Magnes Press, 1965) (thereafter *MEC*), at p. 59.
[47] At pp. 35–9; *Sanctity of Life*, at p. 286; *MEC*, at pp. 15, 24 and 'Oblique Intention', *Cambridge Law Journal*, 46 (1987), 417.

form of negligence.[48] The prosecution must prove both the occurrence and the required degree of fault beyond reasonable doubt.[49] The only significance to be attached, therefore, to the description of a matter as one of defence is that a defendant who invokes it may fail if he does not introduce some credible supporting evidence.[50]

It was not suggested that the courts always adhered to these principles – many a statement is carefully qualified by the phrase 'on the view advanced in this book' or by the word 'generally' – nor that adherence to them would produce fully nuanced moral judgments. All that was contended for was that these were the fairest and most practicable principles for law courts – human tribunals – to follow when what was at stake was liability to state-inflicted punishment. So judges should not pick and choose between the various elements of the prohibited occurrence because, once they started doing that, there was no point at which the slide to liability without fault could be halted.[51] It was, likewise, essential that advertent recklessness should be recognised as a distinct form of fault; for then there would be little reason for law enforcers to strive after any stricter liability.[52] Each principle had its place and its purpose in this carefully constructed scheme.

Much, if not all, of the scheme now sounds boringly orthodox. And, as is the fate of all orthodoxies, its principles are now being attacked by retributivist critics who, as they hanker after those that satisfied eighteenth- and early-nineteenth-century lawyers, sometimes appear to forget that what the argument is all about is not only blame, but liability to state-inflicted punishment and the amount of it that should be ladled out. Deterrence and prevention being, in Glanville's view, the only moral justifications for punishing its citizens that were open to a state, the principles (and rules) of criminal liability should reflect that. This might mean an extension of the criminal law (for instance, to catch intending criminals at an earlier stage,[53] and even those who had made a big mistake[54] or those who dealt in the

---

[48] At pp. 59, 62; *MEC*, at pp. 27, 29, 32; 'Intention and Recklessness Again', *Legal Studies*, 2 (1982), 189.

[49] At pp. 77, 81, 355, 691, 719.

[50] At pp. 173–4; 'Offences and Defences', *Legal Studies*, 2 (1982), 189; 'The Logic of "Exceptions"', *Cambridge Law Journal*, 47 (1988), 261.

[51] *Ibid.*, at p. 159.   [52] At ch. 7 *passim*.

[53] At p. 486; 'A Fresh Start with the Law of Attempt', *Cambridge Law Journal*, 39 (1980), 225; 'The Government's Proposals on Criminal Attempts', *New Law Journal*, 80 (1981), 104, 128.

[54] At pp. 487–503; 'Criminal Attempts: A Reply', *Criminal Law Review*, (1962), 300; 'Attempting the Impossible: A Reply', *Criminal Law Quarterly*, 22 (1980), 49.

proceeds of any sort of crime and not just in stolen goods).[55] Or it might mean the widening of a defence (in favour, for example, of those who unwittingly furthered the enforcement of the criminal law).[56] But either way he was ready to argue for the changes that consistency with his view of the moral justifications for criminal liability and punishment seemed to him to require.

In 1953 the principles of liability for which he was contending were by no means orthodox, as *The General Part* itself, and a decade later, *The Mental Element in Crime* (1965) recognised. Other doctrines had not only historical, but also contemporary support: the latter coming from such powerful judicial figures as Lords Reid, Denning and, most pervasively, Diplock. They rejected a unitary view of the criminal occurrence, did not distinguish between intending and knowingly taking the risk of harm, saw no objection to convicting of serious crimes defendants who were not shown to have been anything worse than negligent, and allowed, where a statute said nothing about fault, no more than that a blameless defendant might go free if he proved that he had not been negligent.[57]

This debate about what Glanville justifiably described as 'the kindergarten part of the criminal law'[58] is not yet at an end. There are even those who question the validity and desirability of the very attempt to generalise.[59] The weakest points in his scheme were the failure to deal sufficiently with (though he touched upon), first, the problem presented when elements of a prohibited occurrence are described adverbially or adjectivally and, second, with applying uniform principles to statutes regulating so many different human activities – from being helpful to the king's enemies to misleading the public about one's medical qualifications – many of these statutes having been drafted without any regard to, or in ignorance of, those principles. And he was perhaps, just a little too ready to extract a 'common law principle' out of a decision interpreting and applying a particular statute.

Remarkably few of the issues of principle that have since come before appellate courts are not touched upon in *The General Part*, and very

---

[55] At p. 183.   [56] At p. 25.

[57] Lord Denning, *Responsibility before the Law* (Hebrew University of Jerusalem, 1961), *passim*; Lord Diplock, *Gould* [1968] 2 QB 65; *Sweet* v. *Paisley* [1970] AC 132, 163; *Hyam* [1975] AC 66; *Caldwell* [1982] AC 341.

[58] *MEC*, preface.

[59] For example, N. Lacey, 'Contingency, Coherence and Conceptualism', in A. Duff (ed.), *Philosophy and the Criminal Law: Principle and Critique* (Cambridge University Press, 1998), pp. 9, 29, 36.

much more often than not these courts have sooner or later gone the way to which it pointed – albeit more quickly and readily in Canada, Australia and New Zealand than in England, though even here there are some indications of a new and more liberal judicial generation, working in and stimulated by the bracing climate of the Human Rights Act 1998, being increasingly receptive of the principles for which the book contended.[60]

For the next forty years Glanville was to defend, reaffirm and exemplify the themes of *The General Part* in an unceasing stream of articles, as well as in its enlarged (by more than 200 pages) second edition and in the 1,000-page *Textbook of Criminal Law* (1st edition 1978, 2nd edition 1983), designed, in the first place, for undergraduate readers. Those themes were combined there with a highly critical survey of the law governing individual offences of personal violence and fraud. Such, however, was his continuing and overriding preoccupation with the fault needed for criminal liability that, somewhat oddly, he discussed it at length before considering the different sorts of occurrence for which that liability might be imposed. And reviewers pointed out (as they had forty years earlier[61]) that 'the line between description and prescription is not always as clear as one might expect from an author who takes Williams' evidently positivist line'.[62] But this is, of course, one of the reasons why his writings have proved to be so enormously influential.

The articles were frequently hard-hitting and a degree of irritation crept into some of the later ones. Most spectacular of all was the attack[63] on the House of Lords' decision[64] that someone who thought, mistakenly, that he was doing something which, if he had in fact been doing it, would have been a crime, did not commit an offence (of 'attempt'). It led the bruised law lords, as they sorrowfully acknowledged, to change their minds within a year and hold that such a criminally intentioned, but mistaken, defendant should indeed be convicted.[65] This was all the more remarkable since the issue is a difficult one, for though such a person is wickedly intentioned, nothing that is legally proscribed will have been

---

[60] Notably in a remarkable trio of House of Lords' decisions: *R. v. DPP* [2000] 1 All ER 561; *K* [2001] 3 All ER 897; *Lambert* [2001] 3 All ER 577.

[61] Text at n. 12 above.

[62] N. Lacey, 'The Territory of the Criminal Law', *Oxford Journal of Legal Studies*, 5 (1985), 453, at p. 454.

[63] Glanville Williams, 'The Lords and Impossible Attempts, or *Quis Custodet Ipsos Cusdodes*', *Cambridge Law Journal*, 46 (1986), 33.

[64] *Anderton v. Ryan* [1985] AC 567.   [65] *Shivpuri* [1987] AC 1.

either done or risked. Much, therefore, can be, and has been, written on
both sides of the question, and courts around the world have reached
different conclusions.[66] What carried the day was Glanville's exhaustive
demonstration that distinguishing between a defendant who was trying
to do what was factually impossible to achieve (whom nearly everyone
agreed ought to be convicted) and one who was mistaken in other ways
was forensically impracticable. This was but the latest occasion on which
his critical analysis had deprived a decision of the House of Lords of all
real authority.[67] Indeed, the abandonment of the quaint convention
forbidding explicit reliance in argument or judgment on the writings of
the living to which English courts were still adhering in the 1960s was
due in some considerable measure to him. His writings were at the head
of those that were just too formidable to be left unacknowledged.

Almost as much attention was devoted to the law governing the
powers of the police, to the procedure followed at criminal trials, and
to the admissibility (and exclusion) of evidence at them, as to the
substantive criminal law, but his work here was never built into a
grand treatise. Instead, there is a shorter book, 'profound and thought-
provoking',[68] *The Proof of Guilt* (1st edition 1955, 3rd edition 1963)
based on his Hamlyn Lectures, together with over two dozen articles.
These writings show him as keen to have laws which would ensure the
conviction of the guilty as well as the acquittal of the innocent. For if the
substantive law took the lean, utilitarian shape he believed it should, it
would be absurd not to remove all obstacles to its effective and accurate
enforcement.[69] This coolly rational approach to highly emotive issues
was to bring the liberal-minded scholar some strange allies, and even
stranger opponents. For here, too, he was, in the comprehensiveness and
comparative sweep of his scrutiny of the rules, procedures and institutions of the English criminal justice system, a pioneer, providing a

---

[66] The legislative history had been lengthy and contentious. The Law Commission had been in
favour of liability, the Home Office's lawyers against it. Glanville's evidence to the House of
Commons' Special Standing Committee persuaded it in favour of the Law Commission's (and
his long-maintained) view, but the draftsman of the Criminal Attempts Act 1981, though then
instructed to do so, had still failed to deal adequately with the point. See P. S. Atiyah,
Pragmatism and Theory in English Law (London: Sweet & Maxwell, 1987), pp. 180–3.

[67] Earlier instances are *Jones* v. *DPP* [1946] AC 347 (see n. 23 above); *DPP* v. *Smith* [1961]
AC 290 after a turn-over article in *The Times*, 12 October 1960, and *Modern Law Review*,
23, 605; and *Shaw* v. *DPP* [1962] AC 220 after *The Listener*, 1961, pp. 66, 275, 280.

[68] J. R. Spencer, 'Obituary: Glanville Williams', *Cambridge Law Journal*, 56 (1997), 456.

[69] See Spencer's persuasive interpretation, *ibid.*, pp. 456–63.

stimulus for other scholars,[70] whose work in its turn generated much public debate which still continues, and to which he was himself, until well into his eighties, a prominent contributor.

There were – and are – many areas of concern. Professor J. R. Spencer has picked out[71] half a dozen of the most salient to which Glanville drew attention. First among them was the need for the police to be given power to detain suspects for questioning. This happened, of course – people were always 'helping the police with their inquiries' – but the practice could be regulated only if it was first legalised. These interviews should, however, he said, always be tape-recorded. Eventually the police came to see that this would be a protection not only for suspects against being manipulated, but also for the police themselves against defence allegations that a confession had been fabricated or obtained by improper means. A quarter of a century later the detentions were authorised, and the tape-recording required, by the Police and Criminal Evidence Act 1984. This requirement has transformed the nature of criminal trials.

Also attacked were the rules that during a trial forbade reference to, and comment on, a defendant's failure to offer any exculpatory explanation of the conduct for which he was being tried, either when he was first arrested and charged or at the trial itself. These rules, like others which excluded relevant and credible evidence and were subjected to similar criticisms, flew in the face of human experience, were a bizarre shackle on the prosecution and could be a trap for the innocent. Here it took even longer to overcome long-standing professional shibboleths, as the Criminal Justice and Public Order Act 1994 to a large extent eventually did.

There was, too, the inherent unreliability of an eye-witness's identification of a suspect, and therefore the need, here and elsewhere, for an effective system of appeal against a jury's findings. Parliament had long since been ready to grant this,[72] but the judges had dragged their feet for fear of undermining the jury system. For, if appellate judges move from overruling the decisions of other judges to overturning jurors' verdicts, who would take those verdicts seriously – why, indeed, should jurors take themselves seriously? It remains to be seen whether the Criminal

---

[70] Notably Professor W. R. Cornish, *The Jury* (London: Allen Lane, 1968) and Professor Michael Zander (who was an undergraduate pupil), who has written extensively on the provision of legal services and on trial procedures.
[71] See above, n. 68.   [72] Criminal Appeal Act 1907.

Cases Review Commission established by the Criminal Appeal Act 1995 will enable the resolution of this dilemma.

Being more alert than most lawyers to technological developments,[73] Glanville also saw that many of the problems that arose when it was necessary to rely on the evidence of children could be met by video-recording it at the first opportunity, when the child's recollection would be fresher, and the surroundings less harrowing and intimidating than a court room many months later. A long campaign, which Spencer was to join,[74] led to the establishment of a government committee[75] and the enactment in the Criminal Justice Act 1997 of some, though not all, of their proposals.

Excoriated, too, were the frequent departures made by Parliament, aided and abetted by the judges, from the principle that proof beyond reasonable doubt by the prosecution of the case it adduced required disproof beyond reasonable doubt of defences raised by a defendant. This, however, was a case that made no progress at all (except with the Criminal Law Revision Committee in its Eleventh Report (1982)) until the Human Rights Act came along in 1998. The law lords were then to find, and to acknowledge that they had found, in Glanville's oft-repeated view[76] that a statute requiring a defendant to prove some exculpatory matter should be read as requiring only that he should adduce credible evidence of it (which the prosecution would then have to disprove), the way to square the intransigence of the Home Office and other government departments, which Parliament had so constantly endorsed, with the protection given to the presumption of innocence by the European Convention.[77] Lord Cooke thought, indeed, that 'one could hardly ask for more than the opinion of Professor Glanville Williams' that such a reading was possible.[78] The argument, as deployed in 'The Logic of "Exceptions"'[79] is, characteristically, as bold as it is elegant and simple.

---

[73] The *Textbook of Criminal Law* (1978) is believed to be the first law book printed in the United Kingdom directly from the author's computer disks.

[74] 'Child Witnesses', in Peter Smith (ed.), *Essays in Honour of J. C. Smith* (London: Butterworths, 1987), p. 188; 'Video-taping Children's Evidence', *New Law Journal*, 137 (1987), 108; 'The Corroboration Question', *ibid.*, p. 131; 'More About Videotaping Children', *ibid.*, 369; 'Child Witnesses and Video-Technology: Thoughts for the Home Office', *Journal of Criminal Law*, 51 (1987), 444, though published under Spencer's name was really, he says, a joint effort.

[75] *Report of the Advisory Group on Video Evidence* (London: Home Office, December 1989).

[76] See above, n. 50.   [77] *Lambert* [2001] 3 All ER 577.

[78] *R. v. DPP, ex parte Kebilene* [2000] 2 AC 326.   [79] See above, n. 17.

The courts read the word 'prove' in a statute, even when occurring within the same section, as meaning 'prove beyond reasonable doubt' when it is the prosecution which is doing the proving, and as 'prove on a balance of probabilities' when it is the defendant. 'Having swallowed this camel, why strain at the remaining gnat', when 'the fate of individual human beings' is at issue, of reading it, as the presumption of innocence demands, as meaning 'adduce sufficient evidence to raise a reasonable doubt'?[80] For, as he exhaustively demonstrated, there was no logic at all in the distinction, so often relied on by the courts, between a rule and the exceptions to it. It was merely a matter of the draftsman's (linguistic) convenience. 'Looking for the line between a rule and an exception is . . . like looking in a dark room for a black cat that isn't there.'[81] There is, in this judicial turn-about, an element of irony. For, as a Benthamite, who like the master considered human rights to be 'nonsense upon stilts', and ever distrustful of the judiciary, Glanville had always been opposed to investing it with the power to overrule or rewrite Parliament's enactments. The judges, it has to be said, continue to express a higher regard for him than he did for them.

IV

It will be apparent that Glanville's legal scholarship was not scholarship done just for scholarship's sake. As Hepple has said, 'he was an accomplished master of the precedents, he could dazzle with his powers of rational analysis, he could be irritatingly logical, but ultimately it was the social justification in modern society for any legal rule which mattered most to him.'[82] His scholarly work was, therefore, seen and almost invariably undertaken as a necessary preliminary to the improvement and reform of especially unsatisfactory or underdeveloped areas of the law. And for this reason it was zealously pursued. And when, as President of the Society of Public (i.e., University) Teachers of Law (1974) he set about transforming it from an ineffective pressure group and social organisation into a learned society; law reform was the theme he proposed for every subject section at the annual meeting. While writing *The General Part* he both served (inevitably) on the [Goddard] Committee on the Law of Civil Liability for Damage Done by Animals (which reported in 1953) and edited *The Reform of the Law* (1951) for the Haldane Society. The book advocated a 'Ministry of Justice' to 'keep

[80] At p. 265.   [81] At p. 278.   [82] See above, n. 3.

the law under review' (which became the Law Commission's terms of reference). By far the longest chapter was devoted to the criminal law. And much of the agenda, it is reassuring to find, has been accomplished. The need for reform is, as has been said, a constant refrain of *The General Part*, and there is scarcely a reform proposal that has not been endorsed by some official body, often at his own prompting, either from within or without.

He lobbied vigorously for the establishment of the Criminal Law Revision Committee,[83] and for twenty-three years (almost all its effective life) was its mainstay and the source of many of its ideas.[84] About half the working papers that the Committee considered came from him. They were often very lengthy and closely detailed, and this, at least at first, irritated its judicial and practitioner members, but increasingly he gained their respect and attention, and persuaded them that they should meet all day, and not just after the courts rose, if they were to do the Committee's business adequately. He did not, however, always get his own way, though he was usually right. The Theft Act 1968 would have been a much less unsatisfactory measure if his advice had been followed. In the years from 1971 to 1975 he was also serving on the [Butler] Committee on Mentally Abnormal Offenders and on the Law Commission's working party on the Codification of the Criminal Law, a cause to which he was passionately devoted, and in which he, like Stephen,[85] was to be most grievously disappointed. When in 1967 the Commission, encouraged by an exceptional Home Secretary (Roy Jenkins), first espoused it, Glanville proceeded to draft a large part of a code to show how he thought it ought to be done. The Commission quailed before it. For the draft was lengthy, detailed and highly systematised, reflecting his belief that if the draftsman could foresee an eventuality and he, of course, could think of a great many, then a rule should be provided to govern it. Thirty-five years, and more than a score of reports, consultation documents and working papers later, very little has, for want of a directing mind with comparable vision, been achieved. One example of his drafting did, however, reach a statute book: Ireland's Civil Liability Act 1961 in substance enacts the 'Suggested Codifying and

---

[83] *The Times*, 10 June 1952; 'Reform of the Criminal Law and its Administration', *Journal of the Society of Public Teachers of Law*, 4 (1958), 217.

[84] Sir John Smith, 'The Sad Fate of the Theft Act 1968', in W. Swadling and G. Jones (eds), *The Search for Principle: Essays in Honour of Lord Goff of Chieveley* (Oxford University Press, 2000), pp. 97, 98.

[85] See above, n. 1.

Amending Measure' in chapter 22 of *Joint Torts and Contributory Negligence*.[86]

It was, perhaps, his many letters to *The Times*[87] in support of one legal reform after another which, like his *Third Programme* broadcasts, best displayed his consummate ability to go directly to the point and expound it to non-lawyers with great succinctness and total clarity. They were matched by 'the closely typed and closely reasoned memoranda which, deaf to every rebuff, he regularly sent to every minister, civil servant or MP who he thought might listen to his views'.[88] But his persistence and patience in law reform causes were nowhere more fully displayed than in the unremitting support he gave to the campaigns for the modification of the criminal law of abortion, and the legalisation of voluntary euthanasia.

He drafted all four parliamentary Bills (1952, 1961, 1965 and 1966) that preceded the one successfully promoted by David Steel in 1967, and he was a member of the widely based committee which Steel formed to advise him. Glanville disapproved, however, of many of the compromises which Steel made in order to secure the support needed for its enactment, notably the dropping of the clause which referred expressly to the mother's incapacity to care for her child, and the requirements for a second medical opinion and notification to the Department of Health.[89] It was natural enough that the author of *The Sanctity of Life and the Criminal Law* should in 1962 have been elected President of the Abortion Law Reform Association, and he thereafter worked closely with its chairman, Vera Houghton, and the parliamentary sponsors of the unsuccessful Bills. But 'his views were always far ahead of those of the [Association's] other members', and he seemed 'indifferent and indeed almost unaware of the outrage' some of his views caused.[90] As he had made clear at the 1963 AGM he favoured a law which would, quite simply, permit a registered medical practitioner to perform an abortion during the first trimester and at any time in order to preserve the mother's life. A third of a century later even the most fervent pro-life campaigner would probably consider this preferable to the irrational and vague provisions of Steel's (now amended) Abortion Act 1967 and the

---

[86] See above, n. 25.

[87] A selection are printed in *Cambridge Law Journal*, 50 (1991), 1.

[88] Spencer, see above, n. 68.

[89] K. Hindell and M. Simms, *Abortion Law Reformed* (London: Peter Owen, 1971), pp. 133–41, 158, 175–8.

[90] *Ibid.*, p. 119.

wide-spread humbug and deceit to which they give rise. Glanville's own satisfaction at the Act's success in driving abortionists from the back streets was mixed with sadness that the medical profession had betrayed the trust placed in it by Parliament.

He wrote and spoke equally tirelessly for the amelioration of the law governing voluntary euthanasia and mercy-killing. His position here was similarly uncomplicated, if over-simple. If it was not unlawful to kill oneself there was, he thought, no good reason for it to be a crime to help someone who wanted to die to do so, and absurd that if he happened no longer to be able to put an end to his own life it should be murder actually to kill him. (His wife, Lorna (nee Lawfield), whom he had first met through a common friend from Bridgend when she was an undergraduate at Newnham College, and who made with him a true and immensely supportive marriage of like minds that lasted for more than fifty-seven years, wishing to spare him the unceasing correspondence and the desperate – and despairing – telephone calls she had good reason to expect would ensue, did, however, persuade him to decline an invitation to become President of the Voluntary Euthanasia Society, which as one of its vice-presidents he long supported.) A deep interest in medical developments and a willingness to meet doctors in debate on their own ground was supported by a wide reading in the current literature. Week by week *The Lancet* and *The Justice of the Peace* were scrutinised with equal care.

V

For lawyers who knew him only in his published writings, their image of Glanville was, no doubt, that of the unrelenting controversialist wielding the scalpel and sometimes the sabre. He certainly found it difficult to resist the temptation to put right a judge, or a fellow academic incautiously venturing into print. Pupils, colleagues and friends encountered a very different person who may also be glimpsed in *Learning the Law*. Written in less than a month in 1944 to meet the needs of students, many of whom were soon to return to their books after the interruptions of war, it combines penetrating insights and astringent comments on legal institutions with astute awareness of what bemuses the student and what he needs to know first, and it offers a host of practical tips on how to set about the whole business, conveyed with a sense of enthusiasm and a slightly conspiratorial air – the author was most definitely on the students' side – in language of marvellous lucidity. '"Rather unconventional" [the author] calls it, and the epithet is justified', commented Lord Macmillan: 'Nothing quite like this has been attempted hitherto.'[91] It was no wonder that it was on every reading list and that its publishers paid their highest royalties ever on it.[92]

Much time and thought was given to how law could be best taught and law students examined, considerable inventiveness was displayed in devising new ways of doing so – the potential here, as in the police station and the court room, of tape- and video-recorders was quickly grasped and utilised – and the methods of American law schools admiringly observed during periods as a Visiting Professor at several of them. He met, it must be said, with rather limited success in persuading his Cambridge colleagues to experiment, and with even less from an inveterately conservative student body. But he was never discouraged and he had, when Chairman of the Faculty, one lasting success: the introduction into the formal structures of the Law Tripos of undergraduate dissertations, seminars and short, examined, lecture courses on new and developing areas of the law. The *Textbook of Criminal Law* published in the year he retired from his Cambridge Chair (1978), which marked a further advance in the scholarly treatment of the criminal law nearly as great as that made by *The General Part*, is constantly interspersed with the questions and comments of a critical and/or incredulous student, with its text divided in the manner of *Les Guides bleus* between large ('what you mustn't miss') and small ('worth seeing if you have a bit more time') print, which shows him as concerned as ever with the learning problems of the law student.

Few of the Cambridge undergraduates whose studies he for a decade (1956–1966) directed at his Cambridge college then realised quite how great a scholar he was.[93] What struck them was his modest manner, the absence of any trace of condescension, the clarity of his exposition, and the simplicity and purity of his Socratic way of teaching. Intellectual

---

[91] *Law Quarterly Review*, 61 (1945), 305.

[92] 11th edition 1982 (this edition was reprinted eleven times), 12th edition (by A. T. H. Smith) 2002.

[93] His initial connection with Jesus College Cambridge was as its external assessor in the search for a Law Fellow to succeed Professor Sir Robert Jennings on the latter's appointment to the Whewell Chair of International Law. None of the three short-listed candidates, all of whom subsequently enjoyed careers of great distinction, succeeded, however, in commanding the majority necessary for election. Faced with this impasse, Glanville, who had continued to live in Cambridge, hesitantly inquired of Jennings whether he thought it would be improper of him to say that if an invitation were extended he would himself be delighted to become a Fellow of Jesus. The candidates whom he had interviewed were, naturally, more than a little surprised at this outcome.

idleness (among either dons or students) was the only failing that he found difficult to forgive. The undergraduates later discovered the trouble he had taken to see that the less as well as the more able among them were placed in suitable solicitors' firms and barristers' chambers. In the faculty at large he was, as he had been in London, alert to identify, encourage and support those wishing to embark on an academic career as several present members of the Academy have testified. He did not hesitate to back his own judgments against those of boards of examiners. For his colleagues there was an old-world courtesy, thoughtful kindly consideration, the notably patient hearing them out, and only then the gentle criticism of their ideas. Uncompromising as he was on many ethical issues – in particular on abortion, euthanasia, population growth and sexual behaviour, and in his pacifism (which was held against him in Cambridge where the Law Faculty's most influential figures had served in one or both World Wars and also strongly disliked the extreme utilitarian views expounded in *The Sanctity of Life and the Criminal Law*) – there was no hint of self-righteousness. He constantly inquired about the safety of a colleague's son sent to the Gulf War.

A total dedication to the life of the mind – the dinner table was an occasion for exploring a new idea or testing the arguments in a new book, not for gossip or idle chatter – the moral seriousness with which he approached every task, and a capacity to work tirelessly and seemingly effortlessly from morning to night, and to abstract himself from his immediate surroundings – he would read while walking in the country and he composed on his portable typewriter while commuting on the train from Cambridge to London – help to explain how a prodigious scholarly output was combined with so much committee work and public activity, without his ever giving the appearance of being busy or pressed for time. And as he approached his eightieth birthday he published articles that were as fresh, forceful and compelling as anything he had written in the previous fifty years.[94]

His tastes and recreations were simple ones: the countryside[95] and especially (earlier) sailing on the Broads and (later) canoeing down rivers

---

[94] For example, '*Finis for Novus Actus?*', *Cambridge Law Journal*, 48 (1989), 391; 'The *Mens Rea* for Murder: Leave it Alone', *Law Quarterly Review*, 104 (1989), 387 (preferred by the House of Lords Select Committee on Murder to one by Lord Goff) and 'Criminal Omissions – The Conventional View', *ibid.*, p. 107.

[95] The reader of the *Textbook* is warned that although picking wild flowers is not theft, she may nonetheless commit an offence under the Conservation of Wild Creatures and Wild Plants Act 1975, s. 4 (as amended), by 'plucking a posy consisting of such listed plants as

(camping or B&B rather than a hotel). Second-hand Jaguar cars were driven sedately. Gadgets of all sorts fascinated. New card and parlour games, some with legal themes, were invented. The classical English poets and novelists were read aloud in the evenings with his wife.

He could be persuaded, just, to accept honours that came after the name. In his fifties, the Middle Temple made him a Bencher, and he was given Silk. There was an Honorary Fellowship from his college, and honorary degrees from half a dozen universities, including the special tribute for one of its own teachers of a LittD from Cambridge in 1995, together with election as a Foreign Honorary member of the American Academy of Arts and Sciences (1985). But the knighthood offered on the recommendation of the lord chancellor and the law lords when he retired from his Cambridge Chair was declined. Although Glanville was not, as his wife is, a member of the Society of Friends, he practised the Quaker virtues, and respected their values and customs. Deeply modest, he 'thought it incongruous that a man who had refused to wield a bayonet should theoretically bear a sword'.[96]

He died peacefully at home on 10 April 1997 at the age of eighty-six.

Note: The writer is most grateful to Glanville Williams' widow, Lorna Williams, and their son, Dr Rendel Williams of the University of Sussex, and also to Sir Roger Toulson, Professor Kurt Lipstein, Professor S. K. C. Milsom and Sir John Smith for information and advice, as well as to Professor B. A. Hepple and Professor J. R. Spencer with whom he joined in the tributes printed in the *Cambridge Law Journal*, 56 (1997), 437–65. These have been heavily drawn on for this Memoir, as has the obituary the author wrote for the *Society of Public Teachers of Law's Reporter* (Autumn 1997), 23–5. There is a (nearly) complete and indexed list of the published writings to 1977 in P. R. Glazebrook (ed.), *Reshaping the Criminal Law: Essays in Honour of Glanville Williams* (1978), pp. 449–68. A supplement to 1997 is available from the writer.

---

ghost orchid, alpine cow-thistle and oblong woodsra': Glanville Williams, *Textbook of Criminal Law*, 2nd edn (London: Stevens, 1983), p. 735.
[96] Spencer, 'Obituary: Glanville Williams', p. 439.

2

Glanville's inspiration

GEORGE P. FLETCHER

When I was a first-year law student at UCLA I developed a quick interest in criminal law. My teacher, Murray Schwartz, was an excellent guide to the basics, and his colleague, later my friend and mentor, Herbert Morris, led me to the philosophical questions on the subject. Criminal law was just then gaining traction as a philosophical subject of interest not only to Morris, but to H. L. A. Hart, Richard Wasserstrom, and Joel Feinberg. The mood was perfect for me to catch the bug as well and develop a life-long commitment to the theory of crime and punishment, then, after my studies in Germany, comparative criminal law, and finally the ICC and international criminal law.

I Williams versus Hall

Circa 1960 the leading theoretical book on criminal law was Glanville Williams' *Criminal Law: The General Part*.[1] This was the first time I had encountered the phrase "general part." So far as I know, no American writer had ever used it. Later I would learn that the term was common in Continental textbooks. Though Williams did not display a knowledge of foreign legal systems in his book, he was obviously familiar with the way his colleagues in Germany, Italy, and France wrote and spoke about the subject. At the time the only serious competition in English was Jerome Hall, who had ambitions of writing a Continental-style book about criminal law. When I studied in Germany in the mid-1960s, I found that the scholars were more

---

[1] See Glanville Williams, *Criminal Law: The General Part*, 2nd edn (London: Stevens, 1961). The first edition was published in 1953.

familiar with his book than any other English work. His problem, however, was that he rejected the basic distinctions of German, Spanish, and Italian legal thought without having replaced them with distinctive concepts of his own.

Hall also thought that in his book on the history of theft[2] he had found the grail sought by all serious thinkers on legal theory: proof that economic and social circumstances shape the law of the time. His leading example was the *Carrier's* case of 1473. The carrier was held for theft of the contents of the bales he was carrying – despite his nominal immunity based on possession of the bales – because he broke open the bales and stole the contents. This generated the famous exception of "breaking bulk" to the rule that someone in possession of goods could not be guilty of larceny of those goods. It was the first of many exceptions that led eventually to breakdown of possession as a relevant line distinguishing between those who could or could not be criminally liable for misappropriation of property. The crime of embezzlement emerged at the end of the eighteenth century – in virtually all legal systems – to create liability for misappropriations by those already in possession.[3]

Hall's work on the *Carrier's* case[4] represented an original form of research, a prologue to current efforts to account for the background influences on the development of the law. Yet it appeared that he had read too much into the *Carrier's* case. There was no way to prove the claim that the 1473 decision demonstrated the triumph of changing economic interests over traditional legal rules. There were economic interests both on the sides of the owner and the carrier that did not line up clearly in favor of a general rule of immunity, plus a narrow exception for "breaking bulk."

Williams was, at this stage, more interested in crimes against the person, the issues of abortion, prolonging life, and even rape – rather than the economic side of the criminal law. Whether this leaves any systematic traces in theory of criminality remains to be seen.

---

[2] Jerome Hall, *Theft, Law, and Society* (Boston, MA: Little, Brown, 1935).
[3] See James Fitzjames Stephen, *A History of the Criminal Law of England* (London: Macmillan, 1883), p. 152; J. W. C. Turner, *Russell on Crime* (London: Stevens, 1958), p. 1203 *et seq.*; Rollin M. Perkins and Ronald N. Boyce, *Criminal Law*, 3rd edn (Mineola, NY: Foundation Press, 1982), p. 351; George P. Fletcher, *Rethinking Criminal Law* (Boston, MA: Little, Brown, 1978), ch. 2.
[4] (1473) YB Pasch 13 Edw IV, f. 9, pl. 5.

II   Mid-century preoccupations

Our central theme is the forging of ideas about criminal law in the middle of the twentieth century. If so, we cannot ignore the critical events of the earlier part of that century: National Socialism in Germany; Prohibition and then the depression in the United States. These events must have had an impact on legal thought at the time and in the cases that came afterward. The Germans submitted to some distortions of the criminal law that I would label "terrifying," except that they are so close to what contemporary thinkers in the common law believe. Two slogans of the time reveal how the system could be understood as corrupt. The first is *Recht ist, was dem Volke nützt* ("Law is whatever is useful to the nation"). The second is *Das Recht und der Wille des Führers sind eins* ("The law and the will of the Führer are one"). I would be much harsher on these doctrines of National Socialism if they did not happen to be very close in meaning to principles found in the utilitarian school of American and English law. The idea that the legally correct solution must be useful is pure Bentham, and the idea that the law is the command of the sovereign is pure Austin. Perhaps the evil represented by National Socialism is the pretense that the politically acceptable scholars knew how to define who was inside and who was outside the nation, and who was to be considered the national leader, *der Führer*.

The major historical watershed for the Americans was not the Second World War, but the experience with Prohibition that occurred a generation earlier. The response to the crimes of selling sugar for distilling and other ingredients for making drugs led to a jurisprudence that was highly sensitive to the overall meaning of "commercial transaction." Not any sugar transaction would do. Emphasizing the *actus reus* side of offenses, the American courts insisted that the physical intrusion into the world should actually contribute to the completion of the crime. It was not enough that the criminal mind of the actor revealed a desire to do harm.

The critical case was *United States* v. *Falcone*,[5] which held that a sugar salesman who knew that his purchasers were planning to use the sugar they purchased illegally to distil alcohol could not be liable unless they had a financial stake in the outcome. That is, their sales would have to be abnormally large and reveal an interest in the transaction beyond doing

---

[5] (1940) 109 F2d 579, aff'd (1940) 311 US 205 (1940).

business as usual. This principle was reaffirmed in 1992 in a Seventh Circuit case, *United States* v. *Blankenship*,[6] which held that a lessor was not complicit in illegal drug activities conducted in an apartment that he leased to the other defendants with full knowledge of their criminal purposes.

The principle behind these cases was influential in the drafting of my brief on behalf of Salim Ahmad Hamdan, bin Laden's driver, who was arrested and prosecuted before a military tribunal for joining a conspiracy to commit the terrorist acts of 9/11. One of the brief's arguments was that he was a driver acting in the ordinary course of business, just as the sugar salesman in *United States* v. *Falcone* and the lessor in *United States* v. *Blankenship* had done. It was never resolved whether Hamdan's emotional "stake" in the outcome could have been sufficient for liability. Five members of the court found themselves convinced by other considerations. The four justice plurality siding with Justice Stevens, was convinced by the argument in my brief that conspiracy did not constitute a crime under the law of war, as required in the jurisdictional definition of the military tribunals. Justice Kennedy was satisfied on procedural grounds alone (the right of the defendant to confront witnesses against him) that the proceedings did not meet the requirements of a fair trial under common Article III of the Geneva Conventions.[7]

It is a pity that there were so many decisive arguments against convicting Hamdan. It would have been good to get a hearing on the general principle suggested by *United States* v. *Falcone* and *United States* v. *Blankenship*. This strikes me as important because the objective factor of criminal conduct – the *actus reus* – is under-theorized in comparison with the enormous attention paid to the factor of *mens rea*.

For good or ill, *Hamdan* v. *Rumsfeld* had a short life. A few months after the decision, Congress intervened with the Military Commissions Act 2006. Some assume that the Act eliminated the conspiracy objection to the military tribunals by defining conspiracy as requiring that every conspirator engage in an overt act. In my opinion, this is no more than a cosmetic change and the illegality of the charge under the law of war remains the same. The Guantanamo regime has generated so much litigation that it is hard to know which part of the detention scheme, if any, remains valid under US constitutional and federal law. The argument based on *United States* v. *Falcone* and *United States* v. *Blankenship*

---

[6] (1992) 970 F2d 283.   [7] See *Hamdan* v. *Rumsfeld* (2006) 548 US 557.

waits in the wings for another possibility to challenge the government's use of extra-legal techniques to circumvent the principles of criminal responsibility.

III   Returning the focus to Williams versus Hall

With some knowledge of the context in which their argument would have an impact on the post-Second World War criminal law, we should turn to some particular differences between Williams and Hall on the smaller doctrinal issues of the times.

A   Inadvertent negligence

Williams and Hall were both strongly opposed to the punishment of negligence. The argument was that inadvertent negligence was not really a form of *mens rea* and the latter, as we all assume, is necessary for criminal liability. Williams referred to negligence as "a half-way house" between *mens rea* and strict liability. The idea apparently was that the *mens rea* had to refer to an actual state of consciousness. It was not a normative judgment of blameworthiness. It was a fact about the perpetrator's mental state.

The Germans had been through this debate in the early part of the twentieth century, and without too much difficulty abandoned the idea that culpability refers to the state of mind that expresses a feeling of guilt. The conclusion of the German debate was that culpability was not a fact at all, but a normative judgment about the criteria that warranted an attribution of guilty.

Though the Continent was not then communicating with the English-speaking world about criminal law, they did think in the same general categories of criminal responsibility. Everybody agreed that you needed an act, some kind of culpability, a harm (in crimes where harm was relevant), and a causal link between the act and the harm. They did not say so, at least not in the English-speaking camp, but they also believed that all crimes presupposed a wrongful violation of the law. A more complete statement would have been that all crimes presuppose a wrongful and unexcused violation of the law. There were other points taken for granted, for example: that the problems of jurisdiction were preliminary to problems of substantive liability; that the violation of procedural rules did not bear on the violation of substantive rules; and other conceptual issues implicitly imparted in the few weeks of any course on criminal law.

It is not clear why theorists on the Continent had no problem with punishing negligent conduct, but it has always been questionable, if not taboo, in the English-speaking world. Notice the way section 2.02 of the Model Penal Code carefully distinguishes between recklessness and negligence. The former, which is a necessary condition for graver offenses, including murder, requires consciousness of the facts that make one's conduct culpable. (In fact, you could argue plausibly that the person oblivious to the risk is more blameworthy than the person who at least makes the effort to find out what the risk is.) The Rome Statute has followed this line of thought by requiring, unless specially provided to the contrary, intention or knowledge as the punishable mental state.

One problem may have been that we in the Anglo-Saxon world have never developed a comprehensive theory of mistake; in particular, a theory that would distinguish in principle between when a mistake should exculpate and when it should be reasonable in order to excuse. Take a case like the attempted murder and battery in the trial of Bernhard Goetz.[8] He thought sincerely – but perhaps unreasonably – that he was about to be attacked. There was a long debate in the case and in the literature about whether his belief that he would be attacked had to be subjectively or objectively unreasonable. Williams would have sympathized with the view that the mistake had to be subjectively unreasonable: in other words, that in order to lose the defense Goetz had to be aware that he was not in danger. He probably would have thought that only a mistake with consciousness of wrongdoing could be considered as *mens rea*. But that view was obviously untenable. It was socially unacceptable to acquit Goetz just because he allegedly believed, however illogically, that the four black youths on the subway had put his life in imminent danger.

The underlying issue here, whether in German, English, or in any other language, is whether the equivalent of *mens rea* is a descriptive state of a state of mind or a normative judgment about what people should know under the circumstances. The analogue to *mens rea* in German is the word *Schuld*, which means debt or guilt. I suppose theorists could once have thought that you could not be guilty unless you felt guilty or at least were aware of the reasons why you should feel

---

[8] *People v. Goetz* (1986) 68 NY2d 96.

guilty. But the language here does not lead us astray as much as the translation of *mens rea* into English does.

The use of "mind" in the English translation of *mens rea* is the problem. It leads theorists to think that some state of consciousness is required for culpability. Even the Rome Statute applies the term "mental element" to the required states of culpability. Behind this way of thinking is an old-fashioned division of the elements of crime into physical and mental elements – plus defenses. This is the outmoded structure we still find in French law, the Rome Statute, and many other jurisdictions around the world.

The connection between negligence and the theory of mistake is very simple. The conventional position is that any mistake will excuse if it negates the intention or knowledge as the required mental states. But when must a mistake be reasonable in order to excuse? It is not a very good answer to reply, as does the Model Penal Code, that it depends on whether negligence is assigned as the particular culpability requirement for the element at stake. The prior question is what culpability element should, in principle, be assigned to that element. In the case of defenses like self-defense, the problem becomes more complicated. The elements of justification are always stated in the negative: the claim of self-defense is justified if the defendant believes that he is about to be attacked. To disprove self-defense it is sufficient that the prosecutor prove that the defendant did not have the requisite belief to sustain a claim of self-defense.

The common law tendency in this area is to treat the problem of knowledge or intention in the case of self-defense as an aspect of *mens rea*. But this is not a *mens rea* problem. The presence of the state of mind does not inculpate, but exculpates the defendant.

The proving area of these theories has been the German jurisprudence on mistake of law. The Americans and the English, not to mention the French and many other countries, have never tried to deal intelligently with mistake of law. The German Supreme Court resolved the problem in 1952 after an extensive debate in the literature. They finally held that only an invincible (or reasonable) mistake of law would excuse.

Note the alternatives to this position:

(1) mistakes of law can never acquit;
(2) mistakes of law can acquit if they negate the required intention (Rome Statute, Article 32(2));
(3) mistakes of law always acquit in intentional offenses (German law before 1952);

(4) mistakes of law can acquit if they are based on certain kinds of reliance on statements made by legal authorities (Model Penal Code);

(5) mistakes of law will acquit sometimes if they are reasonable, invincible, ineluctable, or subject to some other qualifier that renders them free of fault;

(6) mistake of law is never an excuse, because if it were the law would be as the defendant believed it to be and hence there would be no mistake (Hall).

None of these positions will ground in the theory of the criminal law. The biggest problem is not confronting the problem of whether knowledge of wrongdoing should be included in the definition of intention. This uncertainty still plagues the International Criminal Court.

The reason for this complication is that we cannot accept the most appealing standard, namely, that mistake of law is always an excuse for intentional crimes. There are too many people who would want to take advantage of this standard who are not in fact morally innocent. They may not know that they are violating the law, but they could easily have perceived the legal consequences of what they were doing. If you carry a gun, you might inquire whether you need a license. If you hire a dozen undocumented workers, you might think it appropriate to inquire whether this is legal. If you win a million dollars in a lottery, you should inquire whether you have to pay taxes on your winnings. These are cases in which the actor, as it were, is placed on notice. When you are placed on notice and you do not respond to the clues in your situation, you do not intentionally violate the law, but you do so negligently.

All of this is to say that very little supports Williams' effort to ban negligence as a ground of responsibility in the criminal law. The overkill would be too great. Without negligence and its analogues, neither the criminal law nor neighboring fields would be able to function fairly. For one, it would be virtually impossible to construct a coherent theory of mistake of law.

As we have noted, Hall had other problems with regard to mistakes (No. 6 above). His position was more conceptually confused than the other failed attempt to solve the problem. The easy way to see this is to compare mistake of law to insanity. No one would say that a successful claim of insanity redefines the legal standard. Similarly with other excuses, including mistake of law. They do not render the conduct lawful, but merely provide a personal excuse for not punishing someone who has violated the law.

B   The problem of consent and mens rea

In 1975 the English body of criminal theorists confronted a case that they apparently could not solve. In *Director of Public Prosecutions* v. *Morgan*,[9] a group of RAF soldiers encountered the husband of Mrs. Morgan in a bar, all of them presumably a bit drunk. Mr. Morgan convinced the soldiers that his wife enjoyed having sexual intercourse forced on her. Provided with her address, the soldiers broke into her home and raped her, repeatedly. She protested, but they claimed that they understood this is to be part of the game. The soldiers pleaded consent, or at least, mistake about consent. The extraordinary thing about this case is that the House of Lords actually held that they could have been acquitted if the jury had accepted that they genuinely believed that Mrs. Morgan was consenting to the intercourse.

Even more surprising than this decision was that several prominent English theorists of criminal law, including Glanville Williams, supported the decision.[10] Feminists in the United Kingdom were, of course, up in arms. The logic supporting the decision is that rape requires an intent to have intercourse contrary to the will of the victim, and the "poor" deceived soldiers of the RAF did not have this intent and therefore they could not have the intent required for rape. Apart from this case flouting common sense and ordinary sensibilities of justice, the remarkable feature of the Williams' school (if I may generalize) is the assumption that we really know what form of intent is required for the crime of rape. There is nothing specified in the common law or in any statute known to me. The assumption is that the required intent includes not merely the intent to have intercourse, but intercourse against the will of the woman. The model for the *Morgan* definition is larceny, which requires that the taking should be by intercourse against the will of the "owner" of her body. This structure may work fine in theft offenses, but it has no grounding in homicide or other crimes against the person.

<hr/>

[9] [1976] AC 182.
[10] Williams supported the decision because he took the view that a belief as unreasonable as that held by the defendants in *DPP* v. *Morgan* would never be accepted as being genuinely held by a jury. In other words, Williams thought the fact that a jury was unlikely to accept that the defendants held such a belief would be sufficient to obtain a conviction in such cases. This was certainly the case in *DPP* v. *Morgan*, as the House of Lords upheld the conviction on the ground that the jury had found that the defendants had not in fact held the unreasonable belief they claimed to have held. See Glanville Williams, *Textbook of Criminal Law* (London: Stevens, 1983), pp. 128–132.

Williams' position on negligence is obviously linked to his view in the *Morgan* case. If negligence is not really a form of *mens rea*, then it would not do to hold that the defendants were guilty if they were negligent as to the consent of the woman. Either the defendants had to knowingly or intentionally disregard her non-consent or they were not guilty. I am afraid this is the same result we would get under the Rome Statute if someone were charged with rape as a crime against humanity. It is difficult to know whether negligence as to the consent of the women would not be sufficient. The argument would depend on whether the element of non-consent is part of the definition of the offense or a justification to be treated by analogy to self-defense. More about this problem in a moment.

You do not have to be a law student or a lawyer to realize that there is something slightly crazy in the *Morgan* case. These guys stupidly follow the advice of Mr. Morgan and they are immune from liability for rape (attempted rape might be a more complicated story). It is almost as though Mrs. Morgan does not count in the equation of consent. Whatever her husband says and is believed by the culprits counts as a basis for denying the malicious intentions of her rapists. As many critics pointed out at the time, the sensible solution is to create a crime of negligent rape.[11] Another solution would have been to define consent as permission that must emanate directly from the potential victim of the crime. As between these two, the simpler is to recognize negligence as a basis for committing rape.

Perhaps Williams was overly faithful to the concept of *mens rea*. Since negligence was not *mens rea*, it could not qualify as a mode of committing rape. There are three stages to this great error. They proceed in this sequence:

(1) *mens rea* is a descriptive not a normative state;
(2) negligence must be described as an absence of mind (inadvertence);
(3) ergo, negligence is not a form of *mens rea*.

The root error, which the common law has not yet grasped, is that *mens rea*, culpability, *Schuld*, and all equivalent words are normative standards about who should be blamed in order to warrant being punished. The only real insight required for this shift of interpretation is to realize that deciding who should be punished is an irreducibly normative

---

[11] England and Wales now has an offense of negligent rape. See s. 1 of the Sexual Offences Act 2003.

inquiry. If it is, then the syllogism leading to punishment must be based on normative concepts.

C   Distinguishing between acts and omissions

The one place where Glanville and I seem to see eye-to-eye is on the classification of certain difficult prolonging life cases as omissions rather than as commissions.[12] The specific problem is turning off the respirator for a patient who cannot be sustained any other way. There is a great deal in the law to support the simple *sine qua non* test of causation. Any preceding event, such as turning off the switch that leads to death, is a cause of death. The only problem with this standard is that every omission becomes a cause – something obviously not held to be true in the common law or in any legal system. This leaves open the question of how we distinguish among *sine qua non* causes – some being treated as acts causing death, others as omissions failing to prevent death. In an article I wrote early in my career, I ventured to say that in these cases of terminating life support, the action of turning off the switch should be treated as an omission, namely, as the failure to sustain life longer.[13] It should be treated like administering artificial respiration, but getting tired and giving up. The person who gives up does not kill the patient. Call this a form of active omission. It should be treated, as are all omissions, according to whether there is a duty to keep the patient alive.

At the time physicians were terrified of legal liability. The doctors keeping Karen Quinlan alive would not do anything without a court order. Williams saw in my article on "active omissions" a way out and he eagerly picked it up in a collection on euthanasia he was then preparing. I was flattered even though I did not see my article as having the purpose of supporting euthanasia. I thought of it primarily as an exercise in conceptual analysis, with some legal consequences. In that article and in subsequent pieces, I developed a theory in opposition to the conventional view that action was bodily movement expressing the will of the actor. The relevant distinction should be, I have argued, between killing and letting die, not the way the movement of the body entered into the context of killing. Turning off the respirator was clearly a case, I thought, of letting die, and the literature and case law have followed me on this point.

[12] Williams, *Textbook of Criminal Law*, pp. 279–280.
[13] George P. Fletcher, "Prolonging Life," *Washington Law Review*, 42 (1966), 999.

After H. L. A. Hart and Tony Honoré published their influential book *Causation in the Law*,[14] we all have been more sensitive to the role of context in classifying factors bearing on death as acts or omissions. Deliberately not feeding a plant or a child – when expected to do so – could be a cause of death, not just letting die. That the action is expressed in forbearance is not the critical question. The dividing line is between those cases where there is a universal duty not to kill as opposed to a contextual duty to intervene and save life. When we use the words "action of killing," we are assuming we are in the realm where universal duty applies. When the language is one providing care and assistance, we look around for a duty that would make this binding on a specific person. In any event, I appreciate this single point of convergence of my views with those of Glanville Williams. I am afraid, however, that our motives were different. For Glanville, the issue was facilitating euthanasia. I cared less about this than the conceptual problems for their own sake.

D The problem of structure

As it turned out, Williams had a pro-defense position on most issues. This was certainly true in the *Morgan* case. In the case of negligence, his arguments are also restrictive of liability; in the case of omissions, he leans in the same direction: the more killings can be classified as omission, the easier it is to treat them as permissible.

Williams did not realize, however, that many opportunities to fashion claims for the defense derive from the inherent structure of the criminal law. This is not a reference to the distinction between *actus reus* and *mens rea*, or objective and subjective elements of the offense, but rather to the tripartite division between the definition of the offense, the dimension of wrongdoing (absence of justification), and the problem of culpability (absence of excuse), as these dimensions are recognized today in virtually all civilian legal systems. This is not simply the problem of distinguishing between justification and excuse, but recognizing that the entire phenomenon of crime lends itself to analysis according to different questions with different implications.

Two distinctive disputes arise out of these questions of structure. One is whether there is an important difference between definition of the offenses and the elements of justification, and the second is whether claims of justification could be defined in the same objective terms as are

---

[14] *Causation in the Law* (Oxford: Clarendon Press, 1959).

the elements of the definition. Each of these disputes requires some explanation.

E   Definition and justification

My disagreements with Glanville expressed themselves largely in private correspondence and personal conversation. He was too much a gentleman to take on a younger colleague in print simply because he disagreed. But there was one very significant and characteristic issue on which Glanville did express himself in the journals. The question is whether there is a significant distinction between the elements of the definition of the offense (as I call them) and the claims of justification.[15] It is possible to state the issues relevant to homicide in self-defense in the following way. The normal practice today is that the prosecution must prove beyond a reasonable doubt three dimensions of liability, which includes the definition of the offenses, the absence of claims of justification, and the absence of claims of excuse.

It is possible to divide all the issues bearing on liability into those relevant to the definition, those relevant to wrongdoing, and those relevant to excusing wrongdoing. On this trifurcated model, the elements of definition and justification all bear on the question of wrongdoing. It is possible, therefore, to claim that justification is simply a negative formation of an element of the definition the offense. You need an act of killing a human being, and you also need a context in which no one is to try to kill the defender. The argument is that they both bear on wrongdoing and, therefore, there is no critical difference between them.

Williams could go along with the distinction between justification and excuse (after all the distinction was expressed in the ancient common law of homicide), but drawing a sharp line between definition and justification struck Williams as superfluous. He wrote one article for the American law reviews, but it is a very important one: the review of Sanford Kadish's *Encyclopaedia of Crime and Justice* published in the *California Law Review* in 1984. The point of this article was to defend his view on the structure of offenses.[16]

---

[15] See, e.g., Glanville Williams, "Offences and Defences," *Legal Studies*, 2 (1982), 233.
[16] Glanville Williams, "Book Review of Sanford H. Kadish: *Encyclopedia of Crime and Justice*," *California Law Review*, 72 (1984), 1347, 1352.

Williams praises my entries on the theory of justification and excuse, but then turns his critical acumen on what he took as a mistaken distinction between elements of the definition and justification. These are his words:

> George Fletcher's contribution on the theory of Justification appears to me to be blemished. He states as two questions bearing on criminal liability: "(1) Did the defendant's act violate a valid norm of the criminal law?" and "(2) Is the violation of the norm unlawful (unjustified)?" Speaking in friendship and with admiration, and purely on an intellectual level, without a hint of opprobrium, I pronounce the second question to be nonsense. If an act violates a valid norm, it must be unlawful and unjustified. No separate question (2) arises. In my opinion, there are or should be no differences in substantive law between elements of an offence and matters of justification. The distinction between the elements of an offence and justifications is important only in relation to pleading, or to the evidential burden, or (occasionally, and I think improperly) to the burden of persuasion; and it is not necessarily the same for these various purposes.

This claim has a certain superficial appeal. If there is one norm, there can be only one form of violating the norm. Therefore, it seems counterintuitive to think of norms on two levels, and that the person who justifiably kills in self-defense violates one norm but not the other.

A philosopher – Judith Jarvis Thompson – discovered the ideas implicit in the German system on her own. She intuited there are two ways of breaking a rule. You can infringe the rule and you can violate it. The former seemed to her less grievous. It left room for a justification for the infringement, which would preclude a finding of violation. Killing a person in self-defense would infringe the rule protecting life, but it would not violate it. The same thing could be said about promise-keeping. The literature about promise-keeping always adds a *ceteris paribus* clause. Other things being equal, it would be wrong to break a promise. The finding that there is no exception (that nothing has changed between the time of promising and the time of performance) implies that the promise must be performed. As the contract lawyers say, there is no condition of *rebus sic stantibus* and therefore *pacta sunt servanda*. All of these ways of speaking – infringement and violation, *pacta sunt servanda*, and *rebus sic stantibus*, definition, and justification – all express the same idea. There are lower order norms and higher order norms. The space between them provides an opportunity to justify the infringement of the lower order norm.

There are numerous practical implications of the distinction between definition and justification. One of the most important is the possibility of inventing new claims of justification without violating the rule of *nulla poena sine lege*.[17] The statute had defined the prohibited cases of abortion and the permitted exceptions. There was no justification to save the life of the mother, but the court recognized one under the general principle of right, or law as a principle of justice. Whether we are working in the common law or the civil law, we adhere to higher principles of unwritten law that enable us to take the definitions of the statute and submit them to higher claims of justification.

In retrospect it seems that a great scholar like Williams should have thought of views in this regard as "nonsense." It only proves that you cannot make judgments of this type without being exposed to the entire argument.

F   Objective justification

Whether there is a critical difference between definition and justification shapes a second debate, namely, whether claims of self-defense or other justifications like necessity require an intent to act on the justification. If there were no difference between definition and justification, you might argue that the objective circumstances were sufficient either to block the proof of the definition or to establish a justification. If the intended victim is not dead, you cannot establish a case of homicide, even if the actor thinks he is dead. The objective facts are sufficient to block the prosecution for the completed crime, regardless of what the perpetrator might think.

The same is not true in cases of self-defense or other claims of justification or excuse. The objective facts – if unregistered on the person supposedly affected – cannot create a barrier to conviction. To put it another way, the defender's ignorance of the attack is fatal to his claim of self-defense. If he does not know that his life is in danger, his shooting the intending assassin at the right moment is no defense.

This seems clear and straightforward, and it is the prevailing legal rule in every legal system I know of. Nonetheless, this view has generated extraordinary controversy among academics. Apparently both Williams

---

[17] This is the teaching of the famous 1927 abortion case. See George P. Fletcher and Steve Sheppard, *American Law in a Global Context: The Basics* (Oxford University Press, 2005), p. 42.

and Paul Robinson, my student at UCLA in the early1960s, came independently to the view that no knowledge or intention should be required of the circumstances justifying criminal conduct, for example, the fact that you are being attacked in a case of self-defense. I had originally asserted that Robinson convinced Williams of this heresy when Robinson went to study at Cambridge in the early 1960s. But Dennis Baker has corrected me on this point. Williams came to the view earlier, as described by Hall in *Principles of Criminal Law*[18] in a discussion of the famous *Dadson* case.[19]

In the *Dadson* case the crime was apparently defined as akin to shooting someone who was not a felon. Intentionally disarming a felon might be thought of as being covered by the privilege of law enforcement. Dadson had two prior convictions for stealing wood, and therefore if the officer's intent was immaterial when he shot him, he was not guilty of shooting a two-time felon in the act of stealing wood. The prior convictions would function as something like forfeiture. It sounds ridiculous, but the claim would be that the two-time wood-cutting felon must have forfeited his life for his actions.

Dadson was convicted and properly so, but the scholars had their doubts. When we read what Hall had to say about the case, we realize the primitive state of criminal theory in the early 1960s:

> It was held, however, that since Dadson did not know, at the time of the shooting, that P was a felon, he was rightly convicted. Dr. Williams states that the decision "seems hard to reconcile with the requirement of *actus reus*," but he concludes not only that "there was no *actus reus*" but also that the decision in Dadson was wrong.[20]

First of all, it is hard to understand what Williams or anyone might have meant in saying that there was no *actus reus* in shooting the thief. This confusion is a consequence of the point discussed in section E above, the distinction between the definition of the offense and justification. For Williams to be right we have to take those whom the criminal law aims to protect by the relevant offense as persons who have never been convicted of a felony for stealing wood. Accordingly, Dadson was not a protected person and therefore there was no harm cognizable by the criminal law.

The disagreement with Robinson stemmed from the same confusion – or more politely put, the same concept of the interest protected by the

---

[18] Jerome Hall, *General Principles of Criminal Law* (Indianapolis, IN: Bobbs-Merrill, 1947), p. 228.
[19] *R. v. Dadson* (1850) 2 Den 35; 169 ER 407.   [20] Hall, *Principles of Criminal Law*, p. 228.

criminal law. Robinson simply could not see the point of the intent requirement in any justification cases. If you burned down a field with arson on your mind and by accident you save a town, arguably there should be no crime. If you maliciously shoot someone who – unbeknown to you – is about to set off a large explosion resulting in many deaths, there should be no liability. It seemed fairly obvious to me that Robinson was confusing the issues of harm and justification, but it was not so easy to explain what the distinguishing feature of justification was and why it required an intention to effectuate the good end.

The best hypothetical Robinson ever devised was a variation on an incident that occurred in Tel Aviv. A lounger at the beach decided to steal a backpack belonging to the person next to him. He got it a safe distance away, opened the bag and found that it contained a bomb, which he immediately turned over to the police. On these facts, Robinson's view is that it would be absurd to charge this accidentally Good Samaritan with theft. Maybe he is right, but it is hard to see the theft as justified by the defense of lesser evils when the Samaritan had no idea that he was removing the dangerous bomb.

The standard view in all legal systems has always been that justification requires knowledge of the justifying circumstances. This makes sense if you think of justification as a matter of having a good reason for violating the *prima facie* norm prohibiting the conduct. The best case for Robinson and Williams is that whatever the legal systems of the world require, the objectively justified actor does not cause the harm required for liability. That is, the element of justification is built into a lesser conception of interested persons protected by the offenses. It is not all humans who are protected. It is only humans who are not attacking others. The objective justification implies that there is no harm that should be sanctioned by the criminal law.

The flaw in this argument is that if the criteria of justification bear on the required harm, then why isn't every third party equally entitled to kill the aggressor? A similar problem arises in the cases on omissions, where Williams was convinced that pulling the plug on the respirator was an omission. Why, then, would it not be a permissible omission for the night orderly to pull the plug as well?

IV   Concluding observations

As we delve deeper into these cases we see that they are all responses to the problem that arises when three different perspectives on criminal law intersect. One is action, which is the standard focus of the criminal law. The second is status, which comes into play in cases like *Dadson* as well as in the law of war. If killing Dadson is not criminal it is only because his status as a felon makes him a permissible target. The third is relationship, which serves to restrain the open-end consequences of objective justification and omissions in place of actions. Only those who bear a certain relationship to a potential victim should be able to pull the plug or fire the gun in objective justification.

By entering into these abstract considerations that lie at the foundation of the criminal law – action, status, and relationship – we can see how far the theoretical stimulus of Williams, Hall, and Robinson have pushed us. That is a tribute to them and the possible enrichment that their work will reap in the years to come. For the time being, however, it makes sense to temper high-flying theory with some basic considerations of comparative law. The consensus of legal systems is not always right. But the convergence of different cultures who have pondered the same issues should lead us to think that we are close to a stable equilibrium. On most of the issues debated in sections A–F of this chapter there is an obvious consensus:

(A) inadvertent negligence is a basis for liability and disregarding mistakes all over the world;

(B) I find it hard to believe that anyone today would regard the *Morgan* case as correctly decided;

(C) there might be more controversy about whether turning off the respirator is an omission, but this view seems to have been commonly accepted in the leading hospitals of the world;

(D) the principle that structure matters in the analysis of the criminal law is gaining ground, but we can see from the Rome Statute – which invoked a minimal amount of structure – that the debate is still very much alive;

(E) the distinction between definition and justification is still not widely accepted, as is evidenced by the lack of a good word in support of the distinction in the Anglo-American jurisprudence;

(F) objective justification has a following among some of our better theorists, but I predict that with the growing sophistication of structural considerations this view will die out.

Of course, Williams, Hall, and Robinson each has particularities. My purpose here has been to honor Williams, whose instincts are so sound on many points that I am surprised that we disagree at all. In the end, I think, Williams was as good an English lawyer as one can be. If we disagree, it is probably because I pay more attention to the consensus of theorists around the world. There is little doubt in my mind that comparative law serves greatly to avoid errors and to even out our theoretical views with due regard for the community of scholars worldwide.

3

Preventive orders and the rule of law

ANDREW ASHWORTH*

Glanville Williams always supported his arguments of principle with an enormous depth and breadth of detailed understanding of the law. One of the topics on which he brought his learning to bear was 'preventive justice and the rule of law', on which he published an article in 1953.[1] This was a crusading essay, in which he attacked the powers of courts to bind over, to keep the peace, and to be of good behaviour: demonstrating that the powers lacked certainty of definition; that they had come to be used much more widely than authority could support; and that they were afflicted with various procedural defects. Moreover, he objected, the sanction for non-compliance was imprisonment and nothing less, which was inappropriately severe when courts have the power to grant a conditional discharge for actual offences.

I Binding over

The powers to bind a person over take perhaps seven different forms, some at common law, some under various statutes such as the Justices of the Peace Act 1361 and the Magistrates' Courts Act 1980.[2] The details are not necessary here: in essence, when a court decides that the conduct of any person before it (as defendant, complainant or witness) gives it reason to believe that that person may cause a breach of the peace, it

* The work on this chapter forms part of the three-year 'Preventive Justice' project that the author is undertaking with his colleague Professor Lucia Zedner, generously supported by the AHRC, Project No. AH/HO15655/1. I am grateful to Tony Smith for comments on a draft.
[1] Glanville Williams, 'Preventive Justice and the Rule of Law', *Modern Law Review*, 16 (1953), 417–27; the article was substantially reproduced as ch. 16 of his *Criminal Law: The General Part*, 2nd edn (London: Stevens, 1961).
[2] Set out at: www.cps.gov.uk/legal/a_to_c/binding_over_orders.

may ask that person to enter into a recognizance (a sum of money to be forfeited in the event of breach). If the person refuses and is aged 18 or over, imprisonment for up to six months under the 1980 Act or imprisonment for any period under the other powers may follow. A bind-over order does not amount to a criminal conviction, but on breach the recognizance is forfeited.[3]

In this chapter, my aim is to re-visit the principal arguments advanced in Glanville's 1953 article and to consider their application to some contemporary forms of preventive justice. The article has proved influential. In 1994, the Law Commission published a report that recommended the abolition of the bind-over powers, on the grounds that they were substantively and procedurally defective (adopting several of Glanville's arguments), and that they were also unnecessary in view of the availability of other powers.[4] The government of the day took no action on that report, not least because many police officers, prosecutors, magistrates and judges considered the powers to be an important resource. Then, in 1999, the European Court of Human Rights held in *Hashman and Harrup* v. *United Kingdom*[5] that the power to bind a person over 'to be of good behaviour' was insufficiently certain to satisfy the 'quality of law' test under the European Convention on Human Rights, and therefore that this form of binding over could not be regarded as a justifiable interference with the right to freedom of expression. Its particular failing was that the expression 'to be of good behaviour' gave insufficient guidance to citizens: the standard definition referred to behaviour that is 'wrong rather than right in the judgment of the majority of contemporary fellow citizens',[6] and that gave inadequate guidance in that it did not describe the prohibited behaviour by reference to its effect (compared with 'likely to cause a breach of the peace', for example). Four years later, the then government issued a Consultation Paper, taking note of the Strasbourg judgment and of some of the Law Commission's criticisms, but proposing to retain bind-overs and therefore to reject the Law Commission's principal recommendation:

---

[3] There is also a recent statutory power to bind over a parent to ensure proper care and control of a child under 18: Powers of Criminal Courts Act 2000, s. 150.

[4] Law Com. No. 222, *Binding Over* (1994).   [5] (2000) 30 EHRR 241.

[6] Taken from the judgment of Glidewell L J in *Holley* v. *Hughes* (1988) 86 Cr App R 130, at p. 139.

Practitioners argued strongly that the power continued to have a valid place in the sentencing framework as a form of preventive justice. It was seen as effective in defusing difficult situations and settling disputes, often as an alternative to lengthy and contentious court proceedings.[7]

The then government decided that many of the procedural reforms could be effected without primary legislation, and so several changes were incorporated into the Consolidated Practice Direction, and subsequently the Criminal Procedure Rules. Part III.31 of the Criminal Procedure Rules sets out various requirements on evidence, burden of proof, calculating the amount of the recognizance, responding to a refusal to enter into a recognizance and other matters. Above all, the Rules state that courts should no longer bind persons over to be of good behaviour; and that, when they bind persons over to keep the peace, they should specify the types of behaviour from which they should refrain.[8] We will return to the latter issue in due course, but nothing more will be said below about the power to bind a person over to be of good behaviour. That part of the battle appears to have been won, and Glanville's criticisms accepted; but there are several other respects in which the new Rules do not go far enough to meet the 1953 critique.

II What is 'preventive justice'?

English law contains a whole range of measures that might be brought under the umbrella of 'preventive justice'. Some of them form part of the criminal law itself, notably the inchoate offences of attempt and conspiracy – a substantial part of whose rationale is that what has been done so far (with the intent of committing the full offence) is sufficient to justify conviction and thus intervention in order to prevent the occurrence of the prohibited harm. Beyond that, there are preventive measures in criminal procedure, such as arrest and remand in custody pending trial, and also preventive forms of sentence, such as 'discretionary' life imprisonment. The common law doctrines of breach of the peace are different in structure from all these examples, but still preventive in purpose. First, the police have powers to prevent a breach of the peace

---

[7] Home Office, *Bind-Overs: A Power for the 21st Century*, Consultation Document, March 2003, para. 3.8.
[8] Criminal Procedure Rules (2010), Part III.31.3.

from occurring, powers that extend to arrest, entry and restricting people's freedom of movement. The uncertainty surrounding these powers is a matter for reproach in the modern law,[9] not least because Parliament has introduced legislation on police powers (Public Order Act 1986, Criminal Justice and Public Order Act 1994) and yet the common law power is increasingly relied upon and extended.[10] These issues will not be taken further here. Second, a court has various powers, noted above, to bind a person over to keep the peace: the bind-over order enables the court to place a restraint on someone, by virtue of what they have already done (e.g., making a threat, although that need not have constituted an offence), in order to prevent the peace from being broken by the commission of the threatened offence. Binding over sits on the edge of the criminal law, since the making of an order does not require an offence to have been committed, as long as the court is satisfied that the person has done something that gives rise to the apprehension of a future breach of the peace.

The essence of 'preventive justice', in the sense that Glanville Williams and others have used the term, is that it involves measures intended to prevent the likely or imminent commission of an offence. The word 'justice' is used here in one of its broader senses: it cannot be taken to imply that what is done is 'just', but is rather used with the same general meaning as in the phrase 'criminal justice system', to convey that it is part of an authoritative response to (anticipated) wrongdoing. It would be more precise, therefore, to regard binding over as one of many preventive *measures* or *orders*, and to avoid any possible connotation that binding-over orders achieve substantive or procedural justice. Those must remain subjects for enquiry, and it is for that reason that the title of this chapter deviates from that of Glanville's original article by referring to preventive orders.

---

[9] See the critique by R. Stone, 'Breach of the Peace: the Case for Abolition', *Web Journal of Current Legal Issues*, 2 [2001], 3, and by H. Fenwick, 'Breach of the Peace and Kettling', *Public Law* [2009], 737.

[10] See, e.g., *Austin v. Commissioner of Police for the Metropolis* [2009] UKHL 5 and *Austin v. United Kingdom*, judgment, 15 March 2012, on which see A. Ashworth, 'Negotiating the Fundamental Right to Personal Liberty: Four Problem Cases', *Otago Law Review*, 14 (2013) (forthcoming); and *R. (Moos and McClure) v. Commissioner of Police for the Metropolis* [2012] EWCA Civ 12 and R. Glover, 'The Uncertain Blue Line: Police Cordons and the Common Law', *Criminal Law Review* [2012], 245.

III   The rule of law

The other part of the title of Glanville's 1953 article is 'the rule of law'. This is not the place to distinguish the many meanings of this over-worked phrase, but it is important to signal two different senses in which the concept will be relevant to this chapter. First, 'the rule of law' may be taken to indicate an orderly society, not one that is crime-free but one in which the authority of the courts is generally respected. In this sense, 'upholding the rule of law' is regarded as an important objective so as to ensure a reasonable level of security for people living in the relevant country. Among other things, it entails the proper enforcement of orders of the courts, as discussed further in relation to proposition (A) below. Second, we will have occasion to refer to 'rule-of-law' values such as certainty and predictability in the law, fair warning, the avoidance of arbitrary powers and so forth. This is central to the discussion of proposition (D) below.

IV   Six propositions on preventive orders

The substance of the critique of binding-over orders advanced by Glanville Williams in his 1953 article can be re-framed in six propositions, as follows:

(A) It is contrary to principle to punish a person for something that may be done hereafter; there must be some act(s) already done giving rise to the apprehension of a breach of the peace.

(B) The concept of 'breach of the peace' must be held to refer to physical violence of some sort, and not simply to any possible crime.

(C) When Parliament has laid down the maximum punishment for a particular offence, it is not permissible to invoke a different process or different powers in order to circumvent the legislative limitation.

(D) Any court order that, if breached, may have serious consequences must attain the appropriate level of certainty and clarity of definition, so that the subject can know precisely what should not be done.

(E) The powers of the courts, and of the law officers, must be clearly circumscribed; it is not acceptable to allow broad discretion as to the evidence that may be received and the prohibitions that may be imposed.

(F) Reliance on imprisonment as the sole method of enforcement is disproportionate, not least when a court may impose a conditional discharge on a person who (unlike many of those who are bound over) is actually convicted of an offence.

The rest of this chapter will consist of an examination of these propositions in relation to the order binding over a person to keep the peace, and to other forms of preventive order that have been introduced subsequently. It is instructive to see what has become of some propositions, for which Glanville Williams was able to give strong authority from the first half of the twentieth century.

A   Punishment based on proven conduct

The first proposition is that 'it is contrary to principle to punish a person for something that may be done hereafter; there must be some act(s) already done giving rise to the apprehension of a breach of the peace'. This proposition should be explored on two different levels: the principle (or is it an analytical statement?) that a person cannot be punished for conduct not yet done; and the actual requirements for making a binding-over order.

In his 1953 article, Glanville Williams described as 'admirable' the restatement of the relevant law by Denning LJ in *Everett* v. *Ribbands*,[11] which included the following words:

> It would be contrary to all principle for a man to be punished, not for what he had already done, but for what he may hereafter do. Hence there must be something actually done by him, such as threats of violence . . .

What is the 'punishment' to which this passage refers? The immediate context suggests that Denning LJ was referring to the fact that a person who refuses to be bound over may be sentenced to imprisonment (up to six months under section 115 of the Magistrates' Courts Act 1980, but without limit of time under the other powers). But the imprisonment would not be for an offence, since there is no offence of breach of the peace. The imprisonment is for a kind of contempt of court, for the refusal to cooperate with the court and to comply with its authoritative order.

---

[11] [1952] 2 KB 198.

How robust is the analogy with contempt of court? Arlidge, Eady and Smith's authoritative work divides contempts into three principal categories: (i) publication contempts; (ii) other forms of criminal contempt (whether committed in the face of the court or consisting of some other form of interference with the administration of justice); and (iii) civil contempts consisting of non-compliance with court orders.[12] The focus here is on civil contempts, and this brings us to the first meaning of the 'rule of law' mentioned above. The court orders here are generally between private parties, but:

> there is an element of public policy in punishing civil contempt, since the administration of justice would be undermined if the order of any court of law could be disregarded with impunity.[13]

Thus, although the term 'contempt' appears to place the emphasis on affronts to the dignity of the court (as in (ii)), the underlying rationale of civil contempt is to ensure that the authority of the courts is upheld and that court orders are duly carried out. However, conceptually a person who defies a court order may be said to be similar to someone who commits a criminal offence, in the sense of substituting 'the private rationality of pursuit of one's own ends for the public reasonableness of fair terms of interaction'.[14] Moreover, the consequence of a finding of civil contempt may be the deprivation of liberty, and for this reason it has often been said that civil contempts are close to criminal proceedings, or at least should in principle attract the same procedural safeguards as criminal proceedings.[15]

How does this relate to bind-overs? That jurisdiction is clearly *sui generis*, but it seems to partake of elements of (ii) and (iii). It does not fit squarely within (ii), because it is not an interference with the administration of justice as such, but rather a refusal to cooperate with the court. Yet it does not fit squarely within (iii) either, since it does not amount to non-compliance with a court order. It consists of a refusal to consent to a court order, which cannot be made unless the person consents to it being made.

---

[12] *Arlidge, Eady and Smith on Contempt*, 4th edn (London: Sweet & Maxwell, 2012).

[13] *Per* Lord Diplock in *Attorney-General* v. *Times Newspapers Ltd* [1974] AC 273, at p. 308; see also *Ahnee* v. *DPP* [1999] 2 AC 294, *per* Lord Steyn, at p. 303.

[14] A. Ripstein, 'Prohibition and Pre-Emption', *Legal Theory*, 5 (1999), 235, at p. 250.

[15] *Per* Sedley LJ in *Guildford BC* v. *Valler* [1994] JPL 734; see also the recent judgments in the Supreme Court of New Zealand in *Siemer* v. *Solicitor-General* [2010] NZSC 54.

Even though imprisonment for refusal to be bound over is *sui generis*, it comes close to satisfying the definition of punishment. Without entering into a full examination of that question,[16] it may be noted that Hart's famous definition includes the stipulation that 'it must be of an actual or supposed offender for his offence'.[17] As there is plainly no criminal offence here, imprisonment for a refusal to be bound over is not a species of punishment as such, although it may be thought to be analogous, since it is an authoritative deprivation of rights that censures the person for a failure to cooperate in the endeavour of preserving the peace, which is a legitimate concern of the court. 'Punishment', even if it is not for an offence as such, must be for an act done. To impose imprisonment today, on the basis of a prediction that the person imprisoned would otherwise cause a breach of the peace in the coming week, would be a preventive measure, not a punitive measure. When the accepted definition of punishment uses the phrase 'for an offence', it means an offence already committed. Some offences invoke the criminal law largely on the basis of what is likely to happen otherwise, but those offences always require proof of some past conduct – criminal attempts, dishonestly making a false representation with intent to cause gain or loss, or possession of a firearm, for example.[18] Part of Denning LJ's purpose in the passage cited above was to insist on proof of some conduct that justifies the court in 'apprehending' a breach of the peace and therefore seeking to bind the person over to keep the peace. The Criminal Procedure Rules now require a court to give both the prosecutor and the potential subject of the bind-over the opportunity to call evidence and to make representations.[19] This marks a step towards satisfying proposition (A), but it is so closely connected with proposition (B) that we must move on to consider that. The doubts about bind-overs as 'punishment' remain, however.

---

[16] On which see, e.g., C. Steiker, 'Punishment and Procedure: Punishment Theory and the Criminal–Civil Procedural Divide', *Georgetown Law Journal*, 85 (1997), 775, at pp. 800–1.

[17] H. L. A. Hart, *Punishment and Responsibility*, 2nd edn (Oxford University Press, 2008), pp. 4–5. Accord: R. A. Duff, *Punishment, Communication and Community* (Oxford University Press, 2001), pp. xiv–xv.

[18] For broader discussion, see A. Ashworth, 'The Unfairness of Risk-Based Possession Offences', *Criminal Law and Philosophy*, 5 (2011), 237.

[19] Criminal Procedure Rules, III.31.5, 6 and 7; this follows the proposal in the 2003 Consultation Paper, above n. 7, para. 7.5.

B 'Breach of the peace' linked to unlawful violence

The second proposition is that 'the concept of "breach of the peace" must be held to refer to physical violence of some sort, and not simply to any possible crime'. In his 1953 article, Glanville Williams was able to cite overwhelming authority for this proposition,[20] and to draw two instructive distinctions: first, that the concept of peace in 'breach of the peace' has a narrower meaning than in the term 'the Queen's peace', which is indeed violated by the commission of any crime; and, second, that only under the rubric of binding over to be of good behaviour (no longer available, as noted above) could a person be bound over not to commit a non-violent offence. A third point is that the violence must be unlawful, for example, not justifiable by way of self-defence.

Not surprisingly, proposition (B) has been placed under some tension by later decisions. Part of the context for this is that the concept of 'breach of the peace' is central not merely to the courts' power to bind people over, but also to a police officer's power to arrest someone without a warrant if the officer believes that a breach of the peace is likely to be committed. This broad power of arrest, which (unusually) is not dependent on the suspected commission of an offence, has long been regarded by the police as a vital tool in dealing with demonstrations, disturbances and other perceived threats to public order.[21] The legal meaning of the phrase 'breach of the peace' is the same both for the power of arrest and for the power to bind over, as the Court of Appeal held in *Howell*.[22] It is relevant to recall what the court said about the justification for the power of arrest:

> The public expects a policeman not only to apprehend the criminal but to do his best to prevent the commission of crime, to keep the peace, in other words. To deny him, therefore, the right to arrest a person who he reasonably believes is about to breach the peace would be to disable him from preventing that which might cause serious injury to someone or even to many people or to property. The common law, we believe, whilst recognising that a wrongful arrest is a serious invasion of a person's liberty, provides the police with this power in the public interest.[23]

[20] See Williams, 'Preventive Justice and the Rule of Law', pp. 417–18.

[21] Still cited as the *locus classicus* on this is Glanville Williams, 'Arrest for Breach of the Peace', *Criminal Law Review* [1954], 578; see also A. T. H. Smith, *Offences against Public Order* (London: Sweet & Maxwell, 1987), pp. 48–9.

[22] (1981) 73 Cr App R 31.

[23] *Ibid.*, at p. 36, *per* Watkins LJ. As the court recognised, the power of arrest may be exercised by a citizen, not just by a police officer.

This is a striking affirmation of the logic of prevention, and it may also be applied to the inchoate offences in criminal law, which operate to prevent the perpetration of the prohibited harm by enabling the police and the court to intervene before that harm has been caused. Essential to charting the proper boundaries of preventive policing, however, is the scope of this power.

In *Howell* the Court of Appeal was invited by counsel for the prosecution to endorse a wide conception of 'breach of the peace' which would encompass 'public alarm and excitement' and 'disturbance'. Rejecting these broader parameters, the Court concluded that:

> there is a breach of the peace whenever harm is actually done or is likely to be done to a person or in his presence to his property or a person is in fear of being so harmed through an assault, an affray, a riot, unlawful assembly or other disturbance.[24]

Although this definition is a considerable improvement on what went before, it remains relatively broad and uncertain. The context of the inclusion of 'disturbance' in this definition is that Watkins LJ stated that 'the word disturbance when used in isolation cannot constitute a breach of the peace'; however, the mere presence of the term in this definition may be thought to open a door to more expansive interpretations. As for damage to property, this was included without any restriction in the passage cited earlier in relation to the power of arrest; but in the later passage it is restrictively phrased, 'in his presence to his property', so that it might be linked to a fear that violence may be provoked.[25] Further, the reference to putting a person 'in fear' is potentially far-reaching, since it seems apt to include anyone who experiences fear, whether reasonably or not.[26]

A significantly more expansive meaning of 'breach of the peace' was advanced by Lord Denning MR less than a year after the *Howell* judgment, dismissing the view that violence or a threat of violence was necessary and proposing that mere obstruction of people going about their daily work would be sufficient.[27] However, this broader view has

---

[24] *Ibid.*, at p. 37.
[25] This restrictive reading was confirmed in *Percy* v. *DPP* [1995] 3 All ER 124.
[26] K. Kerrigan, 'Breach of the Peace and Binding Over: Continuing Confusion', *Journal of Civil Liberties*, 2 (1997), 30, 33.
[27] In *R.* v. *Chief Constable of Devon and Cornwall, ex parte Central Electricity Generating Board* [1982] QB 458, where it was held that it would be a breach of the peace for protestors to lie in front of contractors' vehicles or to handcuff themselves to machinery. Glanville Williams was critical of Lord Denning's statement in his 'Dealing with

not found favour with the appellate courts. In *Percy* v. *Director of Public Prosecutions*[28] the Divisional Court explicitly followed *Howell*, emphasising the importance of proving violence or the threat of violence, but recognising that a person may be arrested or bound over if the natural consequence of that person's conduct was that there was a real risk that another person would be provoked to use violence.[29] In this case, the appellant had repeatedly entered an airbase, sitting down until she was escorted off the base. The court held that there was no evidence of a likely breach of the peace, in the sense that her actions had not been shown to be likely to provoke violence in others. The House of Lords has subsequently endorsed the *Howell* definition.[30]

However, the application of *Howell* to situations of public protest remains flexible, as the facts and judgment in *Steel* v. *United Kingdom*[31] show. The case concerned the arrest of five people for alleged breach of the peace. The applicants were unsuccessful in their challenge to the certainty and clarity of the legal concept of 'breach of the peace'. Three of the applicants were successful in that the European Court of Human Rights found that their actions in parading with banners and handing out leaflets had not been shown to make a breach of the peace likely. The other two applicants were unsuccessful, one having been arrested for walking in front of members of a grouse shoot to try to prevent them from firing their guns, the other having been arrested for breaking into a construction site and standing in front of a digging machine so as to prevent it from continuing its excavations. Although some members of the court held that those two applicants had been detained after arrest for far too long (forty-four hours and seventeen hours, respectively), a majority disagreed and held that the rulings of the English courts that a breach of the peace was likely to be caused by their behaviour could not be impugned.

Breaches of the Peace', *Justice of the Peace*, 146 (1982), 199 and 217, and (mostly) approving of the effect of *Howell* on bind-overs for breach of the peace.

[28] [1995] 3 All ER 124.

[29] A much-debated aspect of the law on 'breach of the peace', not canvassed in detail here, concerns the circumstances in which a person who is behaving lawfully (e.g., by demonstrating peacefully or by making a speech to advocate a particular point of view), can be said to be likely to cause a breach of the peace if others are likely to react violently to that lawful behaviour. The classic decisions are *Beatty* v. *Gillbanks* (1882) 9 QBD 308 and *Duncan* v. *Jones* [1936] 1 KB 218. For discussion, see D. Mead, *The New Law of Peaceful Protest* (Oxford: Hart, 2010), pp. 325–34.

[30] In *R. (Laporte)* v. *Chief Constable of Gloucestershire Constabulary* [2007] AC 105 and in *Austin* v. *Commissioner of Police for the Metropolis* [2009] UKHL 5.

[31] (1998) 28 EHRR 603.

The result of this survey of legal developments after 1953 shows that proposition (B) may be less secure now than it was then. The Criminal Procedure Rules follow proposition (B) closely:

> Before imposing a binding-over order, the court must be satisfied that a breach of the peace involving violence or an imminent threat of violence has occurred or that there is a real risk of violence in the future. Such violence may be perpetrated by the individual who will be subject to the order or by a third party as a natural consequence of the individual's conduct.[32]

This is narrower in terms than the *Howell* definition of 'breach of the peace', but there are two reasons for believing that courts will feel able to adopt a more expansive approach. First, as a Court of Appeal decision approved by the House of Lords, *Howell* may be treated as the stronger authority. Second, the *Howell* definition allows for significant flexibility at the point of application. It is one thing for the law to presume that, if there is a threat to damage property in its owner's presence, this is to be treated as equivalent to a threat of violence because such action would be highly provocative. That presumption may well be counter-intuitive in certain situations, and surely a real risk of violence should be proved in the normal way. But it is quite another thing to presume that protest by way of direct action (intervening to prevent the continuation of a lawful activity) is properly interpreted as creating a real risk of violence – on the basis that the person(s) obstructed may well resort to violence. There is no suggestion here of an intent to provoke violence. Without that, applying the *Howell* test as it was applied to the first two applicants in *Steel* v. *United Kingdom* (obstructing grouse shooters, obstructing construction work) appears to render the law on breach of the peace malleable enough to make significant inroads into the scope of peaceful protest. The Law Commission's trenchant conclusion bears repetition:

> 'breach of the peace' is an unsatisfactory and potentially oppressive criterion both for determining whether a person should be bound over and for determining whether an order containing an undertaking to keep the peace has been broken.[33]

The Criminal Procedure Rules themselves mark an advance towards the Law Commission's recommendations and the substance of

---

[32] Criminal Procedure Rules 2010, III.31.2; the final sentence refers to the issue identified in n. 29 above.
[33] Law Commission, above n. 4, para. 4.28.

proposition (B). The problem is that many police, prosecutors, magistrates and judges prefer the flexibility of the *Howell* test, and its application in *Steel* may be taken as a clear example of how the law on bind-overs is likely to be applied in practice.

C Legislative limits on punishment should not be circumvented

The third proposition is that 'when Parliament has laid down the maximum punishment for a particular offence, it is not permissible to invoke a different process or different powers in order to circumvent the legislative limitation'. This looks very much like an exemplary piece of constitutional doctrine, but it soon transpires that it has been a site of considerable divergence of opinion. Its immediate application is to the use of binding-over orders against people who persistently flout minor laws – the prime example in former times being trades people who opened their stalls and shops at times forbidden by the law were prosecuted each time and paid the appropriate fine, and continued to trade unlawfully while treating the fines as a business expense. Of course, the order in those cases would be one of binding over to be of good behaviour (since there is no violence or threat involved), and that form of order is now obsolete. But, as we shall see, there may be other ways of dealing with persistent flouting of the law. In terms of its rationale, moreover, this is a significant subcategory of preventive orders – not merely preventing the occurrence of an offence, but preventing its recurrence.

The general principle was stated thus by Lord Tenterden CJ:

> where an Act creates an obligation and enforces the performance in a specified manner, we take it to be the general rule that performance cannot be enforced in any other manner.[34]

The principle was applied by the Court of Appeal in *R. v. Hurle-Hobbs, ex parte Simmons*,[35] where a district auditor had invoked statutory powers to compel the attendance of the applicant at an audit, with documents, and the applicant had refused to attend and had been fined under the statute. The district auditor then obtained a subpoena from the Crown Office to compel the applicant's attendance, but the Court of

---

[34] In *Doe* v. *Bridges* (1831) 1 B & Ald 847, at p. 859, quoted with approval by Lord Halsbury L C in *Pasmore* v. *Oswaldtwistle UDC* [1898] AC 387, at p. 394.

[35] [1945] KB 165, *per* Viscount Caldecote CJ, at p. 172.

Appeal held that this was an unlawful circumvention of the legislative scheme, relying on the principle above.

However, what appears to be a proper constitutional principle may be regarded, from another point of view, as undermining respect for the rule of law. The maximum fine for a particular offence may be so low that it fails to prevent frequent offending and re-offending, and thus jeopardises the law's authority. This was the situation in *R. v. Sandbach Justices, ex parte Williams*,[36] where the applicant had been convicted on several occasions of obstructing a constable by warning bookmakers of the approach of the police and so enabling them to evade arrest. The magistrates bound over the defendant with a surety that was significantly greater than the maximum fine for the offence that he repeatedly committed. The Court of Appeal upheld this. Lord Hewart CJ responded to the argument that there appeared to be no limits on the magistrates' powers if this were allowed, by uttering the extraordinary statement that 'the matter is discretionary and the limits are to be found in discretion'.[37] Although this claim may be dismissed as more rhetorical than reasoned, there is authority for a limited power to grant an injunction to the Attorney-General for the purpose of stifling a continued violation of the law, by traders or by others.[38] Because this power has momentous consequences, often (in effect) subjecting a person to the threat of imprisonment for refusal of this 'offer' rather than to the mere fine provided in the legislation for the offence, the House of Lords in *Gouriet v. Union of Post Office Workers*[39] held that it should be available only on application by the Attorney-General as 'guardian of the public interest'.[40] But, given that imprisonment for a maximum of two years becomes a possibility, the Attorney-General should use the power to apply for an injunction sparingly, and the courts use their power to imprison sparingly. In *Attorney-General v. Harris*,[41] for example, the 'grave and serious injury to the public', as the Court of Appeal described

---

[36] [1935] 2 KB 192.   [37] *Ibid.*, at pp. 195–6.

[38] *Attorney-General v. Harris* [1961] 1 QB 74; see also *Attorney-General v. Chaudry* [1971] 1 WLR 1614.

[39] [1978] AC 435, at p. 471.

[40] The House of Lords went on to hold that the Attorney-General's decision whether or not to apply for an injunction was not reviewable, as an exercise of the royal prerogative. The House subsequently took a narrower view in the *GCHQ* case (*Council of Civil Service Unions v. Minister for the Civil Service* [1985] AC 374), holding that the exercise (or not) of the royal prerogative was reviewable in general, but not where issues of national security or other exceptional considerations arose.

[41] Above, n. 38.

it, was deliberately opening a flower stall in defiance of the law. However, it is defiance of the law that continues to animate this jurisdiction. Thus, Mummery LJ asserted that to suspend a court order that had been deliberately disobeyed would send out the message:

> that the court is prepared to tolerate contempt of its orders . . . The effect of that message would be to diminish respect for court orders, to undermine the authority of the court and to subvert the rule of law.[42]

The issue in that case was the residential occupation of land without the grant of planning permission. Once again, the sanction of imprisonment was available, through the law of contempt, and was used.

Reference to this strong response to the defiance of court orders brings us to the contemporary phenomenon of the civil preventive order. One of the first of these, and probably the best known, is the anti-social behaviour order (ASBO). In essence, a court exercising civil jurisdiction, which is presented with evidence that a person has acted in a manner likely to cause harassment, alarm or distress to one or more other persons, may make an order (an ASBO) prohibiting that person from doing anything described in that order for a minimum of two years. If without reasonable excuse the person contravenes any of the prohibitions in the order, this amounts to a criminal offence for which the maximum sentence is five years' imprisonment.[43] There are many objections of principle to this two-step, civil–criminal procedure,[44] but our concern here is with the possibility that, by prohibiting acts that amount to criminal offences with relatively low maximum penalties, an ASBO may open the way to sentences well beyond those envisaged by the legislature for those acts. An ASBO should not be imposed 'as a kind of device to circumvent maximum penalties that are thought to be too modest';[45] thus, in *Kirby*,[46] where the court had imposed an ASBO because the maximum punishments for driving while disqualified and

---

[42] *Mid-Bedfordshire DC* v. *Brown* [2004] EWCA Civ 1709, at [26]–[27]; see also n. 11 above.

[43] Crime and Disorder Act 1998, s. 1.

[44] For discussion and references, see A. Ashworth and L. Zedner, 'Just Prevention: Preventive Rationales and the Limits of the Criminal Law', in R. A. Duff and Stuart P. Green (eds), *Philosophical Foundations of the Criminal Law* (Oxford University Press, 2011), pp. 297–303.

[45] R. v. *H., Stevens and Lovegrove* [2006] 2 Cr App R (S) 453, *per* Sir Igor Judge P. at p. 462.

[46] [2006] 1 Cr App R (S) 151, followed in *Boness, Bebbington and others* [2006] 1 Cr App R (S) 690.

dangerous driving were regarded as too low to prevent further offences by the defendant, the Court of Appeal held that this was not a proper use of the ASBO. This is clearly a principle with constitutional foundations, in that a prominent objection to the course taken by the lower court was that it was usurping the will of Parliament. The Court of Appeal respected the spirit of proposition (C) here, although without any reference to the line of decisions supporting it.

However, other decisions show the Court of Appeal to be equivocal on the point. In cases where there is no evidence that an ASBO was imposed in order to circumvent a maximum sentence regarded as too low, however, the question of respect for legislative intentions remains relevant. In *Morrison*,[47] the Court of Appeal held that in sentencing for breach of an ASBO a court should not exceed the statutory maximum for an included offence unless the nature of the breach of the ASBO 'goes beyond that offence'. But in *Lamb*[48] the Court of Appeal departed from *Morrison* and gave two reasons why the maximum for an included offence should not be treated as a limit. First, this would be to ignore Parliament's concern for the wider social impact of anti-social behaviour, which was the main reason for the maximum penalty of five years for breach of an ASBO; and, second, the *Morrison* approach would have the perverse result that that maximum would be available where the prohibited act was not a criminal offence, but unavailable where the prohibited act was a criminal offence (albeit with a lower maximum sentence). In *H., Stevens and Lovegrove*,[49] Sir Igor Judge P reaffirmed the place of flexibility on this subject, holding that any lower maximum for an included offence should be 'borne in mind' when sentencing for breach of an ASBO, but that the court should not be limited by the lower maximum because there were two additional elements: that the statutory requirements on harassment, alarm or distress have been fulfilled; and that the offender has breached a court order specifically prohibiting certain conduct.[50]

Would Glanville Williams have been impressed by this judicial reasoning? A major difficulty in accepting it arises from the constitutional dimension, and from the proper approach to determining the legislative

---

[47] [2006] 1 Cr App R (S) 488; the offence was driving while disqualified, maximum sentence six months' imprisonment.
[48] [2006] 2 Cr App R (S) 84, following *Braxton* [2005] 1 Cr App R (S) 167.
[49] Above, n. 45.
[50] In *Anti-Social Behaviour Orders: Guidance* (2007), the Judicial Studies Board is equivocal on this issue in para. 3.2.

purpose. Thus, sections 70 and 71 of the Criminal Justice Act 1982 abolished imprisonment as a maximum sentence for two particular offences: begging and soliciting for prostitution. This was the culmination of long campaigns against the use of prison for these relatively low-level offences, often committed by disadvantaged people. Then the Crime and Disorder Act 1998 introduced the ASBO, because of government concern about anti-social behaviour that reduces substantially the quality of life for citizens. Some courts then began to impose ASBOs on beggars and on people who solicit for prostitution, with the result that some of those who breached their orders were sent to prison – the very consequence that Parliament in 1982 insisted on avoiding. At that time Parliament was well aware that many of those committing these offences are repeaters, and yet it took the step of abolishing imprisonment for all such offenders, no matter how prolific they are. The legislature's decision was clear and informed.

In contrast, the parliamentary debates on the Crime and Disorder Act contained much discussion of noisy neighbours, youths hanging around on street corners and other examples, but no focused discussion of whether beggars and prostitutes should now become subject to imprisonment again. Yet the judicial reasoning in *H., Stevens and Lovegrove* above suggests that, because of Parliament's (undoubted) general concern about the social impact of anything likely to cause 'harassment, alarm or distress', it is justifiable for courts to use imprisonment against beggars and prostitutes.[51] That seems unpersuasive.[52] It is not rendered more persuasive by pointing out that the beggar or prostitute has been made subject to an ASBO that specifically prohibits them from repeating this conduct, because the existing law prohibits the conduct anyway. The high maximum penalty for breaching an ASBO (five years) is disproportionate to most breaches; to emphasise the fact that the offence involves defiance of the law by breaching a specific order of the court (as Sir Igor Judge did in *H., Stevens and Lovegrove*)[53] is unconvincing, because (a) if the prohibited act is an offence the law already sounds a warning to

---

[51] Cf. *Chief Constable of Lancashire* v. *Potter* [2003] EWHC Admin 2272.

[52] Cf. also the Public Order Act 1986, ss. 12–14, which provide a statutory framework intended to balance the various rights and liberties, and of which Lord Bingham said in *R. (Laporte)* v. *Chief Constable of Gloucestershire* [2007] AC 105, at [46], that 'it would be surprising if, alongside these closely defined powers and duties, there existed a common law power and duty … bounded only by an uncertain and undefined condition of reasonableness'.

[53] Above, n. 45, and accompanying text.

everyone, and (b) if the prohibited act is not an offence in these days of rampant criminalisation, then a prison sentence of that length is likely to be disproportionate.[54] However, the courts appear to have adopted a different approach, and proposition (C) appears to be little respected in the current law relating to civil preventive orders. Insofar as it is recognised, it is treated at best as a consideration to be weighed with others, rather than as the distinct barrier that was recognised in decisions such as *Hurle-Hobbs*.[55]

Finally, it should be noted that the current coalition government has declared its intention to abolish the ASBO and to replace it with three new kinds of order: criminal behaviour orders (to be made only on criminal conviction); crime prevention injunctions; and community protection orders.[56] Our particular interest lies with the crime prevention injunction, a new civil order to be made if it is proved on the balance of probabilities that an individual was engaging, had engaged or was likely to engage in anti-social behaviour to one or more persons not of the same household. An injunction could then be made which might include both prohibitions and positive requirements (such as attending an anger management course). Breach of the injunction would not result in a criminal conviction: it would be a civil matter, to be enforced as a civil contempt with a fine or with a maximum prison sentence of six months in a magistrates' court or two years in a higher court. This regime would be preferable to that of the ASBO, but the proposals fail to mention, let alone to prevent, the possibility of undermining proposition (C) by allowing higher penalties than those provided by the legislature for the particular conduct. This point will be taken further when discussing proposition (F) below.

D   Orders with serious consequences should contain only clear and certain prohibitions

Even in their most minimal formulations, the 'rule of law' and the principle of legality require that the criminal law should serve its guidance function by giving fair warning of prohibitions to those affected by them. In order to give fair warning, prohibitions should be as clear and as

---

[54] As the Court of Appeal held in *Lamb*, above n. 48, when substantially reducing the sentence.

[55] Above, n. 35.

[56] Home Office, *Putting Victims First: More Effective Responses to Anti-Social Behaviour*, Cm 8367 (London: HMSO, 2012).

certain as possible, not least when a significant sanction (such as imprisonment) may follow. Thus, proposition (D) is that 'any court order that, if breached, may have serious consequences must attain the appropriate level of certainty and clarity of definition, so that the subject can know precisely what should not be done'. In his 1953 article, Glanville Williams inveighed strongly against the uncertain terms of binding-over orders, mostly in relation to the now obsolete power to bind over to be of good behaviour. The Law Commission raised serious doubts about elements of uncertainty in the power to bind over to keep the peace.[57]

Since the Law Commission issued its report in 1994, there has been a great increase in the creation and use of civil preventive orders – which might be taken as further evidence in favour of the Commission's conclusion that the bind-over power is no longer needed. The ASBO was mentioned earlier, and that has since been joined by around a dozen similar orders, including risk of sexual harm orders,[58] foreign travel orders,[59] serious crime prevention orders[60] and violent offender orders.[61] These vary in their degrees of conformity to the principle of maximum certainty. The ASBO itself shares with certain offences in the Public Order Act 1986 a reliance on whether particular conduct is 'likely to cause harassment, alarm or distress'. The Law Commission raised questions about this phrase, not least because it is not confined to instances of possible violence.[62] Section 5 of the Public Order Act 1986 introduced the offence of using 'threatening, abusive or insulting words or behaviour, or disorderly behaviour' within the hearing or sight of a person 'likely to be caused harassment, alarm or distress thereby'. Both key phrases of this much-used offence have an element of uncertainty. The Joint Committee on Human Rights reviewed the section 5 offence and, having heard evidence from the police and from human rights organisations, concluded that it is open to use in a way that unfairly stifles freedom of expression.[63] The Committee's particular recommendation was that the word 'insulting' should be removed from section 5, on the ground that some protests will inevitably cause other people to be offended, but that this should not be a sufficiently strong reason for

---

[57] Law Com. No. 222, n. 4 above, para. 4.34.   [58] Sexual Offences Act 2003, s. 123.
[59] *Ibid.*, s. 114.   [60] Serious Crime Act 2007, s. 1.
[61] Criminal Justice and Immigration Act 2008, s. 98.
[62] Law Com. No. 222, *Binding Over*, para. 3.10.
[63] Joint Committee on Human Rights, *Demonstrating Respect for Rights? A Human Rights Approach to Policing Protest*, 7th Report (2009), HC 320, para. 84.

criminalising insults. People have a right to be protected from threatening or abusive speech, but criminalising mere insults goes too far in a
democracy.[64] One effect of this would be to place considerable emphasis
on the distinction between 'abusive' and 'insulting', and this might well
require further guidance in order to render it sufficiently certain.
Moreover, there remains the flexibility of the phrase 'harassment,
alarm or distress': even if it is effective to rule out 'mere annoyance or
irritation caused by inconvenience',[65] it is a pivotal phrase with uncertain boundaries. We must therefore conclude that there are doubts
whether proposition (D) is properly respected by the judiciary and the
legislature, a situation particularly regrettable in view of the court's
power to impose imprisonment for refusal to be bound over.[66]

E   Powers of the courts should be clearly circumscribed

Whereas the rationale for proposition (D) resided in the importance of
the law's function of guiding behaviour, the rationale for proposition (E)
is the prevention of arbitrariness by ensuring that powers given to courts
(or to law officers of the Crown) are exercised within a clear and certain
framework. The aim is therefore to ensure that people can predict how
the courts' powers are likely to impinge on them, and to prevent abuse of
those powers. In this context, the statement of Lord Hewart that 'the
matter is discretionary and the limits are to be found in discretion'[67] was
nothing more than an evasion of the issues. Fortunately, the 2003
Consultation Paper proposed to adopt a number of relevant recommendations made by the Law Commission,[68] and accordingly the Criminal
Procedure Rules now provide that the criminal standard of proof be used
throughout, and that courts should have regard to the financial resources
of the individual and hear representations from the individual or legal
adviser.[69] Bind-overs 'should not generally exceed 12 months',[70] and the
Consultation Paper indicated that the recognizance should not normally
be more than £1,000.[71]

The problem has re-emerged in the context of the ASBO. The legislation requires the prohibitions included in an ASBO to be 'necessary for
the purpose of protecting [persons] from further anti-social acts by the

---

[64] *Ibid.*, para. 85.   [65] A. T. H. Smith, *Offences against Public Order*, p. 121.
[66] See proposition F below, suggesting restraint in the use of this power.
[67] See n. 37 above.   [68] Consultation Paper, n. 5 above, paras 7.6.7 and 7.8.5.
[69] Criminal Procedure Rules III.31.8, 9 and 11.   [70] *Ibid.*, III.31.4.
[71] Above, n. 5, para. 7.8.5.

defendant',[72] and there is guidance from the Judicial Studies Board stating that the prohibitions included in an order must be 'precise and capable of being understood by the defendant'.[73] The guidance goes no further than this, but it does include appendices which illustrate prohibitions that would be valid, and prohibitions that have been held to be too wide or badly drafted.[74] This use of illustrations is beneficial, and it is axiomatic that the prohibitions in an ASBO must be tailored to the circumstances of the case. However, that does leave a considerable amount of discretion in the court, which the 'necessity' test (set out above) hardly reduces. Thus, the ASBO, and several other civil preventive orders, leave a great deal of power in the hands of the court making the order. Moreover, the context is one in which breach of an order is a criminal offence carrying a maximum penalty of five years' imprisonment.[75] Thus, it cannot be said that the letter or the spirit of proposition (E) is fully accepted by contemporary law.

F   Reliance on imprisonment is disproportionate

Given the many criticisms of bind-over orders that have been elaborated above, it may be thought superfluous to add the proposition that 'reliance on imprisonment as the sole method of enforcement is disproportionate, not least when a court may grant a conditional discharge to a person who (unlike many of those who are bound over) is actually convicted of an offence'. Yet it is important to make the point that international conventions have long urged that imprisonment should be 'used as a sanction of last resort',[76] and that English law states that:

> The court must not pass a custodial sentence unless it is of the opinion that the offence ... was so serious that neither a fine alone nor a community sentence can be justified for the offence.[77]

---

[72] Crime and Disorder Act 1998, s. 1(6).

[73] *Anti-Social Behaviour Orders: Guidance* (2007), para. 3.2.

[74] *Ibid.*, appendices 2 and 3.

[75] Cf., however, the proposals for replacing the ASBO, above n. 56 and accompanying text.

[76] Resolution VIII of the Eighth United Nations Congress on the Prevention of Crime and the Treatment of Offenders (1990), para. 5(e).

[77] Criminal Justice Act 2003, s. 152(2). See further *Seed and Stark* [2007] 2 Cr App R (S) 436, and A. Ashworth, *Sentencing and Criminal Justice*, 5th edn (Cambridge University Press, 2010), pp. 295–300.

No special justification for confining courts dealing with bind-overs to the sanction of imprisonment has ever been advanced. Glanville Williams was absolutely right to draw attention to this extraordinary position in his 1953 article, and to make the point that courts have a wide range of possible sanctions available when sentencing for offences, including the conditional discharge – which, being conditional, could be as effective as a bind-over in exerting a preventive effect on the future conduct of someone convicted of an offence. Since 1953 there has been a proliferation of other measures, many of them now encompassed by the single community sentence. Moreover, the suspended prison sentence is available for serious cases.

Disappointingly neither the 2003 Consultation Paper nor the Criminal Procedure Rules have tackled this problem directly. The Consultation Paper took the view that this would require primary legislation,[78] and so merely proposed that courts be warned to reserve imprisonment for 'the most exceptional circumstances'.[79] Even this relatively flexible formula failed to make its way into the Criminal Procedure Rules, which merely require courts dealing with someone who refuses to be bound over (i) to consider alternatives to binding over, (ii) to allow the individual to consult a lawyer, and (iii) where the individual declines to take advice, to explain again that imprisonment will be the consequence of failure to accept the bind-over.[80]

It is scandalous that imprisonment can be used in this way, for an order that has only the forfeiture of money as its sanction, particularly given the general statutory provisions on the use of imprisonment.[81] Deprivation of liberty is a negation of one of the most powerful and fundamental rights,[82] and in principle it should be reserved for the most intractable of cases. Moreover, the 'rule of law' rationale here – proper enforcement of orders of the courts, so as to maintain the authority of the law – ought surely to be kept in proportion to the subject matter in the particular case. Is it right to order the deprivation of liberty for defiant

---

[78] Unless s. 63 of the Magistrates' Courts Act 1980 could be used. This provision allows alternative measures of enforcement to be used in certain circumstances, but none of them appeared to apply, and the Strasbourg Court in *Steel* v. *United Kingdom*, above n. 31, acquiesced in the use of imprisonment for refusal to be bound over.

[79] Consultation Paper, above n. 7, para. 7.10.10.

[80] Criminal Procedure Rules III.31.12, 13 and 14.   [81] Above, n. 73.

[82] The European Convention on Human Rights has little to say about this: Art. 5.1 declares the 'right to liberty and security of person', but Art. 5.1(b) creates an exception for detention 'for non-compliance with the lawful order of a court' and, like Art. 5.1(a), fails to articulate any limiting principle.

conduct, conduct for which imprisonment is unavailable? Should the recalcitrant flower-seller ever be sent to prison for contempt?[83] The law ought surely to make imaginative use of other responses, such as distraint of property or other possibilities, rather than resorting to its most severe response. Once the court starts using imprisonment, does logic not compel it to lengthen the periods if the person refuses to comply? If a short period of imprisonment fails to put a stop to the contempt, should the court impose ever longer periods of imprisonment, until it reaches the maximum of two years? Should there not be a limiting role for proportionality here, or should we insist that it is the defiance of the law, not the precise subject matter, that is crucial?

In relation to bind-overs, the simplest and most equitable solution would be to remove the requirement that the individual should consent to be bound over. No such requirement now exists for orders made when sentencing for an offence,[84] and it is not clear why it should be required when imposing a quasi-punishment such as a bind-over order. This would allow the court to impose the bind-over on its own motion, after which the question of compliance is a matter for the person bound over.

V   Conclusions

The 1953 critique of bind-over powers by Glanville Williams has had an enduring effect. His six-point argument against this ancient power raised significant issues of principle, on both substance and procedure. Whereas Blackstone had lauded the bind-over powers as a sound example of the argument that prevention is better than punishment,[85] Glanville took them to task for several failures of natural justice. His criticisms pointed in the direction of abolishing the power, but the conclusion of his 1953 article was that the power was no longer needed against offenders and that therefore the bind-over is 'distinctively a weapon to be used against those who have not broken the criminal law'.[86] The Law Commission was more radical in its recommendations,

---

[83] See *Attorney-General* v. *Harris*, above, nn. 38 and 41 and accompanying text.

[84] For many years the courts could not make a probation order unless the defendant consented to it, but the requirement of consent was abolished in 2001. It was regarded mostly as a sham.

[85] 4 Bla Comm 231–6; at p. 232 Blackstone was particularly keen to establish that the bind-over is not a punishment, merely a 'caution' as to future behaviour.

[86] Above n. 1, p. 427.

but a group referred to as 'practitioners' (police, prosecutors, judges and magistrates – presumably not defence lawyers!) has claimed that abolition of the power to bind over to keep the peace would leave them unable to deal satisfactorily with people who represent a threat to good order. That group's views have largely held sway: the power to bind over to keep the peace has been retained, although (thanks to the European Court of Human Rights) the power to bind over to be of good behaviour has gone. In that context, most of Glanville's arguments seem to have been accepted in the current Criminal Procedure Rules, and the processes for making binding-over orders are much improved – although the use of imprisonment remains a serious blemish.

Since the Law Commission report of 1994 there have been several additions to the powers of the courts, with various civil preventive orders (notably the ASBO) becoming available. It is regrettable that the model for these orders has not followed Glanville's six arguments, and particularly that proposition (C) (with its constitutional dimensions) appears to have been neglected for the most part. Even if proper procedural protections are gradually becoming accepted as the norm, preventive orders will not deserve the appellation 'preventive justice' until respect for legislative decisions (proposition (C)) and reservation of imprisonment as a truly 'last resort' (proposition (F)) are duly confirmed.

4

The specialness of the general part
of the criminal law

MICHAEL S. MOORE

I Glanville Williams and the general part

Glanville Williams is often and rightly credited with the emergence of the idea that criminal law has something aptly called a "general part." This is because of his highly regarded book of 1953, *Criminal Law: The General Part*,[1] reissued in its even better known second edition in 1961.[2] Williams was in truth the originator of neither the idea nor the label. In 1947, Jerome Hall had earlier explored the idea of there being "the 'general part' of the criminal law,"[3] tracing the origins of the idea and the label to Hale's *Pleas of the Crown*, published in 1682.[4] Hall also mentions James Stephen,[5] who (in Stephen's own words) sought to give a systematic treatment of the "general doctrines pervading the whole subject" of criminal law, doctrines "which enter more or less into the definition of all offenses."[6] Still, it was Williams' book that placed the general part of the criminal law squarely in the forefront of the agendas of both academics writing about criminal law,[7] and drafters seeking to

---

[1] Glanville Williams, *Criminal Law: The General Part* (London: Stevens, 1953).
[2] Williams, *The General Part*, 2nd edn, 1961.
[3] Jerome Hall, *General Principles of Criminal Law* (Indianapolis, IN: Bobbs-Merrill, 1947), p. 2.
[4] *Ibid.*, p. 4.   [5] *Ibid.*, p. 8.
[6] Sir James Fitzjames Stephen, *A History of the Criminal Law of England* (New York: Macmillan, 1883), vol. I, p. 3.
[7] Thus, Antony Duff and Stuart Green, in the introduction to their volume on the special part of the criminal law, lament that academics have too exclusively been interested in the general part: "Philosophers and theorists of criminal law have often focused on the 'general part' of the criminal law (the part containing supposedly general doctrines, rules, and definitions) rather than its 'special part' (the part containing the definitions of particular offenses ...) such neglect of the special part has been unfortunate." R. A. Duff and Stuart P. Green (eds.), *Defining Crimes: Essays on the Special Part of the Criminal Law* (Oxford University Press, 2005), p. 1. I also

systematically codify the criminal law.[8] Despite occasional dissents, it is the agenda that we all carry on today.

Williams himself appeared to regard the distinction (between the general and special parts of the criminal law) to be unproblematic. The general part was . . . well, general. As he said in his preface to *Criminal Law: The General Part*, the general part consisted of those "general rules of the criminal law, i.e., those applying to more than one crime."[9] In its reliance on generality to mark the distinction, this was similar to Jerome Hall's conception of the distinction. Hall wrote in 1947 that the general part consisted of "certain generalizations [that] apply to all prescriptions of particular offenses," whereas the rules containing such prescriptions constituted the special part.[10]

Both Williams and Hall devoted the entirety of their respective books to the content of the general part as they each understood it. Each included the principles of *mens rea* within the general part; likewise doctrines about voluntary action, omissions, and causation; likewise doctrines of defense, such as necessity, insanity, and intoxication. Both also included attempt, complicity, solicitation, and conspiracy. Both also included principles of punishment and principles of legality. Others have since added the principles guiding criminalization of behavior such as Mill's harm principle.[11]

This is a rather heterogeneous list, despite each of such doctrines satisfying Williams' and Hall's criteria of generality. Subdividing the general part so as to accommodate this diversity does not help to reduce the heterogeneity, whether it be Hall's tripartite division between principles, doctrines, and rules,[12] or John Gardner's more recent tripartite division between auxiliary, supervisory, and definitional subparts.[13]

happily plead guilty to the charge. Michael S. Moore, *Placing Blame: A General Theory of the Criminal Law* (Oxford University Press, 1997).

[8] The American Law Institute's Model Penal Code thus divides itself between Part I, entitled "General Provisions," and Part II, entitled "Definition of Specific Crimes."

[9] Williams, *The General Part*, 2nd edn, p. v.

[10] Hall, *General Principles*, p. 2. Note that Hall requires much more universality of a doctrine's application to qualify it as being in the general part than does Williams. I shall return to this difference in section V.

[11] Douglas Husak, "Limitations on Criminalisation and the General Part of Criminal Law," in Stephen Shute and A. P. Simester (eds.), *Criminal Law Theory: Doctrines of the General Part* (Oxford University Press, 2002), pp. 14–19.

[12] Hall, *General Principles of Criminal Law*, 2nd edn (Indianapolis, IN: Bobbs-Merrill, 1960), p. 17.

[13] John Gardner, "On the General Part of the Criminal Law," in Antony Duff (ed.), *Philosophy and the Criminal Law* (Cambridge University Press, 1999), pp. 207–209.

Others have divided the general part between that which is descriptive of existing doctrines, and that which is normative in its recommendation of doctrines that ought to exist but do not.[14] Still others divide the general part between propositions of law which are binding on actors within a legal system, and theoretical propositions about the law which are not so binding.[15] Such taxonomization of the general part does not diminish its heterogeneity. That is unfortunate, because such heterogeneity is undesirable in that it disguises what can be of value in conceiving of an area of law such as criminal law as having a "general part."

So I propose to start afresh and ask: how should we conceive of the distinction(s) between the general and the special parts of the criminal law? What is the nature of the general part so conceived? Why is it a fruitful distinction if drawn in the right way? And what should be included as part of the general part? Perhaps in this way we can better bring to heel the quarry chased by Williams and Hall, recognizing that it was they who set us upon the chase some sixty years ago.

II The variety of theories in, about, or of criminal law

I begin negatively by asking what the general part is not. The most obvious thing that it is not is the special part of the criminal law. The special part consists of the primary rules of obligation of the substantive criminal law.[16] It is in this respect like the Ten Commandments, suitably enlarged to the size of a modern penal code. It is the dos and don'ts of a society, backed by the distinctive sanctions of the criminal law. Such doctrines making up the special part of the criminal law are insufficiently general to constitute the general part, because by their nature such doctrines define but one of the 7,000–15,000 substantive crimes typically contained in a modern penal code.

One suggestion is that the general part, while not the special part itself, is nonetheless a *theory* of the special part.[17] This suggestion might make

---

[14] For example, Doug Husak who distinguishes a "normative" from an "inductive" dimension of the general part and who urges that "theorists use the general part *normatively*." Husak, "Limitations on Criminalisation," p. 17.

[15] For example, Hall, *General Principles*, 2nd edn, p. 15, finding the general part to be a descriptive theory of both practitioners and scholars.

[16] On this there seems to be scholarly consensus. See, e.g., the essays collected in Duff and Green (eds.), *Defining Crimes*.

[17] First advanced by Hall, *General Principles*, ch. 1.

one think that the general part is (or at least includes) a theory of punishment, for when one thinks of *theories* of criminal law, the theory of punishment is often the first thing that comes to mind. Yet another thing the general part is not (and that it does not include) is a theory of punishment. To be sure, one can conceive of punishment so narrowly that a theory of "punishment" might well be included in the general part. Suppose one conceived of punishment as the tail of the dog, that is, as the remedy attached to the dog itself, the dog consisting of those prohibitions and requirements that define criminal liability. Then a *theory* of punishment would be seen as a theory of sentencing, a part, although not a central part, of substantive criminal law. By contrast, I take a theory of punishment to be a theory of the whole of criminal law.[18] Punishment, the imposition of moral blame on people in a way that makes them suffer, is the distinctive feature of criminal law as an area of law.[19] A theory of punishment is a theory about what such a system is good for. What good is served by such a blame-and-suffering-imposing institution, a good sufficiently weighty that it can justify this *prima facie* nasty business? The familiar answers, of course, are retributive justice, enhancement of human welfare, or some combination of these two goods.

The theory of punishment is thus the most general theory of the criminal law. It justifies why we are entitled to have criminal law at all. It is not a theory of the special part, nor is it even a theory of the general part (although it should have implications for both). Nor is the theory of punishment a part of the general part. It is too general to play that role or occupy that place.

What is wanted, if the general part is to be a theory of the special part, is some kind of theory that is uniquely a theory of the special part. What would such a "theory" of the special part look like? One possibility would be a *normative* theory, which would be what is standardly called a "theory of criminalization." Such a theory is both substantive and formal. Substantively, the theory of criminalization articulates the proper aims and limits of criminal legislation. Illustrative is Mill's theory, which is that legislators should aim only to prevent harm to those other than the actor(s) in their criminal legislation, and which therefore limits the subject of such legislation to actions harmful to those others.[20]

---

[18] Moore, *Placing Blame*, pp. 27–30.

[19] *Ibid.*, pp. 24–25 (the blaming purpose of suffering-imposing sanctions is what marks those sanctions as criminal).

[20] I discuss Mill's theory as well as its major competitors in Moore, "Liberty's Constraints on What Should be Made Criminal," given at the Stirling University Conference on

Formally, the theory articulates the form such legislation should take, in terms of clarity, publicity, prospectivity, etc. Anglo-American law's principle of legality is illustrative.

Some current commentators include both the formal and the substantive principles of the normative theory of the special part as part of the general part.[21] So conceived, the general part would be, at least in part, a normative theory of the special part. My objection to this is not of the kind that Peter Cane anticipates:[22] that the general part of the criminal law is a natural kind, like the continent of Africa, and that including things that do not belong to the kind is to make a mistake akin to the mistake of classifying Florida as part of the African continent. On the contrary, I assume that the correctness of any distinction between the general and the special parts is hostage to the subtler criterion of theoretical fecundity. What I hope to show by the end of this chapter is how much power the general part has (to serve both theorists and practitioners of the criminal law in their understanding and practice of that law) if it is construed as a descriptive and not a normative theory of the special part. Construing the general part as a normative theory of the special part would rob the general part of the "specialness" to which I refer in my title.

With that promissory note issued, let me turn to what a *descriptive* theory of the special part could look like. We first need to be clear what we mean by a "descriptive theory" of a body of law.

III   Descriptive theories of areas of law

Because I have written about the nature of descriptive theories of areas of law before in some detail, both about areas of law generically[23] and as applied specifically to criminal law,[24] I shall here be brief,

---

Criminalisation, September 2011, and to be published in a forthcoming conference volume, Antony Duff (ed.), *Criminalisation* (Oxford University Press, forthcoming).

[21] For example, Husak, "Limitations on Criminalisation."

[22] Peter Cane, "The General/Special Distinction in Criminal Law, Tort Law, and Legal Theory," *Law and Philosophy*, 26 (2007), 478 n. 28 (accusing Victor Tadros of treating the general part "as if the General Part were a physical object or place").

[23] Michael S. Moore, "Legal Principles Revisited," in M. S. Moore (ed.), *Educating Oneself in Public: Critical Essays in Jurisprudence* (Oxford University Press, 2000), pp. 38–39, 222–233, 239–242.

[24] Moore, "A Theory of Criminal Law Theories," in Moore (ed.), *Placing Blame*, ch. 1.

which means conclusory and with little supporting argumentation. A descriptive theory of an area of law, as I see it, has the following characteristics.

(1) It *describes* the law of which it is a theory. It does not (causally) *explain* why or how the law came to have the content it does, as do historical, psychological, or sociological theories. Nor does it *evaluate* the law of which it is a theory, praising it for its conformities to some normative ideal and condemning it for its deviations from that ideal. A descriptive theory describes.

(2) But it does not issue its descriptions in the same vocabulary as the law that it describes. It gives *more general* descriptions of the legal doctrines than the doctrines use themselves.

(3) This semantic feature (of more general theories compared with less general doctrines) makes possible a *deductive structure*: the theories imply the doctrines but not vice versa. The doctrines become the implications of the theories. Even though psychologically one derives the theory from the doctrines, logically the derivation is the other way.

(4) The theory is *part of the law* of which it is a theory. It is in this sense internal: it is itself a proposition *of* law binding on judges, as much as are the doctrines of which it is a theory; it is not an external theory, which would consist of propositions *about* law of interest to other external theorists, but not binding on those legal professionals working within the legal system(s) in question.

(5) The authority of the theory to be part of the law may stem at least in part from its source in legislative enactment (as when California enacted as "Maxims of Jurisprudence" items such as the well-worn principle, "no one shall profit from his own wrong"). But even without enactment such theories have *the authority of law* due to their service of the virtues distinctive of law, viz, the rule of law values:

  (a) One of these virtues is the *greater determinateness* of an area of law given to it by a descriptive theory, as opposed to the untheorized doctrines by themselves. Theories more general than the doctrines of which they are theories, yield determinate answers to cases that would be indeterminate by recourse to the doctrines alone.

  (b) Another of these virtues is *knowability of the law* of a given area. This epistemic virtue of theories is due to their comparative simplicity and brevity, making the law more easily learned, understood, and applied, and giving rise to greater notice and fewer unpleasant surprises on the part of citizens.

(c) Another of these virtues is *equality*. By isolating more general likenesses between cases, theories can prevent inconsistent treatment of cases that are, at a fundamental level, the same, even while, at a doctrinal level, they look distinct.

(6) Such descriptive theories are *not value-free*; necessarily, they are value-laden. This follows from the rule of law virtues possessed by such theories and which give such theories the authority of binding law. In particular, the ability of such theories to justify decisions in cases not covered by the doctrines depends on the theories describing something of value (and not just some morally arbitrary, formal feature the doctrines might happen to share). Further, the ability of such theories to further equality depends on the deep likenesses discovered by such theories being morally non-arbitrary; for like treatment is worth nothing if the cases demanding like treatment are alike in morally arbitrary ways only.[25] Further, the generality (that such theories must possess if they are to decide cases not decided by already existing doctrines) yields an indeterminacy between competing theories that equally well imply the doctrines, an indeterminacy resolvable only by recourse to evaluative considerations.

(7) The truth-makers for theoretical propositions of law will thus be a *combination of two factors*: how many of the doctrines can be seen to be deductive implications of the theory?; and, how good is the standard articulated by the theory as a rationale for deciding both old cases as they were decided and new cases as they should be decided? These two factors will trade off against one another in their joint determination of the best theory.

With this sketch of descriptive theories of an area of law under our belt, let us now return to the matter at hand. Can the general part of the criminal law be regarded as a descriptive theory of the thousands of doctrines making up the special part of the criminal law in all Anglo-American legal systems?

---

[25] Moore, "Legal Principles Revisited," p. 236.

IV   The general part as a descriptive theory of the special part

A   Describing the doctrines of the special part in general, "content-neutral" terms

More than twenty years ago I urged that there was no interesting descriptive theory of the special part to be found, that the only interesting theory of the special part was normative.[26] Regarded from one angle, this was right, but from another, it was not. What I had in mind was the rudimentary "theory" of the special part that did no more than group crimes into families, such as "crimes against bodily integrity," "crimes against reputation," etc.[27] Such grouping was done by finding similarities in the interests protected by various crimes. This is an enterprise modest in its ambitions. The dominating ambition is simply taxonomic, to display the thousands of crimes there are, by their subject matters. Such a "theory" has no use as a guide to generalizing from examined to unexamined cases. And it has only a modest use as a heuristic, for it makes the learning of the criminal law only moderately easier.

Such an approach to theorizing about the special part has a more ambitious version. Some theorists seek to show how all criminal prohibitions really protect only one interest. George Fletcher, for example, once urged that virtually all crime represented a kind of domination by one person of another and, thus, that the content of almost all criminal prohibitions was really the elimination of interpersonal domination.[28] As another example, some libertarians urge that "liberty can only be limited so as to protect liberty," implying that the wrong done in all crimes is ultimately the deprivation of the victim's liberty. On this view all criminal laws ultimately aim at protecting liberty.

Such univocal schemes for systematizing criminal prohibitions remind one of the instinct theories of bygone psychologies. The latter tried to reduce all the diverse motives for which people act, to just one or two things: sex, aggression, life, death, power, energy-discharge, reduction of birth trauma, etc. In both cases the main problem with such universalizing schemes is that they run roughshod over the diversity of the phenomena that they would

---

[26] Michael S. Moore, "A Theory of Criminal Law Theories," *Tel Aviv University Studies in Law*, 10 (1990), 115–185, at pp. 173–174, reprinted in Moore, *Placing Blame*, pp. 66–67.

[27] See, e.g., Rollin Perkins and Ronald Boyce, *Criminal Law*, 3rd edn (Minneola, NY: Foundation Press, 1982), who organize offenses into families in this way. John Gardner allocates such familial organization of offenses to the special part: Gardner, "On the General Part," p. 205.

[28] George Fletcher, "Domination in Wrongdoing," *Boston University Law Review*, 76 (1996), 347–360.

simplify. The objects sought in crime, the interests harmed in crime, and the motives for suppressing crime are too diverse to be captured by a single formula. Domination, for example, might be plausible as an analysis of the object, interest, or motive for the suppression of extortion and blackmail; it is a poor candidate for those roles *vis-à-vis* homicide.

Such universal schemes do somewhat better if they become very general. The harm, wrong, and wrongful harm principles[29] more plausibly urge univocal standards at what ought to be prevented and punished in criminalizing behavior, and to some extent such principles also describe many of the criminal law doctrines in place in liberal societies. But these are by and large plausible only as reform theories. They would radically alter the special part we have by eliminating many criminal prohibitions as improper uses of the criminal sanction.

Descriptive theories of the special part, if conceived in the ways just described, are thus doomed to the failures of either triviality or falsehood. Yet this is because such theories aim to generalize about the *content* of the rules of the special part. They aim to generalize over something whose variety stubbornly refuses to yield up hidden uniformities. People can wrong, harm, and disserve other people's interests or the interests of the commonweal in far too many ways to be captured by a single general description like "domination."

So what must be done is to prescind away from such content. We should seek neither the trivial familial groupings of such content, nor the grander but false general characterizations of such content. Rather, we should abstract out the conditions that make persons criminally liable for some legally prohibited state of affairs, conditions that hold irrespective of whether that state of affairs is about aborting a foetus, damaging a reputation, not supporting one's children, or whatever. I have elsewhere termed this a "content-neutral" kind of descriptive theory of the special part.[30]

One finds, for example, that the negative prohibitions of criminal codes uniformly prohibit or require *actions*.[31] Whatever commonalities there are to human actions will thus also be commonalities of the liability rules of the criminal law. (On my own theory, to be an act at all an event must consist of a *willing*, that *causes*, a *bodily movement*;[32] to be an action

---

[29] All discussed in Moore, "Liberty's Constraints on What Should be Made Criminal."
[30] Moore, *Placing Blame*, p. 32.
[31] Michael S. Moore, *Act and Crime: The Implications of the Philosophy of Action for the Criminal Law* (Oxford University Press, 1993), ch. 2.
[32] *Ibid.*, chs. 5–6.

of a certain type (such as killing, raping, disfiguring, etc.) an event must possess the *causal* or other properties essential to that type.[33]) Or one finds that liability attaches only for those legally prohibited actions that are accompanied by mental states of *intention* or *belief* of the actor, which states have as their content a representation of the action containing all the aspects of it that make it morally wrong to do.[34] Or one discovers that the rules defining defenses divide between those describing circumstances that render a *prima facie* illegal action not illegal in such circumstances, and those describing circumstances that render a *prima facie* culpable intention or belief not culpable in such circumstances. The first set of defenses, the justificatory defenses, will utilize common elements of *good consequences* and non-consequentialist *privileges*;[35] the second set of defenses, the excuse defenses, will utilize common elements of *capacity, opportunity, ignorance, mistake, compulsion,* and *coercion.*[36]

Such commonalities do not seek to generalize about the content of criminal prohibitions except in the abstract way just described. Rather, liability rules are seen to have a common structure built out of common elements, irrespective of whatever substantive content the rules might contain. It is in this sense that I describe such an abstracting theory as "content-neutral."

Doug Husak queries, specifically to me, "Why *must* the general part be neutral with respect to the special part in order to qualify as general?"[37] From the foregoing the answer should be apparent. It is only by being *neutral* with respect to the content of the special part that anything fruitfully *general* can be discerned and extracted. Action, causation, intentionality, etc., are "content-neutral" in that they are the common building blocks out of which criminal prohibitions as otherwise diverse

---

[33] *Ibid.*, ch. 8.
[34] The *kinds* of mental states required for criminal conviction, and the *content* such mental states must have to make one legally culpable, are explored in Michael S. Moore, "Intention as a Marker of Moral Responsibility and Legal Punishability," in Antony Duff and Stuart Green (eds.), *The Philosophical Foundations of Criminal Law* (Oxford University Press, 2011), pp. 179–205.
[35] Explored by me most recently in Michael S. Moore, "Targeted Killings and the Morality of Hard Choices," in Claire Finkelstein, Jens David Ohlin, and Andrew Altman (eds.), *Targeted Killings: Law and Morality in an Asymmetrical World* (Oxford University Press, 2012). See more generally Michael S. Moore, *Causation and Responsibility: An Essay in Law, Morals, and Metaphysics* (Oxford University Press, 2009), ch. 3.
[36] Moore, *Placing Blame*, chs. 12–13.
[37] Husak, "Limitations on Criminalisation," p. 16 n. 6.

as murder, rape, mayhem, battery, etc., are constructed. The generality of their use in criminal prohibitions stems directly from their content-neutrality.

There is a price for such topic-neutrality of a theory. This is the price that one cannot use the theory so abstracted to generate, by itself, new rules of the special part. For there is not enough content to the theory to serve this purpose. Contrast the content-neutral theory that is the general part of criminal law, to more content-laden theories, such as Posner's theory of negligence in torts (all liability rules induce a minimization of the sum of accident and safety costs),[38] or Langdell's theory of contract-formation (all contracts depend on there being a meeting of the minds).[39] As I asserted in section III, descriptive theories of areas of law like Posner's and Langdell's have the power to generate new rules, usable to decide new sorts of cases. A content-neutral theory such as I have just described, by contrast, has implications only for the *structure* any new rule must have (it should prohibit willed bodily movements that cause legally prohibited results, with accompanying intention or belief with a content matching those results, etc.); the content-neutral theory does not say *what* actions, with *what* objects of intention or belief, should be prohibited.

This is not an unwelcome implication. Criminal law, unlike torts and contracts, is no longer a common law subject in almost all Anglo-American legal systems. In such systems it is an exclusively legislative prerogative to say what should be criminalized. The modesty of a content-neutral theory is thus no disadvantage here, at least as far as courts are concerned. For courts have no need or use for a content-laden theory of criminal law. They, unlike legislatures, are not in the criminalization business and so they do not need a theory that tells them what new crimes to create. Moreover, even legislatures should have little need or use for a content-laden theory of the special part. What legislatures need are *normative* theories of the special part, telling them what they should aim at in their penal legislation, and what substantive and formal limits there are in the manner in which even proper aims may be realized in penal legislation. Conforming to some pattern of existing legislation – if there were one – would be an unduly conservative theory of legislation and thus of little or no help in the legislative task either.

---

[38] Richard Posner, "A Theory of Negligence," *Journal of Legal Studies*, 1 (1972), 29–96.
[39] Christopher Columbus Langdell, *Summary of the Law of Contracts* (Boston, MA: Little, Brown, 1880), pp. 1–2, 12–15.

This brings into focus a second difference between the content-neutral theory sketched here and other, more content-laden descriptive, theories of areas of law like Posner's and Langdell's. The theory here described is "meta" with respect to the rules of the special part, "meta" in the sense of Herbert Hart's secondary rules.[40] The theory is *about* the primary rules of obligation of the special part – how those primary rules are to be interpreted and applied – and is not at the same level as those primary rules (even using more general descriptions). Despite this difference, the theory here sketched is part of the law, just as are more content-laden theories; the secondary rule, "meta" status of the theory does not rob it of its legally binding character, any more than the secondary rule status of constitutional law renders such doctrines not law at all. The result is that the general part is as binding on judges as are the rules of the special part, despite its secondary rule status.

B   The moral aspect to any theory of the special part

I urged in section III that all descriptive theories of areas of law are constituted in part by certain truths of morality, as much as they are constructed by implication from the rules of law distinctive of that area of law. This is dramatically true of the doctrines and principles making up the general part of the criminal law. For what the descriptive theory of the special part has by and large captured (in its doctrines of the general part) is a distinct part of ethics. Indeed, it has pretty much adopted this branch of ethics whole hog, with minor alterations or omissions. The fit is so good that the general part is sometimes mistakenly taken to be an evaluative theory, rather than a description of existing Anglo-American criminal law rules.

Substantive ethics (as opposed to meta-ethics) is standardly divided between deontic and aretaic ethics. The former deals with the morality of right and wrong actions, and the value of the good and bad states of affairs that arguably determine the rightness and wrongness of actions. Its categories are those of the obligatory (the required and the forbidden) and the permissive. Aretaic ethics, by contrast, deals with the morality of virtue, judging both isolated desires and emotions, and long-term character traits, as either having or lacking virtue; although there may be in

---

[40] H. L. A. Hart, *The Concept of Law* (Oxford: Clarendon Press, 1961).

some sense aretaic duties and oughts,[41] and thus aretaic judgments of actions, the distinctive aretaic evaluations are of the supererogatory, the suberogatory, the quasi-erogatory, and the indifferent.[42]

It is tempting to urge that the morality underlying the general part of the criminal law is a third, distinct kind of substantive ethics, to be added to deontic and aretaic ethics. Joseph Raz, for example, urges that we distinguish ascriptive ethics from normative ethics as two "important branches of practical philosophy."[43] Normative ethics for Raz is the study of what our obligations are; ascriptive ethics is the study of when we are blameworthy (or praiseworthy) for breaching (or fulfilling) our obligations. Michael Zimmerman urges that we dub this newly discovered third branch of ethics, "hypological ethics."[44] Yet viewing matters this way exaggerates the distinctness of the morality of responsibility. Such morality is better seen as an aspect of deontic ethics, not as some branch of ethics distinct from, but co-equal with, deontic (or Raz's "normative") ethics.

The content and force of the norms of deontic ethics is, of course, a matter of some considerable disagreement. Deontologists urge that the content of such norms is actions directly, whereas consequentialists urge that the rightness or wrongness of actions is derivative of the more basic locus of value, the states of affairs that actions produce or that omissions fail to prevent; further, deontological prohibitions speak to us categorically: "don't you do action A now." They do not enjoin us to maximize good states of affairs, or to minimize bad ones, as do the obligations of consequentialist theories.[45] But for present purposes we can momentarily prescind from this long-running and wide-ranging debate. Whatever the nature of deontic norms turns out to be in these dimensions, there are two functions for such norms that must be distinguished.

The first is the forward-looking, action-guiding function of moral norms. Injunctions like, "one ought not kill," have as one of their essential features the function of guiding the actions of moral agents

---

[41] See Heidi M. Hurd, "Duties Beyond the Call of Duty," *Annual Review of Law and Ethics*, 6 (1998), 3–39.

[42] Michael S. Moore, "Liberty and Supererogation," *Annual Review of Law and Ethics*, 6 (1998), 111–143.

[43] Joseph Raz, *Practical Reason and Norms* (Oxford University Press, 1975), pp. 11–12.

[44] Michael Zimmerman, "Taking Luck Seriously," *Journal of Philosophy*, 99 (2002), 553–576.

[45] See generally, Larry Alexander and Michael Moore, "Deontological Ethics," *Stanford Encyclopedia of Philosophy* (2007), available at: www.plato.stanford.edu/entries/ethics-deontological.

away from killing. The second function of moral norms is backward-looking: they are to guide the judgment (of the actor and others) about the blameworthiness of an actor for some act of his that has already been performed. They are the book-keeping guides to each person's moral ledger. What Raz and Zimmerman would separate as a distinct kind of ethics is in reality no more than an aspect of deontic ethics, namely, the backward-looking, judgment-guiding aspect of deontic norms.

I should confess that I put this badly in my earlier writings on this topic, and this has misled both friends[46] and critics[47] of the argument. I, too, made it seem as if there were two different norm systems, one being norms of right and wrong action, and the other, norms of attribution of blame for culpably doing wrongful actions.[48] This led scholars like Peter Cane and post-modernists like Nicky Lacey to think that I was distinguishing wrongdoing from culpability. Yet this is not (and never was) the distinction I intended here. In reality there is only one set of moral norms, and those norms have both wrongdoing and culpability as parts of them. The forward- and backward-looking aspects of such norms can make it *look as if* there are two sets of norms, each with a distinctive content. For in the forward-looking use of these norms it may appear that they have no culpability requirements. To serve their action-guiding function, norms have no need to mention culpable mental states such as intent; enjoining agents, "do not kill," presupposes (but does not explicitly assert), "do not try to kill," "do not intend to kill," "do not unreasonably risk killing," etc. Such action-guiding norms also have no need to mention the other part of culpability, the absence of excuse; to be guided by norms about what we should do, it is not necessary or helpful to include descriptions of when we will be excused from blame if we nonetheless make the wrong choices and do the wrong actions.

Yet despite the irrelevance of *mens rea* and excuse to the action-guiding function of moral norms, these items still form part of the content of those norms. True enough, *mens rea* and excuse only come into play *explicitly* in the judgment-guiding function of moral norms. Even so, there is only one set of moral norms in play here. We are guided

---

[46] Cane, "The General/Special Distinction," pp. 469–470.
[47] Nicola Lacey, "Book Review of *Placing Blame*," *Modern Law Review*, 63 (2000), 141–148, at pp. 145–146; Nicola Lacey, "Contingency, Coherence, and Conceptualism," in Antony Duff (ed.), *Philosophy and the Criminal Law* (Cambridge University Press, 1999).
[48] Moore, *Placing Blame*, p. 31.

to correct decisions by the norms by which we are judged, and vice versa. Anything else would be unfair.

Thus, it was misleading to label these two aspects of deontic norms as separate norms of "wrongdoing" and of "attribution," as I did.[49] It encouraged the misinterpretations of friends and critics alike. In any case, the backward-looking, judgment-guiding aspect of deontic norms is the relevant aspect here; for that is where culpability and absence of excuse *explicitly* join wrongdoing and absence of justification to complete the components needed for overall moral blameworthiness.

It may well seem that, even when we restrict our gaze to the backward-looking, judgment-guiding function of deontic norms, there is still a gap between those norms and the "ascriptive" norms making up the theory of responsibility. Yet the "gap" we sense is no more and no different than the "gap" between a more and a less general way of describing the same thing. The *one* thing being described is the deontic norms. Such norms, too, have their "general part," in the sense that if we prescind away from the content of those norms, and seek only the structure of the kind of things they prohibit, we will end up with act intent, cause, etc.: the ingredients in a theory of responsibility.

To illustrate this, let me retract my earlier stepping away from deciding between deontology or consequentialism as competing theories about the most general content and force of deontic norms. Suppose that at least some of the deontic norms of morality are deontological prohibitions: we are categorically forbidden to do (think, intend, etc.) certain things even when doing so would minimize the doing of those things in the future. Suppose further that one wonders about the kind of items marking the content of these deontological prohibition. Are we categorically forbidden to *think* about doing certain things?; to *intend* to do certain things?; to *do* certain *actions*, or *cause* certain *results*?; to do certain actions for certain *reasons*?; to *intentionally act* in certain ways?; to *try* to do certain actions? etc.[50]

It is a well-recognized exercise in substantive ethics to select out and to defend some view about the kind of things categorically forbidden to us by deontological norms of prohibition. My own engagement in this exercise isolated act, cause, intent, and counterfactual dependence as the kind of things around which categorical prohibitions are

---

[49] *Ibid.*
[50] These possibilities are all nicely explored in Heidi M. Hurd, "What in the World is Wrong?," *Journal of Contemporary Legal Issues*, 5 (1994), 157–216.

structured.[51] With a bit of brushing up, these become the key ingredients in a theory of responsibility: we are responsible (for breaching our deontological obligations) when we intentionally cause through our actions some bad state of affairs that would not have happened without our intervention.

The theory of ascription – aka the theory of responsibility – is thus nothing other than the general part of the deontic norms of morality. Raz rightly notes that, "the theory of ascription [responsibility] . . . presupposes that we have a normative theory."[52] Yet we should put the point more strongly than this: the theory of responsibility is nothing other than a theory of the general shape of our deontic norms.

This does not mean that we cannot fruitfully study the theory of responsibility separately from studying the detailed content of deontic norms. For example, we can argue and reach satisfactorily justified conclusions as to why causing the harm you try to cause either does or does not increase your blameworthiness (over and against unsuccessfully trying), without worrying much, if at all, *what* we were trying to cause or did cause. We can fruitfully step away from death, disfigurements, contacts, insults, and defamations to raise this question of "moral luck." Take the argument from control. The argument is that we cannot fully control whether a result we try to cause actually comes into existence. Such argument is perfectly general. It does not depend for its force or cogency on *what* we were causing, death, disfigurement, destruction of property, or whatever.

Peter Cane could be interpreted so as to disagree with this. He writes: "The concept of responsibility devoid of any account of 'to whom we are responsible' and 'what we are responsible for' is a philosopher's dream – or, perhaps, a philosophical nightmare."[53] Cane's example is the late J. L. Mackie's "straight rule of responsibility: an agent is responsible for all and only his intentional actions."[54] Cane's criticism is that: "This rule makes no reference to what our responsibilities are . . . An account of the concept of responsibility which pays no attention to what our responsibilities are is too short by half."[55]

There is a reading of this with which I could agree. This is the idea that, because the truth of Mackie-like statements (such as my own above)

[51] Moore, *Causation and Responsibility*, ch. 3.
[52] Raz, *Practical Reason and Norms*, p. 12.
[53] Peter Cane, *Responsibility in Law and Morality* (Oxford: Hart, 2002), p. 55.
[54] *Ibid.*   [55] *Ibid.*, p. 56.

depends on the general shape of the deontic norms of morality, we should at some point have made sure that these norms indeed have this shape. Yet if the point is that one can make no *general* arguments about the general shape that norms must have to be fair to those subject to them, that seems to me to be false. "Intent matters to responsibility because it is partly constitutive of our agency," is a perfectly general argument in the sense that it is not examining morality norm by norm to see if each has an intent requirement; rather, it proceeds from some general idea about how agency is connected both to intention and to responsibility. Despite this generality, the argument is also, to my mind, a quite cogent one.

We can have our cake and eat it too here. Any theory of responsibility does indeed presuppose that there are deontic norms of a certain shape because it is a theory about that shape; yet we can argue and reach well-justified conclusions about that shape without examining particular moral norms.

In this limited sense, then, we have a somewhat separable set of principles of responsibility. This is what I call the general part of morality's deontic norms. It is this general part of the deontic norms of morality that supplies the moral good at which the general part of the criminal law both does and should aim. Put in more conventional language, it is the nature of moral responsibility that gives moral point and normative guidance to the doctrines of the general part of the criminal law.

V   Can there be a theory of the general part, and if so, by what criteria?

One might well wonder how there can be a *theory* of the general part. After all, the general part itself is a theory of the special part – so a theory of that must be a theory of a theory of the special part. This holds out the promise of full employment for theoreticians: when we tire of this level, maybe we can do a theory of a theory of a theory . . . and on without end?

In truth there is neither nonsense, nor yawning regress, in conceiving of a theory of the general part. We simply need to recognize a shift in the sense of "theory." When we equated the general part with the descriptive theory of the special part we were using "theory" to mean a set of more general statements from which the rules of the special part could be deduced. It would indeed be troublesome to think that there could be some even more general statement(s) from which the general principles of the general part could be deduced. Presumably, we would end up with something pretty vacuous, such as Aquinas' first precept of the natural law: "Do good, and avoid evil."

A more modest, but still idiomatic, usage of "theory" is one whereby a theory of something is just a hypothesis about how the world is in some dimension. "I have a *theory* about who did it" (where "it" is some crime in a detective novel) is nothing more mysterious than a hypothesis about (in this case) a low level matter of fact. In this mundane and everyday sense of "theory" there can be theories of the general part, that is, hypotheses about just what are the principles that best describe and justify the doctrines of the special part. We have already articulated the parameters that any plausible theory of the general part must meet. Any plausible theory about the general part must meet the conditions outlined in section III about the nature of descriptive theories of areas of law. Prominently included are three characteristics that any theory of the general part should honor. One is that the principles of the general part can have their status as part of the law only if they are not value-free. Such principles can perform their internal, justificatory roles (as standards for decision in novel cases or in cases correcting mistakes in structure) only if such principles not only imply the rules of which they are a theory, but also describe some good instrumental to the overall good served by criminal law as a whole. The second is that the principles making up the general part must imply, but not be implied by, the rules of which they are a theory. The general part must have this deductive relationship to the rules of the special part (in addition to serving some good) if the general part can claim the authority of being part of the law. The third characteristic is the dual nature of the criteria for a good theory as to the nature of the general part: a good theory is one that is both actuated by the best moral ideal and that implies the most features of the special part of the criminal law.

The moral and the logical features of a descriptive theory of law do not, of course, always point in the same direction as to the content of such a theory. Except in an ideally just state – that is, no real state – no morally plausible theories perfectly fit their data. The general part is no exception. For any internal, justificatory theory of law some doctrines of law that do exist should not exist, and some doctrines of law that should exist do not in fact exist. Any descriptive theory of an area of law must thus have a means of handling these two types of mistake, which means, seeing them as such, minimizing their impact, or even in some instances eliminating them (by robbing such mistaken doctrines of their status as binding law). An example in the economic theory of negligence law is the doctrine of contributory negligence, which only imperfectly fits the economic theory of negligence.[56]

This feature of descriptive theories of areas of law explains the divergent things theorists of the general part have said about how general some requirements must be to be included in the general part. Jerome Hall ambitiously thought that the general part consists only of "certain general-izations [that] apply to *all* prescriptions of specific offenses," and that "The 'general part' modifies *each* rule in the 'special part.'"[57] George Fletcher has echoed Hall's universalist ambitions for the general part, holding that the general part deals with "issues that cut across all offenses."[58] Glanville Williams, by contrast, much less ambitiously held that to be part of the general part a principle need only apply "to more than one offence."[59] Somewhat in between was J. F. Stephen's intentionally vague idea that for a principle to be part of the general part (which Stephen called "the general doctrines pervading the whole subject"), it must "enter more or less into the definition of nearly all offences."[60] Like Stephen, Peter Cane also hedges his bets here: "a norm can be appropriately included in the general part even if it does not apply to all criminal offences, as long as it applies to a significant number of offences."[61]

Williams', Cane's, and Stephen's kind of hedging (of Hall's and Fletcher's ambitious universalism) is understandable. After all, the prin-ciples requiring causation, *mens rea*, and voluntary act for *prima facie* liability, and the principles allowing provocation, duress, consent, and self-defense as defenses, all seem to be less than universally applicable to the crimes defined in the special part, yet all are standardly included as part of the general part.

There are a variety of ways with which to deal with this worry. To begin with, some of these apparent counterexamples can be written off as the mere appearances of being a counterexample. Take causation as a requirement of criminal liability by way of example. There is an ortho-doxy that has it that causation is a requirement only in so-called "result-

---

[56] See the discussion in Moore, *Placing Blame*, pp. 15–16.

[57] Hall, *General Principles*, p. 2 (emphasis added).

[58] George Fletcher, *Rethinking Criminal Law* (Boston, MA: Little, Brown, 1978), p. 393. See, more recently, George Fletcher, *The Grammar of Criminal Law*, vol. I: *Foundations* (Oxford University Press, 2007), p. 18: "The relatively new general part addresses the issues that might arise in every offence".

[59] Williams, *The General Part*, 2nd edn, p. v.   [60] Stephens, *A History*, vol. I, p. 3.

[61] Cane, "The General/Special Distinction," p. 474.

crimes," but that for "conduct-crimes" there is no such requirement.[62] Yet this lack of universality is an illusion, for in reality all crimes have causal requirements built into their *actus reus* requirements. I do not mean this in the trivial sense that "willings" must cause bodily movements – that causal thesis is already embedded in the voluntary act requirement. I mean that the bodily movements that are the effects of willings, must themselves cause some further state of affairs in the external world for criminal liability to attach. This is, of course, true of battery, homicide, mayhem, and the like; but equally true of theft, rape, burglary, and attempt (the so-called "conduct-crimes").[63] The upshot here is that one can unproblematically assign causation to the general part, because it truly figures in the definition of all crimes, however much conventional orthodoxy thinks to the contrary.

Something like this defense can also be made for the requirement of *mens rea* being assigned to the general part. The problem for making such an assignment arises because fully one-half of the substantive provisions of typical criminal codes in the United States and the United Kingdom are construed so that they define strict liability offenses, that is, offenses with no requirement of *mens rea*.[64] How then can *mens rea* requirements be considered part of criminal law's general part? The moral argument everyone understands: strict liability is anathema to the blaming and suffering-imposing, desert-based institution criminal law is supposed to be. The drafters of the Model Penal Code,[65] and the Supreme Court of Canada,[66] thus got it right in eliminating strict liability from criminal law. But what of the present criminal law in the United States and the United Kingdom? Surely one-half of the criminal codes in each country cannot just be ignored – at least not by any theory holding itself out as *describing* the criminal law we have and not simply evaluating that law in light of the criminal law we ought to have.

Yet even in the law which we have, offenses that require *mens rea* are the real crimes; strict liability offenses are regulatory measures that are almost exclusively forward-looking in their intent: they hope to shape conduct, not to punish it. In the US criminal justice system we recognize the second-class status of strict liability offenses: (1) by presuming

---

[62] The orthodoxy is described in Moore, *Act and Crime*, pp. 214–215.

[63] *Ibid.*, pp. 213–238; Moore, *Causation and Responsibility*, ch. 1.

[64] A. H. Hermann, "In the United Kingdom: Criminal Offences which are not Crime," *Daily Journal*, February 2, 1982.

[65] Model Penal Code, §§1.04(5), 2.05.   [66] *City of Levis* v. *Tetreault*, [2006] SCC 12.

against their existence (via the common law and Model Penal Code presumptions in favor of requiring at least the *mens rea* of recklessness even for statutes that have no explicit *mens rea* requirements);[67] (2) by limiting strict liability crimes to offenses that are (a) not gravely besmirching of reputation (generally meaning non-felonies), (b) not severe in their penalties, and (c) not of common law ancestry;[68] (3) by further limiting strict liability offenses to (a) crimes whose subject matter gives some notice of regulation,[69] (b) crimes whose *actus reus* standard is clear enough that law-abiding citizens can comply with it once they have knowledge of its existence,[70] and (c) crimes where prophylactic actions are possible to those worried about potential criminal liability; and (4) by largely applying strict liability crimes to corporations, who can be sanctioned criminally with no real person being (directly or explicitly) punished. The Model Penal Code's demotion of strict liability "crimes" to non-penal "violations," only makes explicit what is implicit in US criminal law practice: offenses of strict liability are not real crimes.

This move is unavailable to sustain the voluntary act requirement as part of the general part. Morally it is not unfair to attribute responsibility to some who have not performed a voluntary act. There can be serious blame for: (1) failing to prevent a harm that we could easily prevent but which we choose to allow to happen; (2) directing one's thoughts toward temptations that both mar one's character for having them, and enhance the danger that one will act on them; and (3) using mind–brain interface machines to achieve results in the real world which we intend, even though we do not use bodily movements, as our means to achieve such results.[71] Our agency is involved in such omissions, mental actions, and machine-aided actions, and thus there is no strict liability-like objection to be pressed against liability here as there is for true strict liability offenses.

Moreover, the doctrines punishing crimes of omissions (and doctrines that will be created to punish machine-aided actions) are not easily written off as not being real crimes. True, such liability is exceptional; typical is liability for voluntary acts causing harms.[72] Yet when such untypical liability exists, it is a liability based on moral blameworthiness and is thus one that serves the retributive or partly retributive ends of criminal law; it also is not doctrinally

---

[67] Model Penal Code, §2.02(3).   [68] *Morissette* v. *United States*, 342 US 246 (1952).
[69] *Staples* v. *United States*, 511 US 600 (1994).   [70] *Morissette* v. *United States*.
[71] On actions through mind–brain interface machines, see Michael S. Moore, "Libet's Challenge(s) to Responsible Agency," in Walter Sinnott-Armstrong and Lynn Nadel (eds.), *Conscious Will and Responsibility* (Oxford University Press, 2010).
[72] Moore, *Act and Crime*, pp. 80–90.

relegated to second-class citizenship among the crimes of the special part: it is not presumed against, limited to minor punishments and besmirchments, limited to situations giving notice of regulation, or limited in application to corporate defendants. Except for those omission crimes that are also crimes of strict liability, machine-aided actions and omissions are real crimes, even if limited in number in Anglo-American criminal codes.

So how can the voluntary act requirement be part of the general part? The answer lies in seeing the voluntary act requirement as part of a larger, more general requirement – what I call agency,[73] and Husak would call control.[74] One's moral responsibility is limited to the effects of the exercises of one's agency, where agency is constituted by choices, decisions, intentions, willings, and those executed intentions we call tryings or endeavorings. Most of those tryings etc. that have any impact on the real world, do so through causing the movement of our bodies. But not all. Given the existence of mind–brain interface machines, thoughts can cause real-world effects; given our sometimes ability to prevent harms otherwise about to happen, we can will such harms into being by willing not to do those actions that would prevent such harms.

The voluntary act requirement thus should be seen as part of the general part because of its role – as it happens, a still dominant role – within the more general requirement of active agency. In this it is like intention. The requirement of intent is part of the general part even though there are many crimes not requiring such a mental state for conviction. Yet intent is part – indeed, the most important part – of the more general requirement of *mens rea*, which is, as we have seen, part of the general part of the criminal law.

Neither the *mens rea* nor the voluntary act maneuvers seem to work for various, even less universal doctrines of the criminal law. Consider these defenses (in decreasing order of universality): duress, which as a defense does not apply to homicide at common law (although it does under the Model Penal Code); consent by the victim, which is a defense to (or its absence is a part of the *actus reus* of) many crimes, but far from all; self-defense, which is a defense to homicide and assault crimes, but

---

[73] Michael S. Moore, "Renewed Questions about the Causal Theory of Action," in J. H. Aguilar and A. A. Buckareff (eds.), *Causing Human Action: New Perspectives on the Causal Theory of Action* (Cambridge, MA: MIT Press, 2010), pp. 27–44.

[74] Douglas Husak, "Does Criminal Liability Require an Act?," in Antony Duff (ed.), *Philosophy and the Criminal Law* (Cambridge University Press, 1999), pp. 60–100.

not elsewhere; provocation, which is a partial defense to murder, but to nothing else; duress-of-circumstances (or natural necessity), which is an excuse defense to no crimes as a matter of explicit doctrine (as opposed to what one guesses might be the "law in action"). These defenses are standardly regarded as being a part of the general part. But by what criterion?

Antony Duff and Stuart Green consider one of these examples, the partial defense to murder of provocation:

> the fact that the doctrine [of provocation] is applied, in practice, only to homicide is not determinative of its place in the criminal law. What matters is whether the doctrine is in principle capable of general application. Thus, we might say that those criminal law principles that are theoretically capable of general application are part of the general part, and those that are not are part of the special part.[75]

In truth, Duff and Green are on to something, but it is not quite what they think. They think that it is a "conceptual matter" whether some doctrine such as provocation "should nonetheless be viewed as belonging to the general part."[76] I on the contrary think this is much more a moral matter. Recall that the general part, like all descriptive theories of an area of law, answers not only to logic (i.e., whether it implies the doctrines of the special part); it also answers to the general part of deontic morality, what is often called the theory of responsibility. What Duff and Green rightly see about provocation as a partial defense to homicide is that if the provoked emotional state is excusing there, it should equally be excusing of all crimes, not just homicide. The same could be said of self-defense; suitably generalized to the principle that alone can make (moral) sense of the defense,[77] it should apply to many crimes besides murder. Even easier to extend is the excuse defense of duress, which should extend to homicide (as it does under the Model Penal Code) as it does to other crimes.

What Duff and Green see is that the principles that fit and justify the bulk of the doctrines of the special part, sometimes demand

---

[75] R. A. Duff and Stuart Green, "Introduction: The Special Part and its Problems," in Duff and Green (eds.), *Defining Crimes*, p. 3.

[76] *Ibid.*

[77] Namely, the principle that returns the hard end of a hard choice to he who culpably caused the necessity that such a choice be made. See Phil Montague, "Self-Defense and Choosing Among Lives," *Philosophical Studies*, 40 (1981), 207–219.

answers to particular problems different to those supplied by current doctrines of Anglo-American criminal law. In which event one interprets and changes more discrete doctrines so as to achieve greater coherence with the more general principles making sense of the bulk of the criminal law. One thus understands Williams' caution and Cane's and Stephen's wishy-washiness about *how* universally applicable to all crimes a doctrine must be to be part of the general part; for there is no precise threshold of how universal a doctrine must be before it counts as part of the general part of the criminal law. There is only a sliding scale, where universality in instantiation (in the doctrines of the special part) is traded against correspondence with the moral principles of responsibility.

VI   The content of the general part of Anglo-American criminal law

It is time we move from general talk about the general part, and move to describe more particularly Anglo-American criminal law's general part. Necessarily this will be schematic and abbreviatory. After all, Glanville Williams required 929 pages to do this in the second edition of his *Criminal Law: The General Part*. And we come to praise Williams, not to compete with him in the details of his work.

Anglo-American criminal law's general part consists of four theories of liability, each made up of the same four parts.[78] These four parts are best displayed as a four-square matrix, which I do below for the main kind of liability, which is liability as a principal for a completed crime.

		Prima facie	All-out
Wrongdoing	(1)	Voluntary act (or omission where there is a duty not to omit)	Without objectively justifying circumstances being present, such as those involved in:
	(2)	causing (or being counterfactually necessary for)	(1) self-defense; (2) defense of others;
	(3)	in certain circumstances	(3) defense of property; (4) law enforcement needs;

[78] The four theories-four square organization of the general part is the organizing schema for a new criminal law course book edited by thirteen American criminal law theorists: myself, Heidi Hurd, Stephen Morse, Peter Westen, Leo Katz, Doug Husak, Kim Ferzan, Larry Alexander, Chris Kutz, Claire Finkelstein, Ken Simons, Gideon Yaffe, and Mitch Berman.

	Prima facie	All-out
	(4) a legally prohibited state of affairs.	(5) consent; (6) balance of evils.

Culpability	(1) Intent (with respect to result elements of *actus reus*), plus belief as to circumstance elements, or
	(2) knowledge (of such elements), or
	(3) belief of a risk (of such elements), or
	(4) existence of a risk (of such elements) a reasonable person would have known about, or
	(5) none of the above, for minor violations.
		Without excusing circumstances being present, such as:
		(1) coercion/compulsions, as
		  (a) duress, or
		  (b) duress of circumstance (natural necessity), or
		  (c) provocation, or
		  (d) addiction; or
		(2) Ignorance/mistake, about:
		  (a) matters of fact
		    (i) dealing with circumstance elements in the *actus reus* that the defendant believes to a high probability exist,[79] or
		    (ii) dealing with the elements of the justificatory defenses, or
		  (b) matters of law if induced by reliance on official misadvice; or
		(3) Less than full moral agency, as in:
		  (a) insanity, or
		  (b) immaturity, or
		  (c) involuntary intoxication to the point of insanity.

---

[79] Most mistakes of fact re elements of the *actus reus* of an offense are not excuse defenses because they are not defenses at all – they are merely modes of disproving the *prima facie* case for *mens rea* of purpose, knowledge, or recklessness. But under the Model Penal Code's conceptualization of wilful blindness (Model Penal Code §2.02 (7)), mistake operates as a true excuse from liability because a mistaken belief that a circumstance does not exist excuses the actor who knows to a high probability that the circumstance does exist.

There are many items on this list which are controversial; I have simply listed my own view of the matter. For example, I reject the idea that there are "conduct crimes," crimes that do not involve result elements in their *actus reus* requirements;[80] I therefore list causation (or its counterfactual substitute) as a necessary condition for all crimes. As another example, I assume that insanity, immaturity, and involuntary intoxication to the point of insanity all differ from excuses of compulsion or ignorance; these are status excuses, separating out those members of the human species who lack the rational capacities to be full moral agents and thus the proper subjects of blame.[81] As a final example, I assume that mistakes or ignorance about the existence of circumstances which, if they existed, would justify the behavior, are to be classed as negating culpability and not as negating wrongdoing; such mistakes/ignorance are thus classed as excuses, not as justifications. This is to take a position in a long-running debate about how the justification/excuse line is to be drawn.[82]

There are some items that are on this list because current legal doctrine recognizes them even though they do not match the general part of morality, and there are other items on this list even though current law does not recognize them, but the morality of responsibility–ascription urges that it should. The strict liability punishment of acts unaccompanied by any *mens rea* is a glaring example of the first kind, as is (more controversially) the punishment of criminal negligence.[83] The omission in law of any excuse defense of duress of circumstances is an example of the second.

There are also more general divergences between the law we have and that which morality would justify. One example is the possibility that morality radically distinguishes two forms of obligation, distinguishing prohibitions (negative duties) from requirements (positive duties). It is arguable that these two forms of obligation have different force and

---

[80] Moore, *Act and Crime*, ch. 8; Moore, *Causation and Responsibility*, ch. 1.

[81] Michael Moore, *Law and Psychiatry: Rethinking the Relationship* (Cambridge University Press, 1984), ch. 6.

[82] Compare Paul Robinson, "A Theory of Justification: Societal Harms as a Prerequisite to Criminal Liability," *UCLA Law Review*, 23 (1975), 266–292; Paul Robinson, *Structure and Function in Criminal Law* (Oxford: Clarendon Press, 1997), pp. 95–124 (who to my mind clearly has the better of this debate), with Kent Greenawalt, "The Perplexing Borders of Justification and Excuse," *Columbia Law Review*, 84 (1984), 1897–1927.

[83] See Michael Moore and Heidi Hurd, "Punishing the Awkward, the Stupid, the Weak, and the Selfish: The Culpability of Negligence," *Criminal Law and Philosophy*, 5 (2011), 147–198.

different structures. That is, our negative obligation is not to act in ways that cause certain bad states of affairs, and it is often both stringent and categorical in its force; whereas our positive obligation is to prevent certain harms that, counterfactually, would occur but for our intervention, and this obligation is typically both less stringent and consequentialist in its force. The criminal law that we have (with its lumping of causation and counterfactual dependence together as "cause-in-fact") glides over what looks to be a significant moral difference.[84]

Even more generally, there is a question as to whether morality separates *prima facie* wrongdoing from end-of-the-day wrongdoing, *prima facie* culpability from end-of-the-day culpability. One might think that the distinction between *prima facie* and all-out is an artifact of an adversarial legal system with its need to allocate both the burden for producing evidence and the risk of non-persuasion (often called the "burden of proof"). Alternatively, on some views in ethics,[85] obligations are themselves only *prima facie*, as are breaches of them (wrongdoing); on this moral view, what is actually obligatory or actually wrong, separately awaits determination of matters of justification.

Still, whatever the differences between morality's general part and criminal law's general part, they are minor compared with the similarities. Indeed, the general part of Anglo-American criminal law looks like a reasonably (if not perfectly) accurate attempt to write into law morality's theory of responsibility.

The other theories of liability are derivative of the theory of principal liability for a completed crime. Each of such theories should be seen as describing other relations that can exist between an actor's culpable willing of some event, on the one hand, and some state of affairs that the special part of the criminal law condemns, on the other, relations that make the actor responsible for that bad state of affairs. The first theory that we have already examined, that of liability as a principal for a completed crime, involves the relations of causing and of counterfactual dependence, as we have seen. Other relations that can both exist and make one responsible for some bad state of affairs, include the relations of: trying to cause such a state of affairs; culpably risking the causation of such a state of affairs; soliciting or procuring another to cause such a state of affairs, when that other does so; aiding another to cause such a state of affairs, when that other does so; agreeing (or reaching

---

[84] See generally Moore, *Causation and Responsibility*.
[85] W. D. Ross, *The Right and the Good* (Oxford University Press, 1930).

agreement) with another that he will cause such a state of affairs, when that other does so. These various relations are grouped by the law we have into three alternative theories of liability: inchoate liability, complicity, and conspiracy.

A similar four-square box for the second theory, that of inchoate liability as a principal, looks like this:

	Prima facie	All-out
Wrongdoing	(1) Voluntary act (or omission where there is a duty not to omit) (2) causing (or being counterfactually necessary for) (3) in certain circumstances (4) a state of affairs beyond mere preparation toward causing a legally prohibited result, which state of affairs is conceptualized either as a: (a) well-evidenced trying to cause such a result (MPC); or (b) objectively risky proximity to causing such a result (common law).	Without justifying circumstances being present, such as: [same as for completed crimes, above].
Culpability	(1) Intent (with respect to result elements of the *actus reus* of the crime attempted) plus, re circumstances, whatever *mens rea* is required for conviction of the crime attempted. (2) Belief to a reasonable certainty that the result will occur, plus whatever *mens rea* is required for conviction of the crime attempted re circumstances. (3) Belief of a substantiated risk that the result will occur, plus, re circumstances, whatever *mens rea* is required for conviction of the crime attempted.	Without excusing circumstances being present, such as: [same as for completed crimes, above]. Except for: (1) Voluntary abandonment (MPC only). (2) "Legal impossibility" (common law only).

Prima facie	All-out
(4) Substantial risk that the result will occur such that a reasonable person would advert to such risk, plus, re circumstances, whatever *mens rea* is required for conviction of the crime attempted.	

The bracketed items of *mens rea* highlight a peculiar feature of Anglo-American inchoate liability, and that is its focus on the culpability of *trying* to the exclusion of any focus on the culpability of *risking*.[86] Our criminal law is not wrong about the punishable culpability of those who attempt to bring about a harm even though they fail.[87] But that law arguably is incomplete in not having liability for those who culpably risk harm even though that risk does not materialize.[88] There is moral blame attached to such culpable although unrealized risking, and some lesser form of inchoate liability would be created in a general part more closely corresponding to moral responsibility. The Model Penal Code goes only a slight distance down this road with its creation of liability for completed attempts where the actor merely believes (but does not intend) that his actions will cause some legally prohibited result,[89] and in its creation of the crime of reckless endangerment for homicide.[90]

The third theory of liability in the general part is complicity. This is accomplice liability for either completed crimes or for inchoate crimes: one has not caused the harm himself, nor tried to, nor unreasonably risked causing the harm himself; rather, he has procured another to do it, or he has aided that other in the doing of it. The schematic for such a theory is:

---

[86] For a comparison, see Moore, *Causation and Responsibility*, pp. 307–318.

[87] See Gideon Yaffe, "Trying, Acting, and Attempted Crimes," *Law and Philosophy*, 28 (2009), 109–162; Gideon Yaffe, *Attempts* (Oxford University Press, 2010). In both works Yaffe argues that criminal attempt liability rightly focuses on the culpability of tryings.

[88] See Larry Alexander, "Duff on Attempts," in R. Cruft, M. Kramer, and M. Reiff (eds.), *Crime, Punishment and Responsibility* (Oxford University Press, 2011), pp. 236–238.

[89] Model Penal Code §5.01(1)(b).   [90] Model Penal Code §211.2.

	Prima facie	All-out
Wrongdoing	(1) Voluntary act (or omission where there is a duty not to omit) (2) causing (or being counterfactually necessary for) (3) in certain circumstances (4) an aiding or a soliciting (or an attempt to aid, MPC only) (5) of a crime that is actually committed by the one aided or solicited.	Without justifying circumstances being present, such as: [same as for liability for completed crimes as a principal].
Culpability	(1) (a) Intent to promote or facilitate the conduct of another that constitutes the offense: plus: re result elements of the offense aided, whatever *mens rea* is required to be guilty of the offense aided; plus: re circumstance elements, whatever *mens rea* is required to be guilty of the offense aided; or (1) (b) The primary and secondary *mens rea* in (1)(a) above with respect to one offense, and that offense leads to the commission of another offense by the same principal that was reasonably foreseeable to the accomplice (common law minority only). (2) Knowing that one's act will facilitate another in doing an offense. (3) Believing there is a substantial risk that one's act will facilitate another in doing an offense.	Without excusing circumstances being present, such as: [same as for liability for completed crimes as a principal]. Except for: Voluntary abandonment (MPC only)

As with inchoate liability, those who aid or solicit another in doing some crime are not said themselves to cause the harm the substantive offense prohibits. And again, like inchoate liability, this perceived lack of causation by the defendant in complicity is compensated for by requiring the serious culpability of intention for liability as an accomplice. One could (again) imagine a legal system reaching to lesser states of culpability – knowing or reckless aiders – and imposing lesser forms of liability on these less culpable aiders, just as it imposes lesser liability on less culpable causers, that is, principals. That it does not do so is another way in which Anglo-American criminal law's general part deviates from the morality of responsibility.

The alternative *mens rea* (1)(b) bracketed in the scheme above is another deviation of law from morality's general part. This is the common law's "foreseeable second crime" doctrine[91] (an aspect of the "joint enterprise" theory of accomplice liability in England),[92] according to which an accomplice to one crime becomes an accomplice to all other crimes committed by the principal that were foreseeable (or actually foreseen, in England) results of the first crime. The doctrine makes for wildly disproportionate punishments, and thus deviates from morality's dictates. It is bracketed because of its moral undesirability, and because it is rejected by the Model Penal Code[93] and by most American jurisdictions.

Even more dramatic as a deviation from morality is the possibility that what the law calls an accomplice has no separate counterpart in morality. Suppose I am right in the view argued for elsewhere,[94] that those now punished as accomplices are either: (1) causers of the harm through use of another as their means; (2) necessary for the harm to have occurred; (3) attemptors at causing the harm; (4) culpable riskers of causing the harm; (5) none of the above, but liable anyway on a vicarious basis. In such a case the law would not be punishing unjustly (except for the fifth category above), but it would be misjudging the basis for holding "accomplices" to be blameworthy and liable. It would have sliced the pie wrongly, even if most people would be getting the size of piece that they deserve.

The fourth and last theory of liability is that of conspiracy. As is commonly recognized, conspiracy liability is both a form of inchoate liability that punishes the behavior of groups much earlier in their

---

[91] *People* v. *Croy*, 710 P2d 392 (Cal 1985).

[92] *R.* v. *Hyde* [1991] 1 QB 134. On the joint enterprise theory generally, see Sir Roger Toulson, "Sir Michael Foster, Professor Williams and Complicity in Murder," Chapter 10, below.

[93] Model Penal Code §2.06(3)(a).   [94] Moore, *Causation and Responsibility*, ch. 13.

criminal plans than does the law of attempts punish single actors; and a
form of accomplice liability that punishes groups more broadly for the
crimes of any member of the group than would the standard theory of
accomplice liability. Its schematic is below.

	Prima facie	All-out
Wrongdoing	(1) Voluntary act (or omission where there is a duty not to omit) (2) causing (or being counterfactually necessary for) (3) in certain circumstances (4) agreement (common law), or at least an agreeing (MPC) (5) accompanied by an overt act executing the agreement.	Without justifying circumstances being present, such as: [same as for liability as a principal for completed crimes].
Culpability	(1) (a) Intent to promote or facilitate the offense agreed upon, or (1) (b) the *mens rea* in (1)(a) above with respect to one offense, and that offense leads to the commission of another offense by the co-conspirator(s) when the commission of that offense was reasonably foreseeable to the defendant, or (2) knowing that one's agreeing will facilitate another in doing an offense, or (3) believing there is a substantial risk that one's agreeing will facilitate another in doing an offense.	Without excusing circumstances being present, such as: Except for: (1) Voluntary abandonment (MPC only). (2) "Legal impossibility" (common law only).

Conspiracy liability probably goes a long way beyond what the general
part of morality would recommend. For in truth there are large elements
of vicarious liability in conspiracy law as currently practiced in the
United States, particularly under the *Pinkerton* doctrine.[95] Even without

95 *Pinkerton* v. *United States*, 328 US 640 (1946). Rejected by a substantial minority of
American jurisdictions and by the Model Penal Code.

Pinkerton's foreseeable other crimes aspect ((1)(b) in the schema above), mere agreement without more is a quite minor contribution to some criminal result, so that to be punished equally with those who culpably caused that result will often be disproportionate to desert. Still, there is culpability here, even if the wrongdoing is minor. So that if one wishes to have inchoate liability attach this early in the steps leading up to crime, consistency would dictate lesser forms of culpability for conspiracy in line with the lesser forms of culpability for completed crimes as a principal. Since such lesser forms of conspiracy do not exist in current law, those items ((2) and (3) above) are bracketed in the above scheme.

VII   The specialness of the general part

There is a threefold attraction to the general part. For those who practice criminal law the attraction is that of any successful descriptive theory of law: such theories organize and simplify complicated bodies of law so as to make them more easily knowable and usable. The general part of criminal law is particularly successful at this. The four iterations of the four-square matrices above organize the issues, mode of presentation, and decision of every case that can arise in criminal law. Both the issues in such cases, and the resolution of those issues, will be organized along the lines, first, of theories of liability; then, by the *prima facie* case and defense within each theory; then, by the requirements of *actus reus* and *mens rea* within the *prima facie* case; then, by justification and excuse within the defenses; and so on. Not every issue will be a live one in every case; indeed, in real-life cases only one or a few issues will be discussably controversial. But what has to be true *in toto* for a conviction, and how these elements are related to one another, is displayed in a systematic way by the general part. Such systematicity is at once both elegant and highly useful. It is no mean feat to be achieved in an area of law.

I once speculated whether other areas of law such as property, torts, contracts, or constitutional law could be blessed with equally systematic general parts.[96] I now think that that answer is not only in the negative, but that necessarily it has to be so. For the driving force making the general part of the criminal law so systematic is by and large lacking for these other areas of law. That force in criminal law has been the univocal pursuit of one normative ideal rather than several, which single-

---

[96] Moore, *Placing Blame*, pp. 33–35. Peter Cane carries on the speculation vis-à-vis torts in his "The General/Special Distinction."

mindedness allowed the systematicity of that ideal to seep into every nook and cranny of the criminal law over hundreds of years. That ideal is that the blame-imposing and suffering-imposing institution we call criminal law can only fairly be applied to those who deserve to both suffer and be blamed for the wrongs they have culpably done. Such an ideal is part of both retributive theories of punishment, and also of any mixed theory that reserves to desert (versus utility) the role of dictating principles for the distribution of punishment (as opposed to dictating the general justifying aim of punishment).[97]

The point here is not that this ideal is morally correct (although it is). Rather, the point is that *belief* in that ideal (by those thousands of lawyers, judges, and scholars who have shaped Anglo-American criminal law) has *caused* that law to have the shape that it does. No such unanimity of belief has actuated the development of property, contract, tort, or constitutional law. Such areas of law have been constructed piecemeal by the temporary and local victories of three distinct and competing ideals on separate occasions.[98] Sometimes a natural right/corrective justice ideal wins out, as in doctrines of intentional torts, the right against takings of property and other constitutional rights, and promissory estoppel in contract. Sometimes, or more often, the utilitarian ideal of welfare enhancement wins out, as in doctrines of nuisance in tort, consideration in contracts, and *bona fide* purchasers in property. Sometimes the third ideal of distributive justice wins out, as in doctrines of no-fault tort liability, substantive unconscionability in contracts, and non-waivable implied warranties of habitability in landlord–tenant relationships. This cacophony of competing ideals makes it impossible for contracts, torts, constitutional law, or property to cohere into the tightly knit system that is the general part of the criminal law. There is, as a result, no schema for all possible property cases, contract cases, tort cases, etc. like that displayed above for all possible criminal law cases.[99]

---

[97] Herbert Hart's mixed theory of punishment. H. L. A. Hart, *Punishment and Responsibility* (Oxford University Press, 1968).

[98] I sketch this in Michael Moore, "Four Reflections on Law and Morality," *William and Mary Law Review*, 48 (2007), 1523–1569, at pp. 1553–1568.

[99] As Peter Glazebrook has pointed out to me (in private correspondence), in its general doctrines of offer, acceptance, consideration, and excuse Anglo-American contract law comes closest to having a general part analogous to the general part of the criminal law. For these doctrines purport to apply to all kinds of contracts, such as employment contracts, contracts for the sale of goods, government contracts, construction contracts, etc. And, admittedly, there is a universality to such general doctrines of promise-based

To be sure, criminal law has had its share of theoreticians promoting utilitarian or distributive justice ideals (the latter under the guise of "the rehabilitative ideal"). Yet apart from that giant blemish of strict liability for regulatory offenses, these competing ideals have had little sway. They have been what F. H. Bradley once described as the giving of bad reasons for what we believe on instinct anyway.[100] We are all, as I once put it, "closet" retributivists,[101] and the structure of our criminal law shows it.

This close fit of the criminal law we have with the criminal law we ought to have to conform to morality's general part, is the basis of the second attraction possessed by the general part. This is its attractiveness to philosophically minded theoreticians. Because of criminal law's mimicry of the morality of responsibility, the general part becomes a vast reservoir of ready-made thought experiments for moral philosophers. J. L. Austin famously quipped that "fact is richer than diction."[102] Fact is also richer than the imaginations of the most imaginative of theoreticians. The cases that have arisen in criminal law thus vastly outstrip the resources available to any theoretician via his own thought experiments. Moreover, such cases come with provisional resolutions (i.e., judicial opinions) by those whose "thought experiments" have real-world consequences attached to their decisions. Samuel Johnson once remarked that "nothing so focuses a man's mind as the prospect of being hung in the morning." I would add that for decent men and women, nothing so focuses the mind as the prospect of hanging someone in the morning. Real-world cases have real-world consequences turning on their resolution, making those resolutions serious and well-considered. Third, such resolutions are principled and systematic, thanks to the system of precedent that demands that they be so. The collective wisdom of many

---

liability. But (1) contract law is not confined to such promise-based liability (as in its doctrines of "objective contracts," quasi-contract, promissory estoppel, estoppels-en-pais, and the like); and (2) the normative theory underlying such promise-based liability – viz., the theory urging a categorical obligation to keep one's promises – is neither so dominating, nor believed to be so dominating, of the competing utilitarian ideal (of providing a medium for non-simultaneous, efficient exchange) as to uniformly isolate anything like a general theory of personal accountability for keeping one's promise-based obligations.

[100] F. H. Bradley, *Appearance and Reality*, 2nd edn (Oxford University Press, 1897), p. xiv.

[101] Moore, "Closet Retributivism," in *Placing Blame*, ch. 2.

[102] J. L. Austin, "A Plea for Excuses," *Proceedings of the Aristotelian Society*, 57 (1956), 1–30.

judges is not to be sneezed at by solo theoreticians exercising only their own imaginations. Finally, these resolutions are largely congruent with the principles of responsibility in ethics, thanks to the correspondence of criminal law's general part with the general part of deontic morality.

The upshot of these four points is that the general part of the criminal law is philosophically interesting. Moral philosophers have as much to learn from it as the lawyers who practice it have to learn from such philosophers. As J. L. Austin also noted, "it is a perpetual and salutary surprise to discover how much is to be learned from the law" when doing ethics.[103] For this reason, too, criminal law has long been the central home of a happy partnership between legal theory and moral philosophy.

It is interesting to speculate how culturally universal is the general/special distinction that we have explored. Have we charted only Anglo-American criminal law's general part, or something much more universal? George Fletcher's comparative law ventures over the course of a long career have convinced him that "the distinction between the general and the special parts of the criminal law ... is now recognised virtually everywhere in the world."[104] Whether that is so, I leave to others better equipped to expound the doctrines and the structures of criminal codes around the world. But however one answers this comparative law question, Fletcher is spot-on on the universalist aspirations of the moral aspect of the general part of Anglo-American criminal law (what I call deontic morality's general part): it seeks nothing less than to get right the "universal principles of responsibility ... that should be recognised ... in all civilised nations."[105] This is the third attraction of studying the general part of the criminal law separately from any study of the special part. Doing so allows us to isolate a particular kind of injustice that is rank, both in fact and in universal belief. This is the injustice of being condemned and punished for a harm with which one has no wrong-making connection (of causation, counterfactual dependence, aiding, etc.) or about which one has no culpability. It is admittedly one kind of injustice to punish people under laws prohibiting behavior that is not immoral; it is another and a worse form of injustice to punish them for immoralities they did not do. Focusing on the general part isolates this last kind of injustice. Such a general part thus commends itself to all peoples, irrespective of their differing views of substantive morality.

---

[103] *Ibid.*   [104] Fletcher, *The Grammar of Criminal Law*, p. 18.   [105] *Ibid.*, pp. 19–20.

In Book III of the *Nichomachean Ethics* Aristotle was the first to take up the task of articulating the theory of responsibility underlying the general part of criminal law. Neither Glanville Williams, nor those of us like Fletcher, Duff, Husak, or myself who have followed Williams in criminal law theory will be the last. But we can be proud of the progress we have collectively made in the theory of responsibility, as well as in the degree of that theory's realization in the general part of Anglo-American criminal law.

5

Four distinctions that Glanville Williams did not make: the practical benefits of examining the interrelation among criminal law doctrines

PAUL H. ROBINSON*

As a student, I much admired Glanville Williams as one of the greatest living criminal law scholars. He is the reason I went to study at Cambridge after law school. His *General Part* was the most sophisticated criminal law treatise of the day. His *Textbook*, which he published the year after I left Cambridge, seemed a genuine innovation. The historical distance only seems to confirm the importance of his contributions.

As a matter of content, we tend to think of Glanville Williams as the mainstream of criminal law. His books have had such influence that they mark out much of what is now generally accepted. It is easy to forget, perhaps, that in his time he was something of a rebel. He was a free thinker who followed the argument where it led him, with a certain fearlessness about the consequences.

But my topic here concerns an area in which he was much less rebellious: the organizational principles for criminal law doctrines. His approach represents the classic United Kingdom scheme, which essentially follows the evolved common law structure of criminal law. He was largely responsible for popularizing the general part–special part distinction, but he did not go much beyond that in framework innovation.

In the United States, by contrast, there has been an explicit break with the common law framework. In the 1950s, the American Law Institute (ALI) essentially started from a blank slate and produced a structure for criminal law doctrine that it thought was more useful, and used this structure in the organization of its Model Penal Code. Glanville Williams

* The author thanks Melissa Krain, University of Pennsylvania Law School Class of 2013, for her excellent research assistance.

was a consultant to the ALI during this work, but its framework renovation must have had little effect on him. His second edition of the *General Part*, published in 1961, shows apparent indifference to the Model Penal Code framework. His 1982 article, "A Theory of Excuses," concludes that the justification–excuse distinction, which the Model Penal Code drafters thought to be important, was of limited significance. The second edition of his *Textbook*, published the following year, remained uninfluenced by the distinction.

His concern was not that the distinction could not be made or that it was irrational, but rather that it simply had little practical significance, certainly nothing important enough that it should influence his organization of doctrine within his books. In this chapter, I would like to take up Glanville Williams' challenge and show that there is real practical value not just in the justification–excuse distinction, but in the general enterprise of examining the interrelation among different criminal law doctrines. Understanding how different doctrines are similar and are different from one another can improve criminal law in all of its functions. The failure to undertake such an examination can invite error and confusion.

Up front, I would concede that there might be some cost or at least risk in changing the existing framework that current judges, lawyers, and lawmakers have in their minds. Glanville Williams was influential with these people in part, I suspect, because he talked to them in their own terms. His analysis used as its reference points the framework of criminal law that they shared. They were not alienated or distracted by attempts to change that basic framework. But I want to argue that, while there is some risk in the enterprise, the benefits outweigh those risks. Introducing useful categories and distinctions among criminal law doctrines can produce such practical benefits that judges, lawyers, and lawmakers would quickly adapt to the revised framework and soon enough feel comfortable with it.

To illustrate my point that many distinctions can be important and useful, I will look at four distinctions, none of which Glanville Williams used in the organization of criminal law doctrine in his books. None of these distinctions are new with this chapter. Some will be familiar to some readers, but perhaps not all, so I will give some brief background for each.

The first and second distinctions I will look at come from looking at criminal law doctrine from what might be called an "operational" perspective. The first category, general defenses, are doctrines that provide a defense to liability even though the defendant satisfies all the elements of the offense definition. The second category that I will talk about does the reverse: the "doctrines of imputation" impose liability on a defendant even though he does not satisfy all of the elements of the offense definition. That is, doctrines of imputation treat the defendant as if he satisfies an offense element that he in fact does not. Taken together the offense definitions, the general defenses, and the doctrines of imputation organize most of the doctrines within criminal law.

The third and fourth distinctions that I will consider are also related to one another. They look at criminal law doctrine from what might be called the "functional" perspective. Criminal law performs two quite different functions: it announces *ex ante* the rules of conduct for the community, then, upon a violation of those conduct rules, it adjudicates *ex post* the violation.

In this chapter I am not so much trying to sell these distinctions so much as trying to sell the importance of the enterprise – specifically, the practical value of examining the interrelation among criminal law doctrines. Many of these distinctions are at the core of my book *Structure & Function in Criminal Law*, which was dedicated to the memory of Glanville Williams, who died the year the book was published. I offer this short chapter as a rededication to that memory.

I   Conceptual differences among general defenses: justifications, excuses, and non-exculpatory defenses

The first distinction that I would like to discuss distinguishes three kinds of general defenses: justifications, excuses, and non-exculpatory defenses. All general defenses fall into one of these three categories. I would define the categories in the following way. (Others have sometimes defined them differently.) As for the distinction between justification and excuse, which is the most familiar to people, I would define justification defenses as doctrines that give a complete defense, even though the defendant has satisfied all the elements of the offense definition, because his conduct is the right thing to do in the relevant circumstances. The law would be happy to have others do the same conduct under the same circumstances in the future, or at least would be similarly tolerant of it. Excuse defenses, in contrast, are doctrines in which the defendant has done something wrong. The law would wish that others would not repeat such conduct in the future, but this defendant is to be given a defense because he is blameless for doing it. Non-exculpatory defenses are doctrines in which the defendant is given a defense, even though he may satisfy the elements of the offense definition and he is neither justified nor excused, but his acquittal serves to advance some other, typically important, interest.[1]

Justification defenses include defensive force justifications like self-defense and defense of others, public authority justifications like law enforcement authority, and the general justification of lesser evils. Excuse defenses include the disability excuses of insanity, involuntary intoxication, duress, and immaturity, and certain reasonable mistakes that render the defendant blameless (other than by negating an offense element). Non-exculpatory defenses include such doctrines as diplomatic immunity, double jeopardy, the legality doctrines, and the statute limitations, for example.

Glanville Williams understood the distinctions among these three groups of general defenses, but thought them of little importance. Williams noted the historic distinction between justification and excuse defenses, but saw it as being of little value to modern law.[2] "What is the difference between a justification and an excuse? Very little. They are both defenses in the full sense, leading to an acquittal. However, when the act is not justified but only excused it is still regarded as being in some tenuous way wrong, for certain collateral purposes."[3] Similarly, he placed little emphasis on non-exculpatory defenses as a group, referring to them as "certain technical points alleged by the defendant in order to avoid liability,"[4] and devoting little space in both his *Textbook* and his

---

[1] For a more detailed discussion, see Paul H. Robinson, *Structure and Function in Criminal Law* (Oxford: Clarendon Press, 1997), pp. 71–77.

[2] Glanville Williams, *Textbook of Criminal Law* (London: Stevens, 1978), p. 51 (hereinafter Williams, *Textbook*).

[3] Williams, *Textbook*, p. 51. Williams' failure to see the justification–excuse distinction as defined here, together with the lack of recognition of that distinction in the then current law, meant that there was considerable uncertainty about what was a justification and what was an excuse, and whether it mattered. For instance, he differentiated self-defense from a lesser evils defense by saying that: "It is sometimes thought that the difference between private defence [self-defence] and necessity [lesser evils] is that the former presupposes a wrong while the latter does not." Glanville Williams, *Criminal Law: The General Part* (London: Stevens, 1961), pp. 233–234 (hereinafter Williams, *The General Part*). He then goes on to minimize the importance of the distinction saying: "The line is pretty thin, and there is hardly any legal need to draw it." *Ibid.* At another point he says that duress, a defense understood to be an excuse, may also be analogized to a "type of necessity," which could be either a justification or excuse, depending upon how one defines the defense. *Ibid.* at pp. 759–762.

[4] Williams, *Textbook*, p. 51.

General Part to the concept.[5] And when he discussed non-exculpatory defenses, Williams did not note their conceptual difference with other general defenses. For example, he discusses diplomatic immunity in a chapter on criminal capacity that also discusses excuses like immaturity and insanity.[6]

I want to argue that there are important practical benefits that flow from distinguishing these three kinds of general defenses. For example, once one sees that two defenses are the same group – that is, that they play an analogous role – it follows that their formulations ought to be analogous or least consistent.[7] For example, the defenses of insanity and involuntary intoxication provide an excuse where one's disability causes significant dysfunction in the defendant at the time of and in relation to the offense. The dysfunction might be to a defendant's cognitive processes or, as some jurisdictions recognize, the dysfunction might be an impairment to a defendant's capacity to control his conduct. The Model Penal Code in fact uses the exact identical language in defining the excusing conditions for the two defenses: the defendant must "lack substantial capacity to appreciate the criminality of his conduct or to conform his conduct to the requirements of law."

But it is not uncommon for jurisdictions to fail to see the analogy between these two excuses and to define the excusing conditions for the two in inconsistent ways. For example, Alabama recognizes substantial control impairment as a basis for an involuntary intoxication defense, yet denies the same dysfunction a defense when it results from mental illness. Georgia has the reverse asymmetry. It allows the control impairment to provide the basis for an excuse if it results from mental illness, but not if it results from involuntary intoxication.[8] If the extent of a control impairment is identical in two cases, yet one dysfunction is caused by involuntary intoxication and the other by insanity, on what grounds could one provide an excuse in one case and not the other?

A second example of the practical value of these differences between general defenses is in the definition of the triggering conditions for the

---

[5] With the exception of diplomatic immunity and entrapment, Williams did not write any sections in either of his books that focussed exclusively on non-exculpatory defenses (e.g., exclusionary rule, double jeopardy, statute of limitations).

[6] Williams, *Textbook*, ch. 28, pp. 637–645.

[7] See Robinson, *Structure and Function*, pp. 83–92, 98–100.

[8] See Paul H. Robinson, "A System of Excuses: How Criminal Law's Excuses Defenses Do, and Don't Work Together to Exculpate Blameless (and Only Blameless Offenders)," *Texas Tech Law Review*, 42 (2009), 268–270.

use of defensive force. This is an instance where the defense distinctions are simply essential to the proper operation of the doctrine. That is, one simply cannot properly define triggering conditions for defensive force without recognizing the defense distinctions as I have set them out above. We want a defendant to be able to defend against the excused attacker or an attacker with the non-exculpatory defense – the psychotic or the immune diplomat – but we do not want the defendant to be able to lawfully defend against an objectively justified actor – such as the law enforcement officer making a lawful arrest.[9]

A third example of the practical importance of these general defense distinctions is seen in the problem of ambiguous acquittals that arises when these distinctions are not recognized. Note that justification and excuse defenses say directly opposite things about the defendant's conduct: a justification defense announces that the conduct is condoned; an excuse defense announces that the conduct is condemned. Where these two kinds of general defenses are not distinguished, as in a general verdict of acquittal, it is easy for an excuse to be mistaken for a justification.

Recall the Rodney King case in which, after a long car chase, officers surrounded Rodney King and continued to beat him. The jury acquitted the officers, and riots in Los Angeles followed. The jury acquittal may well have been on the theory that the adrenaline build-up during the long car chase, the lack of adequate training to deal with such circumstances, as well as the lack of good supervision on the scene, meant that the conduct was not justified – it was excessive – but that the defendants did not deserve to be punished for it. In other words, the striking conduct on the tape is an example of conduct that we would not want repeated in the same circumstances in the future, but it is not to be punished in this instance because the officers were blameless for it. Yet with an ambiguous general verdict of acquittal, people in the community could easily have come to the conclusion that the conduct they saw on the tape was conduct that the criminal law was condoning (as objectively justified), and that could be quite upsetting.[10] It is easy enough to construct a more nuanced verdict system of a "no violation" verdict and a "blameless

---

[9] Williams seems to concede this: in discussing a person's right to defend against an insane attacker, he explains that "the lunatic has an excuse, on the ground of lack of *mens rea*; but his act of aggression is not authorised by law. It is not *justified*. This is one of the differences in law between a justification and an excuse." Williams, *Textbook*, p. 502.

[10] See Robinson, *Structure and Function*, pp. 119–121.

violation" verdict, but such a solution would be ineffective where the doctrine does not itself distinguish between (objective) justifications and excuses.[11]

A fourth illustration of practical value concerns what one might call post-acquittal collateral consequences. For a justification defense, there ought to be none. What the defendant did was the right thing to do, which others can do in a similar situation in the future. For an excuse defense, one might want to at least ask the question whether the cause of the excusing conditions is recurring. We already do this with insanity acquittals, by having a special verdict for "not guilty by reason of insanity," which is commonly followed by an examination to determine whether civil commitment is appropriate. But there might be any number of situations that give rise to excuse defenses that would benefit from future civil supervision or even just education. Non-exculpatory defenses present an even stronger case for the possible need for collateral consequences. It may well be that we want to give the serial child molester a double jeopardy defense for the case at hand, but that does not mean that we should not be sure that he is denied a license to drive school buses.[12]

Finally, note that non-exculpatory defenses are importantly different from justification and excuse defenses in their potential to undermine the moral credibility of the criminal law. Having justification and excuse defenses that are robust – that fully capture all the nuances of the community views of desert – is important for building and maintaining the criminal law's moral authority with the community, and, as I have discussed elsewhere, that moral credibility can have important implications for the crime-control effectiveness of the criminal law. A criminal law that has earned a reputation for reliably doing justice, no more but no less, is a system that improves its ability to stigmatize and is thus likely to prompt cooperation and acquiescence, rather than subversion and resistance. In turn, this criminal law system is more likely to get

---

[11] See Paul H. Robinson, "Rules of Conduct and Principles of Adjudication," *University of Chicago Law Review*, 57 (1990), 766–767; Paul H. Robinson and Michael T. Cahill, *Law Without Justice: Why Criminal Law Doesn't Give People What They Deserve* (New York: Oxford University Press, 2006), pp. 210–212.

[12] In their current formulation, many non-exculpatory defenses operate to bar a fair adjudication of the case facts. See Robinson, *Structure and Function*, p. 70: "Diplomatic immunity may provide a defense, without regard to the guilt or innocence of the actor, because by forgoing trial and conviction of the offending diplomat our diplomats abroad are free from prosecution by their host countries."

deference in borderline cases where people are unsure about the "condemnability" of the conduct at hand, and, most importantly, will have a greater voice in the shaping of social norms that can harness the powerful forces of social influence.[13]

But every instance of a non-exculpatory defense is a potential failure of justice. Letting a potentially blameworthy offender go free, and doing so intentionally, can seriously undermine the system's moral credibility. It follows then that we should not be quick to make non-exculpatory defenses as robust as possible, thus taking quite a different approach than in the formulation of justifications and excuses. Non-exculpatory defenses, in contrast, ought to be defined as narrowly as possible to achieve their objective. Each aspect of a formulation ought to be tested to see whether the benefits that flow from it can justify the predictable costs to the system's moral credibility that the intentional acquittal of a blameworthy person will cause.[14]

II Doctrines of imputation: complicity, voluntary intoxication, diminished capacity, and *Majewski*

The second distinction that I want to offer as having practical benefit is that which sets apart from offense definitions and general defenses the doctrines of imputation. The most common such doctrines are voluntary intoxication and complicity, but also include causing crime by an innocent, transferred intent, the Pinkerton Doctrine in the United States, the complicity aspect of felony-murder rule, and others.[15] Glanville Williams obviously discusses the important imputation doctrines,[16] but makes no reference to the imputation process as operationally

---

[13] See Paul H. Robinson and John M. Darley, "Intuitions of Justice: Implications for Criminal Law and Justice Policy," *Southern California Law Review*, 81 (2007), 1, 18: "Human beings will demand justice for serious wrongdoing, and [failure to do justice] ... would produce intolerable consequences"; Paul H. Robinson, Geoffrey P. Goodwin, and Michael D. Reisig, "The Disutility of Injustice," *New York University Law Review*, 85 (December 2010), 1940, Pt IV (presenting studies that show how the criminal justice system loses community deference if it fails to align with society's morals and notions of desert).

[14] Robinson, *Structure and Function*, p. 73: "Permitting [non-exculpatory] defenses undermines the purposes for which criminal liability is imposed"; Robinson and Cahill, *Law Without Justice*, Pt III.

[15] See Robinson, *Structure and Function*, pp. 59–64.

[16] See generally, Williams, *General Part*, chs. 9 and 11; Williams, *Textbook*, chs. 15 and 21.

different from other doctrines, nor does he note similarities between the provisions that make up the doctrines of imputation.

As my first exhibit on the practical benefits of recognizing the conceptual category, let me offer a passage from *Director of Public Prosecutions* v. *Majewski*,[17] where the court, quoting Lord Hailsham in *Director of Prosecutions* v. *Morgan*, said:

> Once it be accepted that an intent of whatever description is an ingredient essential to the guilt of the accused I cannot myself see that any other direction [than requiring proof of the intent] can be logically acceptable. Otherwise a jury would in effect be told to find an intent where none existed or where none was proved to have existed. I cannot myself reconcile it with my conscience to sanction as part of the English law what I regard as a logical impossibility, and, if there were any authority which, if accepted, would compel me to do so, I would feel constrained to declare that it was not to be followed.[18]

These are strong words, but they reflect a serious misconception of the process of imputation. The imputation of missing offense elements is not itself a matter for concern. And if doctrines of imputation had been recognized as a doctrinal category, this would have been obvious to Lord Hailsham and "the academics" who share his view and to the court in *Majewski*. Imputation is a common and sensible process that is done in a host of doctrines, such as complicity. Puzzling over the propriety of imputation only distracts from the important issue that should be the point of focus for every doctrine of imputation: is that which is being imputed by the doctrine justified by the conditions that the doctrine sets for that imputation?

That is the central test that must be the focus in all instances of imputation. So, for example, most people seem to think that the requirements of the complicity doctrine do generally justify treating the offender as if he had satisfied the conduct elements of the offense definition, even though he does not in fact. In the case of the doctrine of voluntary intoxication, one can see some basis for an imputation: the defendant's culpability in voluntarily intoxicating himself as he did is seen to justify treating him as if he has some other culpability that might be required for the offense. However, once we announce the "imputation test question," we may be somewhat more critical of the doctrine. Negligence as to becoming intoxicated – typically what is required in

[17] [1976] 2 All ER 142.
[18] *DPP* v. *Morgan* [1975] 2 All ER 347, at p. 360, quoted in *Majewski* [1976] 2 All ER at 166.

the United States to trigger the imputation – may be an adequate moral justification for imputing some missing offense culpability elements, but perhaps not all. For example, such negligence as to becoming intoxicated may not be adequate to justify imputation of recklessness as to causing death, as is required for manslaughter, yet the doctrine would operate to impute such missing culpability.[19] Seeing that the apparently disparate doctrines have the common imputation effect prompts this "imputation test question," which reveals many as coming up short.

Another practical advantage of recognizing the category of imputation doctrines is the help it provides in seeing when such imputation occurs. Imputation takes a variety of forms. In complicity, the doctrine is quite explicit: the rule often explicitly provides that the perpetrator's conduct is being "imputed" to the defendant under the described conditions. In the doctrine of voluntary intoxication, the language is a bit less explicit: where the defendant has voluntarily intoxicated himself, his unawareness of the risk required by the offense definition is said to be "immaterial," yet it is obvious that this means that it is to be imputed – the actor is to be treated as if he satisfied the offense element even though in fact he does not.

In other doctrines, however, the imputation is even more obscured. For example, consider the doctrine that governs what is sometimes called "diminished capacity" or some similar phrase in the United States, that is, the rules governing the use of mental illness to negate an offense culpability element. The Model Penal Code allows evidence of mental illness to be introduced to negate any offense element, but 60 per cent of the jurisdictions in the United States adopt rules that purport to restrict the defendant's ability to introduce evidence of mental illness that would show that he did not have the required offense culpability.[20] These doctrines are sometimes presented as if they were defenses or mitigations but, of course, in practice they are just the reverse; they are doctrines of imputation. They treat the defendant as if he satisfies the required offense element when in fact he does not. That his mental illness negates the required offense element is treated as immaterial.

This operation of the doctrine of diminished capacity serves to illustrate the usefulness of the doctrinal category of imputation in another way. Once the operation of a doctrine shows it to be a doctrine of

---

[19] See Robinson and Cahill, *Criminal Law*, §5.3: "Hypothetical with Buff and Sharon on Voluntary Intoxication."

[20] See authorities collected at Robinson and Cahill, *Criminal Law*, §15.1 (noting "diminished capacity" as a basis for mitigation and the modern rules related to it).

imputation, thus triggering the "imputation test question," the answer to the question for the doctrine of diminished capacity is revealing: are the offense elements imputed by the doctrine in fact justified by the doctrine's conditions? In the case of diminished capacity, there are no conditions other than the character of the evidence being related to mental illness. But on what grounds might one argue that the defendant has some culpability for being mentally ill that justifies imputing to him a required culpability offense element that he does not in fact have? While the doctrine of voluntary intoxication may not be perfect, at least one can point to some prior culpability (as to becoming intoxicated) that provides some arguable basis for imputing of some offense culpability. But the mentally ill defendant is not likely to be culpable for causing his own mental illness (short of a case where he has failed to take his needed medication). Once we understand that diminished capacity is in truth a doctrine of imputation, its impropriety becomes more obvious.

III   Functional differences among doctrines: *ex ante* articulation of rules of conduct versus principles of *ex post* adjudication

A third distinction that has practical benefits arises from taking a "functional" perspective of the doctrine, focusing upon the two different and sometimes competing functions of criminal law: announcing *ex ante* the rules of conduct for the community, and adjudicating *ex post* violations of those rules. What is perhaps most striking about this distinction is that it maps directly onto the doctrines. That is, each doctrine, or part of a doctrine, serves either one function or the other. If one were to review the provisions of a comprehensive criminal code, one would be able to mark out those specific passages that were required to give the community a statement beforehand of what they can, cannot, and must do: the rules of conduct. The remaining code provisions are necessary only for the *ex post* adjudication process. As it turns out, the proportion of the criminal law that serves to set the rules of conduct is quite a small proportion, and this fact, as we shall see, turns out to have practical importance.

Figure 5.1 gives a simplified summary of which doctrines serve which function. A more detailed account is available in my *Structure and Function* book.[21]

---

[21] For a more detailed analysis, see Robinson, *Structure and Function*, Pt III, in particular, see figure at p. 141.

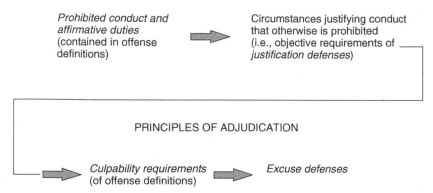

RULES OF CONDUCT

Prohibited conduct and affirmative duties (contained in offense definitions)

Circumstances justifying conduct that otherwise is prohibited (i.e., objective requirements of justification defenses)

PRINCIPLES OF ADJUDICATION

Culpability requirements (of offense definitions)

Excuse defenses

Figure 5.1

In order to state the rules of conduct, one must include a description of the prohibited conduct and affirmative duties, which are typically contained in offense definitions, as well as the objective requirements of justification defenses, which define general exceptions to the prohibitions and duties contained in offense definitions. The primary components of the *ex post* principles of adjudication are found in the culpability requirements within offense definitions and in excuse defenses.

A number of examples of the practical benefits in making these distinctions in the function of doctrines has already been reviewed in section I, above. Note that justification defenses serve to announce the rules of conduct, while excuse defenses serve the principles of adjudication. Thus, all the practical benefits from recognizing that distinction, examined in section I, serve also as illustrations of the practical value of the functional distinction. Recall, for example, the value in seeing different defenses as part of the same general defense category, as in assuring consistency between the excusing conditions of insanity and involuntary intoxication excuses; the essential nature of the distinction in defining the triggering conditions for defensive force; the solution to the problem of ambiguous acquittals; the important differences in implication for post-acquittal collateral consequences; and the differences in effect on the criminal justice system's moral credibility and thereby its crime-control effectiveness.

But let me give several other examples that go beyond these practical benefits of the justification–excuse distinction. For example, mixing the rules of conduct in with the principles of adjudication, which is the standard form in modern criminal codes and is necessarily the case in common law systems, has the detrimental effect of obscuring the rules of conduct within an overlay of principles of adjudication. The rules of conduct represent a relatively small portion of a criminal code, and if they were pulled out into a separate code of conduct, with the other provisions left to be organized into a separate code of adjudication, one could much more effectively perform the function of announcing the rules of conduct to the community. One could imagine a world in which we really took seriously the obligation of government to inform citizens of the rules to which they are bound on pain of criminal conviction. Indeed, one could produce a relatively short pamphlet that sets out all those rules that told citizens what the criminal law expected of them – something that could be carried by officers, and studied by high school students to graduates.[22]

Note, for another example, that the drafting styles one would use in these two documents – code of conduct and code of adjudication – would be quite different because their audiences are different. The code of conduct, addressed as it is to the lay community to guide them in their everyday life, ought to be written in a form that is as simple and as objective as possible. It ought to be easy to understand, remember, and apply. Indeed, its rules will sometimes have to be applied quite quickly and under difficult circumstances, such as the rules governing the use of defensive force. In contrast, the code of adjudication is one that can be, and probably should be, much more subjective and complex. It must capture the complexities of our judgments about blameworthiness. It will be applied only by people who have whatever time they need to apply it, as well as special training or instruction: lawyers, judges, police officers, and jurors acting under their jury instructions.

In addition to these practical benefits of the distinction in permitting codes that more effectively perform their function – drafting rules of conduct that more effectively communicate their demands to those bound to obey them, and drafting principles of adjudication that provide nuanced and thoughtful *ex post* adjudication of violations – let me give a few specific doctrinal examples of practical benefits that can flow from recognizing the functional distinction between doctrines. Consider, for example, the treatment of risk in modern codes.

---

[22] Robinson, *Structure and Function*, pp. 157–164.

Modern codes commonly define offenses as recklessly causing one result or another. The offense of manslaughter is recklessly causing another's death. The offense of endangerment is recklessly endangering another. Thus, the operation of these offenses is wholly dependent upon the definition of recklessness. The Model Penal Code, for example, defines "recklessness" this way:

> A person acts recklessly with respect to a material element of an offense when he consciously disregards a substantial and unjustifiable risk that the material element exists or will result from his conduct. The risk must be *of such a nature and degree that, considering the nature and purpose of the actor's conduct* and the circumstances known to him, its disregard involves a gross deviation from *the standard of conduct that a law-abiding person* would observe in the actor's situation.[23]

The difficulty is that there are two quite different sorts of requirement at issue here, which are being mixed together, creating confusion and error.[24] In the context of rules of conduct, the law must define those *ex ante* risks that are prohibited. Not all risks are prohibited. Presumably this definition will mark out the kinds of harm that ought to be avoided as well as identifying some sliding scale between probability and harm. That is, citizens ought to know that even minor risks of causing another's death ought to be avoided, but that some greater degree of risk may be acceptable for some lesser harm, such as bumping into somebody on the street. The italicized language in the "recklessness" definition above shows some sensitivity to the need for such considerations in defining prohibited risks.

In the context of principles of adjudication, the issue does not concern *ex ante* objective risks at all, but rather subjective risk-taking – that is, a defendant acting with a certain awareness of risk in certain circumstances existing in the real world. Thus, the principles of adjudication may hold a defendant liable for unconsent to intercourse only if, at the time of intercourse, he was aware of a certain possibility that his partner was not consenting.

Yet by failing to appreciate the two quite different functions of criminal law doctrine, by mixing them together throughout the code, by failing to appreciate the difference between the rules of conduct's *ex ante* objective prohibited risk definition and the principles of adjudication's culpable risk-taking definition, the Model Penal Code confuses

---

[23] Model Penal Code, §2.02(2)(c) (emphasis added).
[24] See Robinson, "Rules of Conduct and Principles of Adjudication," pp. 745–749.

the two in a way that is likely to hurt both functions.[25] For example, in the manslaughter and endangerment offenses noted above, the Code simply fails to provide any statement of the needed rule of conduct. That is, it says nothing about what the prohibited risk is. And its principle of adjudication definition of culpable risk-taking ends up being distracted by factors that are relevant primarily to issues of *ex ante* risk definition. By mixing the two functions, the Code invites a similar confusion in its readers. Notions of risk-creation and risk-taking are often used interchangeably.[26]

This can also invite liability errors. Consider, for example, the case where a defendant dumps what he believes are toxic chemicals in a field next to a schoolyard, believing that such dumping will create a risk of death or serious injury to those playing in the schoolyard. If he is correct, and such an *ex ante* risk actually is created, he is properly liable for endangerment and, if somebody becomes sick or dies, he is properly liable for aggravated assault or manslaughter. However, consider the situation where he is mistaken, where the material he dumps has no toxicity because he has been duped in some earlier transaction. A system that cared about the significance of resulting harm and, therefore, probably cared about the existence of a real *ex ante* risk, as opposed to only the subjective belief of risk, would want to punish the actual risk-creation more severely than a simple mistaken belief that a risk was created. Presumably, the liability in the latter case of mistake would be in the nature of attempt liability; the defendant would be liable at most for attempted endangerment, with a lesser offense grade than if he actually had created a real-world risk of harm to the children in the schoolyard. Yet by having only a definition of culpable risk-taking, and by defining offenses purely in terms of culpable state of mind, as the Model Penal Code does, the code treats the latter case as no different from the former and would impose full liability for endangerment even though no *ex ante* risk was ever created.

[25] A better approach is to give independent definitions of criminal risk and of culpable risk-taking. Risk-creation offenses, then, are properly defined to prohibit creation of a "criminal risk" of the specific harm, incorporating by reference the general formula. This replaces the current practice of defining these offenses by using either undefined terms such as "risk" or "substantial risk," or by using culpability terms that drop the requirement that the prohibited risk actually be created. For a proposed formulation, see Robinson, *Structure and Function*, pp. 148–155.

[26] See, e.g., Lawrence Alexander, "Reconsidering the Relationship Among Voluntary Acts, Strict Liability, and Negligence in Criminal Law," in E. Paul, F. Miller, Jr., and J. Paul (eds.), *Crime, Culpability, and Remedy* (Oxford: Blackwell, 1990), pp. 88–89.

This might be a tolerable result if a jurisdiction did not believe in the significance of resulting harm, but would be an inappropriate result for the vast majority of jurisdictions that do. Unfortunately, many states whose codes are based on the Model Penal Code take this view, but are then misled into ignoring the difference between a case of real-world prohibited risk-creation and purely subjective risk-taking.[27]

IV Two kinds of legality: conduct rule legality and adjudication legality

The final distinction to discuss concerns the principle of legality. In its classic form, the legality principle is an umbrella concept for five or six doctrines all of which express a preference for a prior, written, specific statement of criminal law rules. In the United States, these doctrines typically include the statutory prohibition against the judicial creation of offenses, the statutory abolition of common law offenses,[28] the constitutional prohibition against vague statutes,[29] the constitutional prohibition against *ex post facto* application of criminal statutes,[30] as well as a bar on the retroactive application of judicial interpretations of criminal statutes and the rule of strict construction of criminal statutes.[31]

---

[27] For a more detailed discussion, see Paul H. Robinson, *Prohibited Risks and Culpable Disregard or Inattentativeness: Challenge and Confusion in the Formulation of Risk-Creation Offenses*, vol. 4, No. 1, art. 7, available at: http://www.bepress.com/til/default/vol4/iss1/art7.

[28] In the Model Penal Code, both limitations are achieved by the force of section 1.05(1): "No conduct constitutes an offense unless it is a crime or violation under this Code or another statute of this State." The UK and US systems are not the same in this respect. In 1962, for example, the English House of Lords approved the prosecution of a common law offense of "conspiracy to corrupt public morals." *Shaw* v. *Director of Public Prosecutions* [1962] AC 220 (HL) (defendant published *Ladies Directory* that contained names, addresses, and phone numbers of prostitutes).

[29] The *vagueness* prohibition is rooted in the Due Process Clauses of the Fifth and Fourteenth Amendments to the Constitution. The doctrine requires that a statute should give "sufficient warning that men may conform their conduct so as to avoid that which is forbidden." *Rose* v. *Locke*, 423 US 48, 50 (1975) (statutory phrase "crime against nature" gave adequate notice that forced cunnilingus was prohibited).

[30] US Constitution, Art. I, §9, cl. 3: "No bill of attainder or *ex post facto* law shall be passed"; US Constitution, Art. I, §10, cl. 1: "No State shall . . . pass any bill of attainder, [or] *ex post facto* law."

[31] See, e.g., *Rewis* v. *United States*, 401 US 808 (1971) (ambiguity in statute prohibiting interstate travel with intent to "promote, manage, establish . . . certain kinds of illegal activity," could not be construed to extend to operation of illegal establishment frequented by out-of-state customers).

It is appropriate that these doctrines are grouped under the umbrella principle of legality because they share overlapping rationales, of which I will now share five of the commonly presented rationales. A legality principle makes good sense because it helps to provide fair notice to citizens of what the criminal law requires of them; it increases the likelihood of compliance with the criminal law by making the rules clear, thereby improving the effectiveness of deterrence and avoiding over-deterrence that can have an inappropriate chilling effect on conduct; it helps reserve the criminalization authority to the legislature, the most democratic branch; it increases the uniformity in application of criminal law rules; and it reduces the potential for abuse of discretion in the application of those rules. Each of the legality doctrines typically rely on some combination of these rationales, often a different subset for different doctrines.

I want to argue here that there is in fact not a single principle of legality, but rather two quite different principles of legality: conduct rule legality and adjudication legality, which mirror the distinction between rules of conduct and principles of adjudication.[32] If one considers more carefully the legality principle rationales, one sees that the first two concern notice and compliance, which relate almost

[32] Glanville Williams wrote extensively on the legality principle and discussed its rationales (Williams, *The General Part*, ch. 12; Williams, *Textbook*, §§1.3, 1.4, 1.8), but did not suggest that there were two kinds of legality or two different roles or aspects of the legality principle. Nonetheless, he did recognize some of the implications of the differences between conduct rule legality and adjudication legality. For example, he explained that rules of conduct must be accessible to the public, while adjudication rules need not be. "Penal laws should be accessible and intelligible . . . Criminal law is not like the law of procedure, meant for lawyers only, but is addressed to all classes of society as the rules that they are bound to obey on pain of punishment": Williams, *The General Part*, p. 582. Then he later says: "The layman does not need to learn the difference between murder and manslaughter in order to understand that he must not kill others. While everyone should know that he may be punished if he assaults another, he does not, in general, need to be told the scale of punishment that may legally follow each particular kind of aggravated assault," *Ibid*. He notes other distinctions that track the two kinds of legality. Thus, while judicial discretion in the definition of offenses may offend the legality principle, it "does not, in its usual acceptance mean that the actual punishment must be established by law," *Ibid*., at p. 606. Judges have discretion in sentencing and "modern tendency has been to find substitutes for punishment . . . all in the discretion of the court," *Ibid*. Consistent with this, in *The General Part*, Williams provides an entire chapter on legality, but only touches on legality in adjudication in a single section within the chapter on punishment, *Ibid*., at ch. 12, §192. Similarly, in *Textbook*, he has separate sections that touch on legality concepts for conduct rules versus adjudication (e.g., §1.3 is relevant to conduct and §1.8 is relevant to adjudication).

exclusively to the *ex ante* rules of conduct. In contrast, the last two rationales relate almost exclusively to controlling discretion in the *ex post* adjudication process.

To summarize:

Legality rationales as related to ex ante *conduct rules and* ex post *adjudication*

Rationales:	As related to conduct rule legality and adjudication legality:
1 • Providing fair notice. • Gaining compliance with criminal law rules, including effective deterrence and avoiding over-deterrence (chilling effect).	Relate to *ex ante* function of announcing rules of conduct. (*Conduct rule legality* applies.)
2 • Reserving the criminalization authority to the legislature.	Relates to both.
3 • Increasing uniformity in application. • Reducing the potential for abuse of discretion.	Relate to *ex post* function of adjudication of rule violations. (*Adjudication legality* applies.)

The distinct principles of conduct rule legality and adjudication legality have important practical consequences because they suggest that when the classic legality doctrines are applied, they ought to be applied differently to rules of conduct than when applied to principles of adjudication. For example, the standard legality doctrines commonly make sense in their traditional form when applied to the rules of conduct. To assure that citizens have fair notice of the rules of conduct, it follows that vague statutes ought to be barred, that common law rules ought to be abolished, that judicial creation of offenses ought to be prohibited, and that judicial interpretation of broadened statutes should not be retroactive.

But when those same legality doctrines are applied to doctrines that serve the principles of adjudication, where the same notice and compliance concerns do not exist, the proper results are quite different. We may well want to allow what otherwise would be considered a vague statute, if it is necessary to capture the complexity and nuance in our judgments of blameworthiness.[33] For example, in the defenses of insanity and involuntary intoxication discussed above, we are quite comfortable with a standard as vague as "lacks substantial capacity" to appreciate the criminality of one's conduct. We need a relatively vague standard here because it is meant primarily as an invitation to the decision maker to consult intuitions about what can be expected of a defendant under the circumstances of dysfunction in which he committed the offense. Similarly, when considering principles of adjudication, we might well want to allow a common law excuse, to allow a court to create a new or expand an old excuse, or to retroactively apply a broadened excuse defense (as long as the existing criminal code does not have a legislative direction that precludes such judicial exercise of authority).

V   Conclusion

Here, then, are four distinctions that Granville Williams did not make, but which I think have practical benefits that we ought to be, and he would have been, attracted to. Not all distinctions that one could make have practical benefits. A distinction might have some appeal for philosophers, for example, yet have no practical value for the operation of the doctrine, in which case its use would bring only unnecessary cost and confusion.

For example, if one were to rely upon a subjective conception of justification defenses – that is, if one included mistaken justification within the concept of justification, as the Model Penal Code does, and as a host of modern theorists do – then most of the practical benefits discussed above would disappear.[34] Such a subjective conception of justification generally destroys the practical value of the justification–excuse distinction. For example, while we would want to prohibit defensive force against an objectively justified attack, we would not want to prohibit it against an attacker who only mistakenly believes his attack is

---

[33]   See generally, Paul H. Robinson, "Why Does the Criminal Law Care What the Layperson Thinks is Just?: Coercive Versus Normative Crime Control," *Virginia Law Review*, 86 (2000), 1839–1869.

[34]   See Paul H. Robinson, "Objective versus Subjective Justification: A Case Study in Function and Form in Constructing a System of Criminal Law Theory," in P. Robinson, S. Garvey, and K. K. Ferzan (eds.), *Criminal Law Conversations* (Oxford University Press, 2009), p. 343; but see Mitch N. Berman, "In Defence of Subjective Justifications," in Robinson, Garvey, and Ferzan (eds.), *Criminal Law Conversations*, p. 357.

justified, even if that belief were reasonable. By combining the two, into a subjective conception of justification, the resulting conception no longer works as a proper trigger for the use of defensive force.

Similarly, one would want objectively justified conduct to be marked by a "no violation" verdict to signal to others that they can do the same thing under similar objective circumstances in the future, but we would not want to send such a signal for an actor who only mistakenly believes he is justified. If his mistake was reasonable, we might want to acquit him under a "blameless violation" verdict, which serves to condemn, not to condone, his conduct. Indeed, the Rodney King beating case used above to illustrate the confusion sown by general acquittals is exactly this case: a mistake as to a justification, where the conduct should be condemned but the actor excused, is confused for a true objective justification, which condones the conduct, with disastrous results from the confusion.

To give one last example, note that only objective justifications are part of the *ex ante* rules of conduct telling citizens what they can do. The mistaken justification excuse is part of the *ex post* principles of adjudication, and would be appropriate to include only in a code of adjudication and would be drafted in a form appropriate for that audience and purpose. While a code of adjudication needs to earn a reputation within the community for reliably doing justice – giving mistake excuses when deserved – citizens have no need for the details of the mistake excuse, or any other excuse, to know what is expected of them by the rules of conduct.

My larger point here is that there are practical benefits that flow from organizing doctrine around those distinctions that mark useful differences and similarities among different doctrines. While the judges and lawyers may not always like academic attempts to change the basic framework by which the doctrines are organized, if the distinctions used in building the framework have important practical benefits, it seems likely that attempts at modification will be accepted and, in their time, become familiar and comfortable. Glanville Williams may well have been right to demand a showing of practical benefits before incorporating a distinction into the doctrinal framework, but I would like to think that some distinctions, even some he never thought to use, can meet that practical test.

6

Reflections on *Dudley and Stephens* and killing the innocent: taking a wrong conceptual path

JOSHUA DRESSLER[*]

I Introduction

It is an honor to participate in this commemoration of the birth and incredible scholarly life of Glanville Williams. His writings have accurately been described as "prodigious in their quantity, quality and range."[1] His "readable prose," characterized as sometimes "outspoken," and frequently "disdain[ful]" of the "rough and unthinking ways" of the judiciary, has "re-ignited [legal] debates."[2] Those who knew him well have described his "boundless energy and unquenchable optimism."[3] Perhaps because of his optimism, Williams was a reformer at heart. He strived for a law that is "clear, consistent and accessible,"[4] as well as "principled."[5] And, the principles to which Glanville Williams subscribed were unabashedly utilitarian. He was, it has been said, the

---

[*] I gave a version of this chapter on December 4, 2011 at the "Legacy of Glanville Williams" conference, held at the School of Law, King's College London. I thank Dennis Baker for the opportunity to participate at the conference, as well as his courtesies throughout. I received very thoughtful suggestions on ways to strengthen this chapter at faculty workshops at Fordham University, my home institution, and at the Glanville Williams conference itself. Particular thanks are due to Debby Denno, Peter Glazebrook, Jeremy Hoder, Michael Moore, and Marc Spindelman. My research assistants, Dan Anderson (Moritz 2012), Kailee Goold (Moritz 2012), and Nadia Zaiem (Moritz 2013), provided exceptional research assistance.
[1] J. R. Spencer, "Obituary: Professor Glanville Williams," *The Independent*, April 17, 1997, reprinted in "Glanville Williams," *Cambridge Law Journal*, 56 (1997), 437, 437 (a special tribute to Williams).
[2] P. R. Glazebrook, "Glanville Llewelyn Williams, 1911–1997," *Proceedings of the British Academy*, 115 (2002), 411, 411, 420.
[3] Spencer, "Glanville Williams," p. 437.   [4] *Ibid.*, p. 438.
[5] P. R. Glazebrook, "Obituary: Glanville Williams," *Cambridge Law Journal*, 56 (1997), 437, at p. 446 (in the special tribute to Williams).

"illegitimate child of Jeremy Bentham."[6] Although my DNA does not (as far as I know) link me to Bentham or Williams,[7] I and many other criminal law scholars – even those not primarily utilitarian in perspective – are indebted to Williams for his scholarship.

I want to look at one of the many issues about which Professor Williams cared so much: the defense of necessity[8] and, more specifically, the famous case of *The Queen* v. *Dudley and Stephens*[9] (hereafter, "*D & S*"), which confronted the question of whether (and, if so, when) the purposeful killing of an innocent person is justified. As is generally well known, *D & S* ruled that it was murder for two defendants to kill an innocent youth in order that they and a third man could survive by eating his remains.

There is some doubt about what we should take from this case.[10] Is it that there was no general necessity defense at all at common law?[11] Or is such a defense available except in intent to kill murder and attempted

[6] Spencer, "Glanville Williams," p. 438 (quoting Leon Radzinowicz).

[7] I do possess one admittedly trivial link to Williams. He was a Conscientious Objector during *his* war (Second World War) (Glazebrook, "Glanville Llewelyn Williams, 1911–1997," p. 415), as I was during *mine* (Vietnam). He spent his time doing civil defence work while continuing to teach law; I spent mine working as an orderly in a hospital where I met the woman who would become my wife. Overall, I may have gotten the better deal.

[8] Williams' articles on the topic include: "The Defence of Necessity," *Current Legal Problems*, (1953), 216; "A Commentary on *R.* v. *Dudley and Stephens*," *Cambrian Law Review*, 8 (1977) (hereinafter "Commentary"); and "Necessity," *Criminal Law Review* [1978], 128.

[9] (1884) 14 QBD 273.

[10] Perhaps we should take nothing from this case other than that it was meant to send a message against cannibalism. Cannibalism at sea was common, and accepted by seamen as justifiable, at the time of the *D & S* events. According to A. W. Brian Simpson's remarkable book, *Cannibalism and the Common Law* (Chicago University Press, 1984), the *D & S* case was concocted by the government in order to create a precedent against cannibalism on the seas. Through remarkable manipulation, *ibid.*, pp. 195–270, Huddleston B, serving as trial judge, coerced the jury to announce a then obsolete "special verdict," which effectively left the matter to a special court of review (that included Huddleston), on which Lord Coleridge CJ sat as presiding judge. In short, it might fairly be said that "the fix" was in, in *D & S*.

[11] Glanville Williams "somewhat confidently" said that there was a general defense of necessity in English common law. Glanville Williams, *Criminal Law: The General Part*, 2nd edn (London: Stevens, 1961), §231, at p. 724. Various other scholars disagree. For example, J. C. Smith and Brian Hogan, *Criminal Law*, 4th edn (London: Butterworths, 1978), pp. 193–194: "The better view appears to be that a general defence of necessity is not recognized by the English courts at the present time"; D. W. Elliott, "Necessity, Duress, and Self-Defence," *Criminal Law Review*, [1989], 611: "Whether there is any general defence of necessity in English law is at best very doubtful." Glazebrook stated that the answer is a "plain No": P. R. Glazebrook, "The Necessity Plea in English

murder prosecutions? Or can we draw an even narrower reading, namely, that the defence of necessity is available for all crimes, including murder, but it was not proven on the facts in *D & S*?

I will delve into this debate only briefly.[12] It is enough here to say that *D & S* is typically understood to stand for the proposition that the necessity defense is barred in all intent to kill homicide prosecutions, no matter how extreme the circumstances, and even if the killing of an innocent person would save a greater number of innocent lives.[13] And this is the traditional, although today not universal, position in the United States.[14] Moreover, the influence of *D & S* does not end here. It is often seen in the United Kingdom as suggesting or requiring a similar rule when a defendant asserts the defense of duress, and the United States has largely followed the UK's lead in this regard.[15] Put simply, this

Criminal Law," *Cambridge Law Journal*, 30 (1972), 87–119, at p. 87. However, he observed that the concept of necessity was found implicitly in the definition of some offenses; and "there would appear to be no judicial decisions on any of the surviving common law offenses (not even murder) requiring liability to be imposed on a person who in a given predicament chooses the lesser of two evils," *ibid.*, at p. 108. The Commentary to the US Model Penal Code stated that: "although the point has not been entirely free from controversy, necessity seems clearly to have standing as a common law defense; such issue as there was related to its definition and extent." *Model Penal Code and Commentaries*, American Law Institute (July 1985), §3.02 cmt. at p. 10. The drafters of the Model Penal Code believed that a general defense is "essential to the rationality and justice of the criminal law, and is appropriately addressed in a penal code," *ibid.*, at p. 9.

[12] See n. 38, below.

[13] For example, Andrew Ashworth, *Principles of Criminal Law*, 3rd edn (Oxford University Press, 1999), p. 233: "Lord Coleridge CJ held that no defence of necessity was available in a case of taking another person's life"; A. P. Simester and G. R. Sullivan, *Criminal Law: Theory and Doctrine* (Oxford: Hart, 2000), p. 633 (while showing that the case did not need to provide a categorical rule, they assert that "under current law, *Dudley* is regarded as authority that necessity is unavailable to murder"); H. P. Milgate, "Duress and the Criminal Law: Another About Turn by the House of Lords," *Cambridge Law Journal*, 47 (1988), 61–76, at p. 68: "The House of Lords [in *D & S*] decided that necessity could not be a defence to murder, whatever the degree of the participation." But see Glazebrook, "The Necessity Plea in English Criminal Law," p. 114: "*Dudley and Stephens* is not, as is sometimes supposed, an authority against the recognition of a necessity plea on a charge of murder."

[14] The Model Penal Code's "choice of evils" defense, Model Penal Code, §3.02, provides a justification defense for conduct, including murder, "the actor believes to be necessary," if "the harm or evil sought to be avoided by such conduct is greater than that sought to be prevented by the law defining the offense charged." Some American state criminal codes have followed the Code's lead in this regard.

[15] Model Penal Code, §2.09 would recognize a duress defense for all crimes, including murder, as long as the actor was coerced to engage in the criminal conduct "by the use of, or threat to use, unlawful force against his person or the person of another, that a person of reasonable

case has had significant impact on the development of necessity and duress law in the homicide context.

Glanville Williams wrote about *D & S*. I want to consider this case, however, from a perspective that Williams did not consider (indeed, from a perspective that Williams nearly entirely ignored in *all* of his scholarship): the failure of Lord Coleridge to draw a distinction between the question of whether extreme circumstances can *justify* the taking of innocent life, and the separate question of whether such conduct, although unjustifiable, might nonetheless be *excusable*. I submit that this omission – specifically, the failure to focus on the "excuse" possibility, misshaped the law of necessity and duress.

The justification–excuse distinction – in simplest terms, the difference between desirable, good, or, at least, permissible conduct, on the one hand, and conduct that is wrong, but that occurs under circumstances rendering the actor morally blameless, on the other – is a familiar one today, thanks to important scholarship published in the second half of the twentieth century.[16] However, perhaps because of Williams' utilitarian, non-deontological (anti-deontological?) perspective, he almost never focused on this distinction,[17] even after scholarship in the field

firmness in his situation would have been unable to resist." However, most states, by statute or case law, do not permit the defense in intent to kill murder cases, although some jurisdictions permit the defense in felony-murder prosecutions to negate the underlying felony. For example, Alabama Code, §13A-3-30(d)(1) (2005) (expressly providing that the defense is unavailable in murder prosecutions); Arizona Revised Statutes Ann., §13-412(C) (2010) (the defense is "unavailable for offenses involving homicide or serious physical injury"); California Penal Code, §26 (West 1999) (unavailable as a full defense to murder, but available to negate the underlying felony in felony-murder prosecutions, and it may negate the element of deliberation to reduce the offense from first- to second-degree murder, as explained in *People* v. *Anderson*, 50 P3d 368, 379 (Cal 2002)); Georgia Code Ann., §16-3-26 (1982) (expressly excluding murder); 720 Illinois Compiled Statutes Ann., §5/7-11(a) (West 2002) (defense applies to all non-capital offenses; however, it was interpreted in *People* v. *Glecker*, 411 NE2d 849, 849, 955 (Ill 1980), to bar the defense in murder prosecutions even if the death penalty does not apply); Kansas Statutes Ann., §21-5206(a) (2010) (expressly inapplicable to the offenses of murder and voluntary manslaughter, but applicable by case law to felony-murder, in *State* v. *Hunter*, 740 P2d 559, 568 (Kan 1987)); Washington Revised Code Ann., §9A.16.060(2) (does not apply to "murder, manslaughter, or homicide by abuse", and is interpreted also to exclude its use in felony-murder prosecutions, *State* v. *Ng*, 750 P2d 632, 636 (Wash 1988)); *Henry* v. *State*, 613 So2d 429, p. 432 n. 6 (Fla 1992) (duress is not a defense to intentional homicide because "duress will never justify the killing of an innocent third party"); *Pugliese* v. *Commonwealth*, 428 SE2d 16, 24 (Va App 1993) (not a defense to intentional murder, but is a defense to felony-murder).

16 See section III, below.

17 Williams did say in "The Theory of Excuses," *Criminal Law Review* [1982], 732, that: "the distinction is of theoretical significance and of some, though not large, practical importance." Although he minimized the significance of the distinction, he stated just a

flourished.[18] Indeed, at times, Williams himself improperly used the terms interchangeably.[19] Quite simply, he was not a leader, or even much of a follower, in *this* realm.

Williams' lack of attention is unfortunate. He could have been a major force in making English law more consistent and principled in this realm. And I will try to show here by means of a thought experiment what might have happened if the events in *D & S* had occurred *after* scholars focused on the justification–excuse distinction. More specifically, what if Glanville Williams had cared about this dichotomy and had had the opportunity to influence the judiciary in a *D & S*-like case? Might the law have been changed for the better?

II *Dudley and Stephens*: starting down the wrong path

Glanville Williams accurately characterized *D & S* as "one of the most widely discussed of all criminal cases."[20] The case involved terrible circumstances in which the four-person crew of a yacht – Thomas Dudley, Edwin Stephens, Edmund Brooks, and a seventeen-year-old youth, Richard Parker – found themselves forced onto a lifeboat after they were cast away in a storm. Without water or food, except two 1-lb tins of turnips, the four seamen subsisted for the first twelve days on the turnips and a turtle they caught, after which they survived without food or water. After nearly three weeks at

year later, almost as an afterthought, that the newly recognized excuse defense of "duress of circumstances" might be "more palatable to some people on facts like those in [*D & S*], where a moralist may be unwilling to accord a justification but will accord an excuse." Glanville Williams, *Textbook of Criminal Law*, 2nd edn (London: Stevens, 1983), p. 634. Of course, this observation demonstrates that the justification–excuse distinction *does* have "large, practical importance," at least to "moralists." It can mean the difference between conviction and acquittal for defendants in extreme circumstances. Unfortunately, as far as I can tell, Williams never said anything more on the subject.

[18] This should not have been the case, as the distinction has relevance even to a consequentialist. The distinction between conduct that we want (and therefore we should incentivize) and conduct that we do not want, but which arguably is undeterrable, can be understood, roughly, as the line between justification and excuse. But this distinction surely *is* of much greater significance to deontologists ("moralists," as Williams put it, see Williams, *Textbook*) who focus on whether conduct is morally right, tolerable, or wrong, and whether persons who commit wrongs are morally blameless or blameworthy.

[19] In Williams' "The Defence of Necessity," he treated the necessity defense as a lesser harm justification, and yet more than once he used the term "excuse." See, e.g., *ibid.*, pp. 216–217: "Necessity may even *excuse* an interference with a conscious person ... [In the incident he described] D was clearly *justified* in what he did ... D's *justification* rested upon necessity" (emphasis added).

[20] Williams, "Commentary," p. 94.

sea, Dudley suggested to Stephens and Brooks that if no help arrived soon, "lots should be cast who should be put to death [and eaten] to save the rest, but Brooks refused to consent."[21] Finally, with no vessel appearing, Dudley and Stephens killed the youth by cutting his throat. The three survivors "fed upon the body and blood of the boy for four days," until they were discovered by a passing vessel.[22]

Dudley and Stephens were charged with murder. The jury's special findings included the following: (1) "that if the men had not fed upon the body of the boy they would probably not have survived to be . . . rescued"; (2) that Parker, being in much weaker condition, was likely to have died first; (3) at the time of the homicide no vessels were in view, nor was there "any reasonable prospect of relief"; and (4) "there was no appreciable chance of saving life except by killing someone for the others to eat."[23] The jury also found (seemingly contradictorily in light of point (2)) that "there was no greater necessity for killing the boy than any of the other three men."[24]

The Queen's Bench Division, *per* Lord Coleridge CJ, described the "real question in the case" to be "whether killing under the circumstances set forth in the verdict be or be not murder."[25] Lord Coleridge conceded that "the prisoners were subject to terrible temptation, to sufferings which might break down the bodily power of the strongest man, and try the conscience of the best."[26] Nonetheless, the tribunal concluded that the defendants were guilty of murder.

Lord Coleridge affirmed the convictions on grounds of precedent and principle. As a matter of precedent, he rejected the proposition that "in order to save your own life you may lawfully take away the life of another, when that other is neither attempting nor threatening yours, nor is guilty of any illegal act whatever towards you or anyone else."[27] He quoted Lord Hale for the proposition that self-defense was the *only* "private necessity which justified, and alone justified, the taking the life of another."[28] Indeed, according to Lord Hale:

> if a man be desperately assaulted and in peril of death, and cannot otherwise escape unless, to satisfy his assailant's fury, he will kill an innocent person then present, the fear and actual force will not acquit him of the crime and punishment of murder, if he commit the act, for he ought rather to die himself than kill an innocent.[29]

---

[21] *D & S* (1884) 14 QBD 273, at p. 274. [22] *Ibid.* [23] *Ibid.*, at p. 275. [24] *Ibid.*
[25] *Ibid.*, at p. 281. [26] *Ibid.*, at p. 279. [27] *Ibid.*, at p. 281. [28] *Ibid.*, at 282.
[29] *Ibid.*, at p. 283 (quoting Matthew Hale, *Historia Placitorum Coronae: The History of the Pleas of the Crown* (London: printed for F. Gyles, T. Woodward, and C. Davis, vol. I, 1736), at p. 51).

Lord Coleridge quoted other writers as well in support of the proposition that it is never justifiable to kill an innocent person to save one's own life. Only Lord Bacon justified such a homicide,[30] but Lord Coleridge noted that he cited no authority for his proposition and, "if Lord Bacon meant to lay down the broad proposition that a man may save his life by killing, if necessary, an innocent and unoffending neighbour, it certainly is not law at the present day."[31] As Lord Coleridge put the matter:

> now it is admitted that the deliberate killing of this unoffending and unresisting boy was clearly murder, unless the killing can be justified by some well-recognised excuse admitted by the law. It is further admitted that there was in this case no such excuse, unless the killing was justified by what has been called "necessity."[32]

Precedent aside, Lord Coleridge rejected the defendants' plea of necessity on grounds of moral principle. He warned that "the absolute divorce of law from morality would be of fatal consequence; and such divorce would follow if the temptation to murder in this case were to be held by law an absolute defence of it."[33] According to Lord Coleridge, "to preserve one's life is generally speaking a duty, but it may be the plainest and the highest duty to sacrifice it."[34] Indeed, he stated (and I would think this particularly irritated the secular Glanville Williams) that "it is enough in a Christian country to remind ourselves of the Great Example whom we profess to follow."[35] The House of Lords worried that if taking the life of another were allowed,

> who is to be the judge of this sort of necessity? By what measure is the comparative value of lives to be measured? . . . It is plain that the principle leaves to him who is to profit by it to determine the necessity which will justify him in deliberately taking another's life to save his own.[36]

Lord Coleridge closed the delivery of the judgment by stating:

> We are often compelled to set up standards we cannot reach ourselves, and to lay down rules which we could not ourselves satisfy. But a man has no right to declare temptation to be an excuse, though he might himself have yielded to it, nor allow compassion for the criminal to change or weaken in any manner the legal definition of the crime. It is therefore our

---

[30] Bacon's example involved two drowning persons attempting to get on a plank that could hold only one. According to Bacon, if one were to push the other off the plank to save his own life, "this is neither *se defendendo* nor by misadventure, but justifiable." *Ibid.*, at p. 285.

[31] *Ibid.*, at p. 286.   [32] *Ibid.*, at pp. 286–287.   [33] *Ibid.*, at p. 287.   [34] *Ibid.*, at p. 287.
[35] *Ibid.*   [36] *Ibid.*

duty to declare that the prisoners' act in this case was wilful murder, that the facts as stated in the verdict are no legal justification of the homicide.[37]

I will return to Lord Coleridge's analysis, but three points are worth noting here. First, the overall thrust of the judgment seemingly shuts the door on the claim that it is sometimes justifiable to kill an innocent person.[38] Second, a full reading of the judgment demonstrates that, in seeking to determine whether the killing "be or not be murder," Lord Coleridge used the words "justification" or "justify" often and throughout. But – and this third point is important – he also occasionally used the word "excuse" in characterizing the defendants' necessity claim, and (most obviously, at the end of the judgment, quoted in the excerpt

---

[37] *Ibid.*, at p. 288.

[38] It can plausibly be argued that the judgment in *D & S* is limited to its facts – that the need to kill Parker was not yet imminent. After all, the special verdict stated only that if the prisoners had not killed the youth, they "probably" would not have survived. As Coleridge put it: "The prisoners put to death a weak and unoffending boy upon the chance of preserving their own lives . . . and with the certainty of depriving *him* of any possible chance of survival," *ibid.*, at p. 279. See Glazebrook, "The Necessity Plea in English Criminal Law," p. 114 (suggesting that if the issue was not between the certainty of Parker's death and a chance of death by the others, "but between two chances . . . it might have recognised a necessity situation"). The judgment could also be explained on the ground that the defendants chose Parker for death rather than, in the words of a trial judge in instructing an American jury, have the decision of who should be sacrificed among persons in equal relations to each other made by lot. *United States* v. *Holmes*, 26 FCas 360, 367 (No. 15383) (CCED Pa 1842). This explanation, however, fails, since Lord Coleridge stated that the *Holmes* court's "somewhat strange ground . . . can hardly . . . be an authority satisfactory to a court in this country": *D & S* (1884) 14 QBD 273, at p. 285. The strongest argument for the limited nature of Lord Coleridge's judgment is, as Glanville Williams wrote, that "*Dudley* may be distinguished if the facts of a later case are such that necessity not only declares that one at least must die but also indicates who that one is." Williams, "The Theory of Excuses," at p. 744. Thus, in the recent tragic case of Jodie and Mary, conjoined twins, *In re A (Children) (Conjoined Twins: Surgical Separation)*, [2001] 2 WLR 480, [2001] Fam 147, the doctors' decision to separate the twins, although they were aware that Mary would immediately die from the surgery, was the result of their medical knowledge that Mary would die in short time anyway even without separation, but that her death would cause Jodie's death as well in those circumstances.

Although, *D & S* can be explained in limiting terms, probably the fairest reading of Lord Coleridge's words is what seems to be the majority reading of the case (see n. 13 above), namely, that the defence is *never* available when an innocent person is killed. Not only does Lord Coleridge find no precedent for the proposition that killing an innocent person can ever be other than murder, but his fear of "the absolute divorce of law from morality," and his remark about Jesus (the "Great Example"), support the absolutist interpretation.

immediately above) he treated the words "justification" and "excuse" as if they were synonyms, thereby blurring his message.

Professor Williams' critique of *D & S* was insightful, but incomplete. He characterized as "absurd" the claim that a "contrary decision in the case would have created an 'absolute divorce of law from morality.'"[39] After all, even if the killing was immoral, that hardly suggests that the criminal law as a whole would be separated from morality if the men had been granted a defense.

Williams also characterized as "irrelevant" Lord Coleridge's duty to die assertion, because "if the defendants . . . had allowed themselves to die of starvation, they would not have died for others."[40] And he nicely points out that if there were such a duty to sacrifice oneself, then perhaps it was the *youth's* duty to "bare his breast to the knife in order to provide food for the others." To Williams, the question in *D & S*, properly understood "is not of a duty to die but of a liberty to kill."[41]

Williams had other criticisms, large and small, of Lord Coleridge's reasoning, but at its essence Williams comes down differently than Lord Coleridge because the "basic question is whether the law should adopt the utilitarian approach"[42] – elsewhere he calls it the "secular, utilitarian"[43] approach – or instead apply deontological principles, as Lord Coleridge did by relying on Christian values.

Nowhere in Williams' critique, however, does he criticize Lord Coleridge for ignoring the distinction between justifiable and excusable homicide. Indeed, Williams is similarly at fault. Although his commentary primarily analyzes necessity in justificatory terms – sometimes expressly, sometimes by inference, as when he characterized the issue in terms of the "liberty" to kill – he sometimes uses the term "excuse" as if it were nothing more than a synonym for "justification." For example, in discussing necessity as a justification, he states that "judges have constantly invented new crimes; can they not invent new excuses?"[44] And later, Williams observes that "even an 'absolute' pacifist will probably defend himself against a lunatic who attacks him – and a lunatic is not regarded as morally responsible, and is therefore 'innocent.'"[45] This is meant to show that even pacifists will justifiably kill innocent persons. However, Williams misses the point: the "absolute pacifist" who kills the morally innocent insane person would doubtlessly say, "I did the wrong

---

[39] Williams, "Commentary," p. 95.   [40] *Ibid.*   [41] *Ibid.*   [42] *Ibid.*, at p. 98.
[43] *Ibid.*, at p. 97.   [44] *Ibid.*, at p. 94.   [45] Williams, "Commentary," p. 98.

thing [I did not act *justifiably*]," although he might assert an *excuse* for his actions ("I couldn't help myself. I was too weak").

Ultimately, Williams provided a consequentialist criticism of an opinion not based on consequentialism. His critique hardly proves that a non-consequentialist would be compelled to accept the view that no defense should be made available for consideration by a jury in *D & S* circumstances. But the basis for a *non*-utilitarian rejection of the verdict comes from being sensitive to the distinction between justifiable and excusable homicide, a distinction that both legal giants, Lord Coleridge and Williams, ignored.

III   "Justification" versus "excuse": the correct path

This is now a fairly commonplace understanding: a justified act is an act that is right, tolerable, or, at a minimum, not wrong. In contrast, we excuse a person when her conduct was unjustifiable, but when we also believe that she is not morally to blame for her wrongdoing.[46]

At one time, very long ago, this distinction mattered in an obvious way in English law. A justification defense had the effect of outright acquittal, whereas an excused defendant was still subject to the death penalty and forfeiture of his property, although he could avoid execution with a pardon from the Crown. Over time, pardons became *pro forma*, and the excused party could recover his property by means of writ of restitution. Eventually, therefore, there was seemingly no practical difference between acquittal by justification and one by excuse.

Nonetheless, the words "justification" and "excuse" have always had different meanings, and one would have hoped that lawyers, for whom words are their primary tool,[47] would have cared about this. But they largely did not.[48] Consequently, it is unsurprising that courts often used the terms "justification" and "excuse" interchangeably.

---

[46] Joshua Dressler, "Justifications and Excuses: A Brief Review of the Concepts and the Literature," *Wayne Law Review*, 33 (1987), 1155–1167, at pp. 1161–1163.

[47] J. L. Austin, writing about philosophers – but he could just as easily have been writing about lawyers – observed that "words are our tools, and, as a minimum we should use clean tools: we should know what we mean and what we do not, and we must forearm ourselves against the traps that language sets us." J. L. Austin, *A Plea for Excuses*, in Herbert Morris (ed.), *Freedom and Responsibility: Readings in Philosophy and Law* (Stanford University Press, 1961), pp. 6, 9.

[48] Dressler, "Justifications and Excuses," p. 1158.

This insensitivity to the distinction changed, at least among criminal law scholars, in the 1970s in the United States. Professor George Fletcher has been credited with "crying in the wilderness" about the moral and practical importance of the distinction.[49] Glanville Williams credited him as well.[50] Others, of course, deserve mention, most notably Paul Robinson.[51] The two of them in their scholarly writings excited considerable academic interest, including across the Atlantic, in the subject. Consequently, scholars are now well steeped in the literature[52] – "one is tempted to say [that Anglo-American criminal theorists are] 'obsessed over' . . . the distinction"[53] – and today I can report first-hand that most American law school course books sensitize future members of the legal profession to the differences between justifiable and excusable conduct.

This is not to say that there is universal agreement on every aspect of the dichotomy, for there is not. And there are naysayers who contend that the distinction has *no* practical significance.[54] This chapter, although not intended as a rebuttal to naysayers, demonstrates, I believe, the error in that position.

IV A thought experiment

Timing in life – and the law – matters. We all know that. Nonetheless, students often unreflectively assume that the law "that is" was inevitable. To disabuse them, I have them reflect on how some legal doctrines might have turned out differently if a lawyer had made a particular argument to

---

[49] Kent Greenawalt, "The Perplexing Borders of Justification and Excuse," *Columbia Law Review*, 84 (1984), 1897–1927, at pp. 1897–1898 (also describing Fletcher as a "prophetic" voice, and "among . . . the loudest and most eloquent").

[50] Williams, "The Theory of Excuses," at p. 732.

[51] Mitchell N. Berman, "Justification and Excuse, Law and Morality," *Duke Law Journal*, 53 (2003), 3.

[52] Berman, *ibid.*, states that Fletcher and Robinson "are now in crowded company. Indeed, the full list of contributors to the topic reads like a Who's Who of contemporary criminal law theorists on both sides of the Atlantic." A footnote at this point includes "(though is hardly limited to) Larry Alexander, Joshua Dressler, John Gardner, Kent Greenawalt, Heidi Hurd, Douglas Husak, Sanford Kadish, Michael Moore, J. C. Smith, and Jeremy Waldron," *ibid.*, n. 2. Notably absent from this list is Glanville Williams.

[53] *Ibid.*, at p. 1.

[54] For example, Gabriel J. Chin, "Unjustified: The Practical Irrelevance of the Justification/ Excuse Distinction," *University of Michigan Journal of Law Reform*, 43 (2009), 79–115, at p. 80: "Its utility to the criminal justice system – to judges, juries, legislatures, law students, and lawyers – has not yet been demonstrated." Although not so negative, Glanville Williams had little practical use for the distinction. See n. 17, above.

a court, thus putting the law on a potentially different path to the one ultimately taken. Or what if a judge had joined a court at just the right moment, so that she could shape an undeveloped legal field, rather than arrive too late? Or what if a thoughtful scholar, for example, Glanville Williams, had focused attention on an issue early enough to inspire more thoughtful reasoning by courts or legislators?

I provide my students various "what if" examples in American law. I will mention just one here. In 1938, Earl Warren, the future Chief Justice of the United States, was the chief prosecutor in a major California community. That year his father was murdered. Suspicion ultimately focused on a prison inmate who had been near the site of the crime at the time of the homicide. The police wanted to put a hidden recorder and informant in a cell with the suspect in order to elicit incriminating statements. They sought Warren's approval, however, to conduct the eavesdropping. Although Warren knew that the investigation involved his father's murder, he rejected the plan because he considered such surreptitious surveillance to be an inappropriate law enforcement technique. The murder was never solved.[55]

This story is significant because, in 1952, the Supreme Court ruled in *On Lee* v. *United States*,[56] by a vote of 5–4, that the Fourth Amendment to the US Constitution, which prohibits unreasonable searches and seizures, was not violated when the police used an undercover agent, with an electronic transmitter hidden on his body, to befriend a suspect, enter the latter's home, and elicit incriminating statements from him. A year later, Chief Justice Fred Vinson, who voted with the majority in *On Lee*, died. He was replaced by Earl Warren. So, we might ask, what if *On Lee* had come to the Supreme Court in 1953 rather than in 1952, or what if Warren had joined the Court a year earlier than he did? Quite possibly the Warren-for-Vinson replacement would have resulted in an opposite 5–4 ruling. As *On Lee* served as the basis for later Supreme Court rulings expanding the right of police to use undercover agents and electronic surveillance to secure evidence, it is reasonable to speculate that American constitutional jurisprudence and resulting police procedures would have differed significantly but for the one-year timing issue.[57]

---

[55] Bernard Schwartz, *Super Chief, Earl Warren and his Supreme Court: A Judicial Biography* (New York University Press, 1983), pp. 11–12.
[56] 343 US 747 (1952).
[57] For an English example, consider Milgate, "Duress and the Criminal Law: Another About Turn by the House of Lords," p. 65: "It is arguable that three of the five Lords of Appeal [Wilberforce, Edmund-Davies, and Simon] who sat in [*DPP of Northern Ireland* v.]

As timing matters, it is intriguing to reflect on whether necessity and duress law might have developed differently if timing had cooperated. Consider this thought experiment. What if *D & S* – as a case of first impression – had come to the House of Lords in 1984 rather than 1884, and thus was considered at a time when barristers arguing the case could realistically have brought the justification–excuse distinction to the attention of the tribunal? Indeed, what if Glanville Williams, with his great prestige, had drawn frequent attention – well before the hypothetical *D & S* facts reached the judiciary – to the justification–excuse distinction.[58] Or what if a case similar to *D & S* had arisen in 1984, and the House of Lords had been called upon to reconsider its century-old decision?

In any of these versions of the thought experiment, might the case have been decided differently? Perhaps. At a minimum, the case might have been more thoughtfully analyzed. And in this different world about which I am conjecturing, the law of necessity and duress might well have turned out differently and more attuned to what I believe are common moral intuitions. Of course, we will never know if I am right, but at this moment of commemoration of Glanville Williams' life and his "unquenchable optimism" about the role of scholars in reforming the

---

Lynch [[1975] AC 653, which judgment recognized the defence of duress in the case of an accessory to murder] would have allowed the defence of duress to the actual killer if the matter had subsequently come before them." Twelve years later, however, a differently constituted House of Lords in *R. v. Howe and Bannister* [1987] 1 AC 417, ruled that duress *cannot* be pled by the actual killer. And, because it could see no plausible distinction between perpetrators and accessories, *Howe* overruled *Lynch*.

58 This thought experiment assumes that legal scholarship can affect the direction of the law. If one believes the current Chief Justice of the United States, however, this is doubtful. Chief Justice John Roberts recently observed that: "what the legal academy is doing, as far as I can tell, is largely of no use or interest to the people who actually practice law." Adam Liptak, "Keep the Briefs Brief, Literary Justices Advise," *New York Times*, May 21, 2011, pp. A1, A21. It should be noted, however, that justification–excuse scholarship has permeated the course books used to educate the American bar. So, even if the Chief Justice does not think much of legal scholarship, the lawyers arguing before him are influenced by it. Even if this attitude also exists in the United Kingdom, Glanville Williams is not just any academic. In a search I conducted on September 14, 2011 of UK cases in the Westlaw's "UK-Rpts-All" library, Williams was cited in 576 cases. He is cited in a similar number of cases in the United States, and also in Australia, Canada, and New Zealand. (His *Textbook* is listed as the most cited English textbook of criminal law of the twentieth century: Fred R. Shapiro, "The Most-Cited Legal Books Published Since 1978," *Journal of Legal Studies*, 29 (2000), 397.) Thus, it may be hoped that, had Professor Williams shown more interest in the justification–excuse dichotomy, it would have reached the attention of the English judiciary.

law, this seems to be an especially good time to conduct the thought experiment.

V   Correcting the errors of *Dudley and Stephens*

Lord Coleridge in *D & S* almost always wrote in justificatory terms. The issue, as he characterized it at one point, is whether "in order to save your own life you may *lawfully* take away the life of another, when that other is neither attempting nor threatening . . . you or anyone else."[59] One who kills excusably does not do so "lawfully" (at least, if he means by that word "non-wrongfully"). The quoted statements of Lord Coleridge's sources also expressed the non-justifiability of killing innocents. And Lord Coleridge quoted "the learned persons who formed the commission for preparing the Criminal Code" for the view that "we are certainly not prepared to suggest that necessity should in every case be a justification."[60]

That said, Lord Coleridge used the word "justification" – and perhaps others he cited did as well – interchangeably with "excuse." For example, he confusingly wrote, "it is . . . admitted that there was in this case no . . . *excuse* [for the homicide], unless the killing was *justified* by what has been called 'necessity.'"[61] The confusion is magnified at the conclusion of the judgment, set out earlier,[62] where he writes that no man has a "right to declare temptation to be an excuse," and yet in the final sentence he states that it is "our duty to declare . . . that the facts as stated in the verdict are no legal *justification* of the homicide."[63]

Lord Coleridge's 1884 conflation of justifiable and excusable conduct has been repeated, and his analysis and judgment cited in support of the rule that duress, as well, is not a defense to murder. In *R. v. Howe*, Lord Griffiths announced that the principle underlying *D & S* "is the same as that which denies duress as a defence to murder. It is based upon the special sanctity that the law attaches to human life and which denies to a man the right to take an innocent life even at the price of his own or another's life."[64] Similarly, Lord Hailsham in *Howe* cited *D & S*, indicating that "if we were to allow this appeal, we should, I think, also have to say that *Dudley and Stephens* was bad law."[65] Thus, duress

[59] *D & S* (1884) 14 QBD 273, at p. 281 (emphasis added).   [60] *Ibid.*, at p. 286.
[61] *Ibid.*, at p. 287 (emphasis added).   [62] See text accompanying n. 37, above.
[63] *D & S* (1884) 14 QBD 273, at p. 288.   [64] [1987] 1 AC 417, at p. 439.
[65] *Ibid.*, at p. 429.

law – commonly understood today, and for some time in the past, as an excuse defense – has been tainted by the reasoning of *D & S*.

Although there is ample reason to be critical of Lord Coleridge's analysis of *D & S*, he is not alone in his confusion. Courts in the United States have also mishandled the defenses of necessity and duress. The traditional US rule, as in England, is that the necessity defense does not apply to homicides, although there is no evidence that this conclusion was reached after considering the possibility that "necessity" might also serve as an excuse (perhaps labeled "duress by circumstances").[66] There is also ample evidence that many American courts have failed to appreciate that duress, at its core, is an excuse defense,[67] treating it instead as a subspecies of necessity as a justification, subject therefore to the same limits as that of defense.[68] This is seen starkly in a recent California Supreme Court case that held that duress is not a defense to a charge of intentional murder because the "basic rationale behind allowing the defense of duress ... 'is that, for reasons of social policy, it is better that the defendant, faced with a choice of evils, choose to do the lesser evil.'"[69]

---

[66] The Model Penal Code treats the necessity (choice of evils) defense, exclusively as a justification defense. It recognizes duress as an excuse, Model Penal Code, §2.09(1), but it limits the latter defense to responses to "unlawful" threats or force, which thus excludes its use in *D & S* circumstances, in which the actor is responding to non-human (and, therefore not "unlawful") danger.

[67] See generally, Joshua Dressler, "Exegesis of the Law of Duress: Justifying the Excuse and Searching for Its Proper Limits," *Southern California Law Review*, 62 (1989), 1331; Joshua Dressler, "Duress," in John Deigh and David Dolinko (eds.), *The Oxford Handbook of Philosophy of Criminal Law* (New York: Oxford University Press, 2011), ch. 11.

[68] For example, *Jackson* v. *State*, 558 SW2d 816, 820 (Mo Ct App 1977) (recognizing duress as a defense to crimes other than homicide because, with non-homicide offenses, "a harm or crime of greater magnitude is avoided when the subjected person succumbs to the duress"); *Wright* v. *State*, 402 So2d 493, 498 (Fla Dist Ct App 1981) (citing *Jackson* v, *State* with approval, and stating that "the rule that duress will never *justify* the killing of an innocent third party accords with the mores of our society" (emphasis added)); *State* v. *Rocheville*, 425 SE2d 32, 35 (SC 1993): "The rationale of the defense ... is that if the only means of avoiding greater harm is for the defendant to engage in illegal conduct resulting in lesser harm, he should not be held criminally liable"; *Alford* v. *State*, 866 SW2d 619, 624 n. 9 (Tex Crim App 1993) (expressing the rationale of the duress defense in "lesser harm" justificatory terms).

[69] *People* v. *Anderson*, 50 P3d 368, 371 (Cal 2002). The court here is quoting Wayne R. LaFave, *Criminal Law* (St. Paul, MN: West Group, 2000), §5.3. The LaFave treatise is the most prominent criminal law lawyers' treatise in the United States. Through the early editions, it characterized duress as a subspecies of necessity, which in turn was described solely as a justification defense. This particular quotation from LaFave has

So, given all of this confusion, how *should D & S* have been handled? From their perspective, Williams and other utilitarians may very well be right that an absolute bar on the taking of innocent lives, when it will result in a net human savings, is wrong. Perhaps, therefore, Dudley and Stephens or, at least, some persons in imminent danger, *are* legally justified to take innocent human life to save themselves. As the drafters of the utilitarian-oriented Model Penal Code (MPC) put it, "recognizing that the sanctity of life has a supreme place in the hierarchy of values, it is nonetheless true that conduct that results in taking life may promote the very value sought to be protected by the law of homicide."[70] According to this view, although rights often trump lives (as in self-defense), in other cases lives should trump rights,[71] and thus Parker's right to life in *D & S* might have been outweighed by the fact that his body could sustain the lives of his three colleagues on the lifeboat. In a society that applies a cost–benefit calculus to all human undertakings, the necessity defense *should* be applicable in homicide prosecutions, although it should be noted that a balancing of lives requires (as Lord Coleridge worried) confronting the question of whether the law will treat each person equally, notwithstanding differences in health, age, gender, intelligence, occupation, and other factors. To an uncompromising act-utilitarian, the nice sounding "sanctity of life" concept means less than the future differential value to society of each human life on the lifeboat.[72]

Of course, even if the *act* of killing in *D & S* made good consequentialist sense, some utilitarians will worry that a *rule* that justifies a life-counting calculus might weaken the principle that all human life "has a supreme place in the hierarchy of values." Perhaps recognizing the defense of necessity in murder cases would motivate people in hard circumstances to take innocent life too quickly, indeed, unnecessarily, especially when their own life or that of a loved one is in jeopardy. As a rule of law, therefore, the MPC approach, even for some utilitarians,

---

been cited or quoted frequently by state courts in duress cases. Thus, the treatise's error has functioned like a virus contaminating many legal opinions. After the third edition, LaFave correctly stated that the defense is an excuse. *Ibid.*, §9.7, at p. 492 (4th edn, 2006); *ibid.*, §9.7, at p. 519 (5th edn, 2010).

[70] *Model Penal Code and Commentaries*, §3.02 cmt., at p. 14.

[71] Sanford H. Kadish, "Respect for Life and Regard for Rights in the Criminal Law," *California Law Review*, 64 (1976), 871–901, at p. 890.

[72] On the question of whether Parker's weaker health and/or the fact that the defendants had families dependent on them should be part of the cost–benefit calculation, Williams was only willing to say that "even if these facts are put aside as irrelevant": "Commentary," at p. 96.

might go too far. One might sensibly limit the justification defense to situations in which the life of the actor who kills, and that of her family, are not in jeopardy. In such a situation decision making may more objectively be conducted than was possible on the lifeboat.[73] In any case, as with all cost–benefit calculations, utilitarians prefer data. And where, as here, it is impossible to obtain, rule-utilitarians would try to rationally predict the effects, if the law were changed to justify necessitous killings of innocent persons. It is not self-evident that a rule-utilitarian would recognize the defense.

For *non*-utilitarians, Glanville Williams' critique of *D & S* and the preceding analysis is beside the point. Dudley and Stephens surely violated the Kantian principle that a person should never be used as a means to an end. One can hardly imagine a more obvious example of violation of this principle than killing a person to eat his remains in order to survive. Indeed, the power of this moral imperative can be seen in the efforts of the MPC drafters, through the *Code Commentary*, to sugar-coat its broadly drafted, Williams advised, consequentialist-oriented choice of evils provision. For example, the *Commentary* justifies the applicability of the necessity defense in homicide cases in part by providing the example of one who "makes a breach in a dike, knowing that this will inundate a farm [thereby causing the death of those living in the farmhouse], but taking the only course available to save a whole town."[74] As the *Commentary* itself observes,[75] even some non-utilitarian moralists can justify *this* action pursuant to the "double effect" principle: it is always wrong to directly cause evil for the purpose of bringing about a so-called greater good, but it is permissible to act to save lives even though the actor knows that an inevitable indirect effect of her action will be the loss of (fewer) innocent lives.[76] The dike example fits the double-effect principle. One might draw this limiting line in the law – although the MPC does not! – but this leaves Dudley and Stephens without justificatory redress: the youth Parker's demise was not collateral damage; his death was desired outcome.

The *Commentary* to the MPC provides another example that, it claims, justifies rejection of the *D & S* outcome: "A mountaineer, roped to a companion who has fallen over a precipice, who holds on as long as possible but eventually cuts the rope, must certainly be granted the

---

[73] The conjoined twins case, see n. 38, above, in which physicians separated the twins, Jodie and Mary, to save Jodie at Mary's expense rather than let both die, would be an example of such an objective calculation.

[74] *Model Penal Code and Commentaries*, §3.02 cmt., at pp. 14–15.

[75] *Ibid.*, at p. 15, n. 15.

[76] See Suzanne M. Uniacke, "The Doctrine of Double Effect," *Thomist*, 48 (1984), 188.

defense that he accelerated one death slightly but avoided the only alternative, the certain death of both."[77] True enough, but the defense here need not be the justification of necessity. The companion in this hypothetical is fairly characterized as an aggressor (or, better yet, "threatener"[78]) – an innocent one, but one nonetheless. In contrast, Parker did not threaten his killers. The mountaineer arguably should be able to justify his conduct on the ground of self-defense (if one believes that self-defense is based on the principle that every non-aggressor possesses a natural right to protect himself from a lethal aggressor or threatener), or be excused in such defensive circumstances.[79] Similarly, according to this reasoning, the physicians were justified in the conjoined twins case to separate them, in order to save Jodie from "innocent threatener" Mary.[80]

What if one rejects pure consequentialism and puts aside the sugar-coating variations on the theme? I submit that even if the law was to bar a justification necessity defense in all, or even most, criminal homicide prosecutions, an excuse defense should be recognized. The essential point of an excuse defense is that *"even if recognition of excuses has a counter-deterrent effect,* the criminal law is premised on the belief that wrongdoers should not be punished in the absence of moral desert, and moral desert is primarily a deontological, essentially retributive, moral concept."[81] As Professor Kadish has put it so well:

> To blame a person is to express a moral criticism, and if the person's action does not deserve criticism, blaming him is a kind of falsehood and is, to the extent the person is injured by being blamed, unjust to him. It is this feature of our everyday moral practices that lies behind the law's excuses.[82]

---

[77] *Model Penal Code and Commentaries,* §3.02 cmt., at p. 15.

[78] I thank Peter Glazebrook for this suggestion.

[79] Self-defense, as a justification, would not apply if the basis for self-defense is that an aggressor forfeits his right to life because of his culpable aggression. Joshua Dressler, *Understanding Criminal Law* (Newark, NJ: LexisNexis), §17.02[C].

[80] Jodie's aorta fed into Mary's aorta and the circulation ran from Jodie to twin Mary; because of Mary's weak condition, she was irreparably causing harm to Jodie's heart; united, Jodie's heart would have failed in three to six months, causing both to die. *In re A (Children) (Conjoined Twins: Surgical Separation)* [2001] 2 WLR 480.

[81] Joshua Dressler, "Reflections on Wrongdoers: Moral Theory, New Excuses, and the Model Penal Code," *Rutgers Law Journal,* 19 (1988), 671–716, at p. 681 (emphasis added).

[82] Sanford H. Kadish, "Excusing Crime," *California Law Review,* 75 (1987), 257–289, at p. 264.

There are various theoretical explanations offered for why we excuse people in "our everyday moral practices" and in the law.[83] But descriptively, the theory that most closely explains the law of excuses is the "choice" theory. According to this explanation, a person may be blamed for her conduct only if she had the capacity and fair opportunity to choose whether or not to violate society's legal norms. Specifically, blame may not be attributed to an individual if she substantially lacked the capacity or fair opportunity to understand the facts relating to her conduct, appreciate that her conduct violated society's norms, and/or conform her conduct to the dictates of those norms.[84] With some excuses (e.g., insanity), there is something internally wrong with the person that makes her unable to function in a manner that permits a finding of moral responsibility. In contrast, other excuses assume that the actor is normal, but that some external factor has acted on her in a way that causes us to say that she did not have a fair opportunity to act lawfully. Duress is an example of this latter type of excuse. And, surely, this plausibly fits the plight of Dudley and Stephens, who were victims of duress by circumstances.

The case for excusing Dudley and Stephens – or, more precisely, permitting a jury to consider their claim – was laid out by Lord Coleridge himself. The defendants, he wrote, "were subject to terrible temptation, to sufferings which might break down the bodily power of the strongest man, and try the conscience of the best."[85] The law of duress is founded on the principle that, although we should demand reasonable moral firmness by fellow members of our community, we have no right to punish people for being unable to show the strength of a saint.[86] The criminal law should not demand virtue in the form of heroism or martyrdom at the cost of public condemnation and

---

[83] For a brief overview, see Dressler, *Understanding Criminal Law*, at §17.03.

[84] H. L. A. Hart, *Punishment and Responsibility* (Oxford: Clarendon Press, 1968), p. 181: "A primary vindication of the principle of responsibility could rest on the simple idea that unless a man has the capacity and a fair opportunity . . . to adjust his behaviour to the law its penalties ought not to be applied to him"; Dressler, "Reflections on Wrongdoers," p. 701.

[85] *D & S* (1884) 14 QBD 273, at p. 279.

[86] See *S. v. Goliath* 1972 (3) SA 1 (AD) at 6 (S Afr) (in which counsel argued to the South African court that "the law, particularly the criminal law, should not be applied as if it were a blueprint for saintliness but rather in a manner in which it can be obeyed by the reasonable man"). For more complete defense of the proposition in the text, see the sources listed in n. 67, above.

punishment.[87] And yet Lord Coleridge remarkably stated that "we are often compelled to set up standards we cannot reach ourselves, and to lay down rules which we could not ourselves satisfy."[88] Whatever one might say about this observation with regard to a justification defense (and I do not agree with it even there[89]), we do not undermine society's commitment to the sanctity of human life when we recognize an excuse defense in compelling circumstances. As Professor Williams put it so nicely, "the Sermon on the Mount is full of moral prescriptions that cannot be obeyed by ordinary people ... Is there any sense ... in giving a moral ideal the force of law when the finest character – Lord Coleridge perhaps – may be unable to attain it?"[90] Call this a necessity excuse, or call this duress by circumstances, but by whatever label, the men in that lifeboat were entitled to the opportunity to try to persuade a jury of their peers that as a matter of *justice* – not "mere" compassion[91] or exercise of executive mercy[92] – they should be exculpated.[93]

[87] See *United States* v. *Hollingsworth*, 27 F3d 1196, 1203 (7th Cir 1994) (*en banc*) (the purpose of the criminal law is not "to purify thoughts and perfect character").

[88] *D & S* (1884) 14 QBD 273, at p. 288.

[89] To *state* that one has acted unjustifiably if one does not live up to a standard of moral perfection (the behavior of Jesus Christ in Lord Coleridge's mind) may be acceptable, but to restrict a person's liberty or take his life for falling anywhere below that line should trouble us in limited government society. Lying may be morally wrong, but I do not think we want to live in a society where all lies result in condemnation and punishment.

[90] Williams, "Commentary," p. 95.

[91] Lord Coleridge wrote that the law should not "allow compassion for the criminal to change or weaken in any manner the legal definition of the crime": *D & S* (1884) 14 QBD 273, at p. 288. This statement is wrong on two accounts. First, excuses are not recognized out of compassion, but rather, as previously noted (see n. 82, above), as a matter of justice. Second, although it is true that *justification* defenses do, in a sense, "change or weaken" the legal definition of murder by creating a list of exceptions to the proposition that the intentional taking of human life is wrong, excuse defenses do not have this effect. When we excuse an insane actor for his crime, for example, we do not change the definition of murder, nor do we truly undermine the law's denunciation of it, and the same is so with duress.

[92] *D & S* (1884) 14 QBD 273, at p. 288: "If in any case the law appears to be too severe ... [it is] to the Sovereign to exercise that prerogative of mercy which the Constitution has intrusted to the hands fittest to dispense it." The point here is that nobody has a legal right to mercy, but we all have a right to justice, and this should be accorded to a criminal defendant in the guilt phase of a trial, rather than left exclusively to the discretion of a judge in sentencing or to the clemency power of an executive.

[93] It cannot be denied that general verdict exculpations – "not guilty" rather than "not guilty by reason of excuse" – can cause confusion and send a false moral, and counter-utilitarian, message to the public. That is a concern whenever one considers broadening an excuse defense or recognizing a new one. My own hunch is that jury acquittals in compelling circumstances would be rare in homicide cases, so the risk of

And once one understands the errors of *D & S*, it is evident that the English and American courts and legislators are also wrong when they deny the possibility of a duress acquittal in traditional homicide cases. It is reassuring that the drafters of the MPC recognized a full excuse defense of duress in such cases, but even they wrongly limited it to cases involving "unlawful" threats, thereby limiting Dudley and Stephens to a justification claim.[94]

It is also disappointing that English courts, even as they recognize a "duress of circumstances" excuse defense, limit it to non-homicide circumstances.[95] It is unfortunate as well that the Law Commission's recommendations in 1977 and 1993 that the duress defense be extended to murder[96] were not adopted, and that its 2005 Consultation Paper backs away from this position and only calls for a partial excuse, reducing the homicide to a lesser degree of murder. The full defense is no longer proposed, in part because, "even though the [coerced] defendant may have been acting under duress, he has still intentionally taken a life. This is considerably more serious than other offences committed under duress (which result in a complete acquittal)."[97] It is true, of course, that the coerced actor intends to kill, but the response to this observation is to require that the threat or natural circumstances be more severe to excuse a homicide than to excuse a lesser crime. The MPC standard – that the unlawful threat or use of force must be one that would cause a "person of reasonable firmness" to commit the offense – should work nicely as an instruction to the jury.

Even as scholars now demonstrate the errors of *D & S* and its progeny, the law remains stuck in the conceptual quagmire of the nineteenth century. It is time for lawmakers to free themselves of bad case law, think in terms of excuse, and recognize a potential full defense of

---

miscommunication would be minimal. In any case, justice to the defendant should be our predominant concern.

[94] See n. 66, above. The MPC *would* permit Dudley and Stephens to seek to reduce their offense to manslaughter – a partial excuse – on the ground that, at the time of the homicide, they suffered from an "extreme mental or emotional disturbance" for which there was a "reasonable explanation of excuse": Model Penal Code, §210.3(1)(b).

[95] Law Commission, Consultation Paper No. 177, "A New Homicide Act for England and Wales?" 2005, para. 7.13, at p. 180.

[96] Law Commission, Law Com. No. 83, *Criminal Law: Report on Defences of General Application* (London, HMSO, 1977), para. 2.46(2), at p. 16; Law Commission, Law Com. No. 218, *Legislating the Criminal Code: Offences Against the Person and General Principles* (London: HMSO, 1993), para. 31.8, at p. 58.

[97] Law Commission, "A New Homicide Act for England and Wales?" para. 7.32, at p. 185.

whatever name they choose that applies to intentional homicides. If Lord Coleridge may be excused for his errors, modern English and American lawmakers should not be. It is time for them to get it right. And, at least as I see it, when such changes are made, the law will be more just. What better way to honor the memory of Glanville Williams?

7

Intention revisited

ANTONY DUFF*

I Introduction: debating intention

During the 1980s some of us, including Glanville Williams, were exercised about the role of intention in criminal law – about how the criminal
law should define intention, and the role that intention as thus defined
should play in determining criminal liability. Several factors, three of
which should be noted here, contributed to this interest.

First, the Law Commission produced a *Report on the Mental Element
in Crime*, as well as two draft criminal codes, each of which included a
general part that defined relevant *mens rea* terms. The *Report* distinguished 'actually intend[ing]' a result (not further defined) from having
'no substantial doubt' that a result would ensue, but recommended that
in either case the agent 'should be regarded as intending' the result.[1] The
first draft code, produced for the Commission by a small group of
academics, distinguished acting 'purposely' in relation to an element of
an offence from acting 'intentionally': a purposive agent 'wants [the
element] to exist or occur'; an intentional agent need only be 'aware',
or 'almost certain' that it exists or will exist or occur.[2] The second draft
code, which was the Commission's own, reverted to the kind of definition favoured in the *Report*: 'purpose' was dropped; intentional agency
was defined in terms of hoping or knowing that a circumstance exists or
will exist, and of acting 'in order' to bring a result about or 'being aware

---

* Thanks to participants in the 2011 Glanville Williams conference at King's College
London, and to Dennis Baker and Jeremy Horder for helpful comments on an earlier
version of this chapter.
[1] Law Commission, Law Com. No. 89, *Report on the Mental Element in Crime* (London:
HMSO, 1978), para. 44.
[2] Law Commission, Law Com. No. 143, *Codification of the Criminal Law* (London: HMSO,
1985), cl. 22(a).

that it will occur in the ordinary course of events'.[3] These definitions set the scene for continuing uncertainty and confusion about the scope of intention in the criminal law.

Second, in a series of controversial murder cases, of which *Hyam* had been the forerunner in 1974, the law lords seemed incapable of arriving at, or articulating, a clear conception of intention in the law of murder. A woman commits arson at night at a private house, intending to frighten the homeowner (her rival in love) into leaving town, and realising that the fire might cause death or serious injury: is she guilty of murder if someone dies in the fire? If so, is this because she intends, or should be treated by the criminal law as intending, to cause death or serious injury; or because she intends, or should be treated by the criminal law as intending, to expose others to a serious risk of death or serious injury; or because foresight of a (high) probability of death or serious injury, although neither constituting nor establishing an intention to cause such results, is by itself sufficient *mens rea* for murder?[4] If it is proved that the defendant foresaw death or serious injury as a 'natural', or overwhelmingly probable, or morally certain consequence of his act, can or must the jury 'infer' that he intended that consequence – and what kind of 'inference' would that be?[5] If two men push a concrete block off a bridge onto a road, in order merely to frighten a strike-breaking miner being driven along the road to work; or if a man sets fire to the house of a woman against whom he has a grudge: what must be proved if it is to be proved that the act was intended to cause death or serious injury?[6]

Third, the law of attempts was also given statutory form, following a Law Commission report:[7] a criminal attempt requires an 'intent to commit an offence'.[8] But just what does this specification require? In particular, first, should sufficiently certain foresight of the relevant aspects of the *actus reus* of the complete offence be taken to constitute the requisite intent?[9] Second, what constitutes the requisite intent in relation to the circumstantial aspects of the complete offence (in relation, for instance, to the consent or lack of consent of the person whom the

---

[3] Law Commission, Law Com. No. 177, *A Criminal Code for England and Wales* (London: HMSO, 1989), cl. 18(b).

[4] *Hyam v. DPP* [1975] AC 55.   [5] *Moloney* [1985] AC 905.

[6] See *Hancock & Shankland* [1986] AC 455; *Nedrick* [1986] 1 WLR 1025.

[7] Law Commission, Law Com. No. 102, *Attempt, and Impossibility in Relation to Attempt, Conspiracy and Incitement* (London: HMSO, 1980); Criminal Attempts Act 1981.

[8] Criminal Attempts Act 1981, s. 1(1).

[9] See *Pearman* [1985] 80 Cr App R 259; *Walker & Hayles* [1990] 90 Cr App R 226.

defendant tried to sexually penetrate), if recklessness as to those aspects suffices for the complete offence?[10] Third, if the defendant acts in a mistaken belief in the existence of a circumstance whose existence is required for the commission of the complete offence, is she guilty of an attempt to commit the offence; or should she be acquitted on the grounds that she did 'all that she intended to do' without committing the complete offence, and thus could not be said to have attempted (and failed) to commit it?[11]

Glanville Williams took a typically robust view of these matters – robust, but sometimes complicated. He was, to put it mildly, impatient with what he saw as the law lords' lack of clarity on the matter, and was driven on occasion to some fierce criticism. In *Moloney* they 'show no understanding' of the idea of 'oblique intent', or 'express themselves so hazily that one is not quite sure what they think'.[12] *Anderton v. Ryan* provoked an even more magisterial rebuke. The tale of that case is a tale:

> of how the judges invented a rule based upon conceptual misunderstanding; of their determination to use the English language so strangely that they spoke what by normal criteria would be termed untruths; of their invincible ignorance of the mess they had made of the law; and of their immobility on the subject, carried to the extent of subverting an Act of Parliament designed to put them straight.[13]

He also had little time for philosophers who 'arrived on the scene, hoping to help the lawyers to solve their legal problems': we did not 'sufficiently consider the specific requirements of the criminal law'; we were prone to 'mix up the ordinary meaning of the word "intention" with its desirable legal meaning', and to draw distinctions that were 'too subtle ... to be useful for legal purposes'.[14] It seemed to him clear what view the law, and the courts, should take of intention:

[10] See *Breckenridge* [1984] 79 Cr App R 244; *Khan* [1990] 1 WLR 813.
[11] See *Anderton v. Ryan* [1985] 1 AC 560.
[12] Glanville Williams, 'Oblique Intention', *Cambridge Law Journal*, 46 (1987), 417–38, at p. 430.
[13] Glanville Williams, 'The Lords and Impossible Attempts, or *Quis Custodiet Ipsos Custodes?*' *Cambridge Law Journal*, 45 (1986), 33. Lord Bridge responded with admirable humility in overruling that decision a year later, saying of this article that 'the language in which he criticises the decision in *Anderton v. Ryan* is not conspicuous for its moderation, but it would be foolish, on that account, not to recognise the force of the criticism and churlish not to acknowledge the assistance I have derived from it' (*Shivpuri* [1987] AC 1, at p. 23).
[14] Williams, 'Oblique Intention', p. 417 and n. 39: Alan White and I were the philosophers he cited.

(1) Except in one type of case, intention as to a consequence of what is done requires desire of the consequence. Of course, intention, for the lawyer, is not a bare wish; it is a combination of wish and act (or other external element). With one exception, an act is intentional as to a consequence if it is done with (motivated by) the wish, desire, purpose or aim (all synonyms in this context) of producing the result in question. (2) The one type of case in which it is reasonable to say that an undesired consequence can be intended in law is in respect of known certainties. A person can be held (but will not always be held) to intend an undesired event that he knows for sure he is bringing about.[15]

The qualification '(but will not always be held)' marks not Williams' view of what should be held, but his regretful recognition of what courts had said about it: his own view was that what he followed Bentham in calling 'oblique intent' should be classed as a kind of intent, and should generally suffice for criminal liability, save perhaps in three cases: offences of causing mental stress, accessoryship, and treason. In these cases, he thought, the law should require what the 1985 Draft Code defined as 'purpose'; oblique intent should not suffice.[16] As for intention in criminal attempts, it was obvious that Ms Ryan 'intended to commit the ... offence of handling stolen goods', and that her act was 'more than merely preparatory' to the commission of that offence, even if the goods that she handled were not in fact stolen.[17] We can also deal with the question of *mens rea* as to the circumstantial aspects of an attempt in terms of an intent to commit an offence. One who realises that the person whom he attempts to sexually penetrate might not be consenting 'does intend to commit rape', since he acts with 'alternative intents': 'an intention to copulate with her *nolens* or to copulate with her *volens* – to commit rape or to enjoy consensual sex – as matters may turn out'.[18]

The concessions that Williams made to critics of the doctrine of oblique intent, allowing three cases in which the law should require direct intention or purpose, display an admirable intellectual honesty, but have a somewhat ad hoc air. Given the unqualified consequentialism that Williams generally espoused, one might expect a more unqualified insistence that, in the absence of any justification or excuse, foresight of a

---

[15] *Ibid.*, pp. 417–8 (footnotes omitted).

[16] *Ibid.*, pp. 435–8; see Law Commission, *Codification of the Criminal Law*, cl. 22.

[17] Williams, 'The Lords and Impossible Attempts', p. 39; the court in *Anderton* v. *Ryan* had to assume that the goods were not stolen, since the prosecution had failed to prove that they were stolen.

[18] Glanville Williams, 'Intents in the Alternative', *Cambridge Law Journal*, 50 (1991), 120–30, at pp. 121–2.

criminally relevant consequence as being 'morally certain' should always suffice for criminal liability. For what matters, as far as the objective dimension of an offence is concerned, is the extent to which the defendant made it more likely that a relevant harm would ensue; and as far as fault or culpability is concerned, what matters is the extent to which the agent had (and knew that he had) control over the occurrence or non-occurrence of that harm. Both one whose purpose it is to cause harm, and one who is certain that such harm will ensue from his action, can be said to choose to cause the harm; both are surely equally (and equally culpably) responsible for it should it ensue; both, Williams insists, should be guilty of attempting to cause it if it does not ensue;[19] so why should we in these three disparate cases (causing mental stress, accessoryship, treason) suddenly discern a significant difference in culpable responsibility between purpose, or direct intention, and foresight? Williams would perhaps have been impatient with the yearning for systematic consistency that that question displays, and would have reminded us that the law, as a practical institution rather than a philosophical system, can be expected to display such pragmatic inconsistencies; but I will not pursue that argument here – save to suggest that what unites the three kinds of case might be that they illustrate some of the ways in which it might be legitimate for an agent to pay no practical attention to a foreseen outcome of his actions; I return to this point below.

The debates between Williams and others about just how intention should be defined in the criminal law, and about whether, when, and why intention, however defined, should be required for criminal liability, rumbled on. Meanwhile, however, other voices emerged from those who took a more 'critical' stance in legal studies, suggesting that there was something amiss with those debates and with the assumptions that their participants seemed to share. In particular, it was argued, the jurisprudential grail of a clear and coherent account of intention in criminal law might be – as grails tend to be – illusory rather than merely elusive.[20] For we must realise that ascriptions of intention or intentional

---

[19] Williams, 'Oblique Intention', p. 427.
[20] See N. Lacey, 'A Clear Concept of Intention: Elusive or Illusory?' *Modern Law Review*, 56 (1993), 621 (in response see J. Horder, 'Intention in the Criminal Law: a Rejoinder', *Modern Law Review*, 58 (1995), 678). See also A. W. Norrie, 'Oblique Intention and Legal Politics', *Criminal Law Review* [1989], 793; and A. W. Norrie, *Crime, Reason and History*, 2nd edn (London: Butterworths, 2001), ch. 3.

agency are ascriptions of responsible (and culpable) agency, and that as such they mark conclusions rather than premises of the essentially political arguments or ideological postures that lie behind such ascriptions; and when we realise this, we will also come to see that, in a fractured political and ideological context like our own, we cannot hope to agree on or to bring courts to operate with a clear and consistent conception of intention. The courts' unclarities, obscurities, and convolutions over the meaning of 'intention' were due not to judicial stupidity or linguistic or conceptual incompetence; instead, they were symptoms of the underlying political uncertainties and conflicts that are an ineliminable feature of a liberal criminal law. We (or the courts) might be able to find a way, if not to resolve, then at least to live with these conflicts, to negotiate a tolerable way through them; we might then find that the concept of intention can play a useful role in our ascriptions of responsibility and liability:[21] but our understanding of that role, and of the logic of ascriptions of intention, will need to be very different from the understanding that (mis)informed the earlier debates.

There are two responses to this kind of critical argument. One is to insist that we can, through suitably rigorous philosophical effort, provide a clear, coherent account of intention that is independent of, and logically prior to, any particular normative conception of moral or criminal responsibility: that we can, if we are conceptual analysts, produce a clear account of the meaning of 'intention' and its cognates, providing determinate descriptive criteria for the application of the relevant terms; or that we can, if we aspire to a metaphysical account that reaches beyond or beneath the concepts that we use, provide a clear and determinate account of what intentions ('really') are.[22]

A different response is to admit that there is something right in the critics' argument; and in particular to admit that we should not suppose that we could (if we thought clearly enough) provide a clear, consistent set of criteria for the application of 'intention' and its cognates that

---

[21] See, e.g., A. W. Norrie, 'Between Orthodox Subjectivism and Moral Contextualism', *Criminal Law Review* [2006], 486; A. W. Norrie, 'Legal Form and Moral Judgment: The Problem of Euthanasia', in R. A. Duff, L. Farmer, S. E. Marshall, M. Renzo, and V. Tados (eds.), *The Structures of Criminal Law* (Oxford University Press, 2011), p. 134.

[22] See, e.g., M. S. Moore, 'Intention as a Marker of Moral Culpability and Legal Punishability', in R. A. Duff and S. P. Green (eds.), *Philosophical Foundations of Criminal Law* (Oxford University Press, 2011), p. 179, for a robustly 'realist' account of intention as a particular kind of 'representational state'.

would be independent of, and prior to, any normative conception of criminal responsibility and liability. In the context of criminal law (as in other normatively laden contexts), descriptions of what a person intended to do, of her intentions in acting, or of what she did intentionally often reflect judgments about her responsibilities and about the normative significance of her conduct; we should not hope to establish first what she intended or did intentionally, and then ask, as a separate and further question, what she may be held criminally responsible or liable for doing (or failing to do). Ascriptions of intention and of intentional agency do, of course, figure as grounds for ascriptions of criminal responsibility and liability (as for ascriptions of moral responsibility and liability); but they do not figure as purely factual grounds that can be determined in advance of all normative considerations. This is not (yet) to say, however, that we cannot sensibly aspire to work out a clear and coherent account of what intention should mean in (or outside) the criminal law, as long as we are also clear about the logical character of that account. The provision of such an account, as an exercise in applied and contextual conceptual analysis, would not, of course, settle the persisting normative disputes either about what the criminal law should count as being intended (or as brought about intentionally), or about when intention should be required, or as to which aspects of an offence for criminal liability; conceptual analysis cannot resolve genuine normative disagreement. But what such an account could do is to make clear what those normative disagreements are, and precisely where and how they arise – which would itself be a substantial achievement.

My own sympathies, as might already be evident, lie with the second kind of response: but I will not defend it directly here (though I will say a little more about it in section III); nor will I try to offer such an account of intention here. Instead, I will take a more indirect route, one that begins not with intention, but with practical reason, and with the different logical and normative structures of practical reason that might concern the criminal law. The reason for this approach is that we might be better able to see whether, why, and how intention matters if we stand back from the so far inconclusive, often confused debates about what 'intention' means (or about what intention is), and see how far we can get in discussing the grounds and conditions of criminal responsibility without using 'intention' or cognate terms: we will then be better placed to see whether and how we need to talk of intentions and intentional action.

II   Structures of practical reason

Intention is, of course, intimately connected to practical reason: to explain the intentions with which an agent acts is to explain the reasons for which she acts. Perhaps we can achieve greater clarity about the meaning and role of intention in criminal law if we begin by looking not at intention (and especially not at intention as some kind of psychological process or state that precedes or accompanies action), but at the structures of practical reason that inform an agent's actions: not, that is, at whatever psychological processes of practical reasoning might occur before or during our actions, but at the logical structures of practical reason that can be (re)constructed to give the action its meaning and purpose.[23] These should, we can suppose, be relevant to issues of criminal responsibility and liability, since the criminal law addresses us and deals with us as agents who act for reasons, whose conduct can be guided by reasons (normatively guided by good reasons, and also misguided by bad reasons). In defining certain kinds of conduct as criminal, the law claims that we have good, normally conclusive, reasons to refrain from such conduct;[24] when a defendant stands trial to face a criminal charge, he is called to answer an accusation of acting as he had (in the law's eyes) conclusive reason not to act; if he offers a justification or excuse for his admitted or proved commission of an offence, he is claiming that although he committed a kind of action that he would normally have had conclusive reason not to commit, in the particular, exceptional context in which he acted he had good or at least respect-worthy reasons for acting as he did;[25] and if he is convicted, that marks an authoritative judgment that he acted in violation of the normative reasons that, in the law's eyes, bore on his action. The criminal law is thus concerned with the structures of (normative) practical reason that should guide our actions, and with the ways in which the (motivating) reasons that

---

[23] See generally, M. Bratman, *Intention, Plans and Practical Reason* (Cambridge, MA: Harvard University Press, 1987), and M. Bratman, *Structures of Agency* (Oxford University Press, 2007).

[24] Those reasons are not typically created by the criminal law: they are either pre-legal, as are the reasons we have to refrain from so-called *mala in se*; or at least prior to the criminal law, as are the reasons we have to refrain from so-called *mala prohibita*. See R. A. Duff, *Answering for Crime* (Oxford: Hart, 2007), ch. 4.

[25] See, e.g., J. Gardner, 'Fletcher on Offenses and Defenses', *Tulsa Law Review*, 39 (2004), 817; J. Horder, *Excusing Crime* (Oxford University Press, 2004); V. Tadros, *Criminal Responsibility* (Oxford University Press, 2005), esp. ch. 4; also Duff, *Answering for Crime*, ch. 11.

actually guide our actions relate, or fail to relate, to those normative reasons.[26]

Suppose that an agent realises that the course of conduct on which he is embarking will or might amount to φing: to killing (causing the death of) another human being; to sexually penetrating a non-consenting person; to handling goods that were stolen;[27] or to giving false evidence as a sworn witness in court. We can focus now (as the agent himself might or might not focus) on the aspect of that φing that will be especially salient in the eyes of the criminal law: that the action will or might cause death; that the other person does or might not consent to the sexual penetration; that these goods are stolen goods; that this testimony is or might be false. We can distinguish three different ways in which that prospect – call it the prospect that p – could figure, or fail to figure, in the structure of practical reason (of motivating reasons) that informs the agent's action.

First, it might figure as a reason in favour of the action, and as a reason for which he acts: his action is guided by the prospect of causing death, or of the sexual penetration being non-consensual, or of the goods being stolen, or of the testimony being false.[28] To say that he will be guided by that prospect is to say, *inter alia*, that he will be disposed to continue with the action if, but only if, that prospect remains live – that he will be disposed to abandon it if he realises that he will not cause death, or that the sexual penetration will be consensual, that the goods are not stolen, that the testimony will be true; that he will be disposed, *ceteris paribus* and when possible, to adjust his action so as to maximise the chances that that prospect will be realised (to adjust his aim, or the dose of poison, for instance, to maximise the chance of causing death, or to seek out other goods that had been stolen); and that he would count his enterprise as to at least some degree a failure if the prospect was not realised – if he did not cause death, if the penetration proved to have been consensual, if the goods proved not to be stolen goods, or if the testimony proved to have been true. In identifying the prospect that p as a, if not as the, reason for which he acts, we are, of course, picking out (abstracting, as one might

---

[26] On the distinction between normative or justificatory reasons and motivating or explanatory reasons, see J. Lenman, 'Reasons for Action: Justification vs. Explanation', *Stanford Encyclopedia of Philosophy*, Spring 2010 edition, ed. E. N. Zalta, available at: http://plato.stanford.edu/archives/spr2010/entries/reasons-just-vs-expl.

[27] And had not been recovered: see *Haughton* v. *Smith* [1975] AC 476.

[28] Compare, G. Yaffe, *Attempts in the Philosophy of Action and the Criminal Law* (Oxford University Press, 2010), ch. 3 on the 'Guiding Commitment View'.

say) just one aspect of a much larger and more complex structure of practical reason: a fuller account of that structure will tell us more about the reasons why he saw this prospect as a reason for action, and we might then see his action in quite a different light. His immediate reason for firing his gun in this direction is that by doing so he will or might cause V's death, but his reasons for so taking V's death as an immediate aim might be of very different kinds: that V is attacking him, and he sees no other way to ward off the attack; that V is suffering an agonising death, and asks to be shot to have a swifter and less painful death; that he accepted a contract to kill V; that V killed his son by his reckless driving; and so on. We will attend later to the difference that aspects of this larger structure might make to our descriptions of, as well as our judgments on, the agent's action.

Second, the prospect that p (that his action will cause death, that the penetration will be non-consensual, that the goods are stolen, that the testimony is false) might instead figure in the structure of the agent's practical reason as a reason against acting as he does – but as one that is not sufficiently strong, when weighed against the reasons that he sees in favour of the action, to motivate him not to act thus.[29] We can distinguish different possibilities within this category. If he sees no way (without abandoning his enterprise) of avoiding the realisation of that prospect, he might regret it. Indeed, he must regret it if he sees it as providing a reason against acting as he does, at least in the sense that he would prefer to have achieved his goals without bringing this particular result about (to have blown up this building without causing death; to have had consensual intercourse; to have handled non-stolen goods; to have given truthful testimony): for to see something as a reason against my action is to see its presence as rendering the action to that extent less desirable.[30] If he regards the prospect that p as less than certain, he can also hope that it will not be realised; but as his expectation that it will be

---

[29] If it was strong enough to motivate him not to act thus he would no longer be of interest to the criminal law (I leave aside here complicating cases of weakness of will, in which the agent acts against what he sees as the balance of reasons, though many offences are no doubt committed through weakness of will, by agents who do not truly believe that the reasons in favour of their criminal conduct defeat those against it).

[30] The further reason why he sees the prospect that p as rendering his action less desirable might not, of course, be the kind of normative reason that the criminal law expresses: perhaps in his eyes the prospect that p matters only because it increases the chance that he will find himself liable to unwelcome punishment. But while that makes a significant difference to the moral character of his action, all that should matter to the criminal law is whether he recognises and is guided by the appropriate immediate reasons for action.

realised approaches certainty, any such hope must change into some-thing more like wishful thinking or a regretful 'if only'. Furthermore, if he sees the prospect that p as a reason against acting as he does, he must also see it as a reason to adjust his action (if possible) to reduce the chance that it will be realised. He might not adjust his action, for instance, if he thinks that any such adjustment would either unaccept-ably endanger his realisation of his goal or be in some other way too costly; or he might adjust his action so as at least to reduce, if not to eliminate, the chance that the prospect will be realised. If he does adjust his action in this way, he can then regard the realisation of the prospect as rendering his action to some degree a failure: he acted as he did not merely because he thought that this might realise X (the destruction of this building), but because he thought, or hoped, that it might realise X without Y (the destruction of the building without death). Avoiding Y is not his main reason for action; he is prepared to realise Y as the cost of realising X (to cause death as the cost of destroying the building): but the reason that informs his action is better described not just as 'realising X', or as 'realising X despite Y', but as 'realising X, if possible without Y'. If, however, the prospect that p does not guide his action in this way, if he does not adjust his conduct to reduce the chance of its realisation, he can regret its realisation, but he cannot regard it as rendering his enterprise to any degree a failure: for an action fails only if it does not realise some aspect of the goal at which it was aimed – and his action was not even in part aimed at preventing the realisation of the prospect that p.[31] But whether or not the prospect that p plays any such part in guiding his action, we can still say that in acting as he does he accepts the prospect that p: he accepts that he will or might cause death, engage in non-consensual penetration, handle stolen goods, or give false testimony. If he thinks it certain, or highly probable, that that prospect will be realised, we might say simply that he accepts that p – he accepts that he will cause death, that the penetration will be non-consensual. If he thinks it only likely that that prospect will be realised, or more probable that it will not be, we might rather say that he accepts the risk that it will be realised; but

[31] Suppose I am persuaded to play a version of Russian roulette: I will earn £10,000 if I aim a revolver with one bullet in it at V and pull the trigger; there is nothing I can do to reduce the chance that the revolver will fire, and kill V. I think the gamble is worth it, but if the revolver does fire and kills V, I will think the gamble has not paid off. In such a case, I might think that I have lost the bet (the bet that I could pull the trigger without killing V), but cannot think that my enterprise has failed; for it was not guided by a concern not to kill V – it was merely accompanied by a hope that I would not kill V.

to accept a risk that p is still to accept that p if that is how things turn out.[32] He acts as he does despite (the risk that) p: the 'despite' locution marks his recognition of the prospect that p as a reason against acting as he does – but a reason outweighed by what he sees as the reasons in favour of the action.

Third, the prospect that p might not figure in the structure of his practical reason at all. He is aware of that prospect, but sees it neither as a reason for nor as a reason against acting as he does. He might see the prospect that p in this way because he regards p itself as utterly insignificant: perhaps the quality of the goods he is offered, and the asking price, are in his eyes relevant considerations that bear on whether he will buy them; but the fact that they are or might be stolen goods has no practical significance – it is as irrelevant to his decision as is the fact that the seller is wearing a blue shirt. Alternatively, he might see p as intrinsically significant, but as practically irrelevant in this particular context – as something to which he need not, or perhaps should not, attend in deciding and acting. This *might* be how a doctor who administers a pain-relieving drug to a dying patient could see the fact that the drug will also hasten death: the fact that a medication is life-shortening is normally a powerful reason against administering it, but in this special context that fact is not just outweighed by the need to relieve pain, but irrelevant. I will say more about this case below, but for a less arguable example consider someone who opens a shop, knowing that – given her commitment, her marketing skills, and her resources – it is likely that her shop will draw customers away from the long-established shop across the road, with the result that the owner of that shop will lose money, and perhaps even have to close. She might, if sufficiently ruthless, guide her actions partly by the prospect of ruining him, and thus boosting her business; she might plan her sales tactics and marketing campaigns, her special offers, and loss leaders, with a view to taking business away from him. Or she might see the possible effects on his business as a reason against opening her shop – but a reason that is outweighed by the reasons in favour: perhaps she thinks it will benefit the neighbourhood to have a new shop; or she just thinks that it is legitimate for her to pursue her business career in this way, despite the likely impact on other competitors. Or – which is the possibility that concerns us here – she might take an orthodox capitalist view of the market economy, and argue that as long as she stays within the rules of the free (or fairly free) market,

---

[32] Compare the conception(s) of *dolus eventualis* in German criminal law theory.

she need pay no practical attention to the impact her actions might have on her competitors: the prospective closure of the shop across the road might, of course, be a matter of regret, and certainly gives other people reasons for action; but it has no bearing on whether she should open her shop, or on how she should run it. If this is her view, she would deny that she opens her shop 'despite' the impact this will or might have on the other shop: for 'despite' marks a reason against acting; but she denies that the prospect that *p* gives her any reason to modify or abandon her action.

I have talked so far about how the agent might see the prospect that *p*: about how it might figure, or not figure, in the structure of practical reason that guides his conduct. However, we, as interested observers or critics, may also have views about how that prospect *should* figure in that structure of practical reason – views that may differ from his.

First, we might think that far from being a good reason for acting as he does, let alone a reason that should guide his conduct, we might think that the prospect that *p* is a good or even conclusive reason against so acting. An agent who realises that his proposed course of action will cause death, or will amount to non-consensual sexual penetration, should normally see that as a conclusive reason against that course of action; if he realises that it will amount to handling stolen goods, we might think, he should recognise that as at least a strong reason against acting as he does; if he realises that there is a real risk that the prospect that *p* will be realised, he should also see that as at least a strong reason against acting as he does. This agent, by contrast, sees that very prospect as a reason for what he does – a reason significant enough to guide his actions. Again, once we attend to the larger context in which that action and those reasons are set, we might change our view: we might come to agree that he had good reason not merely to act in a way that he realised would or might realise that prospect, but to guide his actions towards its realisation. When we realise, for instance, that he could save his own life only by killing his attacker, or that he was asked to administer a fatal dose of a drug by a terminally ill loved one who earnestly asked for this assistance in securing a better death, we might come to agree that he had good reason not just to do what he realised might cause death, but to orient his action towards death as its immediate aim.[33]

---

[33] I am assuming here that the justified use of defensive violence does sometimes involve aiming to kill, not merely realising that my defensive action will cause death.

Second, when the agent sees the prospect that p as a reason against acting as he does, we might agree that it is a reason against acting thus, but argue that he has attached insufficient weight to it:[34] that his action will or might realise the prospect that p is, we think, not merely a reason against acting thus, but a conclusive reason.

Third, when the agent sees the prospect that p as irrelevant to his action, we might argue that it is relevant, as a reason against acting as he does: that, for instance, the fact that these goods are or might be stolen is significant, and gives him a reason not to handle them; or that the fact that administering this dose of painkiller will hasten the patient's death is relevant to the doctor's decision, as a reason against administering. Sometimes we will think that it is not just a reason, but a conclusive reason, against acting as he did; in other cases, we might agree that the action was on balance justified, but insist that this was only because the reasons that favoured it outweighed or defeated this reason against it – that what he was justified in doing was, for instance, administering a painkiller despite the fact that it would hasten the patient's death.[35]

To illustrate these possible structures of normative and motivating reasons, consider the sad case of Stephen Gough, 'the naked rambler',[36] who lived out his naturist principles by walking naked (apart from woolly hat, rucksack, gloves, socks, and boots) from Land's End to John O'Groats, twice. He has been arrested seventeen times in the last ten years (mainly in Scotland), for conduct liable to cause a breach of the peace; he has served frequent spells in prison, either for that offence or for contempt of court (because he insists on appearing naked in court). Now he is well aware that his conduct, in walking naked through the land, is likely to cause annoyance, if not fear or alarm, to those who see him;[37] but how does that prospect figure (if at all) in the

---

[34] We need not attend here to another possibility: that we think the prospect that p provides no reason at all against acting as he does, but is practically irrelevant (think of what a ruthless free marketeer might say to the would-be shopkeeper who is – as he would see it – squeamish about the possible effects on the existing shops). We can also leave aside the possibility that what he sees as a reason against the action, we see as a reason for the action.

[35] Here, again, there might also be cases in which we see as a reason in favour of the action, perhaps even as one that should guide it, something that the agent saw as irrelevant.

[36] He has a web site at www.nakedwalk.org; there is an informative interview with him in *The Guardian Weekend* magazine, 24 March 2012, available at: www.guardian.co.uk/lifeandstyle/2012/mar/23/naked-rambler-prison.

[37] In Scots law conduct liable to cause a breach of the peace is defined as conduct that is liable to cause fear, alarm, or annoyance: see G. H. Gordon, *The Criminal Law of Scotland*, 3rd edn, ed. M. G. A. Christie (Edinburgh: W. Green, 2000), pp. xxx *et seq*.

practical reasoning that informs his conduct? He could, first, see it as a reason, perhaps the main reason, in favour of acting as he does: he walks naked in public, and appears naked in court, *because* this will offend or annoy people; and he does this not merely for the sake of offending, but in order to provoke a public debate about naturism. Second, he could see it as a reason against acting as he does, but one that is outweighed by the stronger reasons of principle for acting thus: he goes naked for the sake of his naturist principles, despite the (as he sees it) regrettable fact that this will offend and annoy others. Third, he could see it as practically irrelevant to his actions – neither a reason for nor a reason against acting as he does: if others are annoyed or offended, that is their problem, reflecting their blinkered moral attitudes, rather than his problem; their unreasonable reactions, predictable though they are, give him no good reason to alter his conduct. He could similarly see the fact that, if he continues with this course of conduct, he will yet again be arrested and imprisoned as a reason for acting as he does, as a reason (albeit insufficient) against it, or as irrelevant. We, as morally interested observers, might accept or reject his conception of the (ir)relevance of the prospect that his conduct will offend or annoy others; we might think that he is right, or that he is wrong, about the *normative* reasons that bear on his actions.

Two questions now arise. First, what implications (if any) should the differences between these structures of practical reasoning have for the criminal law: for its definitions of offences or of defences; for its determinations of criminal responsibility and liability? Second, how do (how should) our ascriptions of intention, or of intentional agency, map onto these structures?

III   Reasons and criminal responsibility

We have seen that the prospect that p can figure in any one of three ways in the structure of practical reasoning that informs (in the case of motivating reasons) or should inform (in the case of normative reasons) an agent's conduct:[38]

(a) as a reason in favour of acting as he does;
(b) as a reason against acting as he does;
(c) as having no practical relevance as a reason either for or against acting as he does.

---

[38] See n. 26, above, and accompanying text.

How, if at all, should the differences between these possibilities figure in the criminal law's criteria of responsibility and liability?

The distinction between (b) and (c), as a distinction among normative reasons, marks one of the boundaries of responsible agency. If the prospect that p is a reason against acting as I do, it is something to which I should attend in deciding how to act. I can, therefore, be held responsible for acting as I do *despite* the prospect (or fact, or risk) that p: for opening my shop despite the fact that this might ruin my competitor; for handling these goods despite the fact that they might well be stolen goods. If p does ensue or exist, I can be called to answer for my action as described in those terms – for ruining my competitor, for handling stolen goods. I might be able to justify my action, by pointing to stronger reasons in its favour: perhaps the shopkeeper can argue that it is legitimate for her to make a living for herself in this way despite the likely impact on her competitors; or that it is more important to offer potential customers a wider choice of good quality items than to protect established (quite possibly inefficient) shops against competition. The point is, however, that this is something that needs justifying or excusing if she is to avoid criticism: she must now answer not merely for opening her shop, but for ruining (or risking the ruination of) her competitor. By contrast, if she can claim that the prospect that p falls under (c), she can deny responsibility for it: it is not now something to which she should attend as a reason against acting as she does; it is not now true that she acts as she does *despite* the prospect that; she need not answer for ruining her competitor, because the impact of her commercial activity on other shops nearby is not her business.[39]

Does this distinction matter in the criminal law? It might seem at first glance that it does not and cannot, once we recognise that what must matter for the criminal law is not whether the agent herself saw the prospect that p as a reason against acting as she did, but whether she should have done so – that the law's concern in this context is with normative reasons. For the law's offence definitions make clear which factors or prospects are or are not relevant as reasons against an action: if p, or the prospect that p, figures as an element of an offence, it falls under (b); if it does not thus figure, it falls under (c) and is legally irrelevant, whatever the agent might think. D might regard the prospect that in

---

[39] See further Duff, *Answering for Crime*, pp. 30–6.

handling these goods she would be handling stolen goods as irrelevant to her action; but that would not save her from conviction for the offence of handling stolen goods.[40] For in defining this offence in such terms, the law declares the fact that goods are stolen goods to be relevant as a (normally conclusive) reason against handling them, and will count D as handling the goods *despite* their stolen character whether or not that is how D sees the matter. So, too, the fact that an agent regards a prospect as relevant, as a reason against her action, which the law does not count as thus relevant does not bring him within the criminal law's reach: someone who believes that adultery is morally wrong, but gives in to the temptation to commit it, does not render himself criminally liable even if he mistakenly believes that adultery is criminally as well as morally wrong; the law is not interested in the fact that he acts as he thinks he has good reason not to act, but only in whether he acts as in the criminal law's eyes he has good reason not to act.[41]

The matter is not, however, quite that simple, since the prospect that p can be relevant in some contexts but not in others, depending on the responsibilities that citizens have under the criminal law – and there might be disagreement about what responsibilities the criminal law should recognise or impose. For instance, suppose that D enters into 'an arrangement which he knows or suspects facilitates ... the acquisition ... of criminal property by another person': this normally constitutes the commission of an offence, but it is not an offence if D is a 'legal professional' engaged in 'the ordinary conduct of litigation' in 'determin[ing] or secur[ing] legal rights and remedies' for his client.[42] The most plausible way to read this is as holding that citizens should normally see the fact that an arrangement will facilitate the acquisition of criminal property by another as a conclusive reason against entering into it; but that lawyers engaged in litigation on behalf of a client need not attend to such prospects in deciding what arrangements to enter into. The point is not that they will have a defence if charged under this statute, that they may legitimately serve their clients' interests despite the fact that this might facilitate the acquisition of criminal property: for

---

[40] See Theft Act 1968, s. 22.

[41] Which is why this particular species of 'legal impossibility' precludes liability for a criminal attempt: see Williams, 'The Lords and Impossible Attempts', pp. 55–6.

[42] Proceeds of Crime Act 2002, s. 328, as interpreted in *Bowman* v. *Fels* [2005] 1 WLR 3083, paras. 83–4.

that would imply that they must be able to point to legally recognised reasons in favour of allowing them to litigate in this way which outweigh the counter-reasons provided by the prospect that the litigation will help their client acquire criminal property – but the statute implies no such weighing. The point is rather that the law allows lawyers to understand their role and responsibilities in a way that excludes such prospects from consideration: they are a source of authoritative reasons for most citizens in most contexts, but not for lawyers in this context.

We might, of course, criticise this aspect of the law, as we might criticise laws (or readings of laws) that we take to impose unreasonable legal responsibilities on citizens. Someone who sees two male lovers cuddling at a bus stop might feel 'insulted' by such public behaviour, and might breach the peace in response to it: but for a court to convict the lovers for using 'insulting words or behaviour . . . whereby a breach of the peace may be occasioned' is to add to this factual finding the normative claim that the lovers should have attended to such likely reactions as a reason against behaving as they did; whereas we might object that a couple, whether heterosexual or homosexual, engaging in such an ordinary display of mutual love should not have to attend to the unreasonable reactions of others as a reason against acting as they do, and should not be held responsible for provoking such reactions.[43] The general point to notice here, however, is that mere foresight or expectation of an outcome of my action is not by itself sufficient, however certain it might be, to render me criminally responsible for bringing it about: it must also be shown that the prospect of that outcome was normatively relevant to my action, as a reason against acting in that way. The most familiar way that the criminal law operates in this context is to hold us responsible for certain outcomes, whether or not we see them as relevant: given the provisions of section 1 of the Criminal Damage Act 1971, I cannot (I will not be heard to) deny that the prospect that my action will damage another's property is something to which I should attend as a normally conclusive reason against acting thus, or that I am responsible for that damage if I go ahead and cause it. Sometimes, however, the law limits our responsibilities by allowing us to treat as irrelevant, as not our business, prospects that are normally legally relevant as reasons against action: it does this when it allows legal professionals to enter into arrangements which they know might facilitate the

---

[43] See *Masterson v. Holden* (1986) 83 Cr App R 302, applying Metropolitan Police Act 1839, s. 54; and the case of the Naked Rambler, at nn. 36–7, above.

acquisition of criminal property by their clients;[44] it arguably should do this if, among other kinds of case, a person's conduct is likely to lead to a breach of the peace only because of the unreasonable reactions of others.[45]

So much, for the time being, for the distinction between (b) and (c) – a distinction among the prospects or outcomes of which the agent is aware, between those that are and those that are not normatively relevant to her action, and thus between those for which she is and those for which she is not criminally responsible (we will return to this distinction in section IV, since it will throw light on the three exceptions that Williams made to his claim that 'oblique intent' should generally be treated as a species of intent). Suppose, then, that the prospect that p is one to which the agent should attend as a reason against acting as she proposes to act – something that the law declares to be relevant to her action in that way and (to avoid complications) that we can agree should be relevant. This brings us to the distinction between the first two ways in which the prospect that p can figure in the agent's practical reasoning – as a reason against acting as she does or as one of the reasons for which she acts as she does. This is in effect the distinction between so-called 'direct' and so-called 'oblique' intention – but we are avoiding the language of intention, and must ask whether this difference in the structure of the agent's practical reasoning is one that should ever concern the criminal law.

To be more precise, the distinction that concerns us here is that between cases in which the agent sees the prospect that p as a reason in favour of acting as he does, and it is indeed one of the motivating reasons for which he acts, while in the law's eyes, as a matter of the normative reasons bearing on his action, that prospect is a normally conclusive reason against acting as he does (case (a) above); and those in which in the criminal law's eyes the prospect that p constitutes a normally con-clusive reason against acting as he does, but the agent either does not see it as a reason against his action at all or does not allow it sufficient weight, and is thus not motivated by it (case (b) above). The law declares that the

---

[44] Proceeds of Crime Act 2002, s. 328; see at n. 42, above.

[45] See *Masterson* v. *Holden* (1986) 83 Cr App R 302 (n. 43, above); also *Beatty* v. *Gillbanks* [1882] 9 QBD 308 (Williams, *Textbook of Criminal Law*, 2nd edn (London: Stevens, 1983), pp. 338–9). Sometimes the point here might be argued as one of ('proximate') causation: if the relevant outcome would ensue only by virtue of the voluntary responses of others, those responses break the chain of causation: but the more plausible under-lying rationale for such claims about causation is, I think, the one sketched here.

prospect that my action will kill or injure another, or will damage another's property, constitutes a good and normally conclusive reason against acting thus. In case (a), I act as I do *because of* that prospect, or *in order* to bring about that result; that prospect is at least part of what guides my action. In case (b), I act as I do *despite* the prospect of bringing that result about (although if I regard the prospect as practically irrelevant, I will not myself use the language of 'despite'). So is this distinction one to which the criminal law should attach any weight?

It looks like a rather significant distinction. An agent realises that what he is doing will, for instance, cause someone's death, or damage someone's property, or that it will amount to giving false testimony or to handling stolen goods. In one scenario, (b), although he is aware of that prospect, he does not treat it as a reason (or a strong enough reason) against acting as he does: he acts in the expectation that it will be realised, and will not take its realisation to mark the failure of his enterprise, but his action is not oriented towards realising it; he thus fails to be practically moved by what the law declares to be good reasons for action (good reasons for not acting as he does). In the other scenario, (a), he does treat that prospect as a reason for action – but as a reason for, rather than against, acting as he does. He acts not just in the expectation that he will cause death or damage, or give false testimony or handle stolen goods, but in order to achieve that result: not only is he not moved by what the law declares to be good reasons against acting as he does; he treats them as good reasons *for* acting as he does. In (b), his reasons for acting as he does might be perfectly legitimate in themselves, as far as we know; the problem is that he fails to recognise or to take seriously enough the reasons against his action. In (a), the problem is rather that he acts for reasons that are, in the law's eyes, categorically bad reasons for action: categorically bad just because they are, in the law's eyes, reasons against acting as he does. The difference between the two cases is that between failing to be guided by good reasons and being guided by bad reasons; and that is, surely, a significant difference.[46]

It might be replied that, even if that is a morally significant difference in the structures of practical reason that underpin and guide the agents' actions, a difference to which we might pay serious attention in a moral assessment of the agents' characters, it is not a difference to which the

---

[46] See further, Duff, *Answering for Crime*, ch. 7, on the difference between 'attacks' and 'endangerments'. In both cases, the agent might, of course, be able to offer a justification or an excuse; but for present purposes we can ignore that possibility.

criminal law should attend. For the criminal law should be concerned with what we do, not with what we are; and although what we do, if it is to ground criminal liability, must be understood as including more than the purely objective aspects of our conduct, that 'more' need not involve anything beyond the familiar conditions of knowledge and control. We must ask whether the agent realised that he was or might be acting in a way that the law defines as criminal, and whether he had sufficient control over his conduct to avoid acting in that way; but the criminal law should not delve more deeply than that into his practical reasoning or his character.

We cannot embark on a discussion of these competing conceptions of criminal liability here, save to note that what they involve is not so much the question of whether it should be 'action' (or 'choice') rather than 'character' that grounds criminal liability, but instead the question of how we should understand the idea of action in the criminal law: how far, that is, should the criminal law describe and judge our actions in terms of the structures of practical reason that they embody; how far should it take a more superficial view that attends only to the extent to which the agent avoidably failed to act in accordance with what the law declares to be good reasons for action. I have argued elsewhere that the criminal law should at least sometimes attend to such deeper dimensions of our actions – to the difference between attack and endangerment, especially when the crime is not completed, when the character of the agent's action might depend more on what she was trying to do than on what she actually achieved;[47] but I will not revive those arguments here. What matters for present purposes is to realise that if we are to resolve the question of 'oblique intention', and to decide whether Williams was right that the criminal law should not normally distinguish direct from oblique intention,[48] these are the kinds of argument in which we need to engage – arguments not so much about the moral difference between intention and foresight as about the extent to which the criminal law should attend to these differences in the structures of practical reason that inform an agent's (putatively) criminal conduct.

[47] See Duff, *Answering for Crime*, ch. 7; R. A. Duff, *Criminal Attempts* (Oxford University Press, 1996), ch. 13.

[48] As well as whether he had adequate grounds for the exceptions he made to this rule: see at n. 16, above.

IV Intention and practical reason

It is time to return to intention, and to ask how the distinctions discussed in the previous two sections should bear on our, or the criminal law's, ascriptions of intention and intentional agency.

It is obvious that in the first kind of case, (a), when the prospect that p constitutes the, or at least a, reason for which the agent acts, she intends to realise that prospect; she acts with the intention of realising; if it is realised, she has realised it intentionally; if it is not realised, she has attempted to realise it. But how far, if at all, beyond that first kind of case should we, or the criminal law, extend our ascriptions of intentional agency? Should we say that an agent's intentions, or her intentional agency, also encompass cases falling under (b), in which she acts despite the prospect that p – whether or not she sees that prospect as a reason against acting as she does; or that it also encompasses cases falling under both (b) and (c) – which would be to say that I act intentionally in relation to every prospect or outcome of which I am aware? Should we treat 'intention' as encompassing 'oblique' as well as 'direct' intention; if so, how far should 'oblique intent' extend? Here we find ourselves back among the persisting controversies and confusions about the proper scope of 'intention' in the criminal law.

It might seem that we could cut through such confusions, and bypass those controversies and confusions, by dropping the term 'intention' and its cognates from the law's vocabulary in favour of terms that lack the rhetorical baggage that 'intention' has come to carry. Why not, for instance, have the criminal law use the term 'purpose' in relation to results that form part of the agent's reason for action,[49] and the term 'expectation' in relation to those that she foresees as certain to ensue?[50] We could then ask, more clearly, whether and when criminal liability

---

[49] Compare Model Penal Code, §2.02(2)(a), and the 1985 Draft Code, *Codification of the Criminal Law*, cl. 22(a).

[50] 'Expectation' is a better label than 'knowledge', because it covers without strain cases in which the result does not in fact ensue: I can expect, but cannot know, that p will ensue if p does not actually ensue. I leave aside here cases in which the result is foreseen as probable or likely rather than as certain, and assume for present purposes that our intentional agency does not stretch beyond results foreseen as ('practically', 'morally', 'virtually') certain – though, of course, we can be said to have intentionally taken the risk of causing a result whose occurrence we foresaw as merely possible, if we should have seen that risk as a reason against acting as we did. This is not to deny that we are responsible for results that we foresee as merely likely or possible – if we should have seen their likely or possible occurrence as a reason against acting as we did: but insofar as

should require that the agent acted purposely in relation to the relevant result, and whether and when it should require only that he expected it to ensue. But this suggestion ignores a larger underlying question about how we should understand intention (and other *mens rea* concepts). That larger question is whether we should treat intention as a descriptive or as a normative concept. If we are to treat it as a descriptive concept, we must be able to specify criteria for its application that are themselves purely descriptive – criteria that do not involve or depend on any normative judgment. That is indeed how many theorists understand it: thus they argue about whether we should count only 'direct' intention as intention properly speaking, or should also include 'oblique' intention; but they assume that both concept(ion)s of intention can be analysed descriptively, in terms of the reasons for which (or the desires out of which) the agent acted, and in terms of what the agent knew or expected. If we follow this route, however, we will not be able to use the concept of intention to distinguish cases falling under (b) from those falling under (c), since whether a case falls under (b) or under (c) is a normative matter: it depends on whether the prospect that p was something to which the agent *should* have attended was a reason against acting as he did. Nor indeed can we draw that distinction, which we have seen that the criminal law needs to draw, through such concepts as purpose and expectation if they are understood as purely descriptive.

We could instead recognise that intention is not, and should not be, a purely descriptive concept: that it helps to structure our ascriptions of responsibility not by providing a purely factual grounding for such ascriptions, but rather by helping us to determine who should be held retrospectively responsible for what in the light of our normative (and often contested) understandings of the prospective responsibilities that we have in virtue of our positions as moral agents, as citizens, and as filling any of the many roles that we play in our lives.[51] I have offered an account of this kind in the past. An agent intends or acts with the intention of bringing about only those prospects that fall under (a): those that provide at least part of her reason for acting as she does; those whose non-occurrence would render her enterprise, to at least

---

there is room in such cases for a genuine hope that the result will not occur, the structure of the practical reasoning that informs the action is different, thus making room for different judgments of the agent's culpability and responsibility – which is why we distinguish intention from recklessness.

[51] On retrospective and prospective responsibilities, see Duff, *Answering for Crime*, pp. 30–6.

some degree, a failure. However, intentional agency reaches more widely than that: the agent brings about intentionally not only results that she acts with the intention of bringing about, but also those that she foresees as being (virtually or morally) certain, if – but only if – she should see them as providing reasons against what she does.[52] Williams thought this distinction between intended and intentional agency 'too subtle a distinction to be useful for legal purposes',[53] but the distinction itself is hardly subtle. The distinction between intended results and those that, on my account, are brought about intentionally is a distinction between those prospective results that constituted the agent's reasons for acting as she did, and those that constituted normative reasons against acting as she did. The distinction between expected results that are brought about intentionally and expected results that are not brought about intentionally is a distinction between those whose prospective occurrence provided a reason against acting as she did and those that were practically irrelevant, providing no reason either for or against her action. The distinctions are real enough, and in principle clear (though I will note some complications shortly); they can structure a 'Clear Concept of Intention' that does not seem to be either 'Elusive or Illusory'.[54] It will seem elusive, or in despair illusory, if we persist in trying to analyse intention as a purely descriptive concept, while actually using it (or while courts are implicitly using it) as a normative concept.[55] It will also seem elusive or illusory if we try to operate with a single conception of intention, when the criminal law should sometimes require intended agency for criminal liability, but sometimes nothing more than intentional agency.[56] However, once we recognise the essential normative dimension of ascriptions of intentional agency, and distinguish intended from intentional agency in the way suggested here, we can avoid such confusions. That is not to say that the application of the concept will then be straightforward and free from controversy: there will still be plenty of room for controversy about the proper scope of intentional agency, because there is plenty of controversy about the scope of the responsibilities on which our ascriptions of intentional agency depend. But we will at least be clearer about the nature of the controversies that we face;

---

[52] See R. A. Duff, *Intention, Agency and Criminal Liability* (Oxford: Blackwell, 1990), chs 3–4.

[53] 'Oblique Intention', n. 39.   [54] See n. 20, above.

[55] See Norrie, 'Oblique Intention and Legal Politics'.

[56] See Duff, *Intention, Agency and Criminal Liability*, ch. 4.

and we will be able to see that they reflect not confusion about the meaning of intention or the impossibility of finding a clear meaning for the concept, but normative disagreements or uncertainties of a kind that we should not expect to be able to avoid or eliminate.

This is to suggest that we should see intention as one of those 'thick' concepts that help to structure our normative thinking.[57] In particular, it structures ascriptions of responsibility: the scope of an agent's intentional agency is the scope of her responsible agency. It is a thick concept in the sense that, unlike such thin ethical concepts as good and bad, right and wrong, it has some substantial content – as do such thick concepts as courage and honesty; but it is a normative concept in that its applicability (at least in the kinds of context that interest us here) marks a normative judgment about the extent and significance of the agent's responsibility. If I say to the person who opens a shop, and who is (as we both expected) so successful that the shop across the road has to close, 'you intentionally ruined him', she might respond that this was not her aim; if I reply 'but you knew it would ruin him', I am insisting that she must also accept responsibility for this foreseen side-effect of her actions; if she retorts 'but that's not my concern; the market decides who survives', she is denying that responsibility by denying that the effects of her action on the other shop are practically relevant as reasons against her actions. I might then argue that she should attend to such matters – that the effect on existing shops is a reason against opening her shop, and that she is responsible for such effects: this is not yet to claim that it is a conclusive reason against opening her shop – only that if she is to avoid criticism for opening it, she must show how she was justified in opening it *despite* such foreseen effects. If intention is the kind of thick normative concept that I have suggested it is, our disagreements about what she is responsible for, about what should count as reasons for or against her actions, are expressed in part as disagreements about what should be included in her intentional agency – what should be ascribed to her as intentional actions.

If we understand intention in this way, we can make better sense of the three exceptions that Williams suggested to his general claim that expectation ('oblique' intent) should suffice for intention:[58] we could see them not merely as ad hoc exceptions for which no principled

---

[57] On 'thick' concepts see B. Williams, *Ethics and the Limits of Philosophy* (London: Fontana, 1985), ch. 8.
[58] See at nn. 15–16, above.

explanation can be given, but as cases in which the agent might be able to deny intentional agency by denying responsibility. If I act with the ('direct') intention of causing mental stress to another, if I act as I do in part because of the prospect that this will cause mental stress, I cannot, of course, deny that I am responsible for that stress if it ensues. But if I simply realise that what I am doing will cause such stress as a side-effect, I might be able to argue that that is not something to which the criminal law should require me to attend as a reason against my action – that even if I should morally show such sensitivity to the feelings of others, as far as the criminal law is concerned I should be allowed to say that that is not my business.

So, too, in the case of accessories, if part of my reason for acting as I do is the prospect that this will help another commit a crime, I cannot deny responsibility for the part I play in the crime with which I thus associate myself; but if instead I simply foresee that what I do will make it easier for him to commit the crime, I might be able to deny that the law should hold me responsible for that expected side-effect. I sell a customer some tools, realising that he probably (or even certainly) intends to use them to commit a crime: but, I might argue, that that is not my business as a shopkeeper, at least as far as the criminal law is concerned; the law should not require a shopkeeper to attend to the use to which his customers might put their purchases as a source of reasons against selling them.[59] It might now seem that even if the law should allow the shopkeeper to deny responsibility in this way, just as it allows a lawyer to deny responsibility for the way in which his professional conduct as a litigator facilitates his client's acquisition of criminal property,[60] the solution that Williams offers us, to require 'direct' intention for aiding and abetting, is too crude: for surely the law should sometimes hold us responsible, as aiders and abetters, for the assistance that we know our conduct will give to the commission of a crime, even when the prospect of that assistance is not part of our reason for acting as we do. A shopkeeper might be able to argue that in discharging her lawful and valuable role as shopkeeper, she should not be expected to pay practical attention

---

[59] See also *Gillick* v. *West Norfolk & Wisbech Area Health Authority* [1986] AC 112 (Duff, *Answering for Crime*, pp. 85–7); contrast *Khaliq* v. *HM Advocate* (1984) JC 171; *Ulhaq* v. *HM Advocate* (1991) SLT 614. Often the law does in fact hold a person who knows that his conduct will make it easier for another person to commit an offence responsible, as having aided and abetted the commission of that offence (see, e.g., *NCB* v. *Gamble* [1959] 1 QB 11): but the question is whether it *should* do so.

[60] Proceeds of Crime Act 2002, s. 328; see at n. 42, above.

to the use that her customers might make of the ordinary goods that they lawfully purchase: but we might argue that shopkeepers should pay such practical attention when the goods being sold are clearly dangerous (poison, for instance); and in other contexts, when the agent cannot claim to be carrying on a socially valuable enterprise, we might be readier to hold him responsible for the criminal use that others make of what he does. If I lend a handgun to someone, knowing that he intends to use it to commit a serious crime, should the law really allow me to say that I was simply doing a favour to a friend, and that the use to which he would put my gun was not something to which the law should require me to attend as a reason against lending it? There are two ways to deal with this problem: which is better depends in part on whether the law should presume that we do have a general responsibility to attend to the ways in which our actions will foreseeably make it easier for others to commit crimes, although in some special cases (like that of the shopkeeper selling ordinary tools, or a lawyer acting on behalf of a client) that responsibility is removed; or that we have no such general responsibility, although in some special cases (for instance, when the foreseen crime is especially serious) the law may impose a specific responsibility to pay such attention. If the law should presume or impose a general responsibility of this kind, the offence of aiding and abetting should be so defined that it requires only foresight, rather than a 'direct' intention to assist the commission of the crime; the exceptional cases in which such a responsibility can be denied can then be dealt with by special statutory provision, as section 328 of the Proceeds of Crime Act 2002 does for lawyers acting on behalf of their clients. If the law should not impose any such general responsibility, however, it should define aiding and abetting in terms of a 'direct' intention to assist, and deal with exceptional cases by creating specific offences: either of knowingly assisting the commission of particular kinds of crime, or other kinds of 'prophylactic' offence dealing, for instance, with the possession or supply of particular kinds of dangerous implement.[61]

As for treason, and the particular case of *Ahlers*[62] on which Williams focused, if Mr Ahlers could plausibly have claimed that he was just doing his duty as German consul to help German citizens return home after the outbreak of war, he could have denied not just that he intended to assist

---

[61] See A. P. Simester and A. von Hirsch, *Crimes, Harms and Wrongs* (Oxford: Hart, 2011), pp. 79–85.
[62] [1915] 1 KB 616.

the enemy, but that he intentionally assisted the enemy, on the grounds that given his consular duty, the fact that what he was doing would assist the German war effort (by helping potential soldiers return to Germany) gave him no reason not to act thus. In all three cases, a plausible reason for insisting that criminal liability should require a 'direct' intent is that, given a particular view of the agent's responsibilities, mere expectation of the relevant result does not suffice for responsibility, and thus does not suffice for intentional agency.[63] My point here is not that we should accept, or indeed that the criminal law should give formal recognition to, such denials of responsibility; the denial is in each case at least highly arguable. My point is, rather, that the account of intention as a thick normative concept that I have sketched here enables us to see more clearly what the argument is really about in such cases, and why Williams might have been led to make these otherwise unexplained and puzzling exceptions to his insistence on an expansive conception of criminal intention: we should require intended agency (or 'direct' intention) because in these contexts mere foresight or expectation does not guarantee responsibility.

I noted above that, although the two distinctions on which this account of intention rests (the distinctions between cases (a), (b) and (c) drawn earlier) are in principle clear enough, there are complications. I should end by noting two of these – though one has already been touched on.

First, the distinction between (a) and (b), between intended and merely intentional agency (as we can now put it), rests on the distinction between those prospects that provided part of the agent's reasons for acting as he did, and those prospects despite which he acted. But if I am to be able to say that I acted with the intention of bringing X about, despite the prospect that in doing so I would also bring Y about, X and Y must be distinct, separable, results; if instead Y is 'inseparable' from X, then an intention to bring X about must also be an intention to bring Y about. How then are we to determine whether X and Y are separable?[64]

---

[63] Though it was, in fact, hard to deny that Mr Ahlers intended to assist the enemy, since he publicly asked not all German citizens, but German 'men able to bear arms', to report to the consulate for assistance with repatriation ([1915] 1 KB 616, at p. 617); by selecting that group, he must have been aiming to assist those who would strengthen the German war effort.

[64] See A. P. Simester, J. R. Spencer, G. R. Sullivan and G. J. Virgo, *Simester and Sullivan's Criminal Law: Theory and Doctrine*, 4th edn (Oxford: Hart, 2010), p. 134; A. du Bois-Pedain, 'Intention and the Terrorist Example', *Criminal Law Review* [2003], 579.

The doctors in *In re A*,[65] the case of conjoined twins decided in 2001 by the Court of Appeal, knew that if they operated to separate the twins, this being the only chance of saving at least one of them, the weaker twin would die. Could they claim that in operating they would foresee her death as an inevitable side-effect, but would not intend it; or would her death be so 'inseparable' from the operation that to intend the operation would also be to intend her death? In either case, of course, they would need to be able to justify causing her death if they were to avoid a conviction for murder; but it matters whether what they would have to justify would be an intended killing of the weaker twin; or operating despite the fact that this would cause her death. However, the question of (in)separability is a normative, not a purely factual question; to decide whether *X* is 'inseparable' from *Y*, we must attend to the normative significance of each of them, and to their normative bearing on each other.

Second, consider a doctor who administers pain-relieving drugs to a terminally ill patient, knowing that this will also hasten his death.[66] She does not, in my terms, intend to hasten his death, as long as that prospect does not constitute even part of the reason for which she acts; but must she admit to hastening his death intentionally? If so, and if it suffices for murder (as it should) that *D* killed *V* intentionally, then the doctor will need a defence if she is to avoid being liable to a conviction for murder; but perhaps she can deny that she intentionally kills the patient. The fact that a proposed treatment would hasten the patient's death is normally a powerful, even conclusive, reason against it, to which the doctor must attend: but perhaps she could argue that in this context, in which death is anyway and unavoidably imminent, the fact that a treatment will hasten death ceases to be thus relevant; all that should concern her now is the relief of her patient's pain. It might seem that the difference between these two ways of seeing her practical situation is unimportant, if we agree that she should not be condemned for administering the drug: but it matters *why* she should not be condemned. Should she have to answer for an intentional killing by offering a justification for killing her patient? Or can she deny that she killed him, and thus deny that she has a killing to answer for?

---

[65] *In re A (Children) (Conjoined Twins: Surgical Separation)* [2001] 2 WLR 480.
[66] See generally A. J. Ashworth, 'Criminal Liability in a Medical Context: the Treatment of Good Intentions', in A. P. Simester and A. T. H. Smith (eds), *Harm and Culpability* (Oxford University Press, 1996), p. 173; Norrie, 'Legal Form and Moral Judgment'.

These two kinds of complication illustrate the ways in which we might find disagreement or doubt about just how to distinguish intended from intentional agency, or about the scope of intentional agency. I have noted them here not in order to resolve such disagreement or doubt (part of my argument has, indeed, been that they can be resolved only through a normative discussion of the character and scope of our responsibilities); nor in order to undermine the distinctions I have drawn between outcomes that an agent intends to bring about, outcomes that she brings about intentionally, and expected outcomes as to which she can deny even intentional agency. The point of noting them was, rather, to emphasise that such disagreement and doubt reflect normative disagreement or doubt about the scope of our responsibilities – rather than conceptual confusion or empirical uncertainty. If our aim was to articulate a clear, consistent descriptive conception of intention in criminal law, they would mark our failure to achieve that aim, but that does not show that they doom any attempt to articulate a clear and consistent conception of intention to failure. We should instead recognise that intention functions here as a thick normative concept – and that such disagreements and doubts are just what we can expect to find as we argue about the proper applications of such concepts.

8

A disintegrated theory of culpability

A. P. SIMESTER[*]

Many criminal theorists agree that conviction of a criminal offence, or at least of a stigmatic criminal offence, should not normally occur unless the accused is culpable with respect to that offence.[1] Not everyone thinks this. Some writers, for example, hold that once an offender goes through a 'gateway' of wrongdoing, she may legitimately be held criminally liable for consequences that flow from her initial wrongful action,[2] without being culpable specifically for those further consequences.[3] Indeed, similar thinking lies behind traditional doctrines of felony-murder. But even those writers generally accept that the offender should in principle be culpable with respect to the initial action. There must, they agree, be *some* culpability, somewhere, to legitimate conviction for a serious criminal offence.

My concern in this chapter is with the underlying question: when is a person culpable? Conventionally, the ascription of culpability or blame is thought to rest upon findings of *mens rea*.[4] And it is certainly true that *mens rea* elements have a role to play in establishing culpability. Yet how they do so remains obscure. Part of the problem is that many existing

---

[*] I am grateful to the conference organisers for the opportunity to present an early draft of this chapter, and to participants for many helpful comments. Particular thanks to Bob Sullivan for detailed written comments, and to the Singapore MoE Tier One Research Grant (No. R241000100112) for research travel support.

[1] Subject to special cases, e.g., where a justified mistake is made when convicting on the evidence.

[2] For example, J. Gardner, 'Rationality and the Rule of Law in Offences Against the Person', *Cambridge Law Journal*, 53 (1994), 502; J. Horder, 'A Critique of the Correspondence Principle in Criminal Law', *Criminal Law Review* (1995), 759.

[3] Though the extension of liability may be subject to other limitations: e.g., Horder, 'A Critique of the Correspondence Principle in Criminal Law'.

[4] For convenience, I use '*mens rea*' in this chapter to include negligence. Additionally, 'recklessness' refers to advertent recklessness, whereas 'negligence' is presumed to be inadvertent.

accounts seek a comprehensive but false unity. They tend not to separate positive from negative criteria; responsibility from culpability; capacity-based from circumstance-based exculpations; and, most importantly of all, choice-based accounts from other explanations of blame. As we shall see, a less integrated approach, with two alternative bases of culpability, may be more perspicuous.

I Culpability: the basic challenge

Let us start by supposing that D's φing is a wrongful, that is, morally undesirable, act. By this I mean that, 'objectively' speaking, D ought not to φ:[5] that the guiding reasons for D to φ are, all things considered, defeated by the reasons against.[6] This strict usage of 'wrongful' is admittedly stipulative; some may prefer to say that an act cannot be 'wrongful' unless it is culpably done. I will return to this point at the end of the chapter. For now, nothing turns on the linguistic point. My starting point also leaves aside the further distinction between an act's being wrongful and its being *a wrong*: that is, a right violation or breach a duty. It also assumes that the act is not merely *prima facie* wrongful but is, in fact, unjustified on this occasion when performed by D.[7]

In general, that φing be wrongful is an essential condition of D's being blameworthy for doing it. We do not 'blame' D for doing the right thing; although, depending why she did it, we might not praise her. Admittedly, we might blame her for doing something bad – for φing – even though, at the same time, her conduct also had beneficial effects.[8] But that possibility just requires us to be careful about the description under which D's conduct is being assessed; about the act in respect of which we are judging D. If D is to be blamed *for φing*, φing must be something bad or undesirable, something that D ought not to have done.

Given this starting point, the basic challenge of culpability is then to trace our negative evaluation of φing back to D, the person who does it.

---

[5] Note that, by 'objective' or 'guiding' reasons, I do not mean 'universal'. The force of relevant guiding reasons – and thus the moral assessment of φing – will very often be community-dependent.

[6] On the distinction between guiding reasons (which, in fact, apply to the action) and explanatory reasons (by which the agent is, personally, motivated), see J. Raz, *Practical Reason and Norms*, 2nd edn (Princeton University Press, 1990), pp. 16ff.

[7] Thus, we disregard the problems of mistaken or unknown justification; our concern is with the central case.

[8] Albeit not so as to justify D's φing (our starting point).

This is not straightforward because moral evaluations of an act are not the same kind of evaluations as blaming judgments. Their objects of assessment are crucially different. When we blame, we disapprove not of the act by itself, but *of the defendant for doing that act*. It may be necessary, but it is not sufficient, that D's act be wrongful. The burden for ascribing culpability lies in justifying that evaluative link between act and defendant – that link which allows us to transmit judgments of the deed across to the person.

Implicit in this claim is a conceptual unity. I argue in this chapter that there are different grounds of culpability, that its material conditions differ between advertent and inadvertent wrongdoing; not that there are distinct concepts of blame in play. Culpability is a particular kind of moral evaluation.[9] We can also make moral assessments of *people* ('a callous person'), just as we can of actions like φing, or indeed events more generally; but those are not blaming judgments either. To blame someone is to make a moral assessment of that person *in respect of* their action. The challenge for culpability is, one might say, a challenge about how to generate judgments that integrate evaluations of the actor and her act.

For it does not follow from the proposition that D's act is undesirable that D should be blamed for doing it. Imagine that P, a doctor, injects A with a painkiller that produces an allergic reaction and causes his death. P's killing A is undesirable. It is contraindicated by the applicable guiding reasons. It is a matter for regret. But, on these bare facts, it is not a matter for blame. All things considered, A should not have received the injection. But if his allergy is unknown, and unknowable, P is not culpable for injecting him.[10]

P is not culpable because, in a sense, the killing does not reflect badly on her. When we trace back from her φing to an explanation of why she φed, the explanation discloses no shortfall of character, no deficiency of virtue; or, more precisely, none falling below that which would be expected of a normal person in P's position, a so-called 'reasonable' person with decent values and dispositions. In a perfect world, we would always act for undefeated guiding reasons. P did not. So there is a sense in which she failed – at least, as it turned out. But not all failures ground culpability. Whence, then, is blame sourced?

---

[9] I use 'culpability' and 'blameworthiness' interchangeably. We should also note a distinction between blameworthiness and (the act of) blaming. To cast blame might be unjustified, even when the person blamed is actually culpable; and vice versa. But those are secondary issues, and are not pursued here.

[10] The example is taken from A. P. Simester, 'Can Negligence be Culpable?' in J. Horder (ed.), *Oxford Essays in Jurisprudence*, 4th series (Oxford University Press, 2000), p. 85.

Sometimes the answer will be relatively straightforward, in as much as the grounds of blame are embedded in the wrongfulness of φing itself. For example, there are many wrongs that include the intention or motivation of the agent as a defining element of the wrong. As Glanville Williams himself once observed: 'the act constituting a crime may in some circumstances be objectively innocent, and take its criminal colouring entirely from the intent with which it is done'.[11] Thus, it is D's intention to keep the property that helps to explain why picking up V's watch was theft. In such cases, what makes φing wrongful is also, at the very same time, what grounds the attribution of culpability to D. Typically, as we shall see, blame for such wrongs is choice-based; the choice is implicit in the wrong. But other wrongs, like the killing of A, are more basic. In these basic wrongs, it is the bringing about of some (unjustified) harm *per se* that constitutes the undesirable act: indeed, this is typical of so-called 'result crimes'. For both kinds of wrong, it still needs to be shown how they reflect badly on the agent if they are to ground blame. That challenge is more difficult, however, when the wrong is basic; since the grounds for blaming the agent require elements that reach beyond the constituents of the wrong itself.

II   Two negative accounts

A   Blame as the default verdict? Gardner's unifying account

Even so, the challenge may seem simply met. Surely we can derive blame straightforwardly from the conclusion that φing is wrongful? After all, this means that D should not have φed. And if D does what she should not, is that not *prima facie* ground for blame: her failure to act for the very reasons by which she should be guided? This was once suggested by Joseph Raz:

> Other things being equal, [the guiding reasons for an action] are suffi-
> cient grounds for taking the action, and barring reasonable ignorance or
> other excuses, grounds for finding fault with the actor's conduct, if he
> fails to take the action.[12]

---

[11] *Criminal Law: The General Part*, 2nd edn (London: Stevens, 1961), p. 22. For discussion, see W. Chan and A. P. Simester, 'Four Functions of *Mens Rea*', *Cambridge Law Journal*, 70 (2011), 381, 385-8.

[12] J. Raz, *Practical Reason and Norms*, pp. 186-7; cf. also, R. Milo, *Immorality*, Princeton University Press, 1984), p. 224. But see now, J. Raz, 'Responsibility and the Negligence Standard', *Oxford Journal of Legal Studies*, 30 (2010), 1.

Similarly by John Gardner:

> To be blameworthy, one must: (a) have done something wrong and (b)
> have been responsible for doing it, while lacking (c) justification and (d)
> excuse for having done it.[13]

Thus, in our earlier example, P would be blameless only because excused;
not because she lacks *mens rea* as such.[14] Inculpation follows just from
the absence of exculpation. It requires no additional, positive element.
On Gardner's account, the culpability-constituting role of *mens rea* is
primarily to establish the absence of an excuse.[15]

The analysis is attractive. It ties the blaming judgment tightly to the
reasons why D should not φ in the first place. Indeed, φing itself
generates *prima facie* culpability. In turn, culpability for wrongful acts
becomes the default conclusion, a conclusion that follows automatically
unless the actor is excused. No extra, positive element is required,
because the original reasons why φing is wrongful can do all the work
needed to ground blame. The ascription of that blame rests, in turn,
upon D's failure – her omission – to act for understandable (excusatory)
reasons.

What is missing from this approach? At the level of logic, such
an account is capable of giving a *threshold* test for D's culpability.
Provided we have a suitably rich and nuanced understanding of
excuses and their application, we might legitimately conclude that D
has failed to cross from culpability into exculpation when she φs
without any such excuse. A failure-of-excuse account might even, at
least sometimes, tell us the extent to which D fell short of exculpation –
how far short the actor fell of having understandable, excusatory
reasons for her conduct.

---

[13] J. Gardner, *Offences and Defences: Selected Essays in the Philosophy of Criminal Law*
(Oxford University Press, 2007), p. 227. Cf. also at p. 151: 'someone is at fault in
committing a wrong if and only if he commits it without justification or excuse'. On
the distinct nature of irresponsibility conditions, see also below in the text.

[14] Cf. Gardner, *Offences and Defences*, p. 228.

[15] Things would be otherwise if Gardner's definition of 'something wrong' in condition (a)
always included a culpability-generating element. But it does not. Gardner intends the
account to apply to basic wrongs too – an approach that seems to me appropriate if one's
account of doing wrong is to embrace tort as well as crime. In any event, the 'default
verdict' analysis warrants exploration for its own sake. For a fuller discussion of
Gardner's account, see A. P. Simester, 'Wrongs and Reasons', *Modern Law Review*, 72
(2009), 648, 650–9.

Because it is a negative test, however, it cannot tell us anything positive about the grounds on which D is culpable. Whether or not D's φing was advertent, blame is grounded in the reasons D had not to φ, and, at least where the wrong is basic, those reasons are independent of D's awareness of them. So, *if* there is a difference between choice-based and inadvertent negligence-based culpability, a failure-of-excuse account cannot capture it. In a theory of excuses, the positive choice to do wrong has no distinct role to play.

There is a related and more general worry, one that applies even to inadvertent action. In order to show when a person is excused, we need a normative standard by which to measure and delimit excuses. In other words, we can test excuses only once we know what is required for a person to be culpable. (This point may not be obvious. Sometimes it seems that we do not need such a standard, especially when an exculpatory defence operates by putting moral distance between the actor and his act – when it undermines his responsibility for the act. An 'irresponsibility' defence of this sort is not subject to normative standards such as proportionality or reasonableness. But I am not here concerned with irresponsibility defences, and neither is Gardner.) What we might call 'true' excuses, such as duress, concede the actor's responsibility for his act and are concerned to explain *why* he did it.[16] In particular, they aim to explain why in such a way that we refrain from blaming the actor, and conclude that he did not fall short of an expected normative standard when doing something undesirable. Yet that very conclusion demands an explanation of the normative standard and of why it underpins the excuses. How is it that D's falling short of that standard reflects badly on *her*? Even an excuse-driven analysis of culpability cannot avoid the need to give a positive account, one that shows which of the defendant's shortcomings are *in*excusable. Otherwise, grounding blame just in the unexcused wrongfulness of φing cannot tell us what we need to know about D.

B   Capacity-based theories: H. L. A. Hart

A similar problem is found in H. L. A. Hart's analysis, although it is not the only difficulty for that account. In the context of criminal negligence, Hart proposes the following conditions of liability:

---

[16] Gardner, *Offences and Defences*, ch. 6: 'The Gist of Excuses'.

(i) Did the accused fail to take those precautions which any reasonable man with normal capacities would in the circumstances have taken?

(ii) Could the accused, given his mental and physical capacities, have taken those precautions?[17]

Satisfaction of condition (i) is taken by Hart to establish, objectively, a fair opportunity to avoid the relevant harm, while condition (ii) reflects a personalised requirement of capacity.

Once more, condition (ii) is purely negative, and does no positive work to establish culpability. Like all capacity conditions, it is a threshold condition of moral responsibility,[18] a precondition of culpability determinations regarding D's φing. Without it, D is not exposed to assessments of praise or blame, in respect of φing, *at all*. We never get that far. However, its contribution is binomial. Culpability implies capacity; incapacity implies blamelessness. The implication is unidirectional. Once condition (ii) is satisfied, it has nothing more to say. It supplies no reason to think that D is culpable.

At first glance, condition (i) appears to do the culpability work we need. But it does not, for two reasons. First, Hart intends this first condition to be objective, independent of the accused's own capacities and limitations. D may be adjudged negligent when there was a fair opportunity for a 'reasonable person' to avoid φing. Now, if D actually has ordinary powers of intellect, self-control and the like, condition (i) may offer an appropriate test. But what if D has lower than average intelligence?[19] *Prima facie*, we ought to blame people for unreasonably deploying the intelligence they have, not for failing to be reasonably intelligent.

More on that below. It is not the only issue. Like Raz and Gardner, condition (i) too offers a negative test. Again, that might be fine as a baseline test for basic culpability, in particular for negligence (provided we disregard the other difficulty just identified). But it is of no use as a comprehensive explanation of culpability. It cannot distinguish between

---

[17] 'Negligence, *Mens Rea*, and Criminal Responsibility', in *Punishment and Responsibility* (Oxford University Press, 1968), p. 136, at p. 154.

[18] We return to the idea of moral responsibility in section III. As with capacity conditions generally, there are also familiar problems of over-determination. See, e.g., H. Frankfurt, 'Alternate Possibilities and Moral Responsibility', in *The Importance of What We Care About* (Cambridge University Press, 1988), p. 1.

[19] Conversely, an objectively fair opportunity may be too generous where D's capacities exceed those of a normal person.

inadvertent and advertent φing. In effect, it adopts a default position that D is culpable for φing unless she lacked a fair opportunity to do otherwise. Therefore, it cannot differentiate recklessness, or indeed intention, from negligence. Admittedly, Hart was not targeting a comprehensive theory – his concern was specifically to account for negligence. Ultimately, however, his test cannot do even that much, because it fails to demonstrate in positive terms why negligence can be a ground of culpability.

III   Choice and inadvertence

A   Choice theories: Moore

Michael Moore builds on the idea that Hart's capacity plus fair opportunity approach is necessary but not sufficient. In his view, the crucial positive ingredient is choice. What makes intention or recklessness culpable is not the actor's unexercised capacity to do otherwise, but his choice not to exercise that capacity:

> In accommodating responsibility for negligence in this way, Hart, as he recognized, shifted the touchstone of responsibility from choice to capacity. A choice to do a wrongful act then becomes only one way in which the actor's capacity to avoid evil goes unexercised; inadvertence is another. My objection to this shift is a moral one: it relegates choice to a subsidiary role in our responsibility assessments that our judgments won't support. What makes the intentional or reckless wrongdoer so culpable is not unexercised capacity – although that is necessary – but the way such capacity to avoid evil goes unexercised; such wrongdoers are not even trying to get it right. Their capacity goes unexercised because that is what they choose. Choice is essential to their culpability, not one way among others that they could have been seriously culpable.[20]

Moore is right, I think, to emphasise a connection between choice and culpability. Choice can supply the bridge that allows us to transfer judgments about the wrongfulness of φing back to D, underpinning blame. Moreover, the link is not merely permissive but explanatory. When D chooses to act for bad reasons, she accepts and aligns herself

[20] M. S. Moore, 'Choice, Character and Excuse', in E. F. Paul, F. D. Miller, Jr and J. Paul (eds), *Crime, Culpability and Remedy* (Oxford: Blackwell, 1990), p. 57. More recently, see M. S. Moore and H. Hurd, 'Punishing the Awkward, the Stupid, the Weak, and the Selfish: the Culpability of Negligence', *Criminal Law and Philosophy*, 5 (2011), 147, at pp. 172–3.

with those reasons, and in turn with her wrongful act. That act, being chosen, expresses her own inclinations and dispositions, her knowing preference for bad reasons over good ones. Just as we can criticise her, *qua* person, for having such preferences, we can criticise her for acting upon them – which is to say, we can blame her for that act. This is a stronger conclusion than that D has no excuse. It is a positive ground of blame.

Notice that this account does not equate choice with advertence.[21] An actor may be aware of the risk of φing, while not recognising the magnitude of that risk. Suppose, for example:

> John is building a campfire. He has cleared a space around the fire, and notices that there is loose dry grass a further distance away. John believes the risk of sparks carrying is very low and decides it is not worth clearing any further. Unfortunately, given the breeze, the risk is higher than he realises. A spark gives fire to the grass, and the fire spreads to a nearby forest.[22]

John is aware of a fire risk. Yet there is no choice-based fault in choosing to take a risk that, on the facts as perceived, it is reasonable to take. Neither should such a case be regarded as 'reckless', in the subjective sense known to English law.[23] Trade-offs of this sort are a mainstay of surgeons, health and safety regulators, and indeed all of us. John's culpability, if any, lies in his failure to recognise the true risk, not in the decision he made.

Neither can blame for choices persuasively be reduced to a single underlying attitude, such as a desire to humiliate others whenever one assaults them.[24] Moore and Hurd rightly observe that 'someone who renders another unconscious so as to pick his pocket is clearly not motivated by a desire to humiliate; and someone who enjoys embarrassing others is clearly not as culpable as someone who enjoys physically

---

[21] Moore and Hurd, 'Punishing the Awkward, the Stupid, the Weak, and the Selfish', p. 150, attribute this equation to L. Alexander and K. Ferzan, *Crime and Culpability: A Theory of Criminal Law* (New York: Cambridge University Press, 2009), pp. 69, 78 n. 25.

[22] I assume that on the (perceived) risk levels, it would be reasonable to clear no further. The example is based on one developed by W. J. Winslade, 'Brady on Recklessness', *Analysis*, 33 (1972), 31, 32. In Winslade's version, however, the failure to remove the grass is inadvertent.

[23] 'It is however not the taking of every risk which could properly be classified as reckless. The risk must be one which it is in all the circumstances unreasonable for him to take': *Stephenson* [1979] 2 All ER 1198, 1203.

[24] Cf., in the context of assaults, J. Murphy, 'Bias Crimes: What do Haters Deserve?' *Criminal Justice Ethics*, (1992), 20.

torturing others, even though both may be said to be motivated by a desire to humiliate.'[25] We cannot even say, more generally, that one who chooses to φ is 'indifferent' to the interests of others.[26] Certainly, there is acquiescence to the contemplated action. But D may or may not be indifferent. She may choose to risk φing despite wanting strongly not to do so. Perhaps she drove too fast because she wanted to see her children at home before their bedtime, although she was aware that she might skid and crash in the icy conditions. There is acceptance of the danger and hence recklessness even though she very much hopes not to crash. In other scenarios, an actor may positively want to φ – a desire that may or may not motivate her choice to behave as she does.[27] No doubt, in all these cases, we can say the agent does not care *sufficiently* – not indifferent, but insufficiently differing (or worse!). However, that weaker claim adds nothing to the point that she chose to φ when she should not have.

We return to the diversity of motivation and attitude below. So far, one can broadly agree with Moore, whose discussion is insightful and instructive. But no further. Ultimately, it seems to me, his recipe for culpability has too few ingredients.

The first difficulty is that, like Gardner's, Moore's theory of culpability is tied too closely to a theory of excuses.[28] Culpability is presented as the flip side of excuse. The difference is just that excuses are then explained in terms of choice:

---

[25] Moore and Hurd, 'Punishing the Awkward, the Stupid, the Weak, and the Selfish', p. 172.

[26] Cf. J. Brady, 'Indifference and Involuntariness', *Analysis*, 32 (1972), 98, 99: 'indifference distinguishes recklessness from acting purposely'.

[27] Suppose that I shoot my fiancée's father out of an intense dislike for him, realising that this will probably mean the end of my engagement. If I am not motivated to shoot by that realisation, then I advertently – without intending it – cause the abandonment of the wedding; even if I secretly find that prospect a source of relief.

Should choice-based culpability be further divided between intended and reckless φing? Not necessarily. In my view, the main difference between intention and recklessness concerns justifications: see A.P. Simester, 'Why Distinguish Intention from Foresight?', in *Harm and Culpability* (Oxford University Press, 1996), p. 71. However, to the extent that choice-based blame is a placeholder for the underlying attitudes and emotions that motivate one's φing, we may use the intention–advertence divide as a rough proxy for differences in underlying culpability; it being typically worse – and more malignant – to act for the sake of harming others, say, than to do so out of selfishness and a failure of empathy.

[28] Self-consciously (Moore, 'Choice, Character and Excuse', p. 29): 'the excuses are the royal road to theories of responsibility generally'.

> [according to] what I shall call the choice theory of excuse ... one is excused for the doing of a wrongful action because and only because at the moment of such action's performance, one did not have sufficient capacity or opportunity to make the choice to do otherwise. Such a choice theory of excuse instantiates a more general theory of responsibility, according to which we are responsible for wrongs we freely choose to do, and not responsible for wrongs we lacked the freedom (capacity and opportunity) to avoid doing.[29]

Conduct is excused, therefore, by virtue of not being freely chosen. This move effectively eliminates any middle ground on which to defend a separate account of culpability for inadvertent negligence. If there is a free choice to φ the actor is culpable; *aliter*, he is not. Hence, in Moore's account, all the pressure goes onto the question of whether there is a genuinely free choice.

Part of the problem is terminological, and it is worth pausing to clarify an underlying distinction. The quoted passage does not differentiate between being morally responsible and being culpable. If φing is wrongful, and D is 'responsible' for her (freely chosen) act of φing, then on Moore's account D is culpable for it.[30] Just as with the discussion of Hart's two criteria, it is helpful, I think, to separate being morally responsible for φing from being culpable for it.[31] Where one lacks the capacity to not-φ (e.g., when automatic or paralysed), one is then not morally responsible for φing. That is to say, one is not exposed to moral assessments – good, bad, neutral or excused – in respect of that φing. Our assessments never get that far.[32]

---

[29] *Ibid.*

[30] Try, within the quotations in the text of this section, replacing 'responsibility' throughout with 'culpability'.

[31] In ordinary language, there is a natural association of moral responsibility with culpability, and my own usage is admittedly technical. Some may prefer to express the distinction in terms of D's being a 'moral agent' in respect of φing, and as such being eligible for moral appraisal (but not necessarily culpable) for φing. I avoid that alternative primarily because I think one can be morally responsible for an event without being an agent in respect of it. (See, e.g., A. P. Simester, 'On the So-called Requirement for Voluntary Action', *Buffalo Criminal Law Review*, 1 (1998), 403.) For present purposes, however, we can disregard that possibility because nothing here turns on it.

[32] This claim needs at least one qualification, to cover cases where an agent may be blameworthy for becoming incapable of controlling one's bodily movements – that is, where φing is a consequence of D's culpable antecedent μ-ing. See, e.g., A. P. Simester, J. R. Spencer, G. R. Sullivan and G. J. Virgo, *Simester and Sullivan's Criminal Law: Theory and Doctrine*, 4th edn (Oxford: Hart, 2010), §4.3(iii).

On this usage, to be morally responsible for an event is to be eligible for moral assessment in respect of that event's occurrence.[33] This is not the same thing as being culpable or praiseworthy for the event; rather, moral responsibility is a precondition, one that must be satisfied before we can proceed to those moral judgments. It is a necessary, but not a sufficient, condition of blame. As such, capacity conditions such as Hart's are generally relevant to moral responsibility; whereas questions of choice affect findings of culpability, and arise only after moral responsibility is established.

The distinction matters to choice-based accounts because there is a difference between defences that deny moral responsibility and defences that assert responsibility but deny blame.[34] Both are sometimes called 'excuses'. Both affect what Moore calls one's freedom of choice to avoid wrongdoing. But they do so in different ways. The former, which earlier I called 'irresponsibility' defences, are pure capacity-based defences, and are not subject to proportionality constraints. The latter – rationale-based excuses – are. An automaton does not have a choice to make, and is not a moral agent in respect of φing. A person acting under duress does, and is. In the latter case, we then inspect the reasonableness of that choice; whether his reasons reflect badly on him. For Moore, we have noted, what makes φing culpable is the actor's choice not to exercise the capacity he has to do otherwise. But irresponsibility defences tell us nothing about blame. They never get that far: they take the defendant out of the realm of moral agency, of agency susceptible of moral evaluation, altogether. By contrast, where φing is chosen, the structure of rationale-based excuses is closely tied to culpability assessments, and to the content of the choice that was made.

---

[33] It is also important to distinguish D's *moral* responsibility for φing, a *sine qua non* of her eligibility for blame, from other kinds of responsibility which may affect D's obligations to answer for her φing to others. I may not be legally responsible for failing to rescue a drowning person because, say, I owed no legal duty to do so. These latter kinds of responsibility depend on a different variety of arguments, including about what we owe to each other. Unlike moral responsibility, they are not foundational to culpability and can be set to one side here.

[34] Cf. Gardner, *Offences and Defences*, chs 4, 6; A. P. Simester, 'On Justifications and Excuses', in L. Zedner and J. Roberts (eds), *Principles and Values in Criminal Law and Criminal Justice: Essays in Honour of Andrew Ashworth* (Oxford University Press, 2012), p. 95.

B   Inadvertent negligence

But must φing be chosen? Others, not just Moore, think that it must.[35]
Certainly, culpability for inadvertent negligence does not fit easily with a
choice theory of blame. An actor cannot be blamed for negligently
'choosing' to φ, since inadvertent acts are not themselves chosen.[36] So
it should be no surprise that many writers, both before and after Moore,
have denied culpability – and indeed responsibility – for inadvertent
acts. John Mackie did so back in 1977:

> in so far as I am ignorant of what I am doing or bringing about, the
> actions which are for this reason unintentional can be seen not as
> belonging to me as a conscious agent, but to have been foisted upon or
> obtruded into my course of action by the facts or circumstances of which
> I was unaware.[37]

At the level of (what I have called) moral responsibility, this claim seems
too strong. Unintentional acts are capable of 'belonging' to me – at least
as long as they are voluntary and I am a conscious agent at the time of
doing them. Of course, that conclusion depends on what is the point of
an act's 'belonging' to a person. But for present purposes I take it that the
ascription of moral responsibility, or belongingness, serves to mark out
those acts that are tied to us *qua* moral agents: as agents with the rational
capacity to act for reasons, to act for them *qua* reasons, and to deliberate
about those reasons. This is why it is a condition of moral responsibility
that the actor be a moral agent. She must be the kind of agent who is
capable of recognising and acting upon reasons, who has at least a
general capacity to distinguish good reasons from bad, and who can
adjudicate between conflicting reasons, by weighing and contrasting
them, when deciding what to do.

   This differs foundationally from the position adopted by Mackie, and
by Moore. On their view, we are morally responsible only when we

---

[35] For example, J. W. C. Turner, 'The Mental Element of Crimes at Common Law', in
L. Radzinowicz and J. W. C. Turner (eds), *The Modern Approach to Criminal Law*
(London: Macmillan, 1948), p. 195; J. Hall, 'Negligent Behaviour Should be Excluded
from Criminal Liability', *Columbia Law Review*, 63 (1963), 632; C. Finkelstein,
'Responsibility for Unintended Consequences', *Ohio State Journal of Criminal Law*, 2
(2005), 579.

[36] They may be chosen under a different description: as when D deliberately fires a gun (µs)
while out hunting, but does not notice that her colleague has moved into her line of fire.
Here, D chooses to µ, but does not choose to φ (shoot her colleague), even though both
acts are constituted by the same bodily movements.

[37] J. L. Mackie, *Ethics: Inventing Right and Wrong* (London: Penguin, 1977), p. 210.

consciously exercise our capacity to act for reasons – it is only then that our acts truly belong to us as moral agents. So responsibility and fault can lie only when we choose to φ. By contrast, on the account offered here, we are moral agents not by virtue of exercising our rational capacities, but by virtue simply of *having* them. What counts, then, is whether D's φing is susceptible of control by D's rational capacities, not whether it occurs as a conscious exercise of that control.

So far, the difference is primarily formal. Separating the morally responsible from the chosen does not show that the distinction matters, that the gap is populated, that there can be blame without choice. Nonetheless, the gap is crucial. When D φs intentionally or recklessly, we can link our judgment about φing back to an evaluation of D for doing it by reference to D's choice to act for the wrong reasons, something that reflects badly on D *qua* moral agent. The point here is that there may be – and I think that there are – other ways in which inadvertent φing can be linked back to D, so as to reflect badly on D.

Chosen wrongdoing reflects badly on the actor because it shows that he prefers bad reasons to good ones. He would rather stab his opponent than walk away, and so on. By contrast, the complaint when D is negligent is, in a sense, that she fails to act for the right reasons. But this deficiency, too, can reflect badly upon her *qua* rational moral agent. This is because the capacity for rational deliberation does not just involve capacities to assess moral reasons (and act for undefeated ones); it also involves capacities to recognise them.

Reasons for action essentially involve two kinds of proposition: (1) that some outcome or goal is valuable; and (2) that some action (φing) will or may bring about the outcome or goal. When we blame D for choosing to φ, the grounds of our blaming judgment reside in conclusions about D's type (1) evaluations; in particular, that D has acted on personal preferences or evaluations at odds with those she should have acted upon. Such conclusions cannot be avoided if we are to have blaming practices at all, since the very idea of blame involves holding actors to a standard at least partially independent of their own values.[38] D's acting upon morally aberrant values reflects directly upon D and is, in itself, a ground of blame.

By contrast, when we blame D for negligently φing, the grounds for doing so reside in conclusions about type (2) propositions, concerning

---

[38] This is not to suggest that the standard is entirely independent, i.e., that what D ought to do is necessarily independent of what she prefers to do.

the possibility or likelihood that the relevant (undesirable) outcome will occur.[39] Explaining this presents a very different kind of problem from explaining why bad choices are culpable.

For convenience, we might label type (1) failings as *moral preference errors*, whereas type (2) failings might be called *epistemic failings*. An epistemic failing involves some sort of mistake, some inadvertence or ignorance. Since they are not directly concerned with moral evaluations, it is tempting to see type (2) failings as not being the stuff of blame. But that does not follow. There seems no general reason why the explanation of an actor's particular epistemic failing cannot reflect badly on her. Suppose, for example, that D is lying on the beach and does not think to check on her children who are playing in the water. The children drift too far out and are drowned. Here, we might blame D, not for choosing to allow the children to drown, but for failing to think about that risk. In such a case, had D evinced the care she should have shown for her children, *she would have thought* to check on them.

This is not just, although it involves an evaluation of what happened (that, unfortunately, D did not think of the risk and check on the children, with the result that they drowned). It is also an evaluation of D with respect to what happened. D's failure to think about the situation is blameworthy because it tells us about her; it reflects the fact that she lacks sufficient concern for the well-being of her children.[40] And that is a moral shortcoming in D.

I cannot explore such cases in depth here. However, the example serves to suggest that, depending how they came to be made, epistemic failings, too, are capable of reflecting badly on the actor. As such, they are capable of grounding blame. The underlying analysis of this is more complex than for choice-based blame, and nowhere near as direct. Most importantly, the connection between inadvertent φing and blame *does not run through choice*, even indirectly; since we cannot infer from a finding of negligence that D would have φed if she had seen the risk.

Negligence, then, demands a more detailed account of what kinds of failure to advert are culpable. That task is for a different article.[41] The point here is that it is possible. Blame can sometimes lie in D's failure to

---

[39] As was noted in section III.A, negligence may sometimes lie even though D has recognised the possibility of φing; i.e., where she has underestimated it, and the level of risk that D herself perceives is a reasonable one to run.

[40] Conversely, such an evaluation would not follow in cases where D is unaware of the risks at issue, and has no reason to be aware of them.

[41] See, e.g., Simester, 'Can Negligence be Culpable?'.

recognise a risk, where the root of that failure is a moral deficiency of her own preferences and values. Like chosen wrongdoing, the explanation of D's φing may reflect badly on her.

(Incidentally, it is worth observing that the distinction between moral preference and epistemic failings matters in other contexts too. One of the key implications of the distinction between justification and excuse is that chosen official action constituting a *prima facie* crime can normally only be justified. Individual actors may be excused for choosing to φ, on the grounds that their impermissible choice was blameless. But, *qua* officials, state actors cannot claim to be excused for an error of moral preference. Their chosen actions must be either permissible or not. Thus, official torture is inexcusable, even if – conceptually speaking – it might be justifiable.[42] At the same time, epistemic failing by officials is not foreclosed. Provided the official makes a reasonable mistake, for example, when intervening to prevent crime or adjudicating a hearing, the inadvertent error need not undermine the lawfulness of the decision.)

IV   A (thin) moral character flaw theory?

Culpability for negligence commits us to a 'thin' kind of character-based – more precisely, 'character trait' – theory of blame. Any plausible account of culpability for negligence must hold us to blame for our mistakes (only) when the roots of those mistakes lie in certain types of failings. So, for example, inadvertence arising from physical blindness or low intelligence is not normally blameworthy; whereas it may be culpable when arising from the actor's failure to care about his children. Sight and intelligence are not character traits.

At one level, the reference to moral 'character' here is conventional. It is a natural use of language to talk of character flaws, meaning those types of failing that can ground blame for wrongful acts. Low intelligence might comprise a shortfall by reference to standards of an 'ordinary' or average person, but it does not on that usage involve any shortcoming of moral character.[43]

---

[42] I develop these claims further in 'Necessity, Torture and the Rule of Law', in V. Ramraj (ed.), *Emergencies and the Limits of Legality* (Cambridge University Press, 2008), p. 289.

[43] In ordinary language, accusations of 'stupidity' do sometimes attribute culpability. Typically, in such cases, blame (unless misplaced) is not founded on having low intelligence *per se*: cf. Simester, 'Can Negligence be Culpable?' pp. 102–3.

Yet, whatever one calls it, the underlying distinction is one of substance. A moral character-based theory of culpability presents a genuine alternative to choice- and capacity-based theories. It draws a key distinction, being concerned to pick out those kinds of limitation in an actor that *constitute* grounds for ascribing culpability. 'I'm sorry, but I never liked my children,' does not foreclose blame. It founds it.

Suppose that, at the beach, P has been left in charge of a child who then swims too far out to sea and is drowned. Consider three kinds of explanation for P's failure to prevent this disaster:

(1) P fails to rescue the child because he has been paralysed after being attacked suddenly by a swarm of bees;
(2) owing to P's very low intelligence, he does not realise the risk;
(3) P does not pay attention to the child because his attention is absorbed entirely by a radio broadcast of England's winning a cricket match (*mirabile dictu!*).

Case (1) involves no moral responsibility for P's failure to rescue the child. As Hart saw, a capacity-based test of involuntariness shows that no moral evaluation of P is possible with respect to his failure to rescue the child. For that purpose, the event does not 'belong' to P.

Cases (2) and (3) are different. In case (2), when assessing P's potential culpability, our evaluation of P's failure to perceive the risk should be relativised to P's personal intellectual capacities. *But not in case (3).* There, P's failure rests in a flaw of moral character. He falls short of what we expect from a reasonable person, a person who exhibits appropriate – decent – levels of care and concern for those around him. Since this is a shortfall of moral character, blame follows. In case (3), the failure to meet a non-relativised, impersonal standard reflects badly on P, without more.

A   Punishment for character? An objection to mainstream character theories

It is important to emphasise that the kind of 'moral character flaw' theory advocated here is not the same as the kind rightly criticised by Moore, that claims – much more extremely – that blaming judgments are *for* our character traits or dispositions, and only derivatively for the acts that manifest them. As Moore asks:

why not punish people directly for bad character, since that is the locus of their just deserts? Why punish bad character indirectly, only through punishing actions expressive of it? ... If the character theory were correct, the answer given to Molière's Robespierre (when the latter asks why he is being condemned to death) should not be jarring: you are being condemned, Robespierre is told, 'Because you lack grace.' Yet the answer is jarring precisely because no one deserves to be punished for being a poor specimen of humanity ... I have yet to see how the character theorist can deny that character-responsibility alone makes it fair to punish, given his notion that character-responsibility is basic and act-responsibility only derivative.[44]

I agree. One can, of course, make moral evaluations of a person's character. Such a judgment is made here of Robespierre. But those are not blaming judgments. Moreover, blaming judgments do not start there. They start with wrongful acts, and end by linking those acts to a shortfall, a moral character flaw, in the actor. Not the other way around.

Criminal theorists might see an easier reply. There are familiar criminalisation objections to punishing for character alone. A theory of culpability should not be mistaken for a theory of liability. All the worries about enacting thought-crimes apply to punishment for character too. Those worries are compounded if one thinks, as I do (unlike Moore), that punishment is not the motivating purpose of the criminal law.[45] What comes first is the prohibition: and we certainly should not prohibit people from being who they are. Without harmful consequences of some sort, the state's regulatory role is not engaged. So it is no objection to any character theory of *blame* that the criminal law does not, and should not, punish for having a bad character.

But those criminalisation worries are supplementary. Even outside the law, moral evaluations of character flaws are not blaming judgments.[46] My claim, in other words, is not 'that character-responsibility is basic and act-responsibility only derivative'. Blame is *not*, ultimately, for the choice (or character, or whatever) that lies behind the act, as some

---

[44] Moore, 'Choice, Character and Excuse', pp. 55–6. It does not matter to the argument, but Molière died before Robespierre was born. My colleague at Cambridge, Nick McBride, suggests the reference may be misremembered from a Jean Anouilh play, *Poor Bitos*.

[45] A. P. Simester and A. von Hirsch, *Crimes, Harms, and Wrongs: On the Principles of Criminalisation* (Oxford: Hart, 2011), ch. 1.

[46] As it happens, I also think that punishment for mere flaws is unjustified. But this second claim, that punishment (like culpability) must be for φing rather than being, is too large to defend here. Part of the thought is that punishment should involve something for which D is answerable (especially, to the persons on whose behalf punishment is imposed) – and that excludes D's moral character traits, even the flawed ones.

writers seem to think. *Both* the act itself, and the moral flaw(s) by which it is explained, are basic.

Even were this conceded, Moore and Hurd have an administrative objection to the state's punishing according to character-based explanations of blame.[47] It is, they say, unworkable. The seriousness of a defendant's character flaws 'varies considerably across actors and circumstances in a way that defeats the ability of legislators to clearly codify them, and the ability of judges to ensure the like treatment of cases that are morally alike'.[48] Among other things, they think this generates a fair-warning problem, on the grounds that it becomes impossible to codify the law 'so as to make clear and predictable to citizens when and how much they will be punished if they inadvertently invade others' protected interests'.[49]

No one said it would be easy. Assessments of culpability are often highly nuanced, reflecting both the specific circumstances and nature of the wrongdoing itself; and the complex of attributes and motivational impulses of the agent that led her to φ. This is one reason why the state normally signals only a broad range of sentences when it prohibits φing, even as it undertakes to impose a more nuanced, desert-based punishment on particular offenders.[50] It can specify a range based on the general nature of φing, while delegating the more particular assessment *ex post* to a judge. This need not undermine the rule of law, at least not unduly. The criminal law cannot be expected to notify sanctions with exactitude, and its failure to do so hardly leaves potential wrongdoers bereft of notice. A combination of explicit and implicit, desert-based guidance is sufficient for citizens to know broadly where they stand, and how different kinds of φing are likely to be regarded.

Perhaps more importantly, though, much the same worry applies to choice-based wrongdoing. Moore and Hurd seemingly assume that culpability for choosing to φ is grounded in the literal choice itself – the moral preference error made in balancing reasons for and against φing – without more. Yet that may be doubted. Even blame for advertent wrongdoing is, and should be, sensitive to the underlying motivations and attitudes that led D to φ. Someone who does wrong reluctantly (say, because pressured by peers) may not be in the same moral case as

---

[47] Moore and Hurd, 'Punishing the Awkward, the Stupid, the Weak, and the Selfish', pp. 172–3.
[48] *Ibid.*, p. 173.   [49] *Ibid.*, p. 172.
[50] Simester and von Hirsch, *Crimes, Harms, and Wrongs*.

another who, in the same circumstances, does exactly the same wrong callously, or even relishing an opportunity to humiliate the victim. One who smothers his terminally ill parent in anguish is not equally culpable as another who, in identical circumstances, seizes the opportunity to inherit. If that is right, the bare choice is not the whole of the story. Nuanced punishment for φing will take account also of D's underlying motivations, and of how his emotions and values informed and structured the choice he made.[51] Maybe the matter is not quite as complex as it is for inadvertent wrongdoing. But if Moore's and Hurd's administrative worry is a serious one, it is hard to see why it does not apply to choice-based culpability too.

B   The 'out of character' objections

A more important objection to character theories, also pressed by Moore,[52] is the problem of 'out of character' wrongdoing. If the grounds for blame originate in a person's character (understood as a more permanent and stable set of values and dispositions), why do we blame persons whose wrongdoing is 'uncharacteristic' or atypical? Again, I agree with Moore. Isolated instances of wrongdoing, which do not reflect any general tendencies, are not immune from blame. The account presented here does not focus on the actor's own non-transient character, long term or otherwise. Rather, it investigates whether the explanation of her φing reflects badly on her, judged by reference to a generalised, not individualised, standard of character. Notice that much the same holds for chosen wrongdoing. Returning to the beach, suppose two new explanations:

> (4) Q fails to rescue the child because the child has been disobedient and Q is very angry with her. Q has never done such a thing before, and regrets his failure for the rest of his life.

In case (4), we might accept that Q's choice is out of character; although, more usually, such cases will merely reveal a latent aspect of Q's character in an original context.[53] Either way, however, that choice belongs to Q. Judged by reference to the values and priorities Q ought to have, Q falls short on this occasion. Consequently, his failure, however aberrant, is culpable.

---

[51] Cf. R. A. Duff, 'Choice, Character, and Criminal Liability', *Law and Philosophy*, 12 (1993), 345, 362.

[52] Moore, 'Choice, Character and Excuse', p. 57.

[53] See, e.g., Duff, 'Choice, Character, and Criminal Liability'.

Ultimately, therefore, the theory proffered here is not a 'character' theory of blame at all, at least not in the traditional sense. Perhaps we should not even call it a 'thin' type of character theory, although I hope the nature of the account is nonetheless clear. Yet one might still worry that, like some character-based theories, the theory is reductivist. *Contra* Gardner, I claimed that something more is required, in addition to the wrongfulness of φing, to ground blame. I rejected Hart's capacity conditions as doing that work. But if the extra ingredient can be transient and ephemeral, what does it amount to – especially since it is identified by a counterfactual test, of whether a person of good moral character would have done otherwise? Does this test really tell us anything about D? Does it identify any ground of blame, anything that culpability judgments can grip on? At least in Moore's account, one might think, there is something joining D to her φing, something capable of grounding blame. There is D's choice. Where here?

(One riposte is to suggest that Moore's account makes too much of 'choice' as a free-standing wellspring of blame, whereas it is better seen as a placeholder for the underlying moral preference errors, for aberrant values and attitudes that might themselves be ephemeral. As cases like *T* suggest,[54] choice only grounds blame to the extent that it too belongs to D. However, that reply does not meet the 'counterfactual' worry: it just spreads it around.)

Two thoughts by way of response. The first is that the move to blame is not merely a counterfactual one. On the theory articulated here, it involves a positive conclusion that D exhibited (on this occasion) some failing, some flaw of attitude, motivation, values, etc., that led to his epistemic failing. The failing is not *constituted* by the counterfactual. It is a matter of inference. So it is subject to explanations of how D came to φ that defray blame, and must be supported by evidence of a link between moral character flaws and inadvertence. It requires showing the extent to which failures to advert risks can be a function of how much we care about them, and about the interests at stake.[55] Establishing such a link may be probabilistic, admitting of varying levels of confidence.

The second point is to note that the attachment of blame may also, in a sense, be ephemeral. What counts is whether D exhibited some moral shortfall, some character flaw, *on that occasion* – in that moment of acting. Again, this point is tied to the insight that blame is for φing (and, indeed, for exhibiting some moral shortfall in φing); not for having a

---

[54] Discussed below in this section.   [55] Cf. Simester, 'Can Negligence be Culpable?'

poor character. This robs culpability of some depth as a concept, but seems inevitable if we are going to accept that basically good people can sometimes be blamed for momentarily doing wrong. That said, any theory of blame – whether concerned with choice or negligence – will have to leave space for radical disconnection. In *T*, for example,[56] D participated in a violent street robbery. Three days earlier, she had been brutally raped, and was suffering from post-traumatic stress disorder. At least at a superficial level, her conduct was deliberate. She was conscious and responsive to events.[57] Yet something was missing. Her conduct was disengaged from her own values and preferences,[58] and (it seems) unresponsive to any capacity to reason and deliberate about her conduct. Her choices, we may say, did not belong to her.

Distinguish this kind of case from changes in character. Again, this problem is common to advertent and inadvertent culpability. In the well-known example of Patty Hearst, the 18-year-old heiress to William Hearst's publishing empire was kidnapped by the self-styled Symbionese Liberation Army. While in lengthy captivity, during which she was subjected to a programme of abuse and indoctrination, she (unsurprisingly) experienced a personality change. Now endorsing her captors' values, she adopted a new name, Tania, and voluntarily joined in perpetrating an armed bank raid. Here, we cannot blame Patty for being who she became. On the usage identified earlier,[59] we should not even describe her as 'responsible' for being Tania.[60] But she is *answerable* for being who she now is, and open to blame for raiding the bank.

V   Reintegrating choice and character – and capacity?

It emerges from what has been said so far that, in the thin sense of moral character proposed here, choice and character theories are partially (if unidirectionally) reconcilable. Chosen wrongdoing is itself culpable to

---

[56] [1990] Crim LR 256. See J. Horder, 'Pleading Involuntary Lack of Capacity', *Cambridge Law Journal*, 52 (1993), 298, 312–15.

[57] The court allowed D to raise a claim of automatism, a congenial device that involved quite a stretch of legal doctrine.

[58] Potentially, this analysis would allow for cases where D rejects the values by which she is motivated, as in Harry Frankfurt's example of the unwilling drug addict: 'Freedom of the Will and the Concept of a Person', in *The Importance of What We Care About* (Cambridge University Press, 1988), pp. 11, 17.

[59] Above, section III.A.

[60] Cf. Moore, 'Choice, Character and Excuse', pp. 46–7. That qualification apart, I agree with Moore's analysis of this case.

the extent that the actor's choice falls short of what we would expect from
a person of good moral character. We can look behind choice as well as
inadvertence: neither generates culpability save to the extent it reflects
badly on the agent. Consider a final case:

> (5) R fails to rescue the child because he is afraid of cold water (or of a
> tarantula that sits between him and the water, or of the gunmen threat-
> ening the rest of his family, etc.).

In case (5) and its variants, the choice not to rescue the child *does* belong
to R. The excusatory power of duress-type scenarios does not rest on the
premise that, in such situations, the choice to φ does not truly belong to
the actor; that it is not really 'chosen'.

It is chosen. But we are offered a (potential) rationale-based excuse.
Whether R is culpable depends, in turn, on the reasonableness of that
excuse: on whether her choice reflects badly on her. At least where a
reasonable person – a person of decent character – would have acted as
did R, we cannot make the inference of shortcoming that would otherwise ground blame. In such cases, R's choice to act wrongfully merely
discloses an imperfect virtue, not a fault; a limitation characteristic of
humans in general, and not particular to R.

Yet we should not push this reconciliation too far. We should not, for
example, seek to claim that our moral character failings ground blame
because they are themselves, in some sense, chosen. Jean Hampton
makes a move of this variety in defending a choice-based account of
culpability, when she argues that culpable negligence is due to a faulty
character that D 'knew better than to develop in this way'.[61] So, for
example, if D makes a mistake because she is impatient, Hampton would
suggest that her culpability resides in an earlier choice to be an impatient
sort of person. But this is, surely, rarely true. Most of us do not choose to
be bad-tempered, impatient or otherwise flawed persons. Moreover, a
choice-based account requires not merely that the relevant characteristic
be chosen, but that *φing* be chosen. D must be aware of the risk. Thus, in
order to ground culpability for later acts of negligent φing, D's failure to
rectify her character would have to be chosen *in the awareness that* her
later φing is the sort of consequence that might ensue if she does not.
Hampton's analysis is artificial. We blame, rather, because impatience is

---

[61] J. Hampton, 'Mens Rea', *Social Philosophy and Policy*, 7 (1990), 1–28, at p. 27. Attempts
to explain culpability by reference to antecedent fault are nowadays known as 'tracing
strategies'. See Moore and Hurd, 'Punishing the Awkward, the Stupid, the Weak, and the
Selfish', pp. 176–82.

a dispositional trait for which we fault D directly. It is a weakness of moral character.

More generally, it is implicit in the 'thin' character theory of negligence advanced here that one's moral character traits need not be chosen. In practice, attitudes, preferences, values and the like do not usually develop self-consciously, except perhaps at the margins. Rather, they tend to emerge as the product of mixed inputs, including environment, upbringing and genetic inheritance. And moral character is largely settled by the time we become mature agents. Blaming judgments, at least of the kind we have considered here, are not sensitive to such questions. To blame D for φing is not to ask why D is someone who wants to φ, or someone who does not care about φing.[62] It is enough that, chosen or not, D's values and choices are hers. The practice of blaming assumes that D is a moral agent. It operates just to connect that moral agency, on this occasion, to D's wrongful act of φing.

This analysis makes key the category of moral characteristics. It makes them the only kind of shortfall that can ground blame. That such a category exists seems obvious, and necessary if culpability exists at all. The explanation, 'I'm just naturally selfish', grounds rather than excuses blame for φing. But what kinds of characteristic are moral ones? Earlier I noted that mistakes, even unreasonable ones, seem to be blameless where they arise from a lack of intelligence, and I do not think we are generally entitled to expect non-relativised intellectual capacities from wrongdoers. Like deafness, intelligence is not a moral character trait. But we still need an account of *which* incapacities can ground blame. That task lies beyond the scope of this chapter.

VI   Wrongfulness: backwards and forwards with blame

None of what has been said in this chapter contradicts Raz's suggestion that the grounds of blame originate in the guiding reasons not to φ. Indeed, at one level, that proposition seems incontrovertible. We should not choose to φ, and (I would say) we should take care not to φ, *because* φing is a bad thing to do.

Fair enough. Perhaps guiding reasons are primary. However, it is tempting to go further, and think they are primary *simpliciter*. They might, for example, seem to resolve questions of moral luck. After all, we cannot be blamed for φing unless we actually φed, and unless φing was

---

[62] Cf. R. Nozick, *Anarchy, State and Utopia* (New York: Basic Books, 1974), p. 225.

something that, objectively speaking, we ought not to have done. Hence, Gardner endorses a proportionality principle in punishment 'according to which the sentence should be in proportion to the offender's wrongful action, adjusted for his blameworthiness in respect of it'.[63]

I am not sure that follows. There is an important dimension of the idea of wrongfulness that has been concealed by the stipulative usage I have adopted in this chapter. Recall P the doctor, who blamelessly killed A. It is only true that 'P did something wrongful' in this stipulative sense. Killing A was, all things considered, undesirable. But it would be misleading in ordinary language to say that P 'acted wrongfully'.

Part of the distinction might seem to lie in which act we focus upon. Killing A may be inherently wrongful, at least when unjustified, but it is not inherently wrongful to inject A with a painkiller when he needs one. However, that insight does not carry us very far, because whether it is justified to inject the painkiller can also be said to depend on the (objective) guiding reasons for and against doing so; and, in particular, on the fact that injecting A will kill him.

A better way of thinking about the difference is to contrast *ex post* with *ex ante* perspectives. When it comes to blame, guiding reasons are not the only thing that is primary. Certainly, *ex post*, the raw fact of outcomes, lucky or otherwise, determines what we can be blamed for. Φing – killing A – is what P did. But that simple truth does not determine why, or to what extent, she is culpable for it. For that, we must look at P's situation *ex ante* – up to the moment she φs. We must look forward. We must ask, might a reasonable person, a person of decent moral character, have acted (chosen, etc.) like P?

The point is that blame does not originate simply in D's acting wrongfully (doing something that is all things considered undesirable), because it is not the case that, *ex ante, D should actually be guided* by the applicable guiding reasons.[64] D is not perfect or omniscient, and is not expected to be. Guiding reasons tell us whether φing is wrongful. But from the perspective of blame, what counts is D's *actual* practical reasoning when she φed.[65] (Did she choose badly? Did she fail to consider reasons that she should have?) From the perspective of *blame*, D's ultimate obligation is not, as such, to avoid φing *per se*. Her obligation is

---

[63] Gardner, *Offences and Defences*, p. 232.

[64] Hence, the possibility of being vindicated but unjustified.

[65] Importantly, this perspective also allows us to accommodate differentiation in D's reasoning between means, ends, side-effects, etc.

to avoid φing through a shortfall of moral character; to avoid φing in so far as that is reasonable for someone of her capacities.

In our example, P acted for defeated reasons that we would expect any reasonable person (*ex ante*) to act for. She gave the injection because she wanted to alleviate pain. Perhaps A was in extreme pain following a road accident, and it was impossible to test for allergies in the circumstances. P administered a standard palliative drug, but A was one of the very rare persons allergic to it. That A died is tragic. Yet it does not follow that P should refrain from administering the drug again, when confronted with someone in extreme pain who needs immediate palliative relief. Indeed, we would want her to make a similar choice in the future. From an *ex ante* perspective, there is a sense in which P did not fail. She carried out the injection in a manner beyond criticism. And after that, we all must trust to luck.

9

Mental disorder and sexual consent: Williams and after

JOHN STANTON-IFE*

I Introduction

'Every offence', warned Glanville Williams 'has the effect of diminishing the liberty of the defendant, but when a person is convicted on account of consensual activity the practical result is to restrict not only his liberty but that of the person with whom he acts.'[1] It is imperative that the criminal law should endeavour to fix the boundaries of consent correctly, no more so than in the specific context in which Williams was writing, namely, sexual offences against the mentally disordered. Mistakes in this context, in which it is so difficult to say what constitutes consent, are a special concern. Criminalising consensual sexual activity involving the mentally disordered, has the obvious unjust consequence of seriously restricting the liberty of the accused, who may or may not be mentally disordered him- or herself. It also – and this is Williams' main point in the quoted sentence – seriously restricts the liberty of the putative mentally disordered victim. He quoted with approval the view of some doctors that 'even severely impaired people have the right to express their sexuality and to enjoy tender and close relationships'. 'Mentally impaired men and women', he added, 'sometimes marry each other, and together achieve a greater degree of independence than either could do unaided.'[2] Presumably his thought was something like this: criminalise

---

* I am grateful to Dennis Baker and Jeremy Horder, as well as to the (other) organisers of and speakers and participants in the conference on which the volume is based. I received some helpful comments from Antje du-Bois Pedain, Peter Glazebrook and Kiron Reid, to which I have not as yet been able to do full justice; I also benefited from helpful discussion of the subject matter of this chapter with Grant Lamond and Susan Liebeschuetz and many discussions with Alan Bogg.
[1] Glanville Williams, *Textbook of Criminal Law*, 2nd edn (London: Stevens, 1983), p. 571.
[2] Williams, *Textbook*, p. 572.

certain conduct and the state impinges considerably on the availability of the option to persons in general. If sexual conduct involving mentally disordered adults is under certain conditions criminal, not only will that be a disincentive for anyone to engage in the conduct themselves, it will also be a disincentive for third parties as well, for example, staff at care homes, who may conclude they should not encourage such activity and should prevent it where they can. Consent, Williams was implying, has two functions: one protective, the other facilitative. As far as the first is concerned, insisting, with the criminal law as backup, that sexual conduct be consensual protects the freedom of persons from wrongful interference. This point would be readily and widely acknowledged. But it is easier to forget the second function of consent, that wrongly or clumsily criminalising what is, or may in fact be, consensual behaviour can interfere with persons' freedom to engage in activity that is not wrongful and may be valuable. The attempt to protect persons may actually result in harm to their interests. For consent, properly drawn, facilitates freedom too.

A useful warning, one might say. Successive legislators should take note. However, for all that, Williams does not point to any grave problem if consent *has* in its essentials been correctly identified and deployed in the sexual offences involving mentally disordered persons. And this takes us to the question of what it would be to identify the minimum conditions for a valid consent. What are the minimum capacities necessary for it to be possible for a severely mentally disordered adult to give a valid consent? In asking this one immediately runs into the issue of where the threshold for consent should be set. If one fixes the threshold at a relatively low point, so more sexual activity counts as consensual, one is likely to respect more fully the freedom of the mentally disordered persons in question, what we above called the facilitative aspect of consent, but may lose something of the effectiveness of the protective function. On the other hand, if one fixes the threshold at a relatively high point, so less sexual activity counts as consensual, one may achieve more protection at the cost of the sexual freedoms of the mentally disordered persons concerned. Williams favoured the former option: the threshold should be fixed at a relatively low point. The two reasons he gave for this in 1983 were 'First, this is necessary to prevent men who have intercourse with willing but sexually innocent girls from being convicted of rape. Second, it is necessary in order not to forbid sexual expression to women of low intelligence.'[3] As we will see much has changed in the scope and

---

[3] Williams, *Textbook*, p. 571.

nature of the sexual offences since Williams was writing. Williams refers in the just quoted passage only to the offence of rape, but section 30 of the Sexual Offences Act 2003 takes in all potential sexual touching, from what would constitute rape, to kissing and cuddling and everything in between. Moreover, while some ways of committing the offence under section 30 can be carried out only by male defendants the offence in general can be perpetrated by persons of either sex. Victims can be of either sex. My main focus in what follows, with these changes and others in mind, is with Williams' concern with the risk that the law wrongfully forbids sexual activity by means of a misplacing of the threshold for a valid consent.[4]

Below I examine four legal tests for attempting to fix the threshold at which a severely mentally disordered person can give a valid consent to sexual activity. I will have in mind the criminal law of England and Wales, though one of the four understandings I consider is from Australia. There are at least two common law understandings of the minimum conditions for consent that date back to the nineteenth century.[5] Both focus on the relationship between humans and other animals. I shall label the first the 'animal instincts' test. It is derived from R. v. Fletcher,[6] and suggests that a consent can be produced by 'animal instinct'. The second I will call the 'reasoning will' test. Its origin is with the judgment of Palles CB in R. v. Dee, who emphasised the differences between humans and animals. In Palles CB's words: 'Consent is the act of man, in his character of a rational and intelligent being, not in that of an animal. It must proceed from the will . . . sufficiently enlightened by the intellect to make such consent the act of a reasoning being.'[7] Far superior to any understanding developed in Victorian times was, at least in Williams' view,[8] a test that was Victorian in a different sense, namely, that it emanated from the Supreme Court of Victoria in Australia. This

---

[4] Because I believe that s. 30 of the 2003 Act fails to fix the balance correctly between what are described above as the protective and facilitative functions of consent, emphasising the former at the expense of the latter, my focus will exclusively be on the latter. That should certainly not be taken to imply that the protective function of consent is unimportant. Quite the reverse. For some disturbing figures on sexual offences against the mentally disordered, see Peter Rook and Robert Ward, Sexual Offences: Law and Practice, 4th edn (London: Thomson Reuters, 2010), pp. 331–2.

[5] Jennifer Temkin, Rape and the Legal Process, 2nd edn (Oxford University Press, 2002), pp. 112–13.

[6] R. v. Richard Fletcher (1859) Bell 63.   [7] R. v. Dee (1884) 15 Cox CC 579, at p. 593.

[8] And that of Munby J in X City Council v. MB, NA and MAB [2006] EWHC 168 (Fam), para. 73.

was the test contained in *Morgan*,[9] turning on knowledge of the physical facts of the sexual activity in question and knowledge of its sexual nature. As we will see, Williams thought the test would improve with a modification. I will refer to it as the 'physical facts' test. The final test – I shall call it the 'foreseeable consequences' test – is the recent one laid down in section 30 of the Sexual Offences Act 2003. The most important component of this test is the notion of sufficient understanding of the nature and reasonably foreseeable consequences of what is being done in a specific act of sexual touching. The title of this chapter refers to Williams and to what came after he wrote. It may seem odd, then, that three of the tests I am proposing to examine came *before* he was writing, two before he was born. However, I hope to show that there is something to be learned from the confrontation of the new thinking with the old, with Williams positioned somewhere in between.

II   Setting a high threshold: the Sexual Offences Act 2003

I begin with the most recent test, from section 30 of the Sexual Offences Act 2003, the test that sets the threshold at the highest point of the four. This will first require a quick word about one of the other tests, the animal instincts test, which we examine more fully in section VI. It is clear that one of the major motivations in including specific new provisions governing sexual offences against the mentally disordered in the general overhaul of sexual offences in 2003 was the desire to dispense with the *Fletcher* animal instincts test. This had much to do with the fact that the test appears to have been applied in the unreported case of *R. v. Jenkins* in January 2000, something which caused a degree of disquiet.[10] Negatively at least *Fletcher* has influenced the current law.

In *Jenkins* the defendant was a support care worker at a residential unit providing supported housing for about one hundred adults with learning disabilities in London. He admitted having a sexual relationship with a

---

[9] [1970] VR 337 (SC Vic).

[10] Though unreported *R. v. Jenkins* is well documented. Home Office, *Setting the Boundaries: Reforming the Law on Sex Offences*, July 2002, 4.2.4; Law Commission, *Consent in Sex Offences*, Report to the Home Office Sex Offences Review, 27 July 2000; *Hansard*, HL, vol. 647, col. 395, Lord Adebowale (People's Peer), 10 April 2003; and Clare Dyer, 'Care Worker's Release on Rape Charge Prompts CPS to Seek Review of Law', *The Guardian*, 24 January 2000, p. 5. There is also an interesting discussion of the case in relation to issues of paternalism in A. P. Simester and A. von Hirsch, *Crimes, Harms and Wrongs: On the Principles of Criminalisation* (Oxford: Hart, 2011), pp. 173–5.

woman said to have a mental age of under three after she was found to be pregnant and DNA testing had implicated him. He was charged with rape. The judge, it seems, ruled that there was no reason in law why a severely impaired woman should not consent to sex and that the woman could have consented by way of her animal instincts according to the *Fletcher* test. Speaking in the legislative branch of the House of Lords prior to the passing of the 2003 Act, Lord Adebowale (a People's Peer) argued that the facts in *Jenkins* plainly establish the lack of capacity to consent on the part of the learning-disabled woman. He concluded: 'This case alone is a stark reminder of the need for new legislation and for laws to ensure that those who cannot consent have absolute protection of the law.' *Jenkins* was alarming, Adebowale thought, 'not only because it would allow abusers to claim that sexual relations are not abusive, but also because it dehumanises the person with a learning disability and robs them of their privacy and dignity.'[11]

Moreover, according to the report of the Home Office Steering Committee, published in 2002, which led to the Sexual Offences Act 2003, the failure of the prosecution in *Jenkins* established the importance of avoiding any use of 'consent' in the definition of any proposed new offence. In the words of the report:

> The lack of a clear definition in law of capacity to consent to sex makes it particularly hard to prosecute the most serious sex offences such as rape (which rely on proving lack of consent) when the victim is severely impaired and where there is no definition of capacity to consent. The purpose of the law, to protect the most vulnerable, can be lost in consideration of whether or not *actively expressing sexuality* was actually consent. In one recent case (*R. v. Jenkins*), it was held that there was no reason in law why a severely impaired woman should not consent to sex. That is why those offences [i.e., those proposed for adoption in new legislation] intended to protect severely mentally impaired people do not require consent to be proved.[12]

Section 30 of the 2003 Act was to dispense with the requirement that the prosecution prove a lack of consent on the part of the alleged victim. But I have here cited these words from the Home Office Steering Committee and, before that, those of Lord Adebowale in the House of Lords to illustrate the general hostility towards the animal instincts test. It is also interesting to note from the Home Office Steering Committee passage

---

[11] *Hansard*, HL, vol. 647, col. 395, 10 April 2003.
[12] Home Office, *Setting the Boundaries: Reforming the Law on Sex Offences*, July 2002, 4.2.4 (emphasis in the original, last parenthesis added).

just cited that it takes *the* purpose of the law to be to protect the most vulnerable. We saw in the introduction to this chapter that Williams wished to stress a further key purpose of the law of sexual consent, not only to protect but also to facilitate sexual freedom simply by refraining from criminalising certain activity.[13] Lord Adebowale also appears to leave this latter issue out of consideration. Plainly, he is right that the imposition of non-consensual sexual touching on a learning disabled person is a robbery of privacy and dignity and is dehumanising. Unlike Williams, however, he does not appear to notice that these consequences are also risked by forbidding certain sexual activity to such people.

The Sexual Offences Act created a highly complicated series of offences relating to the mentally disordered victim, contained in sections 30–41. Four offences relate to mentally disordered persons who are 'unable to refuse' their consent; four relate to mentally disordered people who are able to agree to sexual activity, but in circumstances in which the agreement is obtained by inducement, threat or deception; and the final batch concern offences perpetrated by care workers. I shall restrict myself to a consideration of section 30, the first and most general of the offences against the mentally disordered.[14] In a nutshell, section 30 proscribes the sexual touching of mentally disordered persons who are unable to refuse consent. My main aim in considering section 30[15] is to

---

[13] To be fair, the Home Office Steering Committee begins its chapter on 'Vulnerable People', with the following words: 'We considered that vulnerable adults shared the universal right to a private life which is specifically protected by the European Convention on Human Rights, and that private life can include a sexual life. On the other hand, those who are vulnerable to exploitation have to be protected by the law', *Setting the Boundaries*, 4.1.3. However, by the time we reach the passage from that chapter quoted in the text the former consideration appears to have fallen entirely out of consideration.

[14] For an account of the offences in general, see Peter Rook and Robert Ward, *Sexual Offences: Law and Practice*, 4th edn (London: Thomson Reuters, 2010), pp. 331–96.

[15] According to s (30)(1) of the Sexual Offences Act, a person (A) commits an offence if:
    (a) he intentionally touches another person (B);
    (b) the touching is sexual;
    (c) B is unable to refuse because of or for a reason relating to a mental disorder; and
    (d) A knows or could reasonably be expected to know that B has a mental disorder and that because of it or for a reason related to it B is likely to be unable to refuse.
Section 30(3) deals with sentences available to a judge on conviction:

    (3) A person guilty of an offence under this section, if the touching involved:

ask where it fixes the threshold for valid consent on the part of a mentally disordered person. First, it is important to note some preliminary points. The wording of the main body of the offence is reproduced in footnote 15. The title given to the offence in the statute is somewhat long-winded: 'Sexual Activity with a Person with a Mental Disorder Impeding Choice'. It is also misleading. The words of the section itself make no mention of choice being 'impeded' or of 'impediments' to choice. Moreover, an impediment is an obstruction, not a barrier; someone with a speech impediment is not someone who cannot speak at all. By contrast, the wording of the section is couched in terms of victims who are 'unable to refuse', that is, barred, blocked or precluded from consenting, not merely impeded. In other words, the situation envisaged is not of someone who consents against the odds or consents with great difficulty; it is of someone who cannot consent at all. The term 'impeding' is thus best ignored.

The conduct element of the offence is met by the intentional touching of another person where the touching is sexual and where the person in question is unable to refuse because of or for a reason relating to a mental disorder. As briefly noted in the Introduction, the offence is extremely wide, covering any form of sexual touching. It is among the most serious it is possible to commit: a sentence of fourteen years can be imposed if the touching is not penetrative, and up to life is available to the judge if the touching is penetrative. Though it contains some interesting issues, I will not here consider the fault element,[16] but turn now to the idea of 'refusal-incapability'.

III   Refusal-incapability

One of the most striking features of the offence in section 30 is that consent is ushered off the scene and replaced with the idea of capacity to

    (a) penetration of B's anus or vagina with a part of A's body or anything else;
    (b) penetration of B's mouth with A's penis;
    (c) penetration of A's anus or vagina with a part of B's body; or
    (d) penetration of A's mouth with B's penis,
is liable, on conviction on indictment, to imprisonment for life.
    (4) Unless subsection (3) applies, a person guilty of an offence under this section is liable:
        (a) on summary conviction, to imprisonment for a term not exceeding 6 months or to a fine not exceeding the statutory maximum or both;
        (b) on conviction on indictment, to imprisonment for a term not exceeding 14 years.
[16] But see Williams, *Textbook*, pp. 571–2 for comment on the fault element which would be pertinent also to s. 30 of the 2003 Act.

consent, or to use the actual terminology, capacity to refuse. Sexual offences, as Williams was certainly assuming, normally contain a clause requiring the absence of consent. The best known offences in the 2003 Act indeed follow this model. The offences of sexual assault, assault by penetration and rape all contain as part of their respective definitions the clause: 'A person (A) commits an offence if . . . (B) does not consent to the penetration/touching.'[17] In place of this, section 30 requires that (B) is 'unable to refuse because of or for a reason relating to a mental disorder'.

What guidance is given by the Act as far as the meaning of refusal-incapability is concerned? According to section 30(2):

> (2) B is unable to refuse if – (a) he lacks the capacity to choose whether to agree to the touching (whether because he lacks sufficient understanding of the nature or reasonably foreseeable consequences of what is being done, or for any other reason), or (b) he is unable to communicate such a choice to A.

Being 'unable to refuse', then, is glossed in terms of *a lack of capacity to choose to agree*. The section can be broken down into a set of conditions, each one sufficient for refusal-incapability in this sense.

(1) B is refusal-incapable if he lacks sufficient understanding of the nature of what is being done.
(2) B is refusal-incapable if he lacks sufficient understanding of the reasonably foreseeable consequences of what is being done.
(3) B, though capable of choosing whether to agree to A's touching, is unable to communicate such a choice to A.
(4) B is refusal-incapable if he is unable to choose to agree for any (other) reason.

(4) makes it clear, if it was not already, that (1)–(3) are sufficient conditions for refusal-incapability, not necessary conditions. The courts may find refusal-incapability for any (other) reason; that is left open. (3) makes it clear that while refusal-incapability is largely conceived as a question of the mental state of B, the complainant, it is not entirely so. For if A, the defendant, has no way of establishing B's mental state even if B is in fact choosing internally to agree, A has no defence.

The conditions in (1) and (2) appear to be the most significant and I now consider how one might understand each of them.

---

[17] Sexual Offences Act, ss. 1–3.

IV 'Sufficient understanding of the nature of what
is being done'

The requirement of sufficient understanding of the nature of the activity presumably relates to the *sexual* nature of the conduct. That the touching is sexual has – as we have seen – also to be established as part of the conduct element of the offence by virtue of section 30(1)(b); the present section makes clear that if B does not understand that what is proposed is sexual, nothing he or she does, or thinks or wants can constitute capacity for consent. When does B understand sufficiently that what is being done is sexual? Are we to understand 'sexual' here in the same way as it is understood in section 30(1)(b) and in the Act in general? The general meaning of 'sexual' in the Act appears in section 78:

> penetration, touching or any other activity is sexual if a reasonable person would consider that (a) whatever its circumstances or any person's purpose in relation to it, it is because of its nature sexual, or (b) because of its nature it may be sexual and because of its circumstances or the purpose of any person in relation to it (or both) it is sexual.

If we are simply to borrow this definition for the purposes of section 30(2), B will understand the (sexual) nature of the behaviour if a reasonable person would think it sexual. More subtly, where a reasonable person would be in some doubt as to whether the activity is sexual, but would think it a possibility that it is, B will need to be able to read the purposes of A and the circumstances of the touching. This may be especially difficult for a mentally disordered person. In *Gosling*, for example, A temporarily placed plastic bags over B's head and took photographs of B, which he admitted was for his later sexual gratification.[18] Had B been a mentally disordered person, there may be extra reason to doubt that she or he appreciated the nature of the activity. Again, it is usually clear to most adults what the difference is between an affectionate caress and a sexual caress. As Roger Scruton puts it: 'A caress of affection is a gesture of reassurance – an attempt to place in the consciousness of the other an image of one's own tender concern for him. Not so, however, the caress of desire, which *outlines* the body of the recipient; its gentleness is not that of reassurance only, but that of

---

[18] *Gosling*, unreported, 4 November 1999 (No. 99/1266/Z5), cited in Peter Rook and Robert Ward, *Sexual Offences: Law and Practice*, 3rd edn (London: Thomson Reuters, 2004), para. 2.65, p. 90.

exploration.'[19] Plainly, it will take some degree of experience and mental capacity on the part of a mentally disordered person to discern the difference.

V   'Sufficient understanding of the reasonably foreseeable consequences of what is being done'

B, if mentally disordered, is refusal-incapable if she or he lacks sufficient understanding of *the reasonably foreseeable consequences* of what is being done. The phrase 'reasonably foreseeable consequences' suggests consequences as seen by the reasonable person, albeit only in 'sufficient' measure. What, then, are the reasonably foreseeable consequences of engaging in sexual touching?

In the case of penetrative, vaginal sex, one obvious consequence is the possibility of pregnancy. There has been much controversy in the last twenty years or so over the question of birth control for mentally disordered women with little or no understanding of the available options: be that the contraceptive pill, perhaps administered by another; or an implantable or injectable contraceptive involving procedures that need to be repeated periodically; or an intra-uterine device, the use of which may not be straightforward in someone who has not had children already; or, most controversially, sterilisation.[20] Presumably, sufficient understanding of the 'reasonably foreseeable consequences' of penetrative, vaginal sex must stretch to knowledge of the possibility of pregnancy and what that involves if the resulting foetus is brought to term. It would also need, presumably, to stretch to some minimal knowledge of the contraceptive possibilities, perhaps involving the help of another. More generally, another relevant consequence, particularly in relation to penetrative sex, but not, of course, restricted to cases where B is a woman, is the possibility of disease.

A third relevant consequence is an especially wide-ranging one given the wide scope of section 30, covering all sexual touching. It is the emotional vulnerability that comes with sexual relations of any sort. Most obviously when people begin to touch one another sexually both parties or one of them becomes vulnerable emotionally to how he or she is treated by the other. From being treated royally one day, one can be

---

[19] Roger Scruton, *Sexual Desire* (London: Continuum, 2006), p. 23 (original emphasis).
[20] I am grateful to Dr Susan Liebeschuetz of Newham Hospital, London for explaining some of the options.

ignored the next. One can be exploited or toyed with in a variety of ways. All this is common human experience; one can be left confused, disorientated and severely depressed (or elated) by the subsequent behaviour of the person with whom one has engaged in sexual touching. When befalling those with very severe mental disorders, this familiar human phenomenon takes on a special poignancy. The section appears to imply that B must have the capacity to comprehend these common tendencies in order to have the capacity to consent. Apart from the most obvious aspect of emotional vulnerability – vulnerability to how A treats B – Niko Kolodny has pointed to a more subtle aspect of emotional vulnerability:

> To say that A is emotionally vulnerable to B . . . is to say, in part, that A is disposed to have a range of favourable emotions in response to A's belief that B . . . has fared or will fare well, and a range of unfavourable emotions in response to A's beliefs that B . . . has fared or will fare poorly. For example, A may feel content when B is well, elated when B meets with unexpected good luck, anxious when it seems that B may come to harm, grief-stricken when B does.[21]

Autonomous adults are aware more or less explicitly of this possible consequence of sexual relations. Ordinary teenagers on the way to becoming fully autonomous learn for the most part that sexual touching brings with it such emotional vulnerability, and in turn brings the power to exploit others. Teenagers, as part of growing up, learn, one hopes, not to exploit the power that comes with the emotional vulnerability of those with whom they are engaging in sexual touching. But how essential is understanding of emotional vulnerability in relation to the lighter forms of non-penetrative sexual touching? How much does it matter, in relation to this lighter touching in particular, whether a mentally disordered person understands, as a relationship becomes more intimate, that this opens her up to emotional vulnerability? Does it matter as much as section 30 appears to imply, to the extent that this added intimacy ought not to be allowed to develop at all?

One could explore more potential candidates for 'reasonably foreseeable consequences of engaging in sexual touching', such as an understanding of the offence that may be caused by carrying out sexual activity

---

[21] Niko Kolodny, 'Love as Valuing a Relationship', *Philosophical Review*, 112 (2003), 135–89, at p. 152.

in public, but we should have said enough by now for it to be abundantly clear that the test is highly *cognitive* in nature. If a mentally disordered person does not have much in the way of understanding of the nature or reasonably foreseeable consequences of any form of sexual touching, he or she lacks the capacity to give, or as the statutory term has it, refuse a consent to it. Its cognitive nature becomes especially evident because the question being asked is not the usual one 'did B consent?'. It is 'did B have the capacity to consent (or refuse)', which turns on what B understood, not what B wanted.

We have seen, then, that no official minimum threshold for consent is set by the section 30 offence. Indirectly, however it is fairly clear where the boundary is. A mentally disordered person who does not have sufficient understanding of the nature or reasonably foreseeable consequences of a given form of sexual touching cannot issue a legally valid consent to sexual touching. If that person never has such understanding that person can never give a valid consent to any form of sexual touching. We mentioned at the outset Williams' concern that 'even severely impaired people have the right to express their sexuality and to enjoy tender and close relationships?'[22] Section 30, however, appears to have the implication that two mentally disordered persons who form an attachment with one another, but in which one or both lacks some of the understanding discussed above, are engaging in criminal behaviour. It seems to be irrelevant as far as the law is concerned whether or not the conduct is mutually desired. That A wishes to touch B and B wishes to be touched by A is neither here nor there if the understanding of one or the other is limited in one of the relevant ways.

Should the cognitive question of what is or is not understood have so much significance? In the case of mutually desired sexual touching of any sort between mentally disordered persons who may not have much of an understanding of the reasonably foreseeable consequences of the touching, it seems plausible to suggest that the key consideration should rather be whether such touching is in the best interests of the person concerned. It might, of course, not be. It may, for example, be exploitative, as where a group of males goad each other to see how far each can go sexually with a mentally disordered woman, who understands little but appears to be enjoying the attention. That is clearly different from Williams' 'tender and close relationship'. It is a serious problem with section 30 that it does not mark the difference between these very different kinds of case; that it

---

[22] Williams, *Textbook*, p. 572.

does not identify a form of behaviour that is itself wrong as opposed to wrong only if other elements not contained in the section, such as exploitation, are part of the story. The Home Office Steering Committee, as previously noted, remarked that 'the purpose of the law, to protect the most vulnerable, can be lost in consideration of whether or not actively expressing sexuality was actually consent'.[23] But one might wonder if some important component of *consent* is itself being lost in consideration of what should be done to protect mentally disordered people. To consider this and other matters further let us now ask what Williams' own view was apropos where the threshold for consent should be set.

VI   Low threshold tests: Williams and animal instinct

We have mentioned already that Williams thought the threshold for the sexual consent of a mentally disordered person ought to be set relatively low. Let us now spell out the test he supported. According to him, the best test available in the common law was the Australian case of *Morgan*:[24]

> *Morgan* test: B must both know the physical facts and know that the [act] is sexual; failing either knowledge, B does not consent in law.

While he thought this the best test available, he doubted the necessity of the second kind of knowledge mentioned in it, knowledge that the act is sexual.[25] Understanding the physical facts alone should, Williams thought, be enough. Accordingly, he seemed to settle on the following, certainly minimal, test:

> *Morgan*-minus test: B must know the physical facts; failing such knowledge, B does not consent in law.

We noted above the desire on the part of the Home Office Steering Committee to reject the low threshold *Fletcher* 'animal instincts' test. Williams, too, dismissed the *Fletcher* test as 'not to the purpose' and added that *Morgan* was 'greatly superior'.[26] However, given it is the *Morgan*-minus test that Williams appears to endorse, it is not at all clear how that test differs from the animal instinct test. For one thing,

[23] Home Office, *Setting the Boundaries: Reforming the Law on Sex Offences*, July 2002, 4.2.4.
[24] [1970] VR 337 (SC Vic).   [25] Williams, *Textbook*, p. 571, n. 2.
[26] Williams, *Textbook*, p. 571, n. 2.

Jennifer Temkin's interpretation of the 'animal instinct' test in *Fletcher* seems to be more or less identical to Williams' *Morgan*-minus test. A consent produced by animal instinct, according to Temkin (in the specific context of a charge of rape) meant:

> that no knowledge or understanding of the meaning or implications of sexual relations was necessary, provided that [B] appreciated that the defendant intended to insert his penis into her vagina.[27]

Many non-human animals, it would seem, can appreciate perfectly well, if non-linguistically, that some part of another entity's anatomy is about to have some causal effect on its own. When my son plays rough-and-tumble with the dog, the dog is very much aware that his arms are about to grab around her neck; that is why she moves sharply and swiftly out of the way, so that he falls over and she can jump on him – all part of the game. Interestingly, as we saw was the case in section 30 of the Sexual Offences Act, the explanation of consent and the threshold for the capacity to consent is in *Morgan* again couched in cognitive terms. What is to be understood is here much more modest, but still the focus is on understanding and not on something else such as desire. *Fletcher*, as mentioned above, appeared to have been significant, if only as something to avoid, in the preparation and passage through Parliament of the Sexual Offences Act. But with the exception of Temkin, whom we have just cited, and Simester and Sullivan, whom we cite below, there seems to have been no attempt to state what 'a consent produced by animal instinct' could and might mean. It now also appears that Williams' '*Morgan*-minus' test may well come down to the same thing as the animal instinct test.

Let us now try then to examine this idea in more detail than is usual. In attempting to understand the idea it might be helpful to take its key words, 'consent', 'animal' and 'instinct' separately. It is surely the word 'animal' that has led to the vilification of the test we noted earlier. Simply stating the test with enough emphasis on 'animal' has been thought enough to establish what is wrong with it. Likening a mentally disordered human in any way to an animal, may seem insulting, hinting at a revolting belief that mentally disordered persons are subhuman, to be regarded and perhaps even treated as such. Of course, if that *is* what the test implies, it deserves all the criticism it has received and a lot more besides. It is axiomatic that we owe equal concern and respect, in Ronald

---

[27] Temkin, *Rape and the Legal Process*, p. 113.

Dworkin's famous phrase, to all.[28] On the other hand, one might think that such a reaction to *Fletcher* is wide of the mark and over the top. Such a response might run in the following way. We are *all* animals. No human has ever escaped that fate. Besides, one loses nothing of the relevant sense of 'a consent by way of animal instinct' if we drop the term 'animal' altogether and speak instead of 'a consent by way of *human* instinct'. Again, quite apart from the fact that there is an appropriate way to view and treat all humans, there is an appropriate way to view and treat non-human animals and any hint to the contrary should also be resisted. In sum, attending to something like a consent by way of animal, more specifically human, instinct may well be a way of granting respect and concern to some aspect of a person that is worthy of respect and concern. It is to focus on the capacities and abilities, indeed the lives, of the individuals concerned.

As for the word 'consent', it may seem out of place in any discussion of non-humans. It is interesting to note that Charles Darwin for one used the term in relation to non-human animals. *Fletcher* was decided in the same year (1859) as the publication of Darwin's best known work, *On the Origin of Species*.[29] In asking how the *Fletcher* test might be best interpreted, however, I am not asking the historical question of what those who devised the test might have meant by it – whether they were influenced by Darwinian or other ideas, for example. But it is interesting to wonder, albeit briefly, what bearing classic Darwinian thinking might have on the question. One of Darwin's many aims was to illuminate aspects of human behaviour by means of comparison with the behaviour of other animals. A consent by way of animal instinct is based on the idea that there are instincts shared by humans and animals. Together with animals, Darwin wrote in his later *The Descent of Man*, 'man has ... some few instincts in common, as those of self-preservation, sexual love, the love of the mother for her new-born offspring, the power possessed by the latter of sucking, and so forth'.[30] As mentioned above, he also found nothing amiss in speaking of consent in relation to animal sexual activity, or of the 'consenting party', although as one would expect

---

[28] Ronald Dworkin, *Taking Rights Seriously* (Cambridge, MA: Harvard University Press, 1977), p. 180. Alternatively put, for those who do not believe in the intrinsic value of equality, we owe appropriate concern and respect to each and every person.
[29] Charles Darwin, *On the Origin of Species* (London: John Murray, 1859).
[30] Charles Darwin, *The Descent of Man and Selection in Relation to Sex*, vol. I (London: John Murray, 1871), ch. II, 'Comparison of the Mental Powers of the Lower Animals'.

consent is not taken by him to have the normative role in the realm of non-human animals as it does for humans.[31] Broadly, Darwinian theory understood animal sexual behaviour according to two models and one might loosely distinguish them by a notion of consent. Male animals, Darwin thought, seek to gain advantage over other males of their own species in two different ways, now sometimes distinguished by ethologists, respectively, by the terms 'intrasexual selection' and 'intersexual selection'. First, a male may fight other males for access to females (intrasexual selection). Second, males may compete indirectly with each other by means of displays made to females or by means of adornments (intersexual selection).[32] The red deer illustrates the first model. Red deer stags grow antlers each year and directly challenge each other for ownership of females, which have no antlers and are herded into harems by successful males. 'The females have little or no choice of sexual partner because the males defend their harems against possible rivals.'[33] The second model was conceived by Darwin as revolving around 'choice exerted by the female'.[34] Here the male seeks to attract the female through displays or adornments, such as the enormous colourful tail of the peacock. Outside of the breeding season a male African Paradise bird, to give another example, looks much like the female; during the season the male, unlike the female, develops elaborate plumage.[35]

On this Darwinian understanding, therefore, there can in a sense be both consensual – where a peahen rejects one peacock in favour of another – and non-consensual activity – where a red deer female is to have the attention of the dominant male whether wanted or not. As already mentioned, the notion of consent is not intended by the ethologists in the normative sense in which it is used, as it must, and rightly, should be used in the human context, but it is interesting to note that even in this non-human context the notion of consent seems to have some clear limits. The activity in question cannot be unwanted and it needs to be with a specific other. Speaking of the *Fletcher* 'animal

---

[31] Darwin, *The Descent of Man*, e.g., in ch. XI, 'Summary and Concluding Remarks on Insects'.

[32] David McFarland, *Animal Behaviour*, 3rd edn (Harlow: Pearson Prentice Hall, 1999), pp. 103–4.

[33] McFarland, *Animal Behaviour*, p. 103.

[34] Darwin, *The Descent of Man*, 'Choice exerted by the Female' is a subheading of ch. VIII, 'Principles of Sexual Selection'.

[35] McFarland, *Animal Behaviour*, p. 107.

instincts' test, Simester and Sullivan suggest that it would be unacceptable for a defendant to be able to defend himself 'by raising the possibility
of sexual arousal' on the part of a learning disabled person prior to the
sexual activity in question.[36] They are right that there is a grave danger in
this context that defence counsel may harp on the undifferentiated
arousal of the complainant in the hope of an unmerited acquittal. But
an undifferentiated arousal is not *consent* by way of anything. It is surely
a constraint on any account of sexual consent, including one based on
instinct, that the consent must be to specific activity (A) with person (P)
at time (T) in location (L). As Baroness Hale has recently stated:

> Any particular choice to engage in sexual activity is, of course, both
> person-specific and occasion-specific; with you here and now, or not
> with you (although possibly with someone else), or not here, or not
> now.[37]

So much for 'animal' and 'consent'; what of the term 'instinct' in
the words 'consent produced by animal instinct'. We observed earlier
the condemnation of the animal instincts test from the Home Office, the
legislative House of Lords and from Williams himself. Munby J also
joined in the chorus of moral condemnation of the animal instincts test,
saying it 'disfigured' the Victorian cases on sexual consent.[38] While the
moral condemnation may be over hasty, as I suggested above, Munby J
also complained of the Victorian cases in general that they were not
'illuminating'.[39] The best reading of the 'consent by way of animal
instinct' test, the reading that makes of it 'the best it can be',[40] takes it
as an attempt to identify something in a severely mentally disordered
human being that is worthy of respect. However, in the end I think
the idea of instinct is indeed too unilluminating to help achieve this aim.
For while the idea of instinct as something like unlearned behaviour is
very much evident in the behaviour of animals, human and otherwise,
so much behaviour is an admixture of learned and unlearned features.
As the ethologists Aubrey Manning and Marian Stamp Dawkins write:

> Instinct is often described as patterns of inherited, pre-set behavioural
> responses which develop along with the developing nervous system and
> can evolve gradually over the generations ... to match an animal's

---

[36] A. P. Simester and G. R. Sullivan, *Criminal Law: Theory and Doctrine* (Oxford: Hart, 2007), p. 436 n. 59.

[37] *Cooper* [2009] UKHL 42.

[38] *X City Council* v. *MB, NA and MAB* [2006] EWHC 168 (Fam), para. 73.   [39] *Ibid.*

[40] Ronald Dworkin, *Law's Empire* (Oxford: Hart, 1998), p. 52 *passim*.

behaviour to its environment. It might be defined in a negative kind of way, as that behaviour which does not require learning or practice, but which appears appropriately the first time it is needed.[41]

The authors observe examples in the animal world. But they go on to suggest that while much animal behaviour can be understood in this way, too often the unlearned, instinctive behaviour is combined with learned behaviour. The passage continues:

> This definition immediately suggests its converse and the other familiar way behaviour can become matched to circumstances. Animals may not have any pre-set responsiveness, but be able to modify their behaviour in the light of their individual experience. They can learn how to behave appropriately and perhaps practice or even copy from others to produce the response.[42]

The message is that while instinct, qua unlearned behaviour, is evident in the animal world it is commonly mixed with learning from experience. In fact, sometimes when we speak informally about human instincts, the sense is not that the activity is exclusively unlearned. For example, one might hear a motorist report that she had 'braked instinctively' while driving, although driving was something that needed to be learned. The idea of instinct, then, is unlikely to be illuminating if understood as unlearned, unthought-out and so on, since so often such behaviour will be combined with learned behaviour. It seems, moreover, prohibitively complicated to operationalise in law any standard based on such instinct.

As far as the idea of a consent produced by animal instinct is concerned a few conclusions emerge. While the invocation of the 'animal' has been emotive in many of allusions made to the test, I have suggested that it could be as well rendered in terms of human instinct. Moreover, the best interpretation of the idea is of one that seeks to identify something worthy of respect in human beings who lack many of the standard capacities of most human beings. There is a sense of consent, we have noted, that has been used, for example, by Darwin to apply to the animal world. However, the stumbling block for the *Fletcher* understanding is the idea of instinct. It is simply too complex a matter to determine in animals, human or non-human, which aspects of their behaviour is

---

[41] Aubrey Manning and Marian Stamp Dawkins, *An Introduction to Animal Behaviour*, 6th edn (Cambridge University Press, 2012), pp. 41–2.

[42] Manning and Stamp Dawkins, *An Introduction to Animal Behaviour*, p. 42.

learned and which unlearned for 'instinct' to lie at the centre of a workable legal test.

VII   From instinct to agency

Is there, in the present context, another route to identifying something worthy of respect in human beings who lack many of the standard capacities of most? What was the animal instincts test trying to capture? In our discussion of the 2003 Act we saw that the threshold for the capacity for consent was fixed cognitively, in terms of an understanding of the nature or reasonably foreseeable consequences of sexual activity. It appeared over-inclusive, taking in some forms of mutually desired sexual touching. This suggests that as well as focusing on cognitive questions of belief we should be focusing on volitional questions of desire. We have also seen that even in the case of non-human animals, Darwinians and others speak quite comfortably about choices and consent. I think this discussion is taking us away from the notion of instinct and on to something else, namely, *agency*. Though animals have sometimes been thought of as automatons, like the traditional Japanese Karakuri doll-like automaton that, when activated, shuffles forward, bows and presents a cup of tea on a tray, automatism is now widely thought to be an untenable model for animal behaviour in general.[43] Many animals, such as dogs or cats, appear to have agency: they have desires and beliefs, and can make certain choices.

Galen Strawson has usefully blocked out the elements of the notion of agency. He is clear that on his understanding many non-human animals, such as dogs, are agents. On his account one is an agent if, and only if, one is:

(1) capable of forming beliefs of certain sorts;
(2) capable of having desires of certain sorts;
(3) capable of self-change (e.g., self-movement);
(4) capable of practical reasoning (in a realistically inclusive sense in which dogs and one-year-old children are capable of practical reasoning).[44]

---

[43] McFarland, *Animal Behaviour*, p. 453.

[44] Galen Strawson, 'Free Agents', in his *Real Materialism* (Oxford University Press, 2008), pp. 359–86. My interest in citing Strawson's work is with his attempt to understand the ordinary notion of agency and to see what, if anything, such a notion of agency lacks if it

In trying to get to grips with the minimum conditions for sexual consent in the context of severe mental disorder, we should turn to such a notion of agency, instead of focusing exclusively on cognitive questions or on the complex unhelpful notion of instinct. I do not here have the space to go in to Strawson's 'realistically inclusive' sense of practical reasoning. In saying more about the notion of agency, I will instead focus now primarily on the notion of desire. It is strange in the tests of sexual consent we have encountered so far to have seen so little of the idea of what is desired as opposed to not desired.

On some philosophical views, something like the account of agency blocked out by Strawson is also sufficient for *freedom*. According to Thomas Hobbes, 'a freeman is he that, in those things which by his strength and wit he is able to do, is not hindered to do what he has a will to do'.[45] Hobbes more or less saw freedom in terms of getting what one wants,[46] stating that his account of freedom applied 'no less to irrational and inanimate creatures than to rational'.[47] His account of free action is developed by means of an analogy with a set of scales:

> The objects, means, &c are the weights, the man is the scale, the under-standing of a convenience or inconvenience is the pressure of those weights, which incline him now one way, now another; and that inclination is the will.[48]

Richard Holton comments:

> Here we can see clearly the sense in which the decision-making process is passive: there is nothing more to the process of decision than letting the weight of one's understanding of the desirability of the various options press upon one. Indeed it is tempting to think that the decision machinery has no role at all. But that would be a mistake. To press the analogy: we need well-working scales if we are to weigh fairly. The point then is not that the scales are redundant; it is rather that they fail to make any *discretionary* contribution to the output. This is the sense in which the inputs *determine* the output: once we know that the scales are true we know how the scales will move simply by knowing the weight of the objects put upon them. Things are parallel on the simple Hobbesian

---

is to be conceived as implying human freedom. I am not concerned with his sceptical arguments about free-will.

[45] Thomas Hobbes, *Leviathan* (London: Printed for Andrew Crooke, 1651), ch. XXI, 'Of the Liberty of Subjects'.

[46] Richard Holton, *Willing, Wanting, Waiting* (Oxford University Press, 2009), p. 56.

[47] Hobbes, *Leviathan*, ch. XXI, 'Of the Liberty of Subjects'.

[48] Thomas Hobbes, *Questions concerning Liberty, Necessity and Chance*, 1656.

model of action. Assuming that agents are well-functioning, their actions
will be determined by the force of the inputs, where these consist of the
agents' understanding of the utility of the various options. There is no
place for an independent contribution from an act of choice. There is just
risk of malfunction.[49]

The Hobbesian account, as Hobbes himself thought, is wide-ranging; it
can be applied to both humans and non-human animals. While we can
talk about choice and by extension consent on the account, it is the
inputs (the desires of the human or the animal based on an understanding of the options) that determine the choice or the consent. The
will, as Hobbes put it, is the 'last appetite in deliberating'.[50] It is something like this sort of account, I think, based on agency that the *Fletcher*
test was really grasping at in trying to block out a minimum notion of
consent, before invoking the unhelpful notion of instinct. In *Fletcher*
itself the conviction of the accused was upheld.[51] Witnesses had said that
the clearly profoundly disordered victim, Jane Jones, had not offered
resistance to Fletcher but had exclaimed that he was hurting her. The
court concluded that Jones was not consenting; although a consent
produced by animal instinct would have sufficed, this was not such a
consent. Surely what is really doing the work here is that Jones did not
want what Fletcher was doing to her. Could the kind of Hobbesian
account we have discussed form the basis of an account of consent
wide enough to take in *both* adult human beings free of any lack of
capacity or any disorder *and* those humans with a severe mental disorder? Consent would turn on the presence of desire for the touching in
question.

The answer, I believe, is certainly not. That would be to go too far, even
if, as I've been suggesting, this seems to be the idea that the animal
instinct test was really trying to capture. For as we have touched on
before, a severely mentally disordered person might desire a form of
sexual touching with a certain person at a certain time, in circumstances
in which they are being gravely exploited or where the sexual touching is
otherwise inappropriate. What should be done in those cases is a complex matter which requires independent discussion. But there remain
cases of what we might call *unopposed sexual desires* for specific forms of
sexual touching with specific people; in other words, Williams' concern
in speaking of the right of severely mentally impaired people to express

---

[49] Holton, *Willing, Wanting, Waiting*, pp. 56–7 (original emphasis).
[50] Hobbes, *Leviathan*, ch. XI.   [51] *R. v. Richard Fletcher* (1859) Bell 63.

their sexuality and enjoy tender and close relationships. Desire for the specific sexual touching could not be *sufficient* then for a valid consent. But in considering it, more modestly, as a *necessary* element in a still to be fully developed account of the threshold of valid consent, we already move beyond the exclusively cognitive understanding of the threshold of refusal-capability under section 30 of the Sexual Offences Act. If A wishes to engage in sexual touching with B, where B wishes to be touched by A in the relevant way, it is no business of the law to criminalise this behaviour in the name of an alleged incapacity to refuse consent.

VIII *Must* consent be intellectual?

I have suggested that the 'foreseeable consequences' threshold of the 2003 Act leaves out important dimensions of agency, in particular the notion of (unopposed) desire, that the test that Williams endorsed – knowledge of the physical facts – was also too focused on the cognitive and at such a limited level that it could not be said to take matters beyond the animal instinct test. The animal instinct test, I think, would be better rendered as a 'human instinct' test, to avoid the emotive noise of the word 'animal', but in any case the idea of 'instinct' is unhelpful. The *Fletcher* test is best understood, I have suggested, in terms not of instinct or automatism, but of agency, with the component capacities for belief, desire and minimal practical reason Strawson suggested. What I called unopposed sexual desires should form a necessary part of a fuller account of minimal consent, about which there are many more questions that I do not pretend to have tackled here, while their presence should not be taken as sufficient for consent.

One might object that the notion of agency I have recommended at least as a starting point for an account of minimal consent is so minimal that it cannot genuinely form an account of any sort of human will worthy of respect. For it was developed in terms of a Hobbesian account of action; and while Hobbes himself thought his account explained the will and human freedom, it is not as if his view has swept all before it. On the contrary, it has decidedly underwhelmed many.[52] In Holton's comment cited above, it was pointed out that the Hobbesian view makes decision making and choice (and we may add consent), essentially passive. There does not, one might claim, seem to be enough for the

---

[52] See, e.g., David Velleman, 'What Happens when Someone Acts?' *Mind*, 101 (1992), 461–81.

chooser or consenter to do. Strawson, moreover, after listing the essential aspects of our conception of agency on which I relied above for my interpretation of *Fletcher*, goes on to say *pace* the Hobbesian view that such agency is still *short* of what we understand to be human freedom. What is missing, he suggests, is some notion of *self-consciousness*. A dog can choose, say between eating some more food or playing with the neighbour's dog who has just appeared. But the dog, lacking self-consciousness, does not know she can choose.

It seems to have been an objection of this kind that Palles CB was expressing in the fourth of our tests, what I referred to earlier as the 'rational will' test of *Dee*.[53] We cited an abridged version of the key sentence of the Chief Baron's judgment early on in the chapter. In full his words are:

> Consent is the act of man, in his character of a rational and intelligent being, not in that of an animal. It must proceed from the will, not when such will is acting without control of reason, as in idiocy or drunkenness, but from the will sufficiently enlightened by the intellect to make such consent the act of a reasoning being.[54]

Palles CB appears to mean that something like the Hobbesian notion of agency sketched above is insufficient for human freedom, which must be more richly conceived. Presumably on this 'rational will' test of minimum consent, what I called the unopposed desires of the mentally disordered would be neither here nor there as far as consent is concerned if not produced by the intellect or rational will. If the animal instincts test and Williams' physical facts tests were low threshold tests, perhaps this should be classified together with the 'foreseeable consequences' threshold of the 2003 Act as a high threshold test. However, this test, as I will now suggest, still falls well short in its implications of the foreseeable consequences test of the 2003 Act. Even if it is right that something like the Hobbesian notion of agency should have *no* place in an account of the minimum conditions of valid consent, it will not follow that the test ought to be the foreseeable consequences test of the 2003 Act. After stating, then, that the rational will test falls short of the foreseeable consequences test, I return finally to the objection that the notion of agency recommended above is just too thin to be of any use in the current context.

---

[53] *R. v. Dee* (1884) 15 Cox CC 579, at p 593.   [54] *Ibid.*

There are a lot of accounts in the philosophical literature of action and the will with which one might profitably compare Palles CB's remarks. One, from R. Jay Wallace, draws a distinction between a motivated and an unmotivated desire.[55] A 'motivated desire' says Wallace, 'is one whose associated evaluative belief admits of a rationalising explanation, where the desire is formed *because* the agent has arrived at the evaluative belief.'[56] When a person has a motivated desire, he suggests, it will always be possible to explain that desire in a way that shows it to be rationalised by other propositional attitudes that the person has. Thus, psychological explanation of motivated desires will go beyond causal claims about the states or conditions that trigger the onset of the desire.[57] Here we can point to a contrast to the interpretation of the animal instincts test suggested above, which does seem to amount to causal claims that trigger the unopposed desires we were discussing. Those desires, it would seem, are triggered in a simpler way, they are caused, they percolate up inside persons so to speak. But in the motivated desire explanation it is being explicitly claimed that the explanation is not restricted to causal claims about the states or conditions that trigger the onset of the desire. 'Rather, motivated desires also (and necessarily) admit of a different kind of psychological explanation, in which the propositional content of the desire is shown to be rationalised or justified by the content of other of the person's attitudes.'[58] Wallace allows that it is possible for one propositional attitude to be rationalised by other attitudes of the agent's without the rationalising attitudes explaining the formation of the state that is rationalised; 'a rationalising explanation requires, more strongly,' he says, 'that the person should be in the rationalising state *because* he has certain other attitudes that rationalise the state.'[59] At this point we might yet again mention Williams' concern that 'severely impaired people ... express their sexuality and ... enjoy tender and close relationships'.[60] The attitudes involved in tender and close relationships seem to furnish examples of potential rationalising explanations, which

---

[55] R. Jay Wallace, 'How to Argue about Practical Reason', in his *Normativity and the Will* (Oxford University Press, 2006), pp. 15–42. Wallace's distinction is, as he says, a development of one devised by Thomas Nagel, *The Possibility of Altruism* (Princeton University Press, 1978), p. 29.

[56] Wallace, 'How to Argue about Practical Reason', p. 26 (original emphasis).

[57] Wallace, 'How to Argue about Practical Reason', pp. 23–4.

[58] Wallace, 'How to Argue about Practical Reason', p. 24.

[59] Wallace, 'How to Argue about Practical Reason', p. 24 (original emphasis).

[60] Williams, *Textbook*, p. 572.

nevertheless fall short of understanding the foreseeable consequences demanded in section 30 of the Sexual Offences Act. A may desire to touch and be touched by B because A finds B desirable and vice versa. An interesting film screened in the United Kingdom by Channel 4 Television, entitled *Richard is my Boyfriend*,[61] contained sensitive performances from actors playing two learning disabled adults embarking on a sexual relationship wanted by both. While the story was fictional it was based on real cases and was analysed in the film by real lawyers and medical professionals. One of the learning disabled characters in particular, Anna, had precious little understanding of the foreseeable consequences of the varying forms of sexual activity involved. But she desired the other character, Richard, and a set of discrete things constituting a 'close and tender relationship' in Williams' phrase. Now the *Dee* 'rational will' test requires that 'the will [be] sufficiently enlightened by the intellect to make such consent the act of a reasoning being'.[62] If that is to be interpreted in Wallace's way as requiring that a (sexual) desire be formed because the agent has arrived at a relevant evaluative belief ('Richard is desirable' and so on), then comfortably more sexual desires will pass the test than would pass the foreseeable consequences test of the 2003 Act.

What, finally, of the objection we floated earlier to the suggestion I made that the idea of agency, as described by Strawson and which can be understood in a Hobbesian manner, should be our starting point for the development of an idea of the minimum threshold for consent? The objection, as we saw, was that the Hobbesian account is too impoverished to be an account of human freedom and the will in general. For one thing, it lacks, as Strawson suggested, the notion of self-consciousness. I would answer this in two parts. First, one should simply concede the main point: the Hobbesian account *is* too impoverished to succeed as a general account of human freedom. Second, however, it does not follow that it can have no role in the *current context* of identifying a minimum

---

[61] Windfall Films, 2007. Commenting on the film, the charity Scope remarked, very much in the spirit of Williams' discussion, that much more thought is needed over how persons in Anna's situation can be 'empowered through supported living to help them make their own choices regarding relationships and sex', available at: www.scope.org.uk/news/scope-statement-on-channel-4-docu-drama-%E2%80%9Crichard-my-boyfriend%E2%80%9D, accessed 4 June 2012.

It hardly helps that these choices may remain criminal in nature if they fall short of the cognitive standards of foresight in s. 30 of the 2003 Act.

[62] *R. v. Dee* (1884) 15 Cox CC 579, at p. 593.

threshold for sexual consent on the part of severely mentally disordered persons. As we saw in our discussion of the 'rational will' test in *Dee* there may be a number of rationalising explanations that the mentally disordered persons in question may have of their sexual desires that fall short of the foresight standards of the 2003 Act. But could there be cases where A wishes to touch B and B wishes to be touched by A (absent circumstances of exploitation and so on) where there is nothing in the way of a rationalising explanation? The answer will depend, of course, on what is actually happening in reality. If there are such cases, it still seems wrong to me that such activity should be criminal in nature. What I called an unopposed sexual desire earlier can then be divided then into two different kinds. In the first kind, there exists some degree of self-consciousness or rationalised explanation of a disordered person's sexual desire which is nevertheless short of understanding the reasonably foreseeable consequences of a specific act of sexual touching. In the second kind, there is no self-consciousness about the sexual desire or no rationalised explanation. In either case surely the key question is not the cognitive one of the 2003 Act, it is the question of what is in the best interests of the mentally disordered person or persons in question.[63] Williams' 'tender and close relationships' may in given cases be an example of precisely that.

---

[63] For the kinds of ways in which one can develop and understand the best interests of persons, see Derek Parfit, 'What Makes Someone's Life go Best?' in his *Reasons and Persons* (Oxford University Press, 1986), pp. 493–502.

10

Sir Michael Foster, Professor Williams and complicity in murder

SIR ROGER TOULSON

I Common purpose: complicity's historical roots

It was an honour to be invited to take part in the conference on the legacy of Glanville Williams. I owe him a great personal debt because he was my first teacher of law. Despite his eminence, he lacked any trace of self-importance. His manner was reserved but kindly. From time to time he displayed impatience towards the House of Lords, but he was remarkably tolerant towards his pupils. I think that he probably had more hope for them. He regarded helping pupils to understand what the law was as a necessary, but not the most important part of being a law teacher. It was more important that his pupils should develop the capacity for questioning why the law should be as it was and how it should be improved. The faculties that he brought to his analysis were a sharply logical and inquisitive mind, a prodigious capacity for research and a deep sense of humanity. His style of teaching was Socratic, but he encouraged his pupils to take an active and constructive role in the discussion. Like Plato, he had the capacity for unpicking complex subjects in simple language.

The opening words of the preface to the second edition of his *magnum opus, Criminal Law: The General Part*,[1] stated its purpose: 'This book is concerned to search out the general rules of the criminal law.' The historical and geographical range of that search was remarkable. He studied the writings of, among others, Hale, Foster, Stephen, Holdsworth and the nineteenth-century Criminal Law Commissioners. The book also contains many references to cases, codes or legal writings from Africa, Australasia, Germany, India and North America.

---

[1] Glanville Williams, *Criminal Law: The General Part*, 2nd edn (London: Stevens, 1961).

The subject of this chapter, complicity in murder, is an old problem which continues to give rise to frequent appeals. In a typical scenario, a group of young men go out either to rob or to fight. In the ensuing violence a member of the group uses a weapon to cause fatal injury. He is charged with murder and convicted. Other members of the group are also charged with murder. Their knowledge may vary. One may have known that the killer was armed with the weapon which he used. Another may have known that he had a stick, but not a knife. A third may have been unaware that the killer had a weapon, but aware that another member of the group had a weapon which was not used. A fourth may have been unaware that anyone had a weapon. What legal test or tests determine whether each co-defendant is guilty of murder, manslaughter or at most a non-fatal offence? This question lies at the interface between the law of secondary liability and the law of homicide.

At the time when the rules about primary and secondary liability were developed, crimes were divided into a number of categories: treasons, felonies and misdemeanours (which were all triable by jury), and petty offences (which could only be tried summarily). That form of classification has been replaced by a simpler classification of offences as either indictable or summary offences. Under the old scheme, for felonies (including murder and manslaughter) there were different categories of participant. A person might be guilty of murder as a principal in the first degree, principal in the second degree or accessory before the fact. The importance of the distinction was twofold. First, no one could be convicted as a principal in the second degree or as an accessory before the fact unless there had been a conviction of a principal in the first degree. Second, the indictment was required to plead the nature of the defendant's involvement. If he was charged as a principal in the first degree, but the evidence showed that he was an aider and abettor, he was entitled to be acquitted on that indictment. Those procedural rules have been abolished, but their abolition was not intended to affect the substance of what gives rise to secondary liability.

Section 8 of the Accessories and Abettors Act 1861, as amended, provides that anyone who 'shall aid, abet counsel or procure the commission of any indictable offence . . . shall be liable to be tried, indicted and punished as a principal offender'. For summary offences the corresponding provision is in section 44 of the Magistrates' Courts Act 1980. Section 8 states in short form the conduct element required for a person to be guilty of an offence as a secondary party. The words 'aid, abet [and] counsel' cover two types of conduct, namely, the provision of assistance or encouragement. The language assumes some degree of link between the conduct of the secondary party and the commission of the offence without further elaboration. The section is silent about the required mental element.

Section 8 of the 1861 Act followed a long line of statutes discussed by Foster in his commentary on the case of *MacDaniel*[2] in his *Crown Law*.[3] Foster was a judge of the King's Bench from 1745 to 1763. His *Crown Law* is in two parts. The first part contains reports made by him on a number of cases in which he was involved. The second part contains a series of discourses or treatises on the criminal law. Foster enjoyed a high reputation. His discourses display a wide knowledge of the criminal law and a keen interest in its principles.

In December 1755, Foster was the trial judge in a remarkable case at the Old Bailey brought against Stephen MacDaniel, John Berry, James Eagen and James Salmon. In that case, and in his commentary on it in *Crown Law*, Foster examined the principles of secondary liability. The defendants were charged with secondary liability for the commission of a robbery by two other men named Peter Kelly and John Ellis. The accusation in the indictment was that they did 'feloniously and maliciously comfort, aid, assist, abet, counsel, hire, and command the said Peter Kelly and John Ellis to commit the said felony and robbery'. The indictment recited that Kelly and Ellis had previously been convicted of the robbery. The peculiarity of the case was that Salmon, one of the defendants, had been the victim of the robbery. The explanation was that the whole operation had been a sting.

The jury in the trial before Foster delivered a special verdict. They found that the four defendants and another man, Thomas Blee, hatched a plan to procure for themselves the rewards given by an Act of Parliament for apprehending robbers on the highway. The plan was that Blee would procure two people to rob Salmon. The wily Blee recruited Ellis and Kelly to go with him to Deptford in order to steal some linen, but he did not at that stage tell them of the intended robbery. Blee led Ellis and Kelly to Deptford, where Salmon was conveniently waiting on the highway. Blee, Ellis and Kelly took the opportunity to assault him and relieve him of the goods in his possession. The defend-

---

[2] (1755) 19 St Tr 745.

[3] Michael Foster, *A Report of Some Proceedings on the Commission of Oyer and Terminer and Goal Delivery for the trial of the Rebels in the year 1746 in the county of Surry, and of other Crown Cases* (Oxford: Clarendon Press, 1762), p. 121.

ants other than Salmon were not present and none of them had any
direct communication with Ellis and Kelly, but the jury found that before
the robbery they had seen Ellis and Kelly and had approved of their
choice as suitable recruits for the purpose of robbing Salmon.

The question argued before all the judges of the King's Bench was
whether on the jury's verdict the defendants were guilty of aiding and
abetting Ellis and Kelly to rob Salmon. That gave rise to two issues. The
first was whether what had happened amounted to robbery of Salmon.
The second was whether, if so, the defendants were guilty of the robbery.

In pronouncing the judgment of the court, Foster dealt first with the
latter issue because, he said, 'the law touching accessories before the fact
is a matter of great and very extensive consequence to the justice of the
kingdom and ought to be well understood'. The court held that Salmon
could not be guilty of robbing himself, but that, if what happened to him
was a robbery by Ellis and Kelly (of which they had been convicted), the
other three defendants were guilty. It was argued on their behalf that they
were not guilty of aiding and abetting Ellis and Kelly because they had no
direct connection with either of them, but it was held that this made no
difference. Foster said:

> MacDaniel, Eagen and Berry, who were the contrivers of this scheme of
> iniquity, agreed upon the place and manner of execution, and conducted
> the whole by the intervention of their instrument Blee, are accessories
> before this robbery, supposing a robbery to have been committed: for in
> construction, and indeed in the language of the law, they did command
> Ellis and Kelly to commit the fact, and did aid and abet them in it.

The court went on to hold that what had happened was not a robbery but
a pretence of a robbery, in that Salmon's property had not been taken
from him against his will. Foster did not record what happened to Ellis
and Kelly, who had been convicted at a previous trial, and there was then
no Court of Criminal Appeal. He did record that the acquitted defendants, MacDaniel, Eagen and Berry, were subsequently convicted of conspiracy, for which they were committed to prison for seven years and
ordered to be set in the pillory twice. On the first occasion, Eagen lost his
life in the pillory through the resentment of the populace, and for that
reason the others were not required to stand in the pillory a second time.

In his commentary on the case in *Crown Law*, at pages 130–1, Foster
said:

> I observe that the legislature in statutes made from time to time con-
> cerning accessories before the fact, hath not confined itself to any certain

mode of expression; but hath rather chosen to make use of a variety of words, all terminating in the same general idea.

Some statutes make use of the word accessories, singly, without any other words descriptive of the offence. Others have the words, abetment, procurement, helping, maintaining and counselling, or, aiders, abettors, procurers and counsellors. One describeth the offence by the words, command, counsel or hire; another calleth the offenders, procurers, or accessories. One, having made use of the words, comfort, aid, abet, assist, counsel, hire or command, immediately afterwards in describing the same offence in another case, useth the words counsel, hire, or command only. One statute calleth them, counsellors and contrivers of felonies; and many others make use of the terms counsellors, aiders and abettors, or barely aiders and abettors.

From these different modes of expression, all plainly descriptive of the same offence, I think one may safely conclude, that in the construction of statutes which oust clergy in the case of *participes criminis* we are not to be governed by the bare sound, but by the true legal import of the words; and also, that every person who cometh within the description of these statutes, various as they are in point of expression, is in the judgment of the legislature an accessory before the fact; unless he is present at the facts, and in that case, he is undoubtedly a principal.

While that case established that the connection between a secondary defendant, D, and the principal offender, P, does not have to be direct, there may be circumstances in which the conduct of D is too remote from the commission of the offence by P for it to be just to hold D guilty of the offence as a secondary party. In his *Crown Law*, at page 369, after observing that he had little to add with regard to accessories before the fact to what had already been said in *MacDaniel*, Foster set out the following much quoted passage:

Sect. 1
Much hath been said by writers who have gone before me, upon cases where a person supposed to commit a felony at the instigation of another hath gone beyond the terms of such instigation, or hath, in the execution, varied from them. If the principal totally and substantially varieth, if being solicited to commit a felony of one kind he wilfully and knowingly committeth a felony of another, he will stand single in that offence, and the person soliciting will not be involved in his guilt. For on his part it was no more than a fruitless ineffectual temptation. *The fact cannot with any propriety be said to have been committed under the influence of that temptation.*

Sect. 2
But if the principal in substance complieth with the temptation, varying only in the circumstance of time or place, or in the manner of execution,

in these cases the person soliciting to the offence will, if absent, be an accessory before the fact, if present a principal. *For the substantial, the criminal part of the temptation, be it advice, command, or hire, is complied with* [emphasis added].

As the emphasised words show, the underlying logic of the distinction was that in one case it would be just to regard the offence as having been committed with the assistance or encouragement of D, but in the other case it would not.

The same principle can be seen in Foster's writing about cases where two or more people set out together to commit a crime. In olden times the distinction between an accessory before the fact and a principal in the second degree depended on whether the person was present at the time of the crime, but presence was sometimes given an enlarged meaning. Since the Accessories and Abettors Act that distinction has ceased to matter, but what does matter is a proper understanding of the basis and extent of what is commonly referred to as joint enterprise liability. Foster explained it in this way, at page 350:

> Several persons set out together, or in small parties, upon one common design, be it murder or other felony, or for any other purpose unlawful in itself, and each taketh the part assigned to him; some to commit the fact, others to watch at proper distances and stations to prevent surprise, or to favour, if need be, the escape of those who are more immediately engaged. They are all, provided the fact be committed, in the eye of the law, present at it; for it was made a common cause with them, each man operated in his station at one and the same instant towards the same common end; *and the part each man took tended to give countenance, encouragement, and protection to the whole gang, and to insure the success of their common enterprise* [emphasis added].

Thus explained, participation in a joint criminal enterprise is an example of mutual assistance and encouragement. It is not a doctrinally separate basis of secondary liability. By contrast, Foster gave instructive examples of cases where D would *not* be liable.

One was the *Three Soldiers'* case, tried at the Sarum Lent Assizes in 1697, which Foster recounted at page 353:

> Three soldiers went together to rob an orchard: two got upon a pear tree, and the third stood at the gate with a drawn sword in his hand. The owner's son coming by collared the man at the gate and asked him what business he had there, and thereupon the soldier stabbed him. It was

ruled by Holt to be murder in him; but that those on the tree were innocent. They came to commit a small inconsiderable trespass, and the man was killed upon a sudden affray without their knowledge. 'It would, said he, have been otherwise, if they had all come thither with a general resolution against all opposers.'

Foster added:

> A general resolution against all opposers, whether such resolution appeareth upon evidence to have been actually and explicitly entered into by the confederates, or may be reasonably collected from their number, arms or behaviour at or before the scene of action – such resolutions so proved have always been considered as strong ingredients in cases of this kind.

A second example was the case of *Hyde*, tried at Newgate in 1672 and cited by Hale.[4] Foster summarised it at page 354:

> A B and C ride out together with intention to rob on the highway. C taketh an opportunity to quit the company, turneth into another road, and never joineth A and B afterwards. They upon the same day commit a robbery. C will not be considered as an accomplice in this fact. Possibly he repented of the engagement, at least he did not pursue it; *nor was there at the time the fact was committed any engagement or reasonable expectation of mutual defence and support, so as to affect him* [emphasis added].

II   Glanville Williams: common purpose homicide then and now

These cases are illustrations of factual situations where it was not just to conclude that the offence committed by P was done with D's assistance or encouragement, for the reasons which Foster gave.

Down the years it has become common to frame the principle in terms of considering whether P's act was 'within the scope of the joint enterprise'. That is a less straightforward way of putting it. One has only to read the often lengthy written directions to juries, which are couched in terms of joint enterprise and incorporate further directions about the 'scope of the enterprise' and acts which are 'fundamentally different' from it, to wish that the expression were not used as a legal formula to be applied by the jury. In many cases it is an artificial legal concept, giving

---

[4] Matthew Hale, *Historia Placitorum Coronae* (London: printed by E. & R. Nutt *et al.*, 1736), p. 537.

rise to complication and confusion, whereas the question whether P should fairly be regarded as having acted with the assistance or encouragement of D is a simpler factual question.

In his *Textbook of Criminal Law*,[5] Glanville Williams was critical of the formulation that an accessory is not responsible for an act going beyond the 'common purpose' for two reasons. He rightly observed that it may lead a jury to suppose that a person is liable because P's crime serves the general unlawful aim of D and P. That is not so, as the *Three Soldiers'* case illustrates. The stabbing of the owner's son assisted the general purpose of the theft of pears. He also rightly observed that it suggests that there must be a common purpose, but that is also incorrect. D may have reasons for assisting or encouraging P to commit a crime without there being any true meeting of minds between them.

Underlying the doctrine of secondary liability is a question which the courts have seldom directly addressed because they have not found it necessary to do so. On what foundation does secondary liability rest? Glanville Williams addressed this question in relation to accessories before the fact in the *Criminal Law: The General Part*:

> A fundamental question as to accessories before has not been fully considered by the courts. Put shortly, the question is whether the law rests on a basis of authorisation or of psychological causation. Is a person responsible as an accessory before the fact in the same way as he becomes principal to a contract in civil law, namely by using a form of words conveying his authority to do the act in question? Or, on the other hand, is it necessary and sufficient to show that the words of the accessory really had an effect on the mind of the principal, and played a part in bringing about the crime? Usually there would be no need to decide between these two theories, for usually the use of words directing another to commit a crime can, where the other actually commits the crime, be presumed to have had some effect on his mind. Sometimes, however, the two theories give different results. Suppose that D suggests to E that he commit a certain crime, and E replies: 'I have already made up my mind to do so.' Here there is the technical counselling, but it appears that (although the crime counselled is afterwards committed) the words of counsel are not an operative factor. Do we require the words of counsel to have had an effect on the principal's mind or not? If it is held that they must, the consequence will be that in the case supposed D is guilty only of the inchoate crime of incitement. On the other hand, it may be contended that the words of advice may well have operated to encourage and reinforce the principal's design. Difficulties of proving causation may

---

[5] Glanville Williams, *Textbook of Criminal Law*, 1st edn (London: Stevens, 1978), p. 299.

well lead to preference for the authorisation theory. But, except in murder, the question is (in England) of little more than technical interest; for the term of imprisonment for incitement may now be as severe as for the consummated crime.[6]

In *Stuart and Schofield*,[7] Hobhouse LJ advanced the view that joint enterprise liability rests on a quite separate foundation from conventional secondary liability and that it is founded on the doctrine of agency. He expressed the same view in the civil case of *Credit Lyonnais Bank Nederland NV* v. *Export Credits Guarantee Department*.[8] This view was criticised by Professor Sir John Smith[9] and has had few supporters. I agree with the critics. The scope for agency or vicarious liability in criminal law is narrow. The agency theory could not apply in any event to a spontaneous joint enterprise except by a legal artificiality. I accept that in a true case of conspiracy the agency theory would fit, but it is unnecessary. The essence of a conspiracy is that conspirators provide mutual encouragement to one another, which falls squarely within ordinary accessory liability.

I have suggested that a better view is that secondary liability is based on a broad theory of causation.[10] I acknowledge that the form of causation theory considered by Glanville Williams would be too narrow, but I would echo the words of Justice Posner in *United States* v. *Oberhellmann*:[11]

> Causation is a complex, contextually variable concept, in law as in life.

And of Lord Bingham in *Kennedy No. 2*,[12] paragraph 15:

> Questions of causation frequently arise in many areas of the law, but causation is not a single, unvarying concept to be mechanically applied without regard to the context in which the question arises.

Two things are clear. First, the prosecution does not have to prove that the offence would not have happened 'but for' the conduct of the secondary party. This was affirmed and explained in *Mendez* at paragraph 23:

---

[6] Williams, *The General Part*, pp. 381–2.   [7] [1995] 1 Cr App R 441.

[8] [1998] 1 Lloyd's Rep 19.

[9] J. C. Smith, 'Secondary Participation in Crime: Can We Do Without It?' *New Law Journal*, 1 (1994), 679.

[10] *Mendez* [2011] 3 WLR 1, at paras 18–23 and *Stringer* [2011] EWCA Crim 1396, at paras 47–51.

[11] 946 F2d 50, 53 (7th Cir 1991).   [12] [2007] UKHL 38.

> Where a victim (V) is attacked by a group, it may well be the case that if any one of the group had not taken part in the attack the outcome would have been the same. If the prosecution had to satisfy a 'but for' test in relation to each defendant, the result would be that no defendant had committed the offence, whereas it is proper to regard each as having contributed to it.

Criminal law is not peculiar in this regard. In civil law it is not uncommon to have a case where separate wrongdoers contribute to causing the same damage. Second, it has been recognised that there must be a 'connecting link' between D's assistance or encouragement and P's act.[13]

It is plainly right and just that there should have to be some 'connecting link'. It would be morally repugnant to find a person guilty of murder for behaving in a way which on a fair view was unconnected with the crime. However, I would regard it as morally and pragmatically justifiable to hold that where P commits an offence with D's knowing assistance or encouragement, D is taken to have contributed to the offence, even if his assistance or encouragement may have been inessential.

This analysis involves a concept of causation which is appropriate to the context. I do not see an alternative foundation on which secondary liability can satisfactorily be said to rest. The verdict of a jury that X murdered Y carries with it a necessary judgment that X was in some way responsible for Y's death.

As with all issues that involve questions of causation and responsibility there may be questions of remoteness. This is not new. The passage cited from Foster in which he spoke of a case where D's conduct was 'no more than a fruitless ineffectual temptation' and the crime could not 'without any propriety be said to have been committed under the influence of that temptation' illustrates this point. So does the language of Lord Parker in *Anderson and Morris*, cited by Lawton LJ in *Reid*, about P's conduct being 'an overwhelmingly supervening event which is of such a character that it will relegate into history matters which would otherwise be looked upon as causative factors'. This is the language of causation.

Questions of remoteness are inextricably interwoven with a sense of what is fair. As Lord Bingham said in *Corr* v. *IBC Vehicles Ltd*:[14] 'The rationale of the principle that a *novus actus interveniens* breaks the chain of causation is fairness.' The question must in each case be whether it is

---

[13] *Attorney-General* v. *Able* [1984] QB 795, at A12 and *Calhaem* [1985] QB 808.
[14] [2008] UKHL 13, [2008] 1 AC 884, at para. 15.

just to regard P's act as done with D's encouragement or assistance, and there may be borderline cases.

For the offence to have been facilitated by D it is not necessary that P should be aware of D's assistance, but encouragement by its nature involves some form of communication of the encouragement to P, although this may be through an intermediary as in the case of *MacDaniel.*

Glanville Williams commented in *The General Part* at page 356 that it is sometimes difficult to know what degree of assistance is regarded as aiding. In *Stringer* the court observed, at paragraph 51, that several centuries of case law have not produced any definitive formula for resolving that question, but that this is unsurprising because the facts of different cases are infinitely variable. It is for the jury, applying their common sense and sense of fairness, to decide whether the prosecution have proved to their satisfaction on the particular facts that P's act was done with D's assistance or encouragement.

In his *Textbook of Criminal Law*, at pages 328–9, Glanville Williams referred to a provision in the US Model Penal Code that a person is not criminally responsible for a result if it is 'too remote and accidental in its occurrence to have a just bearing on the actor's liability or on the gravity of his offence', and he observed that the use of the word 'just' indicated the true nature of the problem. Determining whether it is 'just' to regard a defendant as criminally responsible for what occurred involves in part what he referred to as 'a moral reaction'. It is inevitable in practice, and I do not see it as objectionable, that a jury's decision whether P's act was done with D's assistance or encouragement should involve their judgment whether it is a just conclusion on the facts. This may provide an explanation for differentiating between one who invites a person with a known propensity for violence to accompany him on a lawful expedition in which that person becomes involved in violence, and one who invites another to assist him in carrying out a crime in which the accomplice acts violently. Aside from the mental component of secondary liability, in such cases the approach to causation is inevitably influenced by a moral component whether it is just to consider the defendant culpable for what occurred.[15]

As to the mental ingredient of secondary liability, in principle there is much to be said for requiring that the defendant should have intended to bring about or provide assistance or encouragement towards the com-

[15] *Mendez* [2011] 3 WLR 1, at para. 37.

mission of the offence. The mental element would be parallel to the physical element. In the United States, the principle was stated succinctly in *Bosco* v. *Serhant*:[16]

> Aiding and abetting in the criminal law requires not only knowledge of the principal's objective but a desire to help him attain it.

That principle is consistent with some earlier English authorities, but more recently the law has become increasingly complex and potential liability wider. The wide *mens rea* for murder has led to particular problems in the application of the principles of secondary liability to cases of homicide, including the question of whether D may be guilty of manslaughter when P is guilty of murder. By the 1960s, the courts appeared to have reached a position which was reasonably clear.

In *Wesley Smith*,[17] the appellant and three co-defendants went into a pub and began to cause trouble. The appellant and one co-defendant went outside and began throwing bricks through the glass door. The other two stayed inside and became involved in a fight with the barman, during which one of them drew a knife and inflicted a fatal stab wound. The four were tried for murder. The prosecution's case was that all four acted in concert to make an attack on the bar and on anyone who attempted to prevent them from doing so. The appellant knew that the man who stabbed the barman was carrying a knife. In his directions to the jury the trial judge said:

> a person who takes part in or intentionally encourages conduct which results in a criminal offence will not necessarily share the exact guilt of the one who actually strikes the blow. His foresight of the consequences will not necessarily be the same as that of the man who strikes the blow, the principal assailant, so that each may have a different form of guilt in mind, and that may distinguish their respective criminal liability. Several persons, therefore, present at the death of a man may be guilty of different degrees of crime – one of murder, others of unlawful killing, which is called manslaughter. Only he who intended that unlawful and grievous bodily harm should be done is guilty of murder. He who intended only that the victim should be unlawfully hit and hurt will be guilty of manslaughter if death results.

The appellant was convicted of manslaughter. He appealed on the ground that, on the jury's verdict, the use of the knife to stab the barman was outside the concerted action to which the appellant was a party.

---

[16] 836 F2d 271, 279 (7th Cir 1987). [17] [1963] 1 WLR 1200.

Slade J, giving the judgment of a court of five, described the summing-up as legally unassailable. He acknowledged that there might be 'a case in which there is an act which is wholly outside the scope of the agreement, in which case no doubt different considerations might apply', but he said that this was not such a case, because it must have been within the appellant's contemplation that if the barman did his duty to quell the disturbance, the co-defendant might use the knife on him which the appellant knew that he was carrying.

Betty[18] was a similar case. The appellant and a co-defendant took part in a fight with knives which resulted in the co-defendant inflicting a fatal stab wound. The appellant was convicted of manslaughter. It was argued on the appellant's behalf that his co-defendant was guilty of murder, although he too had been convicted of manslaughter, and that the co-defendant's murderous conduct took the case outside the scope of the concerted action to which the appellant was a party. The Court of Criminal Appeal followed the decision in *Wesley Smith* and dismissed the appeal. In a judgment given by Lord Parker CJ the court approved the direction of the trial judge that:

> if two men attack a third without any intention of killing in the mind of either of them, and, as the fight develops, one or other conceives in his mind an intention to kill and does kill, of course, that does not make the other man guilty of murder, because he never contemplated that was going to be done, he did not intend it, and, in fact, did not do the act of killing. My direction to you is that it does not absolve the other man from facing a charge of manslaughter. It is true that death resulted in that purely hypothetical case I am putting to you from the intentional act of the one, but it was a result of something that resulted and grew out of the initial attack in which two men were engaged.

Lord Parker added that the trial judge had not shown the limits of the doctrine, as indicated by Slade J in *Wesley Smith*, where the death was caused by the use of a weapon which the appellant did not know that the killer had or expected him to use, but that the appellant knew that the killer had a knife and they had both been using knives. In those circumstances, the act which resulted in death was within the scope of the concerted action, namely, a knife attack upon the deceased.

Two years later Lord Parker delivered the judgment of the court in *Anderson and Morris*.[19] The defendants went in pursuit of W and fought with him. In the course of the fight Anderson stabbed W to death.

---

[18] (1963) 48 Cr App R 6.   [19] [1966] 2 QB 110.

Anderson was convicted of murder and Morris of manslaughter. The trial judge directed the jury that if there was common design to attack W, and in the course of the fight Anderson killed him, this was sufficient for Morris to be guilty of manslaughter even if he had no intention of causing W serious harm and no idea that Anderson was armed with a knife. The court reaffirmed that the law was as laid down in *Wesley Smith* and *Betty*, but held that the jury had been misdirected, because Morris was not guilty of manslaughter if Anderson had departed completely from the common design, had suddenly formed an intent to kill and had used a weapon in a way which Morris could not suspect.

Counsel for Morris was Mr Geoffrey Lane QC, later Lord Lane CJ. As Lane LJ he was a member of the Court of Criminal Appeal in the case of *Reid*.[20] The judgment of the court was given by Lawton LJ. Quoting words from the judgment of Lord Parker in *Anderson and Morris*, he treated that case as an example of 'an overwhelmingly supervening event which is of such a character that it will relegate into history matters which would otherwise be looked upon as causative factors'. Contrasting that to a 'mere unforeseen consequence' of the unlawful possession of offensive weapons, Lawton LJ said:

> When two or more men go out together in joint possession of offensive weapons such as revolvers and knives and the circumstances are such as to justify an inference that the very least they intend to do with them is to use them to cause fear in another, there is, in our judgment, always a likelihood that, in the excitement and tensions of the occasion, one of them will use his weapon in some way which will cause death or serious injury. If such injury was not intended by the others, they must be acquitted of murder; but having started out on an enterprise which envisaged some degree of violence, albeit nothing more than causing fright, they will be guilty of manslaughter.

The position established by those cases may be summarised in this way. A person who took part in an attack on another, or in an attempt to put him in fear of violence, which resulted in death, would ordinarily be guilty at least of manslaughter, whether or not the consequences were foreseen. He would be guilty of murder if, but only if, he had the *mens rea* for murder. However, he would not be guilty of any fatal offence if the conduct of the killer went altogether beyond anything which he could have foreseen. The jury in such a case would therefore have a choice of verdicts: guilty of murder, guilty of manslaughter or not guilty of any

[20] (1975) 62 Cr App R 108.

fatal offence. Glanville Williams observed in *The General Part*, at pages 397–8, that: 'it seems that a common intent to threaten violence is equivalent to a common intent to use violence, for the one so easily leads to the other', and this approach was followed in *Reid*. A manslaughter conviction in such circumstances may be seen as a form of unlawful act manslaughter.

III   The current law

The law changed with the decisions of the Privy Council in *Chan Wing-Sui*[21] and the House of Lords in *Powell and English*.[22] It is now the law that the mental element required for D to be guilty of murder as a secondary party is satisfied if D entered into a criminal enterprise with foresight that it was possible that someone else might deliberately cause death or serious bodily harm, subject to the proviso that D will not be guilty of any offence of homicide if P's act in killing the victim was fundamentally different from anything foreseen by D. However, if D lacks such foresight, he is not guilty of either murder or manslaughter even though he took part in an attack which carried an obvious risk of resulting in someone suffering serious injury or death. The possibility of a manslaughter verdict has therefore been removed in many cases, and those who would formerly have been convicted of that offence are either convicted of murder or acquitted of both murder and manslaughter. *Reid* was cited in argument in *Powell and English*, but it was not referred to in any of the speeches, although it was a judgment of a strong Court of Appeal following a line of previous authorities. It is right to say that reference was made in the speeches to *Wesley Smith* and to *Anderson and Morris*, but not to the way in which *Anderson and Morris* was interpreted by the Court of Appeal in *Reid*.

As is apparent from the flow of appeals, this area of the law is a continuing source of problems. One difficulty is that in a case of unplanned group violence, typically fuelled by alcohol, there is often something rather artificial about trying to identify the level of violence and associated risk of injury which the defendant foresaw. It is one thing for a jury to assess what was his intention, which can generally be judged from his actions. It is another thing to attempt to assess what he foresaw as a possibility in circumstances where it may be unlikely that he paused to ponder about how far others might go. Second, courts have continued

---

[21] [1985] AC 168.   [22] [1999] 1 AC 1.

to have difficulties in applying the 'fundamentally different' test, which can make all the difference between a conviction for murder with a mandatory life sentence and outright acquittal. Third, prosecuting authorities have responded to the removal of the manslaughter option by including a count in the indictment of violent disorder, as an alternative to murder, but the upshot has not been entirely satisfactory. In many cases where a defendant takes part in a joint attack, but others go further than he intended and cause death, there is much to be said for the view that the defendant should have some culpability for the victim's death, but culpability of a different kind from that of the killer. Manslaughter provided that route.

When the Law Commission conducted its review of the law of murder, manslaughter and infanticide[23] there was virtual unanimity among consultees that the law in this area need to be reformed. In its report the Commission recommended that D should be liable for manslaughter if the following conditions are met:

(1) D and P were parties to a joint venture to commit an offence;
(2) P committed the offence of murder in relation to the fulfilment of that venture;
(3) D intended or foresaw that (non-serious) harm or the fear of harm might be caused by a party to the venture; and
(4) a reasonable person in D's position, with D's knowledge of the relevant facts, would have foreseen an obvious risk of death or serious injury being caused by a party to the venture.

There is good precedent for adopting a partially objective test in determining whether there has been unlawful act manslaughter.[24] The Government has not yet decided whether to adopt this recommendation.

IV Conclusion

If Glanville Williams were alive today, I doubt that he would change the statement in the preface to his *Textbook of Criminal Law* that 'the present state of criminal law is such that major problems abound'. In the particular area under discussion the problems have certainly not abated; if anything they have become more acute, as is reflected by the constant stream of appeals.

[23] Law Commission, *Murder, Manslaughter and Infanticide*, Law Com. 304, 2006.
[24] *Church* [1966] 1 QB 59.

I doubt also that he would change what he wrote in the first chapter of the same book at page 8:

> Parliament has been industrious in multiplying offences, very inartistically drawn, but it is slow to remedy clear absurdities and deficiencies in the law as they come to light ... Also, we have in England no criminal code superseding the protean rules of the common law and enabling the whole body of law to be regularly checked by a supervisory commission. Two great efforts to produce such a code were made in the 19th century, but they failed, largely because of the opposition of the judges themselves, who wished to retain their discretionary powers. The position was somewhat improved by the setting up of the Criminal Law Revision Committee in 1959 and of the Law Commission in 1965; the latter is now making a fresh effort to draft a code, but the prospects are doubtful because the legal profession as a whole remains indifferent, while some of its most influential members are hostile.

That was over thirty years ago. While much of it remains true, it would be wrong now to describe the legal profession or the judges as indifferent to the state of the law about complicity in murder or hostile to reform. On the contrary, there was widespread support from the judiciary, legal scholars and the legal profession for much of the Law Commission's recommendations for statutory reform of the law of homicide, including the particular recommendation to which I have referred. The topic of complicity in murder is particularly problematic. Signs of this are the lengthy written directions which judges now feel it necessary to give and the appeals which they continue to generate. Although the courts may, and should, be able to improve things by some simplification, there are limits to what can be done by judicial tinkering. Most serious crimes are now governed by statute. Murder and manslaughter are the major exceptions. There remains a pressing case for Parliament to consider what the law should be and to put it on a statutory basis.

11

Williams versus Kamisar on euthanasia: a classic debate revisited

JOHN KEOWN*

Professor Glanville Williams is rightly regarded as one of the leading jurists of the twentieth century. Although best known for his writing on criminal law, he also made a foundational contribution to the discipline of the law and ethics of medicine. It is therefore fitting that a volume commemorating the centenary of his birth should reflect his influence on that new discipline.

Williams' foundational contribution took the form of his controversial volume *The Sanctity of Life and the Criminal Law* (1957).[1] This book has recently been the subject of a comprehensive and critical re-evaluation.[2] The focus of this chapter will not, therefore, be the book but the celebrated debate it provoked, with fellow lawyer Professor Yale Kamisar, on the decriminalization of voluntary euthanasia. The relevance of their classic debate to the euthanasia debate today should not be overlooked.

The chapter is divided into five parts which respectively outline and evaluate Williams' case for decriminalization; summarize Kamisar's response; evaluate Williams' rejoinder; consider the current relevance of their debate; and offer some brief conclusions.

---

* I am grateful to Professors Christopher Kaczor and Luke Gormally for their comments on a draft of this chapter. I remain solely responsible for its accuracy and argument.

[1] Glanville Williams, *The Sanctity of Life and the Criminal Law* (New York: Alfred A. Knopf, 1957). References in this chapter are to the revised volume published in 1958 (London: Faber & Faber, 1958). Hereafter "*SOL*."

[2] John Keown and David Jones, "Surveying the Foundations of Medical Law: A Reassessment of Glanville Williams's *The Sanctity of Life and the Criminal Law*," *Medical Law Review*, 16 (2008), 85.

I   Williams' case for decriminalization

In *The Sanctity of Life* Williams argued, uncontroversially, against the criminal prohibition of suicide, urging that the prohibition could serve to hinder medical treatment and that even if some powers of official restraint were necessary, they need not involve the use of the criminal law.[3] He proceeded to argue, controversially, that acceptance of this case required acceptance of the decriminalization of both assisted suicide and homicide on request.

His analysis began by asserting that the basis of the legal prohibition of suicide was Christian theology.[4] He omitted to confront the philosophical case against suicide, just as he had omitted earlier in the book to rebut the philosophical case against abortion. The natural law criticism of suicide was caricatured as an argument from natural instinct.[5] Williams had the argument the wrong way round: the natural law argument is not that human life is a good because of our instinct to preserve it; it is that because human life is a basic good it is gravely wrong to try to take it, and we ought therefore to feel strongly against so doing. Williams proceeded to argue that, according to "common sense," the rightfulness of suicide depended on the circumstances.[6] He cited approvingly one writer who observed that the greatest happiness of the greatest number may sometimes be attained by personal sacrifice, as the annals of heroism and martyrdom suggested.[7] Heroism and martyrdom need not, however, involve suicide. It does not follow that because heroes or martyrs foresee death they therefore intend death, but Williams' conflation of foreseen and intended consequences led him to think otherwise. In his world, both Judas and Jesus were suicides.[8]

Though Williams' principled argument for decriminalizing suicide was flawed, his prudential case for decriminalization was persuasive.

---

[3] *SOL*, pp. 259–260.   [4] *Ibid.*, p. 231, see also, at p. 278.

[5] *Ibid.*, p. 237. For a classic contemporary exposition of natural law theory see John Finnis, *Natural Law and Natural Rights*, 2nd edn (Oxford: Clarendon Press, 2011). A valuable introduction is Alfonso Gómez-Lobo, *Morality and the Human Goods* (Washington, DC: Georgetown University Press, 2002).

[6] *SOL*, p. 241.   [7] *Ibid.*

[8] *Ibid.*, p. 242. Williams quoted Durkheim's definition of suicide as: "any cause of death which results directly or indirectly from the positive or negative act of the victim who knew that it was bound to produce this result," *ibid.*, n. 2. On Williams' conflation of intention and foresight see John Keown, *The Law and Ethics of Medicine* (Oxford University Press, 2012), pp. 9–10.

He was, however, largely pushing at an open door. He noted that since the First World War policy had in general shifted to one of non-prosecution of attempted suicides.[9] The decriminalization of suicide by the Suicide Act 1961, only a few years after the publication of *The Sanctity of Life*, was the culmination of a change in attitude which had dawned long before. Williams did not, however, confine himself to the decriminalization of suicide. The tail of his chapter on suicide contained a sting. Although the bulk of the fifty-page chapter was devoted to making an uncontroversial, prudential case for the decriminalization of suicide, its final five pages argued, almost as an afterthought, for something much more radical: the decriminalization of assisting suicide and of homicide on request.

His argument ran that if it were no longer illegal to commit suicide, it should no longer be illegal to assist someone to commit suicide.[10] He claimed that it was "universally conceded" that one who incited a young person to suicide was "properly punishable," but that a physician who assisted his dying patient in suicide might well be regarded as beyond "any intelligently conceived prohibition."[11] These "sensible" results could be achieved by punishing only those who acted from "selfish motives."[12] Such a move would, in turn, require the endorsement of unselfish homicide by consent, for it would be absurd to distinguish between the doctor who supplied a lethal poison to the patient and the doctor who poured it down the patient's throat.[13] Williams concluded, therefore, "that the law might well exempt from punishment the unselfish abetment of suicide and the unselfish homicide upon request."[14]

Williams' case invited several responses. First, his proposal was far from modest. He urged that the law permit anyone to kill anyone from "unselfish" motives on request.[15] Motive is, of course, generally irrelevant to criminal liability, and for good reason. What limits would the notion of "unselfishness" place on killing? Moreover, if a killer were to claim that his motives had been "unselfish," how could the prosecution prove otherwise? Further, Williams espoused an elastic notion of

---

[9] *SOL*, p. 249.   [10] *Ibid.*, p. 274.   [11] *Ibid.*   [12] *Ibid.*   [13] *Ibid.*, p. 275.
[14] *Ibid.*, p. 276.
[15] It seems clear that Williams, who used "request" and "consent" interchangeably, was proposing that an "unselfish" killing be permitted provided the victim consented, even if the victim did not request it. This is indicated by a passage indicating that his proposal would protect a person who suggested suicide. *Ibid.*, p. 274.

"consent." He evidently regarded consent to sterilization as a condition of discharge from a mental institution as free as consent to a flu jab.[16]

Second, it does not follow that the decriminalization of suicide requires the decriminalization of assisted suicide, let alone consensual murder. The decriminalization of suicide need involve no moral condonation of suicide and can be justified on prudential grounds. Indeed, such grounds were central to the case Williams himself advanced for decriminalization.[17] Moreover, he noted, but did not respond to, the argument that while the threat of punishment might not be effective against a potential suicide, it might be effective against a potential abettor.[18] Indeed, this argument helps to account for preservation of the offense of assisting or encouraging suicide in the Suicide Act 1961. It is clear from the parliamentary debate leading up to the Act that the government did not intend decriminalization to signal condonation of suicide.[19] In *Pretty* Lord Bingham confirmed that suicide was decriminalized for other reasons.[20]

---

[16] *Ibid.*, pp. 88–89. He wrote: "few if any choices in life are voluntary, for every choice involves the acceptance of a course that is more preferred in place of one that is less preferred," *ibid.*, p. 88.

[17] *Ibid.*, pp. 259–260. Moreover, it does not follow that because suicide was decriminalized it therefore became "lawful." See John Keown, *Euthanasia, Ethics and Public Policy* (Cambridge University Press, 2002), p. 65; G. E. M. Anscombe, "Prolegomenon to a Pursuit of the Definition of Murder," in Mary Geach and Luke Gormally (eds.), *Human Life, Action and Ethics* (Exeter: Imprint Academic, St Andrews Studies in Philosophy and Public Affairs), pp. 253–260.

[18] *SOL*, p. 274.

[19] Addressing concerns that decriminalization might give the impression that suicide was no longer regarded as wrong, the Joint Under-Secretary of State for the Home Department declared: "I should like to state as solemnly as I can that that is certainly not the view of the Government ... I hope that nothing I have said will give the impression that the act of self-murder, of self-destruction, is regarded at all lightly by the Home Office or the Government" (1960–61) 644 Parl Deb HC 1425–6.

[20] "Suicide itself (and with it attempted suicide) was decriminalised because recognition of the common law offence was not thought to act as a deterrent, because it cast an unwarranted stigma on innocent members of the suicide's family and because it led to the distasteful result that patients recovering in hospital from a failed suicide attempt were prosecuted, in effect, for their lack of success. But while the 1961 Act abrogated the rule of law whereby it was a crime for a person to commit (or attempt to commit) suicide, it conferred no right on anyone to do so. Had that been its object there would have been no justification for penalising by a potentially very long term of imprisonment one who aided, abetted, counselled or procured the exercise or attempted exercise by another of that right. The policy of the law remained firmly adverse to suicide, as section 2(1) makes clear": *R. (Pretty) v. Director of Public Prosecutions (Secretary of State for the Home Department intervening)* [2001] UKHL 61 [35].

Third, even if one took the view that suicide were not immoral there would be sound prudential reasons for not adopting Williams' proposal to decriminalize "unselfish" assistance in suicide and consensual homicide. Oddly for an ostensible utilitarian, Williams did not explain why his proposal would maximize human happiness. Indeed, he had earlier approvingly cited evidence that seemed to undermine his proposal, including one study that indicated that four-fifths of students had sometimes wished for death. Williams had observed: "Common sense suggests the unwisdom of having an institutionalized means of gratifying such a passing fancy promptly and painlessly."[21] Yet his proposal would have permitted rendering assistance in suicide even though the request was merely a passing fancy. He also seemed to have forgotten his earlier statement that it was "universally conceded" that one who incited a young person to commit suicide was "properly punishable."[22] He noted that, besides resulting in the loss of a young life, "the suicide of an only son or daughter will almost infallibly destroy the mother's happiness for the rest of her life."[23] Yet his proposal would have permitted "unselfishly" assisting a young person in suicide and thereby destroying not only a young life, but also parental happiness. Further, he recognized that suicide was frequently the outcome of a "passing impulse or temporary depression,"[24] and that there was a significant correlation between committing suicide and being lonely, divorced or an immigrant.[25] Rather than advocating improved social support or psychiatric help for such vulnerable people, Williams' only proposal was to make it easier to kill them or help them kill themselves. One might have expected that he would at least have required psychiatric evidence that requests were not the result of a "passing impulse or temporary depression," but were free and well-considered;[26] he did not do so.

---

[21] SOL, p. 240.   [22] Ibid., p. 274.

[23] Ibid., p. 243. And the father's? See, e.g., Peter Evans, "Richard Todd: The Dam Busters Star who Never got over the Suicide of his Two Sons," Daily Mail, December 6, 2009, available at: www.dailymail.co.uk/news/article-1233181/Richard-Todd-The-Dam-Busters-star-got-suicide-sons.html.

[24] SOL, p. 261.   [25] Ibid., p. 264.

[26] Earlier he had argued that society should make sure that a determination to commit suicide was "fixed and unalterable," ibid., p. 262. How his proposal for decriminalization would have ensured this he failed to explain. In its consultation paper on the law of homicide the Law Commission noted that "Suicide pacts are strongly linked with illness, both mental and physical, in one or both of the participants," that depression was the most frequent mental illness, and that this finding tied in with studies of individual

We may illustrate the laxity of Williams' proposal with reference to two hypothetical cases drawn from the Law Commission's discussion of suicide pacts in its consultation paper on the law of homicide, published in 2006. In the first:

> D and V are involved in a shoot-out with the police. Eventually, they realise that capture is inevitable. D and V agree that D will kill V and then turn the gun on himself. D kills V but is arrested before he can turn the gun on himself as agreed.[27]

In the second case:

> D is the leader of a fringe religious cult. He persuades his followers to meet to commit suicide together. At the meeting, with his followers' consent, he pours a lethal poison down their throats but finds he cannot summon the courage to do the same to himself when the moment comes.[28]

The Law Commission observed that in relation to such cases it was "hard to see a reason" for reducing the crime in these cases below first degree murder.[29] Under the proposal advanced by Glanville Williams, however, D would commit no offense whatever. This would be so even if D never intended to commit suicide. Indeed, Williams' proposed reform appears to have been so lax that it would have allowed anyone to tour the country persuading the elderly, sick, and disabled to have a plastic bag held over their head to reduce government expenditure on pensions, healthcare, and social support.[30]

Finally, what of the danger of abuse from purely selfish killing, such as the killing by husbands of wives they wanted to dispose of as expeditiously as possible, or of children killing elderly parents to accelerate an inheritance? Williams recognized that his proposal might allow relatives to dispatch "invalids" and then plead their consent, safe in the knowledge that their victims could not testify.[31] His response to this risk was far from reassuring. He wrote: "the danger of false evidence is one that the

suicide among the elderly in which 50–60 per cent were physically ill and 79 per cent suffered mental disturbance from depression. Law Commission, *A New Homicide Act for England and Wales?*, Consultation Paper No. 177 (2006) (hereafter "L.C."), L.C. para. 8.63. The Commission quoted another study indicating that "Homicides-suicides in older people are not acts of love or altruism. They are acts of depression and desperation," *ibid.*, para. 8.80.

[27] L.C., para. 8.21.   [28] *Ibid.*   [29] *Ibid.*

[30] He had observed earlier that society would "fall to pieces if men could murder with impunity," *SOL*, pp. 11–12. Would his proposal not have facilitated such killing?

[31] *Ibid.*, p. 275.

law has to meet in almost all situations, and it is not otherwise a sufficient reason for opposing a change that is otherwise desirable."[32] In arguing that the risk (of murder) was one the law had to meet and that the change in the law was "otherwise desirable," Williams begged the question. The highest purpose of the criminal law is to protect the lives of innocent people. Why was it desirable to expose members of society, not least its most vulnerable members like the "elderly, lonely, sick, or distressed,"[33] those with disabilities, and women,[34] to the risk of being killed with impunity? Because, it appears, Williams simply thought that it followed logically from the case for decriminalizing suicide.

Williams recognized that his proposal was probably too radical for public opinion, and he therefore offered a more limited proposal which would have permitted doctors to perform voluntary euthanasia to end severe pain in terminal illness.[35] He rejected the vulnerability of this proposal to the "slippery slope" argument:

> Logically, the only "general line of conduct" involved in permitting a particular case of voluntary euthanasia of a suffering patient in a fatal illness is that all suffering patients in fatal illnesses may have voluntary euthanasia.[36]

In fact, his proposal was highly vulnerable to "slippery slope" concerns.

There are two "slippery slope" arguments against voluntary euthanasia.[37] The first is that, practically, safeguards to ensure that euthanasia is

---

[32] *Ibid.* He added that the killer would, for his own protection, call witnesses to hear the victim's request. *Ibid.*, pp. 275–276. But if the killer did not, how could the Crown prove beyond reasonable doubt that the request had not been made? And what if a witness simply lied that he or she had been present and that a request had been made?

[33] *Report of the Select Committee on Medical Ethics*, HL Paper 21-I of 1993–94, para. 239 (1994).

[34] The Law Commission observed that: "Gender differences are at work in both suicide pact and homicide-suicide cases." It added: "in many cases men remain 'in control' of decision-making within the relationship, which explains the suspicion that, in many suicide pacts cases, men are taking the lead or even using coercion," L.C., para. 8.78. There is evidence that even ostensibly voluntary requests by women for hastened death may not in fact be so. George writes of "a risk that the decisions of some women for assisted death are rooted in oppressive influences inimical to genuine autonomy, such as structural factors, for instance, social and economic disadvantage, and stereotypes that idealise feminine self-sacrifice, passivity and compliance." Katrina George, "A Woman's Choice? The Gendered Risks of Voluntary Euthanasia and Physician-Assisted Suicide," *Medical Law Review*, 15 (2007), 1–33, at p. 33.

[35] See text at n. 52, below.   [36] *SOL*, p. 281.

[37] For a fuller explanation of these arguments see Keown, *Euthanasia, Ethics and Public Policy*, ch. 7.

carried out only at the free and informed request of the patient, who is terminally ill and suffering, cannot in practice be made effective, not least because of the imprecision of the criteria (what, for example, constitutes a "free and informed request" or "unbearable suffering"?); the difficulty of determining whether they have been satisfied in a given case (how is a doctor to know whether a request is not the result of depression or pressure from relatives?); and the inherently confidential nature of the doctor–patient relationship which resists external regulation. By "effective" is meant sufficient to achieve the degree of control and protection that is warranted by the importance of the rights and interests to be protected, and that has been regularly accepted by proponents of voluntary euthanasia to be desirable, and asserted by them to be attainable, by virtue of the safeguards stipulated in the proposals themselves. The second argument is that, logically, the case for voluntary euthanasia is also a case for non-voluntary euthanasia, the euthanasia of incompetent patients. If the principal reason for voluntary euthanasia is that death can benefit a suffering patient who can request it, why deprive a suffering patient of this benefit merely because the patient is unable to request it? Why should medical compassion be limited by patient incompetence?

Williams' case for decriminalization was vulnerable to both "slippery slope" arguments. First, his "safeguard" against abuse amounted simply to trusting in the competence and good faith of at most two doctors. Second, he admitted that his proposal's limiting conditions were dictated solely by political expediency and that he had no objection in principle to euthanizing those unable to consent, whether adults or children.[38] The only reservations he mentioned to non-voluntary euthanasia were pragmatic, including a concern about the infliction of "a traumatic injury upon the accepted code of behaviour built up by two thousand years of the Christian religion."[39] Given that *The Sanctity of Life* was a wholesale assault on the Christian code of behavior, this concern was distinctly odd.

The vulnerabilities to the "slippery slope" arguments of Williams' case for the decriminalization of voluntary euthanasia for those suffering painful, terminal illness were forensically exposed by Yale Kamisar.[40]

---

[38] *SOL*, pp. 310–312. Any such objection would, moreover, have been difficult to square with his endorsement of "oblique" intent (see n. 8, above). If he had no objection to palliative treatment of the incompetent which had the foreseeable effect of shortening their lives, how could he object to the purposeful ending of their lives?

[39] *Ibid.*, p. 310.

[40] Yale Kamisar, "Some Non-Religious Views against Proposed 'Mercy-Killing' Legislation," *Minnesota Law Review*, 42 (1958), 969.

II Kamisar's reply to Williams

In the now voluminous literature on euthanasia, Professor Yale Kamisar's argument against decriminalization, published in the *Minnesota Law Review* in 1958,[41] remains a reference point. It began by noting Williams' call for decriminalization in *The Sanctity of Life*, adding that when a scholar of Williams' stature joined a number of other formidable criminal law scholars in calling for decriminalization, a major exploration of the basis of the criminal prohibition was in order.[42]

Kamisar, like Williams, adopted a utilitarian perspective. He rightly questioned Williams' representation of the debate as one between Catholics and Liberals. As a "non-Catholic and self-styled liberal," Kamisar identified "substantial utilitarian obstacles" to the decriminalization of voluntary euthanasia.[43] While not wanting to argue against euthanasia in the case where a patient was incurably ill, suffering intolerable and unrelievable pain, and had a fixed desire to die, Kamisar noted that while carefully formed hypotheticals were one thing, specific proposals for everyday situations were another.[44] He questioned Williams' proposal that euthanasia should be allowed for such a patient by giving physicians wide discretion and trusting to their good sense.[45] Such a proposal involved too great a risk of abuse and mistake to warrant changing the law. Possible radiations from voluntary to non-voluntary euthanasia, and the emergence of the legal precedent that there were lives not "worth living," gave additional cause to pause.[46] Tracking the practical and logical "slippery slope" arguments outlined above, Kamisar wrote:

> I see the issue, then, as the need for voluntary euthanasia versus (1) the incidence of mistake and abuse; and (2) the danger that the machinery initially designed to kill those who are a nuisance to themselves may someday engulf those who are a nuisance to others.[47]

Reflecting these two concerns, his paper considered the objections to decriminalization from a "close-up view" and a "long-range view."

---

[41] *Ibid.* The paper is reprinted in Dennis J. Horan and David Mall (eds.), *Death, Dying and Euthanasia* (Frederick, MD: University Publications of America, 1980), p. 406.
[42] Kamisar, "Some Non-Religious Views against Proposed 'Mercy-Killing' Legislation," pp. 969–970.
[43] *Ibid.*, p. 974.   [44] *Ibid.*, p. 975.   [45] *Ibid.*, pp. 975–976.   [46] *Ibid.*, p. 976.
[47] *Ibid.* (footnote omitted).

A   The "close-up view"

Kamisar noted that proposals to permit voluntary euthanasia ranged from those granting a wide immunity to anyone to those imposing elaborate procedural requirements.[48] Nothing, he observed, aroused Williams' ire more than the argument of opponents that the proposals were either too lax or too elaborate.[49] Yet Kamisar suggested that the "euthanasiasts" were pursuing a goal that was inherently inconsistent: "a procedure for death which *both* (1) provides ample safeguards against abuse and mistake; and (2) is 'quick' and 'easy' in operation."[50] He described this tension as the "euthanasiasts' dilemma." Williams, who favored giving the medical practitioner "a wide discretion and trusting to his good sense,"[51] had proposed:

> It shall be lawful for a physician, after consultation with another physician, to accelerate by any merciful means the death of a patient who is seriously ill, unless it is proved that the act was not done in good faith with the consent of the patient and for the purpose of saving him from severe pain in an illness believed to be of an incurable and fatal character.[52]

It would be for the physician, if charged, to show that the patient was seriously ill, but for the prosecution to prove that the physician did not act from a humanitarian motive.[53] There would be "no formalities" and "everything should be left to the discretion of the doctor."[54]

Kamisar noted that Williams' proposal was not limited to adults.[55] Williams wrote that euthanasia for minors would be "best left to the good sense of the doctor," taking into account the wishes of the parents and the child.[56] Kamisar wrote that the dubious voluntariness of euthanasia for minors did not need to be labored.[57] Kamisar also observed that it was difficult to discuss the consultation feature of Williams' proposal because Williams himself did not discuss it. This, together with Williams' emphasis on giving the general practitioner a free hand, suggested that it was not intended to be a significant feature of the

---

[48] *Ibid.*, p. 978.   [49] *Ibid.*, p. 981.   [50] *Ibid.*, pp. 981–982 (original italics).
[51] *SOL*, p. 302.   [52] *Ibid.*, p. 308.   [53] *Ibid.*, p. 303.
[54] *Ibid.* It "would bring the whole subject within ordinary medical practice," *ibid.*, p. 305.
[55] Kamisar, "Some Non-Religious Views against Proposed 'Mercy-Killing' Legislation," p. 985 n. 43.
[56] *SOL*, p. 303 n. 1.
[57] Kamisar, "Some Non-Religious Views against Proposed 'Mercy-Killing' Legislation," p. 985 n. 43.

proposal.[58] Consultation could simply be with another general practitioner; was probably limited to the matter of diagnosis; and there was no requirement of a concurrence in diagnosis or of a written report.[59] Williams had proposed no other safeguards. Kamisar commented that Williams' proposal assumed a great deal about general practitioners' abilities and their willingness to assume the burdens it would impose upon them.[60]

Kamisar proceeded to question how voluntary and informed patients' requests for euthanasia would likely be. Was the patient's request to be made while under the influence of narcotics, or in pain after the narcotics had been suspended for the purpose?[61] Leaving aside this problem, was someone who was so severely ill as to be thought a candidate for euthanasia capable of requesting it? If someone in that state of mind were to decline the assistance of counsel, would the courts hold that he had "intelligently and understandingly" waived the benefit of counsel?[62] Kamisar continued:

> Undoubtedly, some euthanasia candidates will have their lucid moments. How they are to be distinguished from fellow-sufferers who do not, or how these instances are to be distinguished from others when the patient is exercising irrational judgment is not an easy matter. Particularly is this so under Williams' proposal, where no specially qualified persons, psychiatrically trained or otherwise, are to assist in the process.[63]

Even if the mind of the pain-racked might occasionally be clear, was it not also likely to be "uncertain and variable"?[64] Williams' proposal was, Kamisar added, particularly vulnerable to this objection as it did not stipulate a time period to provide evidence of a settled intention.[65] Williams sought to cater for requests which were "clear and incontrovertible," but when, if ever, would they be so?[66] Even if they were "clear and incontrovertible" asked Kamisar,

> Is this the kind of choice, assuming that it can be made in a fixed and rational manner, that we want to offer a gravely ill person? Will we not sweep up, in the process, some who are not really tired of life, but think others are tired of them?[67]

Was there not also a risk of the relatives influencing the patient or the doctor?[68] Williams banked all on the "good sense" of the doctor, but "no

---

[58] *Ibid.*, p. 983 n. 41.   [59] *Ibid.*   [60] *Ibid.*, p. 984.   [61] *Ibid.*, pp. 986–987.
[62] *Ibid.*, pp. 987–988.   [63] *Ibid.*, p. 988.   [64] *Ibid.*   [65] *Ibid.*, pp. 988–989.
[66] *Ibid.*, p. 989.   [67] *Ibid.*, p. 990.   [68] *Ibid.*, pp. 990–992.

man is immune to the fear, anxieties, and frustrations engendered by the apparently helpless, hopeless patient."[69] Kamisar cited a "mercy-killing" prosecution of a physician who said that he had "snapped" under the burden of caring for his patient.[70]

Kamisar then turned to the possibilities of error in diagnosis and of a cure being discovered. He noted Williams' criticism that medical grounds were often invoked by those who objected to euthanasia on theological grounds, but he replied that errors in diagnosis, even by eminent physicians, were real.[71] Yet Williams' proposal would allow even the minimally competent physician to perform euthanasia. Kamisar continued:

> If the range of skill and judgment among licensed physicians approaches the wide gap between the very best and the very worst members of the bar – and I have no reason to think it does not – then the minimally competent physician is hardly the man to be given the responsibility for ending another's life.[72]

Williams' reply to the possibility of error was that mistakes were possible in relation to any of the affairs of life.[73] Kamisar questioned the need to alter a fundamental precept of the criminal law and to risk the fatal mistakes that would inevitably occur.[74] The need was not to save life, but only to ease pain, and while an appreciable number of patients suffered intolerable pain, it was highly doubtful whether they needed to: the medical profession had neglected the field of palliative care.[75] Moreover, Kamisar doubted whether many of those who must necessarily suffer intolerable pain really wanted death, or had a fixed and rational desire for death.[76] Even if the need for voluntary euthanasia were to outweigh the risk of mistake, he added, it was not too much to expect that something approaching the protection afforded someone suspected of a criminal offense be thrown around someone who appeared to have an incurable disease, and Williams' proposal fell far short of this standard.[77]

Having identified the "euthanasiast's dilemma"; the problem of ensuring a voluntary, informed choice; and the possibility of mistakes in diagnosis and prognosis, and having questioned the need for voluntary

---

[69] *Ibid.*, p. 992.   [70] *Ibid.*, pp. 992–993.   [71] *Ibid.*, pp. 993–994.

[72] *Ibid.*, p. 996 (footnote omitted).   [73] *SOL*, p. 283.

[74] Kamisar, "Some Non-Religious Views against Proposed 'Mercy-Killing' Legislation," p. 1007.

[75] *Ibid.*, pp. 1008–1009.   [76] *Ibid.*, p. 1011.   [77] *Ibid.*, p. 1013.

euthanasia, Kamisar proceeded to consider the likelihood of a "slippery slope" to non-voluntary euthanasia.

B   The "long-range view"

Kamisar began by noting that Williams, in defending what the latter described as the "studiously moderate and restrictive" bill introduced in 1936 which excluded non-voluntary euthanasia, rejected the "thin end of the wedge" or "slippery slope" argument.[78] Kamisar aptly enquired why the bill had excluded non-voluntary euthanasia. If it had done so merely for reasons of political expediency, to pave the way for less restrictive bills, then Williams' rejection of the "wedge" argument failed: "No cry of righteous indignation could ring more hollow," wrote Kamisar, "than the protest from those utilizing the 'wedge' principle themselves that their opponents are making the wedge objection."[79]

Kamisar pointed out that, historically, advocates of voluntary euthanasia in both the United Kingdom and the United States had endorsed non-voluntary euthanasia. In 1936, at the inaugural meeting of the Voluntary Euthanasia Legalisation Society in the United Kingdom, the chairman of its Executive Committee said that they were initially concerned to promote voluntary euthanasia, but that, as public opinion developed, "further progress" would become possible as an ageing population increased the number of "useless lives."[80] Two years later the Euthanasia Society of America was formed. At its first annual meeting its treasurer explained that its proposed legislation was *limited purposely to voluntary euthanasia because public opinion is not ready to accept the broader principle*," and that the Society hoped eventually to legalize non-voluntary euthanasia.[81] Moreover, cases cited by advocates to illustrate the case for relaxing the law, including cases cited by Williams himself, were often of the non-voluntary type.[82]

Kamisar also identified inconsistencies in Williams' case for decriminalizing voluntary, but not non-voluntary, euthanasia. In relation to the senile, Williams wrote that the problem had not reached the degree of seriousness to justify changing the law, a change which would "inflict a traumatic injury" upon the accepted code of behavior built up by 2,000 years of Christianity.[83] Given, as we noted above, that *The Sanctity of Life* sought to debunk that code, Kamisar not unreasonably identified this as

[78] *Ibid.*, p. 1014.   [79] *Ibid.*, p. 1015.   [80] *Ibid.*   [81] *Ibid.*, 1016 (Kamisar's emphasis).
[82] *Ibid.*, pp. 1017–1023.   [83] *SOL*, p. 310.

the most startling passage in the book.[84] Moreover, Kamisar was puzzled by Williams' claim that the problem of senility was not sufficiently serious, given that Williams had noted that senile dementia was "increasingly common."[85] Indeed, was not the problem of dementia greater numerically than that of the cancer victim in intolerable, unrelievable pain?[86] And what of disabled infants? Williams had downplayed the case for paediatric euthanasia on the ground that it was proposed by a "very small minority" and could be dismissed as "politically insignificant."[87] Kamisar observed that if the only advantage Williams saw for voluntary over non-voluntary euthanasia lay in the existence of an organized movement, that advantage could be readily wiped out.[88] Kamisar also questioned whether only a "very small minority" had advocated non-voluntary euthanasia: until euthanasia societies in the United Kingdom and the United States began to focus on voluntary euthanasia, and until the Nazi atrocities embarrassed, if only temporarily, advocates of non-voluntary euthanasia, about as many writers had favored each type.[89] He concluded:

> Williams' reasons for not extending euthanasia – once we legalize it in the narrow "voluntary" area – to the senile and the defective are much less forceful and much less persuasive than his arguments for legalizing voluntary euthanasia in the first place. I regard this as another reason for not legalizing voluntary euthanasia in the first place.[90]

Kamisar accepted that the "wedge" or "slippery slope" argument could be abused, but he concluded that, given the endorsement of non-voluntary euthanasia by many advocates of voluntary euthanasia, the argument had traction.[91] Another reason it had traction was that what he described as the "parade of horrors" had actually happened, during the Nazi era. He quoted Dr. Leo Alexander's famous observation that the Nazi parade began with "the acceptance of the attitude, basic in the euthanasia movement, that there is such a thing as a life not worthy to be lived."[92] Kamisar noted that Williams made no attempt to distinguish

---

[84] Kamisar, "Some Non-Religious Views against Proposed 'Mercy-Killing' Legislation," p. 1025. See text at nn. 39–40, above.

[85] Ibid., p. 1025.   [86] Ibid., pp. 1025–1026.   [87] SOL, p. 312.

[88] Kamisar, "Some Non-Religious Views against Proposed 'Mercy-Killing' Legislation," p. 1027.

[89] Ibid.   [90] Ibid., p. 1030.   [91] Ibid., p. 1031.

[92] Leo Alexander, "Medical Science under Dictatorship," New England Journal of Medicine, 241 (1949), 39–47, at p. 44, quoted in Kamisar, "Some Non-Religious Views against Proposed 'Mercy-Killing' Legislation," pp. 1031–1032.

or minimize the Nazi experience.[93] Kamisar considered the counter-argument that such gross breaches of human rights could not happen in a country like the United States, but he pointed to the internment of Japanese Americans during the Second World War.[94] No small part of US constitutional law was, he wrote, shaped by the concern that abuses can happen unless lines are adamantly held and small beginnings snuffed out. He concluded:

> To flick off, as Professor Williams does, the fears about legalized euthanasia as so much nonsense, as a chimerical "parade of horrors," is to sweep away much of the ground on which all our civil liberties rest.[95]

III   Williams' rejoinder

Glanville Williams penned a spirited rejoinder to Kamisar in the pages of the same law journal.[96] He began by summarizing the case for the decriminalization of "voluntary euthanasia in the terminal stages of painful diseases."[97] The case, which echoed the case he had made in *The Sanctity of Life*, rested on two values. The first was the prevention of cruelty, to both the patient and the patient's relatives.[98] The second was liberty.[99] What social interest, asked Williams, was there in preventing the sufferer from accelerating his death by a few months? What "positive value" did his life still possess for society? There was also the liberty of the doctor. It was the doctor's duty "to prolong worth-while life" and "to ease his patient's passage."[100]

Williams omitted to explain why these values did not support the decriminalization of euthanasia in a much wider range of cases. First, cruelty. If it was cruel to deny a terminally ill patient's request to be released from suffering, why was it not cruel to deny the request of a patient who was not terminally ill and who (with his relatives) faced the prospect of more protracted suffering? And what of patients who were suffering, but incapable of making a request? Was it not cruel to allow them (and their relatives) to suffer? Second, liberty. If there was no social interest in preventing a terminally ill patient from choosing to accelerate

---

[93] Kamisar, "Some Non-Religious Views against Proposed 'Mercy-Killing' Legislation," p. 1033.
[94] *Ibid.*, pp. 1036–1037.   [95] *Ibid.*, p. 1038.
[96] Glanville Williams, "'Mercy-Killing' Legislation: A Rejoinder," *Minnesota Law Review*, 43 (1958), 1 (reprinted in Horan and Mall (eds.), *Death, Dying and Euthanasia*, p. 480).
[97] Williams, "'Mercy-Killing' Legislation: A Rejoinder," p. 1.   [98] *Ibid.*, p. 2.
[99] *Ibid.*   [100] *Ibid.*

his death by a few months, what of the patient who sought to accelerate
death by a few years? And if it was the doctor's duty to do all he could "to
prolong worth-while life" or, in the last resort, "to ease his patient's
passage," why did this duty apply only to the patient who was terminally
ill and able to request death?

Williams proceeded to criticize opponents of decriminalization,
including Kamisar, for winking at the practice of euthanasia rather
than accommodating it by legislation. Williams claimed that he had
shown in *The Sanctity of Life* that the eminent physician Lord Dawson
had admitted in the House of Lords debate on the euthanasia bill of 1936
that there was a practice of euthanasia among reputable doctors and that
this practice did away with the need for legislation.[101] Williams claimed
that his own legislative proposal for voluntary euthanasia would bring
the law into line with "the ethical feeling of most doctors and with the
actual practice of many of them."[102] This bold claim, that most doctors
ethically approved of voluntary euthanasia and that many of them
practised it, seemed to rely largely on Lord Dawson's speech, but it is
questionable whether the speech substantiates the claim. Moreover,
Williams' reliance on Lord Dawson was double-edged. In 1936,
Dawson intentionally administered a lethal injection of morphine and
cocaine to hasten the death of the moribund King George V, and did so
in order that the king's death would be reported first in the morning
edition of *The Times* and not in some lesser publication later in the day.
His actions were later described by a medical reviewer as an arrogant
"convenience killing."[103] This case of non-voluntary euthanasia, in order
to meet a newspaper deadline, went way beyond Williams' proposal to
allow voluntary euthanasia to relieve severe pain, and illustrated the
dangers of trusting to the "good sense" of doctors, even eminent doctors.

Williams did land a blow when he proceeded to criticize Kamisar for
the latter's evident endorsement of juries violating their oaths in hard
cases,[104] but the "sentimental acquittal" was only one of the ways in
which Kamisar illustrated the law's merciful flexibility, the others being a

---

[101] *Ibid.* See pp. 334–339 of the 1957 edition of the *SOL*. Williams, "'Mercy-Killing'
Legislation: A Rejoinder," p. 2 n. 3. The corresponding pages in the 1958 edition (the
edition used in this chapter) are pp. 297–302.

[102] *Ibid.*, p. 304.

[103] J. H. R. Ramsey, "A King, a Doctor and a Convenient Death," *British Medical Journal*,
308 (1994), 1445.

[104] Williams, "'Mercy-Killing' Legislation: A Rejoinder," p. 3.

decision not to prosecute, leniency in sentencing, and reprieve.[105] And Kamisar made the telling response that if inequality of application were enough to damn a particular provision of the criminal law, then we might as well tear up all our codes.[106]

Williams turned to address the "euthanasiast's dilemma" at the heart of Kamisar's case which is, we will recall, that advocates of voluntary euthanasia are pursuing a goal which is inherently inconsistent: a procedure for death which contains ample safeguards against abuse and which is quick and easy in operation.[107] Williams' answer took the form of an analogy.

In the state of Ruritania, he wrote, many live a life of poverty and misery. They would happily emigrate, but the state bans all emigration for fear that the population would be decimated by the numbers seeking to leave.[108] Senator White proposes that people be allowed to emigrate provided they complete a questionnaire stating their income and prospects, and satisfy an official referee that they are living at or near starvation-level.[109] Senator Black, a member of the government party, opposes the proposal on the ground that it is intolerable that a free citizen should be required to disclose these humiliating details and, in particular, be subjected to investigation by an official referee. Williams concluded that Senator Black's objection would be reasonable if he were prepared to admit that citizens should be able to emigrate without formality, "But if he uses his objections to formality in order to support the existing ban on emigration, one can only say that he must be muddle-headed, or self-deceptive, or hypocritical."[110] Any unbiased mind, Williams continued, could see that it was better to be allowed to emigrate on condition of form-filling than not to be allowed to emigrate at all.[111] Kamisar's position on euthanasia was, he thought, identical to Senator Black's on emigration.

Williams' analogy is unconvincing. First, it is widely agreed that there is a right to emigrate; it is not widely agreed there is a right to be euthanized. Second, it does not follow that it is better to be allowed to do X on condition Y than not to be allowed to do X at all. It may be that condition Y is unprincipled or impractical.

---

[105] Kamisar, "Some Non-Religious Views against Proposed 'Mercy-Killing' Legislation," p. 971.
[106] Ibid., p. 972.   [107] Ibid., pp. 981–982. See text at nn. 50–51, above.
[108] Williams, "'Mercy-Killing' Legislation: A Rejoinder," pp. 3–4.   [109] Ibid., p. 4.
[110] Ibid.   [111] Ibid.

What if, for example, there were good reason to believe that formalities required for voluntary euthanasia would in practice be ignored by a significant proportion of doctors, perhaps because they would regard them as overly bureaucratic or as too intrusive an interference with their medical judgment? Why would it be "muddle-headed" to oppose a proposal to permit voluntary euthanasia subject to those formalities? Indeed, Williams wrote: "I agree with Kamisar and the critics in thinking that the procedure of the Euthanasia Bill was over-elaborate, and that it would probably fail to operate in many cases for this reason."[112] He went on to write that this was no argument for rejecting the measure if it was the most that public opinion would accept.[113] But if procedures laid down to ensure that the patient had indeed made a free and informed request would fail to operate in many cases – and it is surely more difficult to ensure that requests for euthanasia are free and informed than it is to ensure that someone is financially at or near starvation level[114] – why was this not a sound argument for rejecting a proposal containing those procedures? Opponents of decriminalization are not, like Senator Black, concerned about formalities being humiliating to applicants: they are centrally concerned about their enforceability. Third, if preservation of the state of Ruritania would justify allowing the starving to emigrate, why would it not justify requiring, or at least encouraging, them to emigrate?[115] If, to quote Williams, a person's life has no "positive value" for society,[116] why not require or at least encourage that person to request euthanasia?

Williams proceeded to defend the proposal for decriminalizing voluntary euthanasia advanced in *The Sanctity of Life*. He noted that Kamisar's first objection related to the voluntariness of the patient's request, and that Kamisar questioned whether the patient's request might be uninformed or the product of an unsound mind.[117] Williams' breezy response to this central objection was the unreferenced claim that

---

[112] *Ibid.*   [113] *Ibid.*

[114] In an important *Statement* in 2006 critical of a bill to allow physician-assisted suicide, the Royal College of Psychiatrists cautioned that there was a clear association between depression and requests by the terminally ill for hastened death. The Royal College also highlighted the difficulties of non-psychiatrists diagnosing depression and noted that, when depression was treated, almost all patients changed their minds about wanting to die. Royal College of Psychiatrists, *Statement on Physician-Assisted Suicide* (2006). The *Statement* is currently under review and is no longer available on the Royal College's web site.

[115] I am grateful to Lord Justice Toulson for this point.

[116] Williams, "'Mercy-Killing' Legislation: A Rejoinder," p. 2.   [117] *Ibid.*, pp. 4–5.

he had "dealt with this problem" in his book. The reader could be forgiven for wondering where and how.

Williams then addressed Kamisar's related concern that a patient might consent to euthanasia only to relieve his relatives of the burden of caring for him. Williams replied that if a patient suffering pain in a terminal illness wanted euthanasia partly because of the pain and partly because he saw his loved ones breaking under the strain of caring for him, it was not clear how this discredited either the patient or his relatives; there were limits to human endurance.[118] Williams omitted to explain how a doctor was to determine in any given case whether a patient's request was motivated by altruism or by pressure.

Williams next turned to Kamisar's concern about the possibility of mistaken diagnosis. Williams wrote that the possibility would have to be considered by the two doctors his proposal envisaged.[119] But how searching could their consideration be, especially if they were neither specialists nor experienced? He asked, in any event, whether such "medical questions" had "any real relevance to the legal discussion."[120] How was it, he asked, that lawyers such as himself and Kamisar had to examine the medical literature to assess the advantages and disadvantages of a medical practice?[121] Developing this point, he invited the reader to return to Ruritania and to imagine that, many years ago, before Pasteur's discoveries, surgery in Ruritania killed as often as it cured. The legislature had passed a law that criminalized all surgical operations, but allowed specific exceptions to be made by statute.[122] Because of the practical difficulties of enacting statutes permitting surgery – the lack of public interest, the conservatism of lawyers and politicians, and the fact that surgery was thought inimical to established religion – even appendicectomy was still illegal.[123] Williams observed that in the United States and England there was no such absurd general law, but there were two medical procedures which were subject to "the Ruritanian principle": abortion and euthanasia.[124] Instead of legalizing voluntary euthanasia in order to see if the predicted dangers materialized, society was required to make a social judgment on the probabilities of good and evil before doctors were allowed to embark on empirical tests.[125] He wrote that the question whether euthanasia would effect a net saving of pain and distress was, perhaps, one that could be answered only by trying it.[126] It was "obscurantist" to forbid the "experiment" on the

---

[118] *Ibid.*, p. 5.   [119] *Ibid.*, pp. 5–6.   [120] *Ibid.*, p. 6.   [121] *Ibid.*   [122] *Ibid.*
[123] *Ibid.*, pp. 6–7.   [124] *Ibid.*, p. 7.   [125] *Ibid.*   [126] *Ibid.*

ground that until it was performed we could not certainly know its results. "Such an attitude, in any other field of medical endeavour, would have inhibited progress."[127]

Williams' return to Ruritania was unhelpful. First, as he recognized, the object of euthanasia was not to prolong life, but the reverse.[128] Analogizing appendicectomy, which is intended to save life, with euthanasia, which is intended to end it, simply begged the question. Second, the utilitarian objection to decriminalization need not be that until the law is relaxed we cannot certainly know the consequences. The objection could be that we have good reasons now to believe – reasons of the sort deployed by Kamisar – that the consequences of decriminalization would be negative. Williams wrote that while Kamisar's argument that the need for voluntary euthanasia was not large might be true, it was irrelevant: "So long as there are any persons *dying in weakness and grief who are refused their request for a speeding of their end*, the argument for legalization remains."[129] And to Kamisar's point that there was no great need for euthanasia because of advances in palliative care, Williams' retort was that palliative care often failed to save patients from "an artificial, twilight existence" with unpleasant symptoms.[130] Williams appeared to believe that it was irrelevant to the strength of the case for legalizing voluntary euthanasia whether palliative care could alleviate serious pain in all cases and left just one person in a "twilight existence." Surely, the smaller the number wanting euthanasia to alleviate suffering which they claimed could not otherwise be alleviated, the weaker his utilitarian case? It is revealing that Williams, who accepted most of Kamisar's valuable footnotes substantiating the risks of legalizing voluntary euthanasia,[131] scarcely began to establish the need for voluntary euthanasia.

Williams then addressed the "slippery slope" argument at the heart of Kamisar's contention. Williams' response was twofold. First, he pointed to the laws in several US states permitting voluntary and involuntary sterilization. A few states had used such laws, he wrote, but in practice their use had been progressively restricted and it was virtually confined to voluntary sterilization, as in North Carolina.[132] Williams (an avowed eugenicist who evidently had no objection to the compulsory sterilization of gays and habitual criminals)[133] was mistaken. Under the US laws

---

[127] *Ibid.*, pp. 6–7.   [128] *Ibid.*, p. 7.   [129] *Ibid.*, p. 8 (original emphasis).
[130] *Ibid.*, pp. 8–9.   [131] *Ibid.*, p. 1.   [132] *Ibid.*, p. 10.   [133] *SOL*, p. 91.

tens of thousands were sterilized without consent.[134] In 2010, in North Carolina, the state singled out for praise by Williams, the governor established the Justice for Sterilization Victims Foundation to provide justice and compensation for those compulsorily sterilized since 1929. The Foundation's website reports:

> North Carolina law during the eugenics period endorsed sterilization of people who had epilepsy, sickness, "feeblemindedness" and other disabilities. Eugenics was a popular movement, especially prior to ... World War II, and other states had similar programs. However, North Carolina was the only state that allowed social workers to petition for the sterilization of members of the public. These local social workers would petition the board to sterilize a person, and the board would make the final decision. Over 70% of North Carolina's sterilization victims were sterilized after 1945 in contrast to other states that conducted the majority of their sterilizations prior to World War II and 1945.[135]

Early in 2012 the Eugenics Compensation Task Force appointed by the governor recommended compensation of US$50,000 per victim.[136] The governor responded:

> While no amount of money will ever make up for the fact that government officials deprived North Carolinians, mostly women, of the possibility of having children – and officials did so, in most cases, without the victims' consent or against their will – we must do something. I support the task force's compensation proposal. I also agree that we should establish a permanent exhibit so that this shameful period is never forgotten.[137]

In short, the experience of the US sterilization laws does little to refute the "slippery slope" argument.

Second, Williams addressed Kamisar's concerns about the non-voluntary euthanasia of disabled children and of the senile, but inadequately. Williams merely commented that a proposal to permit infanticide might be put forward some day, but it would have "distinct limits."[138] As for the senile,

---

[134] See Keown and Jones, "Surveying the Foundations of Medical Law," pp. 109–110.

[135] North Carolina Department of Administration, NC Justice for Sterilization Victims Foundation, available at: www.sterilizationvictims.nc.gov/aboutus.aspx.

[136] North Carolina Department of Administration, "Eugenics Compensation Task Force Votes on Recommendations Including Lump Sum Payment of $50,000 to Living Victims," January 10, 2012, available at: www.doa.nc.gov/media/releases/showrelease.asp?id=0001-10JAN12.

[137] State of North Carolina, Office of the Governor, "Gov Perdue's Statement on Eugenics Task Force Recommendations," January 10, 2012, available at: www.doa.nc.gov/media/releases/showrelease.asp?id=0002-10JAN12.

[138] Williams, "'Mercy-Killing' Legislation: A Rejoinder," p. 11. He did not vouchsafe what these limits might be.

Williams wrote that he was not proposing euthanasia of the aged "in present society" and that the problem of maintaining those with senile dementia was economically manageable as matters stood.[139] To Kamisar's questions about how "serious" a problem had to become to warrant changing traditional attitudes, and whether senile dementia was not already numerically a more serious problem than that of the suffering cancer patient,[140] Williams offered no reply. Moreover, we will recall that in his rejoinder to Kamisar, Williams argued that if any patient wanted death to escape suffering, the case for voluntary euthanasia stood.[141] Why, then, did the existence of any suffering infant or any patient with senile dementia not ground an argument for non-voluntary euthanasia? Further, Williams judged that maintaining the senile was "economically manageable," but on what utilitarian basis did he arrive at this conclusion? Where was the "positive benefit" to society in maintaining such lives? Could those resources not have been deployed to better effect?

In sum, Kamisar offered a rigorous, well-referenced utilitarian response to Williams' argument for the decriminalization of voluntary euthanasia. Williams' rejoinder, by contrast, tended toward the superficial and evasive, centring on strained analogies with emigration and appendicectomies. In particular, the rejoinder did little to rebut Kamisar's effective deployment of both the practical and the logical "slippery slope" arguments.

IV   The Kamisar versus Williams debate today

Although this classic debate took place over half a century ago, it resonates today. While the issue of mistaken diagnosis and new cures has faded into the background, the issues of whether voluntary euthanasia can be effectively controlled (the practical "slippery slope" argument) and whether the decriminalization of voluntary euthanasia leads in principle to the decriminalization of non-voluntary euthanasia (the logical "slippery slope" argument) remain center-stage. The passage of time has served only to confirm the strength of Kamisar's case and the weakness of Williams'.[142] This is so for at least three main reasons. First,

---

[139] *Ibid.*, pp. 11–12.   [140] See text at nn. 85–86, above.   [141] See text at n. 129, above.

[142] Kamisar has continued to make major contributions to the ongoing debate. See, e.g., Yale Kamisar, "Physician-Assisted Suicide: The Last Bridge to Active Voluntary Euthanasia," in John Keown (ed.), *Euthanasia Examined* (Cambridge University Press, 1995), ch. 15.

the ongoing debate has resulted in the reports of several expert committees, which have examined the issue closely. Second, we now have the
benefit of the "experiment" urged by Glanville Williams, chiefly in the
form of over twenty-five years' experience of legalized voluntary euthanasia in the Netherlands. Third, empirical evidence has emerged concerning the extent of the practice of euthanasia by medical practitioners
in the United Kingdom.

A   Expert reports

The reports of expert committees on euthanasia have, with eccentric
exceptions,[143] confirmed the cogency of Kamisar's concerns. Two land-
mark reports appeared in 1994. In the first, the House of Lords Select
Committee on Medical Ethics, chaired by the eminent physician Lord
Walton, unanimously recommended against legalizing voluntary euthanasia.[144] Having closely considered the arguments for decriminalization,
the Committee found them insufficient to justify weakening the law's
prohibition on intentional killing. The Committee concluded:

> We acknowledge that there are individual cases in which euthanasia may
> be seen by some to be appropriate. But individual cases cannot reason-
> ably establish the foundation of a policy which would have such serious
> and widespread repercussions.[145]

A major reason for its opposition to legalization was that "It would be
next to impossible to ensure that all acts of euthanasia were truly
voluntary, and that any liberalisation of the law was not abused."[146]
The report continued:

---

[143] Such as the report in 2012 of a committee, almost all of whose members were known
supporters of legalization, which was sponsored by Dignity in Dying (formerly the
Voluntary Euthanasia Society), funded by a patron of that pressure-group, and chaired
by an outspoken activist for legalization, Lord Falconer. Available at: www.demos.co.
uk/publications/thecommissiononassisteddying. The Royal College of Physicians and
the British Medical Association were just two organizations that declined to give
evidence to this self-styled "independent commission."
[144] *Report of the Select Committee on Medical Ethics.*   [145] *Ibid.*, para. 237.
[146] *Ibid.*, para. 238. Significantly, the Committee also opposed legalization on the principled ground – which is immune to Williams' utilitarian case – that it would offend the
prohibition on intentional killing which was "the cornerstone of law and of social
relationships" and which "protects each one of us impartially, embodying the belief that
all are equal," *ibid.*, para. 237.

> Moreover to create an exception to the general prohibition of intentional
> killing would inevitably open the way to its further erosion whether by
> design, by inadvertence, or by the human tendency to test the limits of
> any regulation. These dangers are such that we believe that any decrim-
> inalisation of voluntary euthanasia would give rise to more, and more
> grave, problems than those it sought to address.[147]

The Committee went on: "We are also concerned that vulnerable people – the elderly, lonely, sick or distressed – would feel pressure, whether
real or imagined, to request early death."[148] The message society sent out
to such vulnerable and disadvantaged people should not, however
obliquely, encourage them to seek death, but should assure them of
care and support in life.[149] There was, moreover, good evidence that
through the outstanding achievement of palliative care the pain and
distress of terminal illness could be adequately relieved in the vast
majority of cases and, with the necessary political will, such care could
be made available to all who could benefit from it.[150]

The same year, the New York State Task Force on Life and the Law
published its impressive report on euthanasia.[151] The report noted that
the Task Force members were divided on the ethical acceptability of
voluntary euthanasia, but that, nevertheless, they were unanimously
opposed to its decriminalization.[152] The Task Force concluded that:

> the dangers of such a dramatic change in public policy would far out-
> weigh any possible benefits. In light of the pervasive failure of our health
> care system to treat pain and diagnose and treat depression, legalizing
> assisted suicide and euthanasia would be profoundly dangerous for many
> individuals who are ill and vulnerable. The risks would be most severe for
> those who are elderly, poor, socially disadvantaged, or without access to
> good medical care.[153]

Many members were particularly struck by the degree to which requests
for assistance in suicide by terminally ill patients were correlated with
clinical depression or unmanaged pain, both of which could ordinarily
be treated effectively.[154] Legalizing euthanasia and assisted suicide
"would pose profound risks to many patients."[155] Positing an "ideal
case" was not sufficient for public policy if it bore little relation to
prevalent medical and social practices.[156] The criteria and safeguards

---

[147] Ibid., para. 238.   [148] Ibid.   [149] Ibid.   [150] Ibid., para. 241.
[151] New York State Task Force on Life and the Law, When Death is Sought. Assisted Suicide
and Euthanasia in the Medical Context (New York: New York State Task Force on Life
and the Law, 1994).
[152] Ibid., pp. xii–xiii.   [153] Ibid., p. ix.   [154] Ibid.   [155] Ibid., p. xiii.   [156] Ibid.

that had been proposed would prove elastic in clinical practice and the law. As long as they hinged on pain or suffering they were uncontainable, and euthanasia to cover the incompetent would be a likely, if not inevitable, extension of permitting voluntary euthanasia.[157] The Task Force noted that these concerns had been heightened by the experience of the Netherlands.[158]

B   The Netherlands

In 1984, the Dutch Supreme Court declared voluntary euthanasia and physician-assisted suicide lawful in certain circumstances. The Royal Dutch Medical Association formulated guidelines for doctors. In 2001, the Dutch legislature essentially translated these guidelines into statutory form. The Dutch experience has been extensively considered elsewhere.[159] Suffice it to observe here that it amply illustrates both "slippery slope" arguments. Official surveys carried out by the Dutch themselves have disclosed widespread and persistent breach of the "safeguards," with virtual impunity, including the euthanasia of thousands of patients without request and the failure of doctors in thousands of cases to file reports with the authorities.[160] Since voluntary euthanasia was permitted, moreover, non-voluntary euthanasia has come to be condoned: Dutch appellate courts have held that it is now lawful to administer lethal injections to disabled infants.[161] The Dutch euthanasia regime has twice drawn criticism from the UN Human Rights Committee.[162]

C   The extent of medical euthanasia in the United Kingdom

We will recall Glanville Williams' bold claim that most doctors approved of voluntary euthanasia and that many of them practised it.[163] The claim appears to rest on little more than anecdote. It is, moreover, difficult to

---

[157] *Ibid.*, p. xv.   [158] *Ibid.*
[159] See, e.g., Keown, *Euthanasia, Ethics and Public Policy*, Pt III; John Keown, *Considering Physician-Assisted Suicide* (London: Carenotkilling, 2006), Pt I, s. 1; Emily Jackson and John Keown, *Debating Euthanasia* (Oxford: Hart, 2012), pp. 118–128; Herbert Hendin, *Seduced by Death: Doctors, Patients and Assisted Suicide* (New York: W. W. Norton, 1998); Raphael Cohen-Almagor, *Euthanasia in the Netherlands* (Dordrecht: Kluwer, 2004); John Griffiths *et al.*, *Euthanasia and Law in the Netherlands* (Amsterdam University Press, 1998); John Griffiths *et al.*, *Euthanasia and Law in Europe* (Oxford: Hart, 2008), Pt I.
[160] See generally, Jackson and Keown, *Debating Euthanasia*, pp. 118–128.
[161] *Ibid.*, p. 121.   [162] *Ibid.*, p. 124.   [163] See text at n. 102, above.

square with the consistent opposition of the medical profession, not only the British Medical Association but also the World Medical Association, to decriminalization.[164] It is no less easy to square with recent surveys of UK medical practice indicating that voluntary euthanasia, non-voluntary euthanasia, and assisting suicide are "rare or non-existent."[165]

V   Conclusions

The Williams versus Kamisar debate, which in many ways has served to frame the public policy debate to this day, richly repays a revisit. Kamisar exposed the fragility of Williams' argument that voluntary euthanasia can be effectively policed by the law. Kamisar skillfully highlighted "the 'euthanasiasts' dilemma'" and showed how Williams was caught in it. Williams' proposal for legalization, which trusted to the "good sense" of the doctor, made no serious attempt to incorporate effective safeguards. It made an inviting target for Kamisar's concerns about the influence on patients of pain, drugs, pressure, and depression; about mistaken diagnosis and new cures; about the limited need for euthanasia; and about the risks of legalization to the vulnerable, both competent and incompetent. Kamisar could also have targeted Williams' faulty logic, noted in the first part of this chapter, which fancied a link between decriminalizing suicide and decriminalizing consensual murder.

Williams' relatively brief rejoinder to Kamisar, which centered around strained Ruritanian analogies, did little to answer Kamisar's concerns. The practical and logical "slippery slope" arguments at the heart of Kamisar's case remained essentially unanswered.

Over half a century on, they still are. A battery of expert committees in the intervening years, which have examined the case for legalizing voluntary euthanasia, of which Lord Walton's Select Committee and the New York State Task Force merit particular mention, have repeatedly found it unpersuasive. The failure of the Dutch, over the last quarter of a century, effectively to control voluntary euthanasia and to prevent the slide, in practice and in logic, to non-voluntary euthanasia, helps to explain why.

Kamisar deftly demonstrated that Williams' case for the legalization of voluntary euthanasia was largely a conclusion in search of an argument.

---

[164] See Keown, *Euthanasia, Ethics and Public Policy*, ch. 18.
[165] C. Seale, "End-of-life Decisions in the UK Involving Medical Practitioners," *Palliative Medicine*, 23 (2009), 198–204, at p. 201.

Their debate also confirmed what *The Sanctity of Life* had shown: that when Williams moved from his familiar terrain of criminal law, on which few could equal his prowess, to other disciplines such as medical ethics, theology, and social policy, his scholarly standards slipped, sometimes precipitously.

12

The failure of the defence of necessity as a mechanism of legal change on assisted dying in the common law world

PENNEY LEWIS

I Introduction

In his 1953 Current Legal Problems lecture on necessity, Williams described the defence of necessity in now familiar utilitarian terms as involving:

> a choice of the lesser evil. It requires a judgment of value, an adjudication between competing 'goods' and a sacrifice of one to the other. The language of necessity disguises the selection of values that is really involved.[1]

Williams saw the defence as 'an implied exception to particular rules of law' which would be available to defendants charged with any criminal offence, even a statutory offence which does not mention necessity as a defence.[2]

II A necessity defence for voluntary active euthanasia

Although that early lecture did not mention euthanasia as an example of the suitable use of the defence, Williams advocated its use at some length in *The Sanctity of Life and the Criminal Law*. The bulk of his analysis concerned cases involving the administration of pain relief which may also hasten death, but Williams began with the classic case of voluntary active euthanasia:

---

[1] Glanville Williams, 'Defence of Necessity', *Current Legal Problems*, 6 (1953), 216–35, at p. 224.

[2] Williams, 'Defence of Necessity', at p. 224.

If the doctor gives the patient a fatal injection with the intention of killing him, and the patient dies in consequence, the doctor is a common murderer because it is his hand that has caused the death. Neither the consent of the patient, nor the extremity of his suffering, nor the imminence of death by natural causes, nor all these factors taken together is a defence. This, at any rate, is always assumed by lawyers, though there is no case in which the argument that the concurrence of all three factors may present a defence has been actually advanced and decided. It is by no means beyond the bounds of imagination that a bold and humane judge might direct the jury, if the question were presented, that voluntary euthanasia might in extreme circumstances be justified under the general doctrine of necessity. Just as, in the case of *Rex* v. *Bourne*,[3] the jury were directed that the unborn child may be destroyed for the purpose of preserving the yet more precious life of the mother, so, in the case of voluntary euthanasia, it is possible to imagine the jury being directed that the sanctity of life may be submerged by *the overwhelming necessity of relieving unbearable suffering in the last extremity, where the patient consents to what is done and where in any event no span of useful life is left to him.* Although a persuasive argument can be advanced in support of such a direction, it must be emphasised that no hint of it appears in the existing legal authorities. On the contrary, the authorities precisely exclude, on a charge of murder, any defence that the deceased consented to the extinction of his life, any defence of good motive, and any defence that the deceased would shortly have died in any event.[4]

For Williams, then, the criteria proposed for successful use of the defence of necessity in termination of life cases were: consent; terminal illness; and unbearable suffering.

A   Could the necessity defence be limited in this way?

Williams' formulation of the necessity defence was as a choice of the lesser evil between competing evils. He argued that the law should permit the doctor to prefer the evil of terminating the patient's life to the evil of unbearable suffering. While unbearable suffering forms a key part of such an assessment, the requirements of consent and terminal illness are more difficult to embed in a 'lesser evils' analysis.

---

[3] *Bourne* [1939] 1 KB 687, [1938] 3 All ER 615 (the two reports are different in substantial respects).

[4] Glanville Williams, *The Sanctity of Life and the Criminal Law* (London: Faber & Faber, 1958), pp. 283–4 (added emphasis).

1   Consent

Those who are not able to consent for themselves may also experience unbearable suffering. The 'lesser evil' formulation would apparently permit termination of life without request.

Williams was, though, not necessarily wedded to consent as an essential requirement. He returned to the possible use of necessity in the euthanasia context in a 1973 article in the *Medico-Legal Journal*, in which he discussed the trial in Liège of parents who had killed their physically disabled infant:

> English law, according to the general opinion, would admit no justification in such circumstances, but a sufficiently courageous judge might create a justification, either by following the ancient rule that a 'monster' is not within the protection of the law of homicide, or by invoking the doctrine of necessity. I am not suggesting that such a ruling is likely.[5]

2   Terminal illness

Those who are not terminally ill may also experience unbearable suffering. One might try to embed terminal illness as a criterion by arguing that one can consider the termination of life to be a lesser evil than unbearable suffering only if 'no span of useful life is left'[6] to the patient. The 'lesser evil' formulation does not necessarily require such an interpretation: while the level of suffering must be greater than the evil of shortening the patient's life, the more unbearable the patient's suffering, the longer the span of useful life left to the patient one could reasonably shorten. Whether the patient has a terminal illness is nonetheless *relevant* to the assessment of whether the patient's suffering is unbearable, the prospect of improvement in that suffering, and whether there is a reasonable alternative to euthanasia.

---

[5] Glanville Williams, 'Euthanasia', *Medico-Legal Journal*, 41 (1973), 14–34, at p. 22. See also, Glanville Williams, 'When Sentences are Excessive', letter to the editor, *The Times*, 19 November 1962, p. 11, reacting to the acquittals at Liège. On the 'monster' argument in relation to conjoined twins, see Williams, *The Sanctity of Life and the Criminal Law*, pp. 31–2, discussed in *Re A (Children) (Conjoined Twins: Surgical Separation)* [2001] Fam 147, at p. 213 (CA).

[6] Williams, *The Sanctity of Life and the Criminal Law*, p. 284.

B   Alternative formulations of necessity

Perhaps an alternative formulation of necessity would permit such restrictions? The 'lesser evil' formulation adopted by Williams is one of a number of justificatory formulations considered by the common law.[7]

1   A proportionality approach

In *In re A (Children) (Conjoined Twins: Surgical Separation)*, Brooke LJ adopted Sir James Stephen's formulation of the defence of necessity:

> there are three necessary requirements for the application of the doctrine of necessity: (i) the act is needed to avoid inevitable and irreparable evil; (ii) no more should be done than is reasonably necessary for the purpose to be achieved; (iii) the evil inflicted must not be disproportionate to the evil avoided.[8]

Instead of a requirement that the defendant's conduct constitute a 'lesser evil', the slightly less onerous third requirement[9] is that the evil perpetrated must not be disproportionate to the evil avoided.

This formulation is nonetheless consistent with the defence advocated by Williams[10] and could be used to justify euthanasia: (i) the 'inevitable and irreparable evil' would be the patient's 'unbearable suffering';[11] (ii) the second element can surely only be met if there were no reasonable alternative way of ending the patient's suffering other than terminating her life, that is, her suffering could not be assuaged by other means than euthanasia;[12] and (iii) death would not be disproportionate to the relief of suffering when the patient was 'in the last extremity' with 'no span of useful life . . . left to him.'[13] The possibility of restricting this defence to

---

[7] Here I am considering only justificatory necessity and not excusatory necessity, which is not a workable model for physician-committed euthanasia. See George Fletcher, 'The Individualization of Excusing Conditions', *Southern California Law Review*, 47 (1974), 1269–309, at p. 1278.

[8] *Re A*, at p. 240, derived from Sir James Fitzjames Stephen, *A Digest of the Criminal Law (Crimes and Punishments)*, 4th edn (London: Macmillan, 1887), p. 24.

[9] Ian Dennis, 'On Necessity as a Defence to Crime: Possibilities, Problems and the Limits of Justification and Excuse', *Criminal Law and Philosophy*, 3 (2009), 29–49, at p. 32 n. 27.

[10] Williams, 'Defence of Necessity', p. 224.

[11] Williams, *The Sanctity of Life and the Criminal Law*, p. 284.

[12] Williams, *The Sanctity of Life and the Criminal Law*, p. 290.

[13] Williams, *The Sanctity of Life and the Criminal Law*, p. 284. See the discussion of the proportionality requirement in the Canadian case of *Latimer* [2001] 1 SCR 3 in Penney Lewis, *Assisted Dying and Legal Change* (Oxford University Press, 2007), pp. 91–2.

cases involving consent and terminal illness seems just as remote as for the 'lesser evil' defence.

2   A conflict of duties approach

In *In re A*, all three judges relied on the concurring reasons of Wilson J in the Canadian Supreme Court case of *Perka*.[14] In that case, the defendants were transporting cannabis from Colombia to Alaska by sea. Due to bad weather and mechanical problems they were forced to land in Canada to make repairs and the cargo was off-loaded in case the ship capsized. The defendants were acquitted at trial on the grounds that they had been forced to bring the cargo onto Canadian soil by necessity. The prosecution appealed in part on the basis that the trial judge had made errors in his charge to the jury on the defence of necessity. While the majority restricted necessity solely to an excuse, Wilson J was prepared to allow for a justification of necessity in limited circumstances:

> the justification must be premised on the need to fulfil a duty conflicting with the one which the accused is charged with having breached.[15]
>
> In some circumstances defence counsel may be able to point to a conflicting duty which courts can and do recognize. For example, one may break the law in circumstances where it is necessary to rescue someone to whom one owes a positive duty of rescue (see *R.* v. *Walker* (1979), 48 CCC (2d) 126 (Ont. CCt)), since failure to act in such a situation may itself constitute a culpable act or omission (see *R.* v. *Instan* [1893] 1 QB 450). Similarly, if one subscribes to the viewpoint articulated by Laskin CJC in *Morgentaler* [[1976] 1 SCR 616] and perceives a doctor's defence to an abortion charge as his legal obligation to treat the mother rather than his alleged ethical duty to perform an unauthorized abortion, then the defence may be invoked without violating the prohibition enunciated by Dickson J in *Morgentaler* against choosing a non-legal duty over a legal one.[16]
>
> Where necessity is invoked as a justification for violation of the law, the justification must, in my view, be restricted to situations where the accused's act constitutes the discharge of a duty recognized by law. The justification is not, however, established simply by showing a conflict of legal duties. The rule of proportionality is central to the evaluation of a justification premised on two conflicting duties since the defence rests on the rightfulness of the accused's choice of one over the other.[17]

For Wilson J, the justification of necessity could not extend to murder. She agreed with Lord Coleridge in *Dudley and Stephens*[18] 'that necessity

---

[14] *Perka* [1984] 2 SCR 232.   [15] Wilson J in *Perka*, at p. 274.   [16] *Perka*, at p. 276.
[17] *Perka*, at pp. 277–8.   [18] Discussed below, text accompanying nn. 23–4.

can provide no justification for the taking of a life, such an act representing the most extreme form of rights violation'.[19]

The conflict of duties analysis appealed to the judges in Re A as the doctors clearly owed conflicting duties to each twin to preserve their lives.[20] Having adopted Wilson J's approach, each judge in Re A then distinguished her refusal to apply it in murder cases.[21]

The 'conflict of duties' approach clearly permits, in theory at least, the scenario envisaged by Williams. The doctor is faced with a conflict between the duties to preserve life and to relieve suffering.[22] The latter duty forms part of the doctor's duty of care. Clearly, the patient's suffering must be unbearable without any reasonable alternative to relieve it before the duties can be said to be conflicting. But would a conflict of duties approach provide a greater opportunity for limitations to consent and terminal illness in the euthanasia context? Again, as an incompetent patient could be suffering unbearably, a restriction to consent is difficult to embed within a conflict of duties approach. And similar problems exist for a restriction to terminal illness. The conflict of duties may be present in cases where the patient does not suffer from a terminal illness, if the patient is suffering unbearably from a condition which is not terminal.

None of the common law formulations of necessity permit only a limited form of euthanasia. They would all appear to permit termination of life without request and outside the terminal illness context, provided that causing the patient's death is a lesser evil or not disproportionate to the unbearable suffering experienced by the patient. In the face of a necessity defence on which it is difficult to enforce limitations, the common law has responded in two ways. First, by creating rules which exclude the defence of necessity in all euthanasia cases, and, second, by

[19] *Perka*, at p. 276. Wilson J's limited 'conflict of duties' approach has been criticised by academics who favour a rights-based approach to necessity: Simon Gardner, 'Necessity's Newest Inventions', *Oxford Journal of Legal Studies*, 11 (1991), 125–35, at pp. 131–2; Donald Galloway, 'Necessity as a Justification: A Critique of Perka', *Dalhousie Law Journal*, 10 (1986), 158–72, at pp. 170–1.

[20] The abortion case of *Bourne* (discussed below, text accompanying nn. 37–9) also contains hints of a conflict of duties approach. At three points in his summing up, the trial judge referred to the doctor's duty to perform the abortion. *Bourne*, at pp. 616, 618.

[21] *Re A*, at pp. 202–3, 237–8, 255.

[22] One advantage of the conflict of duties approach to necessity is that the requirement of a duty to prevent suffering (as part of the physician's duty of care) would limit the availability of the defence to physicians. This is further discussed below, text accompanying nn. 70–2, 85–6, 92–5.

creating alternative means of exonerating doctors who perform euthanasia or termination of life without request.

III Preventing the use of the defence of necessity in euthanasia cases

A variety of rules have been developed that prevent recourse to the defence of necessity in euthanasia cases, ranging from a ban on the defence in all murder cases, to more specific prohibitions.

A The common law prohibition on necessity as a defence to murder

In *Dudley and Stephens*, two sailors who had been shipwrecked were convicted of the murder of a cabin boy whom they had killed and eaten. It was held that necessity was unavailable as a defence to murder.[23] Williams had to distinguish this authority in order for his proposal to stand a chance. He did so on the basis that *Dudley and Stephens* involved a choice as to who was to die, which would not exist in the oft-cited mountaineering example (or indeed in the subsequent conjoined twins case):

> Even as regards murder, the decision should not stand in the way of accepting the defence in a mountaineering case where the choice is between cutting the rope and causing some to perish immediately, or not cutting it and allowing all to perish slightly later. Here there is no choice as to who is to die.[24]

For Williams, then, a necessary condition for the successful use of the defence of necessity in a murder case was that the defendant must *not* choose who is to die between competing alternatives. Euthanasia does not involve such a choice, so his proposal still had a chance.

The unavailability of the defence of necessity in murder cases was confirmed in *Howe*,[25] which involved a choice made by the defendants between their own lives and those of their innocent victims, analogous to

---

[23] *Dudley and Stephens* (1884) 14 QBD 273.

[24] Glanville Williams, 'A Commentary on *R. v. Dudley and Stephens*', *Cambrian Law Review*, 8 (1977), 94–99, at p. 99.

[25] *Howe* [1987] AC 417, at pp. 429, 439, 453. Although only duress was argued on the facts of the case, the decision addressed the availability of both duress and necessity. See also *Pommell* [1995] Cr App R 607; *Rodger* [1998] 1 Cr App R 143.

the choice made in *Dudley and Stephens*.[26] The judges in *Howe* confirmed the significance of the distinction drawn by Williams between *Dudley and Stephens* and his mountaineering example:

> It seems to me plain that the reason that it was for so long stated by writers of authority that the defence of duress was not available in a charge of murder was because of the supreme importance that the law afforded to the protection of human life and that it seemed repugnant that the law should recognise in any individual in any circumstances, however extreme, the right to choose that one innocent person should be killed rather than another. In my opinion, that is the question which we still must face. Is it right that the law should confer this right in any circumstances, however extreme?[27]

The House of Lords did not, however, restrict the prohibition on necessity as a defence to murder to cases which involved such a choice. Lord Hailsham's *obiter* reference to mercy killing as an 'almost venial, if objectively immoral' kind of murder made clear that the prohibition extended to *all* cases of murder.[28]

1 Legal change to remove the common law prohibition on necessity as a defence to murder

Although it once contemplated a general defence of necessity which could be available in murder cases,[29] the Law Commission rejected this possibility in part on the grounds of its 'imping[ement] ... on the unresolved question of euthanasia',[30] and has subsequently been reluctant to intervene for similar reasons.[31] It appears that the Law Commission is unwilling to examine this issue without an explicit reference from Parliament, which seems unlikely given the recent failure

---

[26] *Howe*, at pp. 432 (Lord Hailsham), 439 (Lord Griffiths), 453 (Lord Mackay).

[27] *Howe*, at p. 456 (Lord Mackay). See also *Howe*, at p. 430 (Lord Hailsham).

[28] *Howe*, at p. 433.

[29] Law Commission, *Defences of General Application*, White Paper No. 55 (1974), pp. 20–42.

[30] Law Commission, Law Com. No. 83, *Report on Defences of General Application* (London: HMSO, 1977), pp. 25–32. For criticism, see Glanville Williams, 'Necessity', *Criminal Law Review*, [1978], 128; P. H. J. Huxley, 'Proposals and Counter Proposals on the Defence of Necessity', *Criminal Law Review*, [1978], 141.

[31] Law Commission, *A New Homicide Act for England and Wales*, Consultation Paper No. 177 (2005), paras 1.1(3), 1.3(1), 8.3 (exempting the issues surrounding necessity and euthanasia from the most recent proposals on homicide), confirmed in Law Commission, Law Com. No. 304, *Murder, Manslaughter and Infanticide* (London: TSO, 2006), paras 7.26–7.33.

of attempts to amend the Suicide Act 1961 to exempt assistance with travel to a permissive jurisdiction for assisted suicide.[32]

B   A requirement that the defendant must not choose who is to die

An exception to the common law prohibition on necessity as a defence to murder *was* made in *Re A*. The Court of Appeal allowed the use of the defence of necessity prospectively in a case of an operation to separate conjoined twins which would result in the death of one of them. The case meets Williams' necessary condition for the successful use of the defence of necessity in a murder case: the defendant must not choose who is to die between competing alternatives. In *Re A*, the choice would not be made by the potential defendant, but rather determined by the poor prognosis of one of the twins.[33] It is therefore closer to Williams' mountaineering example than to the facts of *Dudley and Stephens* or *Howe*. Without the operation to separate them, both infant twins would die within a few months. If the operation were performed, Mary (the

---

[32] 'Acts not capable of encouraging or assisting suicide (exception for travel abroad)', proposed amendment to Coroners and Justice Bill, 19 March 2009, available at: www.publications.parliament.uk/pa/cm200809/cmbills/072/amend/pbc0720319a.456-460.html, accessed 16 February 2012; 'Acts not capable of encouraging or assisting suicide', proposed amendment to Coroners and Justice Bill, 1 June 2009, available at: www.publications.parliament.uk/pa/ld200809/ldbills/033/amend/am033-g.htm, accessed 16 February 2012. See also the recent defeat of the End of Life Assistance (Scotland) Bill, SP Bill No. 38, 20 January 2010 by eighty-five votes to sixteen in the Scottish Parliament. Scottish Parliament Information Centre, *End of Life Assistance (Scotland) Bill Summary* (2010), available at: www.scottish.parliament.uk/S3_Bills/End%20of%20Life%20Assistance%20%28Scotland%29%20Bill/EndofLifeAssistanceBillsummary.pdf, accessed 16 February 2012.

[33] *Re A*, at p. 239 (Brooke LJ) (describing the weaker twin as 'self-designated for a very early death'). See also J.C. Smith, 'Surgical Separation: Whether Surgical Separation of Conjoined Twins that Would Lead to Death of Non-viable Twin Lawful', *Criminal Law Review*, [2001], 400, at p. 404. One could argue that the victim in *Dudley and Stephens* was also 'self-designated for death' as he had drunk salt-water and was, according to the defendants, extremely unwell at the time that they decided to kill him. *Dudley and Stephens*, at p. 274. See Winnie Chan and A.P. Simester, 'Duress, Necessity: How Many Defences?' *King's College Law Journal*, 16 (2005), 121–32, at p. 130. Chan and Simester also identify another distinction between *Dudley and Stephens* and *Re A*: 'In *Dudley and Stephens*, the cabin boy's death was directly intended: the defendants aimed to kill him, in order then to eat him. In *Re A*, [the weaker twin's] death was no part of the doctors' aim or purpose, although it was an inevitable consequence of what they sought to achieve.' This distinction was not one relied upon by the court in *Re A*. As death is directly intended in cases of euthanasia, such a limitation on the defence of necessity would prevent the application of the defence to euthanasia cases.

twin with the poor prognosis) would die immediately, but it was hoped that Jodie (the remaining twin) would survive to lead a 'relatively normal life'.[34]

C   A requirement for a net saving of life

In *Re A*, when choosing the lesser evil, to use Williams' phrase, one is choosing the death of one twin over the death of both twins, or the deaths of a few mountaineers over the deaths of those few and one or more additional mountaineers.[35] Is this 'net saving of lives' aspect of *Re A* a necessary condition for the successful use of the defence of necessity in a case of murder? If so, it would exclude the case of euthanasia in which one is choosing the death of a person over their unbearable suffering.

Ward LJ specifically excluded the possibility that the defence of necessity could be used to justify or excuse euthanasia, restricting it solely to the conjoined twins scenario which does involve a net saving of lives:

> Lest it be thought that this decision could become authority for wider propositions, such as that a doctor, once he has determined that a patient cannot survive, can kill the patient, it is important to restate the unique circumstances for which this case is authority. They are that it must be impossible to preserve the life of X without bringing about the death of Y, that Y by his or her very continued existence will inevitably bring about the death of X within a short period of time, and that X is capable of living an independent life but Y is incapable under any circumstances, including all forms of medical intervention, of viable independent existence. As I said at the beginning of this judgment, this is a very unique case.[36]

The abortion case of *Bourne*, which Williams had used in support of his necessity proposal, could also be seen as a case involving a net saving of life, as the life of the woman was described by the judge as 'yet more precious' than the life of the foetus. In *Bourne*, the defendant obstetric surgeon was charged with procuring a miscarriage of a fourteen-year-old girl who had been violently raped. The defendant and two medical experts had testified that the continuance of the pregnancy would probably cause serious injury to the girl resulting in her becoming a 'mental wreck'. The defence in section 1(1) of the Infant Life Preservation Act

---

[34] *Re A*, at p. 197. See Sandra Laville, 'Surviving Siamese twin Gracie goes Home to Gozo', *Daily Telegraph*, 16 June 2001.

[35] See also the Zeebrugge example in *Re A*, at pp. 229–30.   [36] *Re A*, at pp. 204–5.

1929 permitting abortion where essential to preserve the life of the
mother was incorporated into section 58 of the Offences Against the
Person Act 1861, and this defence was interpreted 'in an extended sense
to include preserving the longevity of the mother'.[37] Williams argued
that 'the only legal principle on which the exception could be based ...
[and] the only principle indicating the extent of legality is the defence of
necessity'.[38] Returning again to the 'judgment of value' outlined in the
1953 Current Legal Problems lecture, Williams concluded that 'the
defence of necessity involves a choice of values and a choice of evils,
and the choice made by the judge appears clearly from his statement that
"the unborn child in the womb must not be destroyed unless the
destruction of that child is for the purpose of preserving the yet more
precious life of the mother"'.[39]

D An explicit exclusion of euthanasia

In *Re A*, the court limited its holding carefully, and Ward LJ specifically
excluded the possibility that the defence of necessity could be used to
justify or excuse euthanasia, restricting it solely to the conjoined twins
scenario.[40] Brooke LJ described the availability of the defence of necessity as 'unique' to the circumstances of the present case. He also observed
that 'successive governments, and Parliaments, have set their face against
euthanasia'.[41]

Doubts have been raised about the effectiveness of the limitations
proposed in *Re A*, coupled with either enthusiastic[42] or horrified[43]
suggestions that the decision might be used to justify euthanasia. In an
earlier work, I argued that these suggestions are unconvincing as they fail
to recognise the key distinction between the facts of *Re A* and a case of

---

[37] Williams, *The Sanctity of Life and the Criminal Law*, p. 151.
[38] Williams, *The Sanctity of Life and the Criminal Law*, p. 152. See also *London Borough of Southwark v. Williams* [1971] Ch 734, at p. 746, in which the Court of Appeal treated *Bourne* as based on the defence of necessity.
[39] Williams, *The Sanctity of Life and the Criminal Law*, p. 152, citing *Bourne*, at p. 620.
[40] *Re A*, at pp. 204–5.   [41] *Re A*, at pp. 239, 211.
[42] Richard Huxtable, 'Separation of Conjoined Twins: Where Next for English Law', *Criminal Law Review*, [2002], 459, at p. 468; Suzanne Ost, 'Euthanasia and the Defence of Necessity: Advocating a More Appropriate Legal Response', *Criminal Law Review*, [2005], 355, at pp. 367–9.
[43] Elizabeth Wicks, 'The Greater Good? Issues of Proportionality and Democracy in the Doctrine of Necessity as Applied in *Re A*', *Common Law World Review*, 32 (2003), 15–34, at p. 22; Jenny McEwan, 'Murder by Design: the "Feel-Good Factor" and the Criminal Law', *Medical Law Review*, 9 (2001), 246–58, at p. 248.

euthanasia. In *Re A* (and in Williams' mountaineering example): (1) the act is needed to avoid the death of one person; (2) the separation (or cutting the rope) is reasonably necessary to avoid that death; and (3) the death of the person who will die as a result of the act is inevitable and therefore not disproportionate to the death avoided (either both twins would die in a few months, or Jodie might be saved if Mary were killed by the operation to separate them).[44]

Some of these critics envisage, as Williams did, an application of the defence of necessity in euthanasia cases which would be limited to cases involving consent. Wicks, for example, states that after *Re A*, 'there remains a lingering fear that, in the absence of stronger authority, *Re A* could be used in the future as persuasive authority for voluntary active euthanasia'.[45] Huxtable posits that faced with a different factual scenario, a later court might utilise the defence of consent coupled with the doctrine of necessity from *Re A* to legitimise active voluntary euthanasia.[46]

Ost goes even further, suggesting that the 'lesser evil' formulation of necessity could be limited to doctors *and* to cases involving consent:

> The defence of necessity, as currently understood, would require a certain amount of restructuring in order to encapsulate the situation where a physician commits euthanasia. Thus, a physician could rely upon the defence of necessity if he acts both reasonably and proportionately and ends the patient's life because he believes that it is immediately necessary to prevent the continuation of severe pain and suffering of the patient, this belief being reasonable and held in good faith. An issue that could particularly be relevant to ascertaining whether the physician acts reasonably and proportionately is the level of pain the patient is experiencing ... The nature of the patient's request for death could also be a significant issue – has this request been made repeatedly over a period of time and is the patient fully competent when making this request?[47]

Consent, as we have seen, is not a viable limitation on a necessity defence based on unbearable suffering, whether in the 'lesser evil', proportionality or conflict of duties formulation. Ost provides no justification for the restriction to doctors, although, as we will see, the conflict of duties approach is compatible with such a restriction. Ost rejects the conflict of

---

[44] Lewis, *Assisted Dying and Legal Change*, pp. 87–8.
[45] Wicks, 'The Greater Good?' p. 22.
[46] Huxtable, 'Separation of Conjoined Twins', p. 468.
[47] Ost, 'Euthanasia and the Defence of Necessity', p. 368.

duties formulation of necessity,[48] but neither the 'lesser evil' nor proportionality formulation of necessity could accommodate a restriction to doctors and would be available to anyone confronted with unbearable suffering.

IV Disguising the defence of necessity in cases of pain relief which may hasten death

In 1957, in *Bodkin Adams*, Devlin J had stated in his address to the jury that 'the doctor is entitled to relieve pain and suffering even if the measures he takes may incidentally shorten life'.[49] In *The Sanctity of Life and the Criminal Law*, Williams rejected both of the methods by which this holding (and those which have followed it)[50] are commonly rationalised: intention and causation. He dismissed the intention argument in terms similar to those we would use today:[51]

> There is no legal difference between desiring or intending a consequence as following from your conduct, and persisting in your conduct with a knowledge that the consequence will inevitably follow from it, though not desiring that consequence. When a result is foreseen as certain, it is

---

[48] Ost, 'Euthanasia and the Defence of Necessity', n. 56. Ost's reason for doing so 'confuses the utilitarian doctrine of necessity which Brooke LJ preferred [in *Re A*] with the more limited doctrine of necessity which has already been recognised by the common law', in *Re F (Mental Patient: Sterilisation)* [1990] 2 AC 1. Jonathan Rogers, 'Necessity, Private Defence and the Killing of Mary', *Criminal Law Review*, [2001], 515, at p. 517.

[49] Quoted in Williams, *The Sanctity of Life and the Criminal Law*, p. 289. See also Henry Palmer, 'Dr. Adams' Trial for Murder', *Criminal Law Review*, [1957], 365, at p. 375.

[50] See *Re J* [1991] Fam 33, at p. 46: 'the use of drugs to reduce pain will often be fully justified, notwithstanding that this will hasten the moment of death. What can never be justified is the use of drugs or surgical procedures with the primary purpose of doing so'; *Airedale NHS Trust v. Bland* [1993] AC 789 (HL), at pp. 867–8 (Lord Goff); *Re A*, at p. 199; Anthony Arlidge, 'The Trial of Dr David Moor', *Criminal Law Review*, [2000], 31; J. C. Smith, 'A Comment on Moor's Case', *Criminal Law Review*, [2000], 41. See also House of Lords Select Committee on Medical Ethics, *Report*, HL Paper 21-I (1993–94), paras [242]–[244]; House of Lords Select Committee on Assisted Dying for the Terminally Ill Bill, *Report*, HL Paper 86-I (2005), para. [15] (quoting the Attorney-General that it is not murder 'where a doctor acts to do all that is proper and necessary to relieve pain with the incidental effect that this will shorten a patient's life').

[51] Today, we would say that a consequence is intended if the consequence either is the actor's purpose or desire, or is foreseen by the actor as morally certain to occur. *Woollin* [1999] AC 92. The general criminal law concept of intention therefore includes an undesired but known consequence, as in the case where a doctor knows that death will be hastened by the administration of pain-relieving medication.

the same as if it were desired or intended. It would be an undue refinement to distinguish between the two.[52]

The causation argument was the one used by Devlin J, who instructed the jury that:

> no act is murder which does not cause death. 'Cause' means nothing philosophical or technical or scientific. It means what you twelve men and women sitting as a jury in the jury box would regard in a common-sense way as the cause ... If, for example, because a doctor has done something or has omitted to do something death occurs, it can be scientifically proved – if it could – at eleven o'clock instead of twelve o'clock, or even on Monday instead of Tuesday, no people of common sense would say, 'Oh, the doctor caused her death.' They would say the cause of her death was the illness or the injury, or whatever it was, which brought her into hospital, and the proper medical treatment that is administered and that has an incidental effect of determining the exact moment of death, or may have, is not the cause of death in any sensible use of the term.[53]

Williams found this argument unconvincing:

> While I am reluctant to criticise a legal doctrine that gives a beneficial result, the use of the language of causation seems here to conceal rather than to reveal the valuation that is being made. To take an example, suppose that it were shown that the administration of morphine in regular medical practice caused a patient to die of respiratory failure or pneumonia. Medically speaking, this death would not be caused by the disease: it would be caused by the administration of morphine. There seems to be some difficulty in asserting that for legal purposes the causation is precisely the opposite.[54]

Instead, Williams preferred to recognise the choice at the heart of the pain relief dilemma:

> a physician may give any amount of drug necessary to deaden pain, even though he knows that that amount will bring about speedy or indeed immediate death. His legal excuse does not rest upon the Roman Church's doctrine of 'double effect', for it would be both human and right for him in these circumstances to welcome his patient's death as a

[52] Williams, *The Sanctity of Life and the Criminal Law*, p. 286.
[53] Palmer, 'Dr. Adams' Trial for Murder', cited in Williams, *The Sanctity of Life and the Criminal Law*, p. 288.
[54] Williams, *The Sanctity of Life and the Criminal Law*, pp. 289–90.

merciful release. The excuse rests upon the doctrine of necessity, there being at this juncture no way of relieving pain without ending life.[55]

In his *Criminal Law: The General Part*, Williams put the case for necessity more simply: 'the value of saving the dying patient from pain is preferred to the value of postponing death'.[56]

If one agrees with Williams that the doctrine of double effect is simply a covert use of the defence of necessity, then the courts have found a way to limit the use of the defence. It applies only to doctors, and is restricted to cases where the medication used can be used to relieve pain, in addition to causing or hastening death. This latter restriction is not, however, one of principle, nor is it one of those restrictions advocated by Williams.

V   Avoiding the defence of necessity altogether

In addition to the doctrine of double effect, jury nullification, the acceptance of guilty pleas to lesser offences, selective charging decisions or decisions not to prosecute may all play a role in avoiding the defence of necessity altogether.[57]

VI   Can the defence of necessity be effectively limited in euthanasia cases?

The successful use of the defence of necessity in euthanasia cases seems unlikely unless it can be effectively limited. An examination of the use of this defence in Dutch euthanasia cases suggests a different sort of limitation might be feasible, one reliant on the medical profession to determine (some of) its contours.

---

[55] Williams, *The Sanctity of Life and the Criminal Law*, p. 288. See also Glanville Williams, *Textbook of Criminal Law* (London: Sweet & Maxwell, 1983), p. 581. The Church of England also supported this analysis: E. Garth Moore, 'Appendix 2: The Common Law Doctrine of Necessity', in Board for Social Responsibility of the Church of England (ed.), *Decisions about Life and Death: A Problem in Modern Medicine* (London: Church Information Office, 1965), p. 50, cited by the Archbishop of Canterbury (H. D. Coggan) in, 'On Dying and Dying Well. Moral and Spiritual Aspects', *Proceedings of the Royal Society of Medicine*, 70 (1977), 75–81, at p. 76.

[56] Glanville Williams, *Criminal Law: The General Part*, 2nd edn (London: Stevens, 1961), p. 727.

[57] See Lewis, *Assisted Dying and Legal Change*, pp. 95–7.

A   The Dutch defence of necessity in termination of life cases

In the Netherlands, a doctor can rely on the defence of necessity when faced with conflicting duties, namely, the duty to preserve life and her professional duty to relieve her patient's suffering.[58] The defence was developed through a series of court cases.[59] Doctors could use the defence in cases of termination of life on request (which is a separate, lesser homicide offence)[60] and murder, when the patient was unable to make a request.[61] The former use (in cases of termination of life on request, which the Dutch call 'euthanasia'[62]) was codified in 2001.[63]

B   Limiting the Dutch defence of necessity

The limits proposed by Williams were consent, terminal illness and suffering. Only the latter is compatible with any of the common law versions of necessity. The Dutch defence of necessity, based on the doctor's conflict of duties, is similar.

The defence is not restricted to cases involving consent or request, as is evidenced from its successful use as a defence to murder in two appellate cases involving seriously ill neonates whose suffering was found to be unbearable.[64] In 2004, the defence was held by the Supreme Court to be available, in principle, in cases of termination of life without request. However, the defendant had not faced conflicting duties as the patient was comatose and therefore not suffering unbearably, and her death was imminent.[65] As a reasonable alternative, the defendant could have given

---

[58] Maurice Adams and Herman Nys, 'Euthanasia in the Low Countries: Comparative Reflections on the Belgian and Dutch Euthanasia Act', in Paul Schotsmans and Tom Meulenbergs (eds), *Euthanasia and Palliative Care in the Low Countries* (Leuven: Peeters, 2005), p. 5.

[59] See John Griffiths, Alex Bood and Heleen Weyers, *Euthanasia and Law in the Netherlands* (Amsterdam University Press, 1998), pp. 51–67, and sources listed in Lewis, *Assisted Dying and Legal Change*, p. 78 n. 15.

[60] Lewis, *Assisted Dying and Legal Change*, pp. 76–81, 124–7.

[61] Lewis, *Assisted Dying and Legal Change*, pp. 127–36.

[62] Lewis, *Assisted Dying and Legal Change*, p. 77.

[63] Lewis, *Assisted Dying and Legal Change*, pp. 81–3, 124–7.

[64] See the discussions of *Prins* and *Kadijk* in Lewis, *Assisted Dying and Legal Change*, pp. 127–36.

[65] *Van Oijen* Nederlandse Jurisprudentie 2005, No. 217 (Supreme Court). See the case comment by Michael Bohlander, 'Hoge Raad der Nederlanden (Supreme Court of the Netherlands) Murder: Euthanasia', *Journal of Criminal Law*, 69 (2005), 401. The patient suffered from a heart condition and osteoporosis. She was bedridden and developed necrotic bedsores. Palliative pain relief was provided and the patient eventually became unconscious. With the consent of her daughters, the defendant injected the patient with

the patient a further sedative injection, as he himself had recognised. Thus, the defendant had not found himself in a situation of necessity and he was found guilty of murder.[66]

The defence of necessity is not restricted to cases involving a terminal illness,[67] although whether the patient is suffering from a terminal illness will affect 'the extent to which the patient's life is shortened by euthanasia [and thereby] the extent, for example, to which [the doctor] should insist on exploring treatment alternatives or should engage in more than the minimum consultation'.[68] However, the Dutch defence has inherent limits by virtue of the nature of the duty to prevent suffering. First, it is a duty which applies only to doctors. Second, doctors have a duty to prevent suffering only when its alleviation falls within their 'field of expertise'.[69]

1   The restriction to doctors

Only a doctor can be faced with the required conflict of duties to preserve life and prevent suffering. The doctor must be acting in her capacity as the patient's physician; being professionally qualified as a doctor is not sufficient.[70] Neither laypersons (including relatives) nor nurses are thought to be faced with a professional duty to relieve suffering which may conflict with their duty to preserve life and to abide by the criminal prohibition against killing.[71] Although there has been much public

a euthanaticum and she died almost immediately. Van Oijen's patient had, when competent, expressed a desire to be kept alive.

[66] The court upheld the sentence imposed by the Court of Appeals, Amsterdam of one week's imprisonment, suspended for two years. Bohlander, 'Murder: Euthanasia'.

[67] *Admiraal* Nederlandse Jurisprudentie 1985, No. 709 (District Court, The Hague); *Postma* Nederlandse Jurisprudentie 1973, No. 183, 560 (District Court, Leeuwarden), trans. Walter Lagerwey, 'Euthanasia Case Leeuwarden: 1973', *Issues in Law and Medicine*, 3 (1987–88), 439, at p. 440; *Pols* Nederlandse Jurisprudentie 1987, No. 607 (Supreme Court) at p. 2124. See also Barney Sneiderman and Marja Verhoef, 'Patient Autonomy and the Defence of Medical Necessity: Five Dutch Euthanasia Cases', *Alberta Law Review*, 34 (1996), 374, text accompanying n. 51.

[68] Griffiths *et al.*, *Euthanasia and Law in the Netherlands*, p. 104.

[69] Koninklijke Nederlandse Maatschappij ter Bevordering van de Geneeskunst (KNMG), *Op zoek naar normen voor het handelen van artsen bij vragen om hulp bij levensbeëinding in geval van lijden aan het leven* (2005), pp. 39–40.

[70] District Court, Rotterdam, 7 December 1992 (denying the defence of necessity to a physician working for the Dutch Society for Voluntary Euthanasia who had assisted in the suicide of a patient whose own doctors had refused to help him), discussed in J. K. Gevers, 'Physician-assisted Suicide and the Dutch Courts', *Cambridge Quarterly of Healthcare Ethics*, 5 (1996), 93–9, at p. 94.

[71] Griffiths *et al.* cite a number of lower court decisions in support of the proposition that neither laypersons nor nurses may avail themselves of the defence of necessity. Griffiths

debate over the possibility of lawful lay assistance, there has been no legal change in this direction and prosecutions of lay assisters continue.[72]

2   Suffering within the medical domain

The archetypal euthanasia case involves suffering the source of which is somatic, that is, stemming from a physiological disorder.[73] In *Chabot*, a psychiatrist assisted the suicide of his patient who was suffering from severe depression which had not responded to treatment. The Dutch Supreme Court decided that alleviating suffering of non-somatic origin might also fall within the doctor's duty, relying on the Court of Appeal's finding that 'from the point of view of medical ethics the legitimacy of euthanasia or assistance with suicide in such circumstances is not categorically excluded'.[74]

In a subsequent case, the Supreme Court explored the boundaries of a doctor's duty to prevent suffering. Edward Brongersma was an elderly retired senator whose suicide was assisted by his physician on the grounds of his '"existential suffering", which was defined by one of the experts at the [subsequent] trial as the unbearable suffering of life in the absence of any clinical cause and without hope of any improvement'.[75] Brongersma's general practitioner, Sutorius, believed that his

---

et al., *Euthanasia and Law in the Netherlands*, p. 103 n. 40. See further sources in Lewis, *Assisted Dying and Legal Change*, p. 81 n. 27.

[72]   John Griffiths, Heleen Weyers and Maurice Adams, *Euthanasia and Law in Europe* (Oxford: Hart, 2008), pp. 46–7; Suzanne Ost and Alexandra Mullock, 'Pushing the Boundaries of Lawful Assisted Dying in the Netherlands? Existential Suffering and Lay Assistance', *European Journal of Health Law*, 18 (2011), 163.

[73]   Over 80 per cent of all reported cases of euthanasia or assisted suicide in the Netherlands involve cancer patients. Regionale Toetsingscommissies Euthanasie, *Jaarverslag 2010* (2011), 58 (81.25 per cent).

[74]   See, e.g., *Chabot* Nederlandse Jurisprudentie 1994, No. 656 (Supreme Court), trans. in Griffiths *et al.*, *Euthanasia and Law in the Netherlands*, p. 334, app. II-2.

[75]   Ubaldus de Vries, 'A Dutch Perspective: The Limits of Lawful Euthanasia', *Annals of Health Law*, 13 (2004), 365–92, at p. 384. See also Maike Möller and Richard Huxtable, 'Euthanasia in the Netherlands: The Case of "Life Fatigue"', *New Law Journal*, 151 (2001), 1600; Tony Sheldon, '"Existential" Suffering not a Justification for Euthanasia', *British Medical Journal*, 323 (2001), 1384; Tony Sheldon, 'Doctor Convicted of Helping Patient to Commit Suicide may be Retried', *British Medical Journal*, 325 (2002), 924; Margo Trappenburg and Joop van Holsteyn, 'The Quest for Limits: Law and Public Opinion on Euthanasia in the Netherlands', in Albert Klijn (ed.), *Regulating Physician-Negotiated Death* (Amsterdam: Elsevier, 2001), p. 115; Gerrit K. Kimsma and Evert van Leeuwen, 'Shifts in the Direction of Dutch Bioethics: Forward or Backward?' *Cambridge Quarterly of Healthcare Ethics*, 14 (2005), 292–7, at pp. 294–6.

patient 'was suffering unbearably because of his obsession with his physical decline and hopeless existence'.[76]

The prosecution appealed the doctor's acquittal[77] on the grounds that the doctor had acted outside his professional domain, as the patient's suffering had no clinical origin.[78] If this were the case, the defence of necessity would be unavailable: 'if there is no disease, there is no patient and, it would seem, no medical duty to alleviate suffering such as to place a physician in a potential conflict of duties'.[79] The Appeals Court commissioned two expert witnesses to answer three questions:

> (1) whether a doctor could legitimately honour a request for euthanasia in the absence of any physical or psychological illness; (2) whether it is part of a doctor's function to assist people, whose suffering is primarily characterized by psychological factors, such as the daily experience of an empty and lonely existence and the fear that it may continue for many years; and (3) whether there is a consensus among doctors about the answer to these [two] questions.[80]

Thus, according to the court, by virtue of her professional role, the doctor has a duty to relieve only certain kinds of suffering. In the absence of consensus that the doctor's duty to relieve suffering includes a duty to relieve existential suffering, the necessity defence cannot be used in cases of existential suffering.[81] As the experts agreed that no such consensus

---

[76] Tony Sheldon, 'Being "Tired of Life" is not Grounds for Euthanasia', *British Medical Journal*, 326 (2003), 71.

[77] *Brongersma* Tijdschrift voor Gezondheidsrecht 2001, No. 21 (District Court, Haarlem).

[78] Donald van Tol, 'Physician-Assisted Suicide: The Brongersma Case', *Newsletter MBPSL*, 5 (2001), 3.

[79] Gevers, 'Physician-Assisted Suicide and the Dutch Courts', p. 97.

[80] de Vries, 'A Dutch Perspective', pp. 386–7, citing *Brongersma* Tijdschrift voor Gezondheidsrecht 2002, No. 17 (Court of Appeals, Amsterdam).

[81] The distinction between existential and other types of psychological suffering may be exceedingly hard to draw. Rob Schwitters, 'Medical Competence as a Restriction on Physician-Assisted Suicide: The Brongersma case', *Newsletter MBPSL*, 7 (2003), 2. The distinction may also be easily manipulable. Schwitters argues that 'in the case of elderly people, it is almost always possible to identify a medical cause to their suffering. Some have suggested that if Brongersma's doctor had emphasized the various medical problems the elderly man experienced, he would have had no difficulty in securing legal acceptance of his decision.' See also Sheldon, 'Being "Tired of Life" is not Grounds for Euthanasia': 'Doctors and ethicists have already attacked the judgment ... GPs, they argue, treat patients every day whose complaints cannot be linked to a classifiable disorder.'

existed among doctors, the doctor was convicted.[82] Were such a consensus to develop, the position could be revisited.[83]

VII   Conclusion

Glanville Williams' proposal to use the common law defence of necessity in cases of euthanasia has not been taken up. Williams saw the best chance for his proposal in cases where the doctor is faced with 'the overwhelming necessity of relieving unbearable suffering in the last extremity, where the patient consents to what is done and where in any event no span of useful life is left to him'.[84] But if the defence of necessity is used as the route to legalisation of euthanasia, successfully limiting its availability to patients who request it or to patients who suffer from a terminal illness is unlikely.

Using a conflict of duties approach, following the Dutch model, the defence could be limited to doctors acting within the medical domain. In relation to the 'medical exception',[85] Williams argued that 'controls exercised by the medical profession itself should be accepted as sufficient'.[86] A similar approach has been taken by the Dutch courts, in relation to the defence of necessity, in accepting that the boundaries of the duty to prevent suffering are determined by the existence of medical consensus.

[82] The experts in the trial court had also reported a lack of such consensus. See van Tol, 'The Brongersma Case', p. 4; Tony Sheldon, 'Dutch GP Cleared after Helping to End Man's "Hopeless Existence"', *BMJ*, 321 (2000), 1174.

[83] 'The court appears to keep the door open for lawful euthanasia if and when there is a consensus among doctors as to whether existential suffering is suffering of a medical or clinical nature. If so, it may well be that the necessity defence could extend to such cases': de Vries, 'A Dutch Perspective', n. 126. For the situation in practice, see Mette L. Rurup, B. D. Onwuteaka-Philipsen, M. C. Jansen-van der Weide and G. van der Wal, 'When being "Tired of Living" Plays an Important Role in a Request for Euthanasia or Physician-Assisted Suicide: Patient Characteristics and the Physician's Decision', *Health Policy*, 74 (2005), 157; Mette L. Rurup, M. T. Muller, B. D. Onwuteaka-Philipsen, A. van der Heide, G. van der Wal and P. J. van der Maas, 'Requests for Euthanasia or Physician-Assisted Suicide from Older Persons Who Do Not have a Severe Disease: An Interview Study', *Psychological Medicine*, 35 (2005), 665.

[84] Williams, *The Sanctity of Life and the Criminal Law*, p. 284.

[85] Either at common law or in statute, a 'medical exception' exists which removes most medical treatment from criminal law regulation by the law governing offences against the person. See Penney Lewis, 'The Medical Exception', *Current Legal Problems*, 65 (2012) (forthcoming).

[86] Williams, *Textbook of Criminal Law*, p. 590. I have recently argued that this does appear to be the way in which the medical exception operated in relation to contraceptive sterilisation in the United Kingdom. Penney Lewis, 'Legal Change on Contraceptive Sterilisation', *Journal of Legal History*, 32 (2011), 295.

Interestingly, this consensus has evolved over the last ten years in the Netherlands. In 2005, the Royal Dutch Medical Association published the report of the Dijkhuis Commission on existential suffering or 'suffering from life',[87] which stated that 'no reason can be given to exclude situations of such suffering from a doctor's area of competence'.[88] The Commission proposed 'a more open, but not unbounded, definition of the medical professional domain of the physician',[89] rejecting the more limited approach of the Supreme Court in *Brongersma*.[90] In 2011, the Royal Dutch Medical Association took the view that cases in which some patients who could be described as experiencing suffering from life, 'are sufficiently linked to the medical domain to permit a physician to act within the confines of the Euthanasia Law'.[91]

This professionally focused approach to the defence of necessity looks remarkably as though the medical exception has been applied to cases of termination of life from which it has historically been excluded. In the Netherlands, the use of the 'medical exception' was rejected by the Supreme Court in *Pols*.[92] The defendant argued that her actions were justified 'since she acted in accordance with the demands of appropriate professional practice'.[93] The court held that no medical exception for euthanasia existed, as it was 'evident that even in medical circles in the

---

[87] KNMG, *Lijden aan het leven*, p. 14.

[88] KNMG, *Lijden aan het leven*, discussed in Tony Sheldon, 'Dutch Euthanasia Law Should Apply to Patients "Suffering through Living", Report Says', *British Medical Journal*, 330 (2005), 61. The report does not suggest that consensus has already been achieved. 'The report recommends caution, saying that doctors currently lack sufficient expertise and that their roles remain unclear. It recommends drawing up protocols by which to judge "suffering through living" cases and collecting and analysing further data. In the meantime it recommends an "extra phase" to treatment, where therapeutic and social solutions can first be sought.' Sheldon, 'Dutch Euthanasia Law Should Apply to Patients "Suffering through Living," Report Says'.

[89] Koninklijke Nederlandse Maatschappij ter Bevordering van de Geneeskunst (KNMG), *The Role of the Physician in the Voluntary Termination of Life*, (2011), 11.

[90] In *Brongersma*, the Supreme Court held that the defence applies only if the patient is suffering as a result of a 'classifiable physical or mental condition'. *Brongersma* Nederlandse Jurisprudentie 2003, No. 167 (Supreme Court), discussed in Sheldon, 'Dutch Euthanasia Law Should Apply to Patients "Suffering through Living," Report Says'.

[91] KNMG, *The Role of the Physician in the Voluntary Termination of Life*, p. 23.

[92] *Pols*, English summary in Barry Bostrom and Walter Lagerwey, 'The High Court of The Hague Case No. 79065, October 21, 1986', *Issues in Law and Medicine*, 3 (1987–88), 445, 445–6.

[93] Bostrom and Lagerwey, 'The High Court of The Hague Case No. 79065', p. 445 (2122–3 of the original).

Netherlands there is no general agreement regarding the permissibility of euthanasia and the manner in which, and the conditions under which, it might be carried out'.[94] The defence of necessity would, though, be available in appropriate cases.

Although it is no longer necessary to revisit this issue in the Netherlands following the codification of the necessity defence in euthanasia cases, it seems clear that a Dutch court would no longer reach this conclusion regarding the medical exception. In contrast, in light of the lack of consensus on euthanasia among the medical profession in the United Kingdom,[95] it is unsurprising that neither the defence of necessity nor the medical exception have proved to be viable routes towards the legalisation of euthanasia.

---

[94] Bostrom and Lagerwey, 'The High Court of The Hague Case No. 79065', p. 446 (2123 of the original). The medical exception is discussed in H. J. J. Leenen, 'The Development of Euthanasia in the Netherlands', *European Journal of Health Law*, 8 (2001), 125–33, at p. 126; J. V. Welie, 'The Medical Exception: Physicians, Euthanasia and the Dutch Criminal Law', *Journal of Medicine and Philosophy*, 17 (1992), 419–37, at pp. 429–32; Griffiths et al., *Euthanasia and Law in the Netherlands*, pp. 91–7; Heleen Weyers, 'Euthanasia: The Process of Legal Change in the Netherlands', in Albert Klijn (ed.), *Regulating Physician-Negotiated Death* (Amsterdam: Elsevier, 2001), p. 19; Adams and Nys, 'Euthanasia in the Low Countries: Comparative Reflections on the Belgian and Dutch Euthanasia Act', p. 14 n. 21.

[95] Clive Seale, 'Legalisation of Euthanasia or Physician-Assisted Suicide: Survey of Doctors' Attitudes', *Palliative Medicine*, 23 (2009), 205.

13

The duty to preserve life and its limits in English criminal law

ANTJE DU BOIS-PEDAIN

I Introduction

The decision of the House of Lords in *Airedale NHS Trust* v. *Bland*[1] remains central to the way in which the duty to preserve life and its limits are understood in English criminal law. It allows, indeed it requires, the withdrawal of life-sustaining artificial nutrition and hydration (ANH) from an insensate patient when it cannot be shown that their continued provision would benefit the patient. The result is presented as an upshot of the act–omission distinction. Since a person may not interfere with the bodily integrity of another without lawful authority to do so, an insensate patient can be provided with invasive treatment, including 'invasive basic care', only if such treatment is positively in the patient's best interests. Where this cannot be shown the doctor must stay her hand.

The ethical criticisms directed at this reasoning are well known and remain largely unanswered. If it is indeed true, as Lord Keith stated, that 'to an individual with no cognitive capacity whatever, and no prospect of ever recovering any such capacity in this world, it must be a matter of complete indifference whether he lives or dies',[2] then it must equally be a matter of complete indifference to this person whether or not someone interferes with his body with a view to prolonging his biological life. That the integrity of a body whose owner has as much, or as little, interest in maintaining his bodily integrity as he has in preserving his life, should

---

[1] [1993] AC 789. The report of the first instance judgment may be found at pp. 795–806; the report of the judgments in the Court of Appeal may be found at pp. 806–34; and the report of the argument before and judgments of the House of Lords may be found at pp. 835–55 and 856–99, respectively.

[2] [1993] AC 789, at p. 858.

mandate the withdrawal of treatment from that person, thus convinces neither the supporters nor the opponents of this course of conduct.

But the discomfort with the reasoning in the case goes deeper still. The problem is not just that the biological fact of the inaccessibility of any dimension of human experience is taken to remove *one* interest rooted in the experiential aspects of human existence – that in the preservation of life – whereas *another* interest flowing from the same elements of human existence – that in the inviolability of the body – is said to persist. At its heart is the fact that the judgment makes the act–omission distinction the linchpin of its outcome. In doing so, I argue, the decision relies on the wrong moral register – it draws on the act–omission distinction in a context where this distinction holds no sway. This is so because the duty of care towards the patient concerned has not simply evaporated. Staff would not be free to abandon his insensate body on the street as if he was a mere thing. He is still a patient receiving treatment, even though the appropriateness of the particular treatments being offered has been thrown into doubt.

In this perspective, the duty to preserve life is but an instantiation of the more foundational, relationship-defining duty of care. Life-preserving actions are not categorically different from other specific actions which the duty of care may require a medical practitioner to perform in the context of the doctor–patient relationship. In order to make sense of the rights and obligations of the medical practitioner towards the patient, we therefore need to focus on the doctor–patient relationship as a moral and legal concept.

I argue that the organising framework of the 'duty of care' should be understood as giving rise to a distinct moral, and consequently also to a distinct legal regime. As a moral regime, it makes the choice of actions and inactions subject to a 'care morality' that differs in significant ways from the 'stranger morality' that governs the encounters between humans outside duty-governed relationships. What is distinctive of this moral regime is that it prioritises welfare over rights. This, in turn, reflects the internal structure of duty-governed relationships, their orientation towards certain interests of the protégée, interests whose protection and realisation become to an extent the duty-holder's project and task.

When this moral regime is carried across into a legal framework, duties of care not only have obligation-imposing, but also power-conferring and permission-generating dimensions. In their power-conferring dimensions, duties of care entitle the duty-holder to be involved in the process of making certain determinations regarding the protégée's rights and circumstances. In their permission-generating dimensions, duties of care are a source of substantive entitlements to do certain things the duty requires that, in the absence of the duty, one would not be morally or legally permitted to do. Consequently, the criminal law implications of a duty of care are far from exhausted by the possibility that duty-holders may be held criminally liable for omissions that violate their duty of care. Within the criminal law, the duty of care may also furnish the duty-holder with role-related permissions and with decision-making powers. In that particular legal setting, there is no room for a fallback preference for 'doing nothing' over 'doing something'. The duty of care has primacy over the act–omission distinction.

This has important implications for the interpretation and demarcation of the duty to preserve life and its limits in English criminal law. Its content and scope differ according to the moral relationship between the parties to the interaction. Where 'stranger morality' rules, the arm's-length distance between the parties puts the focus firmly on the integrity rights of the affected party as barriers to intervention. By contrast, interactions that stand to be evaluated under the 'care morality' distinctive of duty-governed relationships occur in a framework where the 'default setting' is pro-interventionist. This means that the duty-holder can be morally required and legally permitted to do what would otherwise be considered morally invasive and legally prohibited.

My argument develops in three parts. Section II challenges the orthodox understanding of *Bland* as marking the point at which the duty to preserve life ceases to exist. The judgment should instead be read as delineating the content of the duty of care in respect of an insensate patient – an interpretation which I label 'the continuation view of duty' in contrast to the 'cessation view of duty'. Section III sets out the morality of duty-governed relationships, whereas section IV investigates the extent to which the moral assessments and obligations that flow from these relationships are, and can be, reflected in law. The conclusion returns to the relevance of these insights for our understanding of the reach of the duty to preserve life and its limits in English criminal law. The fundamental distinction, even for the criminal law, is not between acts and omissions, but between conduct performed within or outside a duty-governed relationship. The decision in *Bland* understands that relationship to be continuing until the patient's death. In practical terms, this explains why the patient may not be abandoned or left to die without any form of ongoing medical attendance. In doctrinal terms, this shows the need for the decision to withdraw treatment to be based on positive grounds in favour of that choice.

II   The judgment in *Bland*: an exercise in doctrinal reconstruction

In *Airedale NHS Trust* v. *Bland*,[3] the House of Lords held that it would be lawful for the applicant hospital trust to discontinue feeding their patient Anthony Bland through a naso-gastric tube. Bland had been injured three years earlier in a stampede at a public sporting event and sustained extensive brain damage. He had been diagnosed as existing in a 'persistent vegetative state' (PVS). A 'vegetative state' results from severe neurological damage to parts of the cerebral hemisphere of the brain related to consciousness and awareness, as well as to voluntary purposeful action. The brain stem still functions, however, which means that the patient can breathe unaided and his vital organs continue to operate. The condition is diagnosed through clinical observation of the patient. Reliance is put on criteria such as: no evidence of awareness of self or environment and an inability to interact with others; no evidence of sustained, reproducible, purposeful or voluntary behavioural responses to visual, auditory, tactile or noxious stimuli; no evidence of language comprehension or expression; intermittent wakefulness manifested by the presence of sleep–wake cycles; sufficiently preserved hypothalamic and brain stem automatic function to permit survival with medical and nursing care; bowel and bladder incontinence; and variably preserved cranial-nerve reflexes (pupillary, oculo-cephalic, corneal, vistibulo-ocular and gag) and spinal reflexes. These diagnostic criteria imply that there is a range of dysfunction among patients judged as being in a vegetative state. The state is classified as 'persistent' when it has lasted for more than six months without improvement. There are, however, rare reported cases of slight improvement after more than one year. 'Persistent' is therefore not to be confused with 'permanent'. It simply means enduring, with an uncertain but (in terms of probabilities) negative prognosis for future improvement.[4]

---

[3] [1993] AC 789.

[4] For details, see Joseph T. Giacino and Kathleen Kalmar, 'Diagnostic and Prognostic Guidelines for Vegetative and Minimally Conscious States', *Neuropsychological Rehabilitation*, 15 (2005), 166; Andrew Grubb, Pat Walsh and Neil Lambe, 'Reporting on the Persistent Vegetative State in Europe', *Medical Law Review*, 6 (1998), 161, esp. at pp. 168–74.

The factual findings of the lower courts in Bland's case placed this patient at the extreme end of actual dysfunction and negative prognosis. Brain scans had revealed such extensive damage to the tissue of the higher brain that the medical professionals giving evidence to the court felt confident completely to rule out both the possibility of any actual sensate experience on the part of this patient and any future prospect of him regaining even minimal levels of awareness of self and environment.[5] Faced with 'the awful certainty of [Bland's] fate',[6] the judges were left with the quandary of how to apply the 'best interests test' – the basis on which the medical professionals are, in law, entitled to treat an incapacitated patient – with regard to this patient. The three judges in the Court of Appeal were all attracted to a broader notion of best interests, which would stretch to include a rather wide range of non-medical and even non-experiential interests and could found a positive case for the discontinuation of life-prolonging treatment. Sir Thomas Bingham MR (as he then was) opined that weight should be given to 'the constant invasions and humiliations to which his inert body is subject; to the desire he would naturally have to be remembered as a cheerful, carefree, gregarious teenager and not an object of pity; to the prolonged ordeal imposed on all members of his family, but particularly on his parents; even, perhaps, if altruism still lives, to a belief that finite resources are better devoted to enhancing life than simply averting death'.[7] Butler-Sloss LJ (as she then was) pointed *inter alia* to Bland's 'right to be well regarded by others, and to be well remembered by his family' as well as the 'right to avoid unnecessary humiliation and degrading invasion of his body for no good purpose'.[8] Hoffmann LJ (as he then was) admonished the Official Solicitor for offering 'a seriously incomplete picture of Anthony Bland's interests when he confines them to animal feelings of pain and pleasure', adding that: 'It is demeaning to the human spirit to say that, being unconscious, he can have no interest in his personal privacy and dignity, in how he lives or dies.'[9] In the Court of Appeal these wider interests were seen as tipping the balance in favour of discontinuing the feeding regime of a patient 'immune to suffering' in the present and 'with no hope of recovery' in the future.[10]

But the positive case for treatment withdrawal that was built on these arguments was not one that the House of Lords was prepared to

---

[5] [1993] AC 789, at pp. 799–800.   [6] [1993] AC 789, at p. 828 (Hoffmann LJ).
[7] [1993] AC 789, at p. 813.   [8] [1993] AC 789, at p. 822.
[9] [1993] AC 789, at p. 829.   [10] [1993] AC 789, at p. 809 (Sir Thomas Bingham MR).

embrace. Lord Mustill rebuffed the notion that the sorts of interests recognised by the Court of Appeal could be ascribed to an insensate patient. Even if it was true – as it obviously was – that Bland's relatives were suffering in seeing their son and brother in his hopeless state, Lord Mustill thought it was:

> stretching the concept of personal rights beyond breaking point to say that Anthony Bland has an interest in ending these sources of others' distress. Unlike the conscious patient he does not know what is happening to his body, and cannot be affronted by it; he does not know of his family's continuing sorrow. By ending his life the doctors will not relieve him of a burden that has become intolerable, for others carry the burden and he has none. What other considerations could make it better for him to die now rather than later? None that we can measure, for of death we know nothing.[11]

He therefore concluded that: 'The distressing truth which must not be shirked is that the proposed conduct is not in the best interests of Anthony Bland, for he has no best interests of any kind.'[12] Lord Keith agreed that: 'In the case of a permanently insensate being, who if continuing to live would never experience the slightest actual discomfort, it is difficult, if not impossible, to make any relevant comparison between continued existence and the absence of it.'[13] Lord Goff of Chieveley thought it a case where 'there is in reality no weighing operation [of the burdens and benefits of the proposed treatment] to be performed'.[14]

This insecurity regarding the application of the 'best interests' standard in Bland's case does not arise because of any remaining *factual* uncertainties about whether Bland's condition may improve with time. Factual uncertainty, as the later case of *Burke* reminds us,[15] *must* be resolved in favour of the patient. That is, where the doctor is unsure whether the patient feels or perceives anything at all, he must assume that the patient could have this ability. In assessing the potential burdens

---

[11] [1993] AC 789, at p. 897.   [12] [1993] AC 789, at p. 897.
[13] [1993] AC 789, at p. 858.
[14] [1993] AC 789, at p. 869. The remaining two law lords motivated their conclusions by deferring to the doctors' actual – and defensible – conclusions as to the patient's best interests. Lord Browne-Wilkinson thought that no continuing interest in staying alive could be ascribed to Bland because none of the doctors treating him thought that there was some benefit to him in staying alive (at p. 884). Lord Lowry placed reliance on the fact that the doctors had concluded that in this patient's best interests they ought not to feed him (at p. 876).
[15] *R. (on the application of Burke)* v. *General Medical Council* [2005] EWCA Civ 1003, [2006] QB 273, esp. at [44]–[45] and [67]–[68].

of treatment and non-treatment, the potential for increased suffering that may be caused through either course of conduct if the patient were to have some remaining cognitive ability, must be factored into the balance. Similarly, a doctor who has the option of attempting a treatment when he is uncertain whether the treatment might work, but considers it possible that it could have some positive effect, and the treatment itself involves no or only mild burdens for the patient, would be failing in his duty if he did not 'give it a shot'. In Bland's case, however, the judges were certain that Bland's condition made any self-awareness and experience impossible. The results of the brain scan suggested that not only was there no current higher brain activity, but that the damage to the brain tissue had been so extensive and profound that even partial improvement or regeneration over time could be ruled out. Hence, the judges' arguments must be understood as an admission of *normative* uncertainty: given that Bland exists but did not and could not know that he exists, nor experience any aspect of his existence, the judges found it impossible to ascribe to him any interest that could inform and guide the application of the medical 'best interests' standard. They responded to what they saw as a normative impasse: the impossibility of making a best interests assessment in respect of a person for whom, as Lord Keith put it, 'it must be a matter of complete indifference whether he lives or dies'. It is *for this reason* that the best interests standard could no longer mandate the continuation of Bland's treatment. The standard implodes due to the fact that Bland was beyond having interests.

This reasoning in effect recognises the existence of a class of cases where the best interests assessment involving the balancing of interests for and against continuance of treatment cannot be performed, because all one can say is that 'so far as the living patient is concerned, treatment is of no benefit to him because he is totally unconscious and there is no prospect of any improvement of his condition'.[16] The interest in the prolongation of life that the law would protect is seen not as an interest in bodily existence as such, but as an interest in continued experience of self and environment to some perceptible degree.

Yet the House of Lords was equally clear that the inconclusiveness of the 'best interests' assessment as such did not provide a resolution to the case. Now everything depended on how one poses the question to be answered. Is it: 'Is it in Bland's best interests that feeding is discontinued so he may die more quickly than he otherwise would?' Or is it: 'Is it in

---

[16] [1993] AC 789, at p. 686 (Lord Goff).

Bland's best interests that feeding is continued so he may live longer than he otherwise would?' The perplexing reality is that although these two questions are really just different ways of asking after the same substantive point, they appear to lead to diametrically opposed legal outcomes. The answer to the first question – 'One cannot say that discontinuing the feeding is in Bland's best interests' – suggests that there is no case for feeding to be withdrawn. The answer to the second question – 'One cannot say that continuing to feed him is in Bland's best interests' – suggests that neither is there a case for feeding to be continued.[17] What, then, is the doctor to do?

The House of Lords suggested that the doctor must remind herself that the question to be asked is the second question – after all, she needs to make the case for the continuation of a bodily intervention in the form of a feeding tube. She should then, they stated, realise that the fact that there is no active case to be made for a continuation of the feeding regime means that she no longer has the right to continue with it, as she now lacks the authority to perpetuate the bodily invasion involved.[18]

At first sight, this analysis is in stark contrast to the Court of Appeal's reliance on the continuing duty of care, the source not only of the positive authority to discontinue the feeding regime as contrary to the patient's best interests once his wider, non-medical interests have been taken into account, but also of the right and duty to continue caring for the patient in different ways, ensuring a non-distressing death.[19] It is therefore easily overlooked that the argument in the House of Lords equally depends on an assumption that the duty of care continues throughout this period of time until the patient's death. For what, if not the continuation of the duty of care, could in their lordships' view authorise the doctor to withdraw the feeding tube? It is precisely their case that the doctor's conduct in withdrawing the feeding tube is to be viewed differently than if the same act were performed by an outsider – as an omission rather than an act.[20] If it was an active intervention, it would be prohibited under the judges' own analysis. This means that the very solution favoured by the House of Lords depends on their acceptance that because of the persistence of the doctor–patient relationship,

[17] See esp. [1993] AC 789, at p. 897 (Lord Mustill).
[18] See esp. [1993] AC 789, at pp. 868 (Lord Goff) and 884 (Lord Browne-Wilkinson).
[19] For the Court of Appeal's approach, see esp. [1993] AC 789, at pp. 824 (Butler-Sloss LJ) and 833 (Hoffmann LJ).
[20] The most elaborate argument on this point was made by Lord Goff, [1993] AC 789, at p. 866.

the duty of care continues to exist. Only *that* assumption can explain why the doctor could conceivably withdraw the feeding tube. Absent that special relationship between the doctor and the patient, the doctor would be no different from an interloper who switches off a life-support machine.

There is, in other words, an important similarity between the judgments in the House of Lords and in the Court of Appeal. All the judges accepted that the duty of care was still in place – regardless of whether, as Lords Keith, Goff and Mustill argued, the point is reached where the patient's medical 'best interests' no longer offer intelligible guidance.

Once it is appreciated that the doctor–patient relationship and its guiding framework, the overarching duty of care of the doctor towards the patient, continue to exist, the straight move from the unworkability of the best interests standard in respect of PVS patients to the absence of a duty to continue to provide the treatment, comes under pressure. At the core of the House of Lords' judgment there now appears to be a contradiction: on the one hand, the special context in which the act of withdrawing the feeding tube occurs allows us to evaluate it as in substance not an act, but an omission, thus slipping past the general law's prohibition against harmful interventions causing death. On the other hand, it is precisely the general law's evaluation of the presence of the feeding tube as a bodily invasion that allegedly commands the tube's removal, without any further need for justification within the doctor–patient relationship. But if the doctor–patient relationship takes priority over the general law's analytical framework – as, by implication, the House of Lords' 'rebranding' of an action into an omission accepts – then the decisive question is not how the general law views the doctor's actions, but how they are to be viewed within the doctor–patient relationship. The House of Lords' judgment therefore cannot mark the point at which 'the duty to preserve life' ceases to exist. What the doctor must do to prolong the life of the patient, is merely an upshot of what her overarching duty of care requires her to do in the individual patient's specific circumstances. That duty does not cease, but continues until the doctor–patient relationship ends (say, through the transfer of the patient, the patient's discharge or release, or the patient's death). If the doctor is indeed entitled to discontinue a treatment, the justification for this must be found within the doctor–patient relationship.

Bland has been applied to only a fairly narrow group of patients who were believed no longer to have *any* form of sensate experience, nor the capacity to regain it. By contrast, patients with (even minimal) consciousness and sensate experience of the outer world have not been treated as having lost any legally recognisable interest in their own continued existence. In relation to these patients, treatment decisions continue to be based on a weighing of the burdens against the benefits for the patient, and the courts have held treatment withdrawals to be impermissible where the treatment (such as ANH) was not onerous for the patient, and effective at keeping a patient of extremely limited cognitive capacity alive.[21] Moreover, the medical profession's understanding of PVS has shifted in recent years, putting the medical soundness of 'PVS exceptionalism' into question. Few would now say that they are sure that a patient who betrays no signs of awareness of self or environment, has indeed no 'mental life' or experiences of any sort.[22] But the general questions of what the doctor–patient relationship morally requires, and how these moral requirements influence the application of the general law to the duty-holders in duty-governed relationships, remain central to any assessment of the duty to preserve life and its limits in the criminal law. I address these two questions in sections III and IV, below.

III   The morality of duty-governed relationships

This section is concerned with the doctor–patient relationship as a moral relationship. It argues that we have to understand the 'duty of care' as an overarching, relationship-defining concept that provides the framework for every interaction between doctor and patient within that relationship. Specific duties to perform particular actions arise on the basis of this general, relationship-defining duty. (Not all duties to perform

---

[21] See *W* v. *M, S and a NHS Primary Care Trust* [2011] EWHC 2443 (Baker J) (permission to withdraw ANH from a patient in a minimally conscious – as opposed to vegetative – state refused). This application was heard and decided by the Court of Protection under the Mental Capacity Act 2005. The facts of this case, incidentally, demonstrate the continuing disagreement among medical professionals about how strictly the criteria for a diagnosis that a patient is in a PVS state should be applied. A leading expert thought it was not inconsistent with a PVS diagnosis that nursing staff had observed 'inconsistent islands of function' in the patient over a number of years. When further assessments clarified that the patient was able to press a buzzer when asked to do so, all experts concurred that she was not in a PVS, but rather a minimally conscious state.

[22] Cf. Ronald T. Seel *et al.*, 'Assessment Scales for Disorders of Consciousness: Evidence-Based Recommendations for Clinical Practice and Research', *Archives of Physical Medicine and Rehabilitation*, 91 (2010), 1795; J. Luauté *et al.*, 'Long-Term Outcomes of Chronic Minimally Conscious and Vegetative States', *Neurology*, 75 (2010), 246.

particular actions have this complex, contextually generated structure, but those arising from 'duties of care' do.) Section A introduces the concept of a duty-governed relationship and contrasts it to other uses of the notion of duty. Section B elaborates on the kind of morality applicable in duty-governed relationships: a 'care morality' which is significantly different from the moral regime applicable to arm's-length interactions of independent individuals. Section C looks at the doctor–patient relationship from a care morality paradigm, highlighting the important differences between the moral requirements generated within 'care morality' and 'stranger morality' as distinct moral regimes.

A   The concept of a duty-governed relationship

A duty-governed relationship exists when one person owes a broadly conceived duty of care towards another. Such duties are best thought of as background duties or relationship-defining duties. They provide a stable normative framework for an open-ended number of interactions between the duty-holder and the protégée (or, in the case of area-limited and hence not necessarily all-encompassing background duties, for an open-ended subgroup of these interactions). Examples are the relationship between doctor and patient, wherein the doctor takes on a fairly general responsibility to attend to the medical needs and concerns of the patient (or, as in the case of specialist care, a particular subset of these), and the relationship between parent and child, where the general responsibility of the parent pertains to a far wider range of needs of the child (nutritional, educational, safety-providing, to name but a few), but also allows for greater flexibility and imperfection in what counts as an appropriate discharge of the duty.

A background or relationship-defining duty of this sort operates at the level of the objectives we may set ourselves for our conduct. Suddenly, we are not free to do whatever takes our fancy, provided we can do it without coming into conflict with the rights of others; instead, we have to strive towards a particular objective. The course of conduct we adopt will be measured against the standard set by the duty, and whether we fulfil our duty in the concrete situation through 'an act' or 'an omission' is irrelevant.

Duty-governed relationships are, therefore, structured in such a way that participants in them acquire 'role responsibilities'. Some roles, to be sure, are more malleable than others. What 'being X's boyfriend' requires of Y, the boyfriend, has a lot more to do with the kind of people X and Y are and with the kinds of needs and expectations they communicate to and recognise in each other, than it does with generalisable features of being 'someone's boyfriend'. Generalisable expectations can, however, already be described more concretely – at something like an intermediate level of abstraction – when we ask what 'being the mother of S, a five-year-old child' requires of his mother, Q. Finally, many professional roles, such as that of a teacher, lawyer or dentist, come with a clearly defined set of tasks and responsibilities which allow for extensive generalisable determinations of their requirements at the concrete level of 'duty implementation'.

Note that when the word 'duty' is used to signify a relationship-defining duty, it means something different from the definite, single instance obligations that are the correlatives of specific rights to performance. Rather, this kind of duty is the rootstock from which particular act requirements grow. It is also important to distinguish this notion of a duty from another use of the term 'duty' in philosophical discourse. Sometimes the fact that I am not allowed to hit or injure others in ways which would violate their rights, is referred to as me having a 'duty' not to hit or injure others. In statements such as these the word 'duty' is used only in a weak sense. It refers to the general restrictions of our freedom of action which result from the fact that, in pursuing our lives as we wish, we owe others respect for their liberty and personal integrity, and have no right to interfere with their rights. The way in which a duty-governed relationship is ruled by duty is very different from this. I will subsequently refer to a 'duty' only when our being under such a duty means that we now have to orient our conduct towards the achievement of particular objectives for which we have become responsible.

B   The morality applicable to duty-governed relationships

How we should treat others is, of course, a central question for moral philosophy. Many classic philosophical approaches are universalist and impersonal in that they want to furnish guidance for our behaviour that is applicable to our interactions with other persons regardless of who they are.[23] They reject the notion that there may be different moral

---

[23] The enlightenment philosophies of Immanuel Kant and John Stuart Mill belong to this group. Among contemporary philosophers, see especially Thomas Scanlon, *What We Owe to Each Other* (Cambridge, MA: Harvard University Press, 1998). It is important to note that many philosophers support some sort of separation of the public and private spheres – a move which makes it possible for them to develop separate accounts of how

domains in which the standards of moral rightness and wrongness by which we measure our actions also differ, and baulk even more at the thought that such systems of moral assessment might overlap and generate contradictory demands for the same situation. By contrast, other philosophers with universalist leanings insist that any complete depiction of the requirements of morality must make space for legitimate priority to be given to certain particular others. To the extent that they do not make particularity paramount or generate necessary privileges for the near and dear through some general impersonal rule or principle,[24] they may become attracted to the recognition of different moral regimes[25] (construed variously as mutually exclusive or as overlapping, and with or without a strategy for resolving possible contradictions).

In this section, I draw upon a tradition of moral thought that places care and empathy at the centre of a person's moral obligations. Such theories of morality – developed in recent decades predominantly, but

---

we should treat others 'as citizens' and 'as persons' while retaining their universalist meta-ethical position.

[24] For an interesting essay that contrasts 'moral universalism' as a meta-ethical view about the possibility of formulating moral obligations through general rules and principles for 'like cases' with the position that moral obligations always arise from the situatedness and irreducible specificity of the concrete agent ('moral particularity'), see Margaret Urban Walker, 'Moral Particularity', *Metaphilosophy*, 18 (1987), 171–85. For different accommodations of the special proximity of some others by theorists who remain attracted to meta-ethical 'moral universalism', see Thomas Nagel, *Equality and Partiality* (Oxford University Press, 1991); Samuel Scheffler, *Boundaries and Allegiances* (Oxford University Press, 2001); and Martha C. Nussbaum, 'Patriotism and Cosmopolitanism', in Joshua Cohen (ed.), *For Love of Country: Debating the Limits of Patriotism* (Richmond, VA: Beacon Press, 1996). For discussion of the related problem of how to make universalist morality accommodate reasonable partiality towards oneself, see Samuel Scheffler, *The Rejection of Consequentialism* (Oxford University Press, 1982).

[25] For an interesting account of different moral regimes that resonates with the present focus on the morality of duty-governed relationships, see James Kellenberger, *Relationship Morality* (University Park, PA: Pennsylvania State University Press, 1995) (distinguishing guilt morality, shame morality and sin morality as forms of moral assessment; stressing, however, that 'relationship morality sees human relationships as foundational to all of morality, including the moral rights of others' (p. 40)). Lawrence Blum sets out a view that is compatible with the concurrent existence of other valid regimes of moral assessment. Contrasting his own view with Bernard Williams' attempt (in *Ethics and the Limits of Philosophy* (Cambridge, MA: Harvard University Press, 1985)) to hive off non-impartialist claims to a separate domain of the 'ethical', distinguished by Williams from the impartially/objectively 'moral', Blum writes: 'My own argument is that the category of the moral should be broadened to include at least some of what Williams puts in the domain of the ethical' (*Moral Perception and Particularity* (Cambridge University Press, 1994), p. 26).

not exclusively, by feminist writers – set out their demands either in competition with, or in addition to, traditional universalist theories of morality.[26] Their proponents share a belief that to reduce morality's requirements of interpersonal interaction to standards such as Kantian categorical imperative(s) or to utilitarian injunctions to bring about 'the greatest good for the greatest number', is a doomed enterprise. These 'objective' or 'impersonal' approaches to determining the requirements of the moral life should either be supplemented or replaced wholesale by different ways of thinking and different modes of engaging with the other, compatible with and demanded by a distinct 'morality of care'.[27]

This morality of care is said to differ from a morality of justice (or, as one might say instead, from a morality of rights) by its recognition of the affected person as a concrete individual who, in his or her irreducible specificity of self, situatedness and needs, makes particular and concrete claims upon the agent. These claims are immediate and direct, unfiltered through any generally formulated rules or principles supposedly applicable to 'all persons'. Partly, this is so because the obligated individual – the one who cares or, in Nel Noddings' usage, the 'one-caring' – is called upon also as a specific individual irreducible to some sort of abstract 'moral agent', as a real person with a specific relational link to the other.[28]

This is not the place to develop a complete account and critique of the various strands of thinking about a morality of care. In particular, I do not want to be drawn on the question of whether a morality of care is of universal application or whether it binds us only in our interactions with certain selected others.[29] For the purposes of this chapter, it is helpful to think of care morality and justice/rights morality – a morality I also refer

---

[26] See esp. Michael Slote, *The Ethics of Care and Empathy* (London: Routledge, 2007); Virginia Held, *The Ethics of Care: Personal, Political, Global* (New York: Oxford University Press, 2006); Nel Noddings, *Caring: A Feminine Approach to Ethics and Moral Education* (Berkeley, CA: University of California Press, 1984); Selma Sevenhuijsen, *Citizenship and the Ethics of Care: Feminist Considerations in Justice, Morality and Politics* (London: Routledge, 1998).

[27] See particularly, Held, *Ethics of Care*, and Margaret Urban Walker, 'Moral Understandings: Alternative "Epistemology" for a Feminist Ethics', in Virginia Held (ed.), *Justice and Care: Essential Readings in Feminist Ethics* (Boulder, CO: Westview Press, 1995), pp. 139–52.

[28] See Nel Noddings, 'Caring', in Held (ed.), *Justice and Care*, p. 9.

[29] For discussion, see Held, *Ethics of Care*. Walker cautions philosophers 'not to be too tempted by the "separate spheres" move of endorsing particularism for personal or intimate relations, universalism for the large-scale or genuinely administrative context, or for dealings with unknown or little-known persons', insisting on the importance of

to as 'stranger morality'[30] – as different moral domains. These moralities can generate contradictory conclusions about how a particular individual ought to act in a particular situation. But since care morality treats more information about the situation and the agent as relevant to its analysis than stranger morality does, where care morality applies it overrides and displaces stranger morality.

If one conceives of duty-governed relationships not just as specific sites of moral interaction, but as settings governed by a distinct kind of morality, then these relationships are important in precisely the way James Kellenberger stresses in his account of relationship morality. Specific relationships matter in that they 'determine the individual form of the obligation appropriate to the relationship in question ... and also in that they are the very source of the type of obligation that obtains'.[31] Kellenberger labels this kind of morality 'sin morality'. What he means by this is that the wrong-making component of the agent's conduct lies in his violation of his relationship with the other: to 'sin' against another means to fall short of the ethical demands that our relationship with the other imposes on us – and in some of these demands we may fail invisibly, as in cases where we ought to have thought of the other and his needs, but allowed ourselves to be distracted instead. 'Success in sin morality', Kellenberger explains:

> is a matter of respecting and living up to all the relationships with persons that one has ... Living up to a relationship ... is not just a matter of not violating obligations that exist – not if 'obligation' means what it means in a guilt morality.[32] [It means] attention to needs and desires, the exercise of sensitivity, and more. As opposed to not breaking a moral rule, living up to a relationship is something one can draw near to and draw nearer to.[33]

'preserv[ing] a lively sense of the *moral incompleteness* or inadequacy' of resorts to generalised treatments even in contexts where this is the best we can manage' ('Moral Understandings', p. 147; original emphasis). However, Kellenberger's distinction (in *Relationship Morality*, chs 10–12) between the concurrent regimes of moral assessment he calls guilt morality, shame morality and sin morality, seems both theoretically attractive and practically challenging.

[30] Cf. Held, *Ethics of Care*, p. 80.   [31] Kellenberger, *Relationship Morality*, p. 39.

[32] For Kellenberger, 'those who follow a guilt morality live in accord with their morality so long as they do not inexcusably violate any moral rules' (*Relationship Morality*, p. 277), hence, the 'obligations' recognised by guilt morality are only those imposed on us by general rules concerning the rights of others.

[33] Kellenberger, *Relationship Morality*, p. 278.

In Lawrence Blum's account, what is ethically required of a person is to act 'from loving attention to particular persons'[34] – something that is integral to any committed human relationship. While the central image for such a relationship is a connection of the personal, even intimate, kind, the expectation holds true (in a somewhat weakened and formalised form) also for the relationships formed through certain kinds of professional connection. To 'take on a case' for a client as a lawyer, or to 'accept a patient for treatment' as a doctor, are relationship-forming decisions that instantiate a variant of that special obligation of attentiveness to which Blum refers. It is not, to be sure, the fullness of 'loving attention', but a more limited yet, nevertheless, foundational 'professional attention' that the protégée may now expect to receive. It is true for all these relationships that they are, as Blum says, 'expressive of a good internal to those special relationships' and that 'the moral dimension of those relationships, as generators for reasons of action, is bound up with this particularity, at least the particularity of that type of relationship'.[35]

Moreover, as Blum explains with reference to friendships, the reasons for action generated within such relationships are not always or even typically 'reasons of special obligation' in that what we do for our friend 'is often not demanded by any obligation, either because it is more than what is demanded (giving up one's vacation to help a friend move), or because it consists in doing something lying outside the obligation structure altogether (phoning one's friend to see how he is doing, simply because one has not spoken to him in a long time)'.[36]

What, then, does care morality require of the one caring? This differs somewhat between relationships formed between equals (friends, siblings, life partners) and relationships marked by an asymmetrical need. But let us look first to what is true for all relationship-governed interaction:

> Within the context of relationship, the self as a moral agent perceives and responds to the perception of need. The shift in moral perspective is manifest by a change in the moral question from 'What is just?' to 'How to respond?'[37]

In figuring out how to respond, the one caring, as Michael Slote explains, does not 'simply impose [her] own ideas about what is good in general,

---

[34] Blum, *Moral Perception*, p. 25.   [35] Blum, *Moral Perception*, p. 21.

[36] Blum, *Moral Perception*, p. 21.

[37] Carol Gilligan, 'Moral Orientation and Moral Development', in Held (ed.), *Justice and Care*, pp. 31–46, at p. 35.

or what would be good for the individual cared about. Rather, [she pays] attention to . . . the way the other person structures the world and his or her relationship to that world – in the process of helping that person.'[38]

Margaret Urban Walker elaborates on this:

> This view does not imagine our moral understandings congealed into a compact theoretical instrument of impersonal decision for each person, but as deployed in shared processes of discovery, expression, interpretation, and adjustment between persons. Facets ... which appear repeatedly ... are: attention to the particular; a way of constructing morally relevant understandings which is 'contextual and narrative'... ; a picture of deliberation as a site of expression and communication.[39]

Whereas stranger morality would have us structure our social interactions in terms that are symmetrical, reciprocal, rights-based and focused on preventing unwanted interference, care morality is very different. Starting not from rights but from needs, and with not independence but interconnectedness in mind, it does not reason from general principle or value but from the individual case. What is morally demanded of me is always a question of what is needed by a specific other and the relation in which I stand to this specific other; it is irreducible to any generalised formula. Our moral obligations must respond to this reality of asymmetrical relationships. Whether the other party can reciprocate or whether we could treat others in need alike, are unimportant considerations. Moral deliberation focuses on the question of what best advances the welfare of the other, and in this context on the other's precise configuration of needs (say, to acquire greater independence and self-sufficiency, or to be given stronger support and guidance for a while) regardless of whether it ultimately counsels non-intervention or welfare-advancing intervention.

C   The doctor–patient relationship from a care morality paradigm

Care morality provides a useful paradigm for understanding the moral requirements of duty-governed relationships of the sort which are my focus in this chapter. If one were to line up possible relationship

---

[38] Slote, *Care and Empathy*, p. 12.
[39] Walker, 'Moral Understandings', p. 140. The quotation within the quotation is to Carol Gilligan, *In a Different Voice* (Cambridge, MA: Harvard University Press, 1982), p. 19.

structures according to the degree in which the roles of the parties linked through them are reversible – that is, according to the degree of symmetry and mutuality possible within them – then the doctor–patient relationship (like the relationship parents have with their minor children) is at the asymmetrical end in that the roles of 'care-giver' and 'cared-for' are fixed within it. This is not to say that the cared-for cannot give anything back to the care-giver, or that the relationship does not impose moral requirements upon the former, too. What counts is that the very raison d'être of the relationship is not a coming together of equals for their mutual development and advancement, but a strong need or welfare interest on the part of the one cared-for that the care-giver commits himself to meeting as best he can. It is thus appropriate to think of one party to that relationship as a duty-holder and the other party as the protégée.

In asymmetrically structured, needs-based relationships, it is, of course, often unavoidable that the duty-holder decides certain issues for the protégée. But care morality requires that this is not done as a mere imposition of power. Rather, decisions taken are negotiated outcomes in the sense that they follow from a procedure of meaningful, responsive engagement, in which dialogue and participation are not mere boxes to be ticked before power is imposed. 'How to respond' is not a question the answer to which can be channelled through fixed structures of rules, powers and entitlements. The moral task is to engage with the other person in the right, caring attitude,[40] in a process which is attuned to the other's self and needs, and usually results in agreed outcomes. To follow principles or generalised reasoning is, from this vantage point, but to take a lazy shortcut towards making a decision, skipping some of the hard work involved in being fully responsive to the other person.[41]

The doctor–patient relationship arises in a context where the duty-holder is called upon in his professional role. This has certain implications for the care morality which governs it. First, it makes sense to approach the question of what *this* relationship requires while remaining mindful of the institutional context. The relationship is, from the perspective of the duty-holder as the one caring, less about personal fulfilment and more about the fulfilment of a particular role. Certain matters pertaining to the cared-for, the patient, remain outside this relational

---

[40] Recall the discussion of Blum's 'attentiveness to Murdochian reasons' above.

[41] Noddings is quite correct to point out that care morality is more demanding than stranger morality ('Caring', p. 21).

setting and, consequently, outwith the remit of the duty-holder's legitimate consideration. Whether the patient lies to his landlord about the sort of things he is physically able to do (pretending to the landlord that he is physically unable to take the bins outside, etc.), is not the sort of issue in respect of which the doctor–patient relationship affects the moral rights and obligations of the parties within it. Even within the duty-governed relationship some matters are simply not the duty-holder's business.

Moreover, where the duty-governed relationship is defined by the professional role in which the duty-holder stands towards the protégée, the decision-making process appropriate in this context will typically fall somewhat short of the full responsiveness to the self and needs of the other that advocates of care morality posit as the ideal.[42] Many doctors have limited knowledge of the personal values and beliefs of the patient and have to rely on assumptions about them when performing urgent interventions while the patient is incommunicado. At the same time, this institutionalised form of care morality still conforms to the basic features of such a morality in that it invokes a particular mode of reasoning – not from abstract principles, but from concrete needs and concrete options, and possibilities of meeting those needs – and advocates particular forms of decision making – consultative and dialogical rather than deductive and enforcement-based.[43] This explains, incidentally, why notions such as 'the sanctity of life' or 'respect for autonomy' provide such inconclusive guidance to medical decision making. There is no free-floating value 'of life' (or anything else for that matter) that could be attended to independently of what the patient can, or at least has the capacity to come to, value. Everything done is done to a particular person, to be lived through by that person. The realisation of a lofty abstract value of the 'preservation of life' begins to look nasty in a concrete situation where a suffering person who deeply and strongly wishes to die is forced to continue living.[44] Equally, there is no such thing as a bright line between

---

[42] Walker, therefore, thinks of these cases as impoverished examples of care morality ('Moral Understandings', p. 147). But I prefer to regard these as settings in which a semi-structured blending of individual responsiveness and modes of communication, and reference to expectations and rules-of-thumb that can be cast in some generalised mould, is entirely appropriate.

[43] They also require a proper attitude, and arriving at decisions concerning the patient with such an attitude of concerned involvement forms part of the moral requirements of this relationship.

[44] I discuss this from a human rights perspective in Antje Pedain, 'The Human Rights Dimension of the *Diane Pretty* Case', *Cambridge Law Journal*, 62 (2003), 181.

competence and incompetence that is treated as assigning absolute decision-making powers. The reality is one of guided decision making by which medical practitioners and their patients move forward through the different phases of treatment. Resort to a formal determination of the competence of a patient usually signals that the communicative process is failing to such an extent that the ideal of negotiated and agreed outcomes can no longer be lived up to.

One should also not overlook the fact that the concrete doctor–patient relationships which are formed cannot be pressed into a completely standardised expectation framework.[45] True, the asymmetrical feature of need versus non-need at the founding occasion is present in all of them. But the actual relation can come much closer to the reciprocal and equality-based end of the scale. Over time, it may even acquire elements of friendship with its different boundaries of what matters concerning the other are for me, the friend, to involve myself in, and in what respects I must, qua friend, defer to the other when it comes to deciding important questions concerning him. Some cases in which doctors have heeded the requests of their patients to be actively killed by them appear to have come about within this complicated moral structure of a doctor-cum-friend relationship in which deference to the patient-cum-friend's strongly expressed preferred resolution to an otherwise unresolvable predicament may have been what, for the doctor-cum-friend, was morally called for.[46]

One important feature of duty-governed relationships is that in this relational setting, the act–omission distinction loses its value as a 'moral heuristic'.[47] Within an ethics that prioritises welfare over rights, the

---

[45] Even though handbooks on professional ethics do, of course, try their best.

[46] Dr Cox's case appears to have the features of such a doctor/friend case, by reason of which Dr Cox becomes subject to our moral assessment not simply as 'a doctor who kills his patient at her request' but, more specifically, as 'a doctor who kills his patient and friend at her behest'. The moral issue is not fundamentally different from the one raised by the first case in which the practice of terminal sedation was recognised as lawful, *R. v. Adams* [1957] Crim LR 365. For an account of his trial, see Patrick Devlin, *Easing the Passing: The Trial of Dr John Bodkin Adams* (London: Faber & Faber, 1986).

[47] The expression is Sunstein's, who argues that 'the act–omission distinction operates as a heuristic for a more complex and difficult assessment of the moral issues at stake'. This shortcut to moral judgment works well enough when the more complex issues excluded from view would not lead us to a different moral conclusion. But sometimes they would, and for these cases it is true that 'a moral mistake pervades both common-sense morality and law ... by treating harmful omissions as morally unproblematic or categorically different from harmful actions': Cass R. Sunstein, 'Moral Heuristics', *Behavioral and Brain Sciences*, 28 (2005), 531–43, at pp. 540–1.

argument that 'doing nothing needs no justification' whereas any active intervention is in need of such justification, holds no sway.[48] A positive case has to be made for any chosen course of conduct, wherever it falls on the range from multi-pronged and intense interventions to more selective and limited ones, until eventually mere presence and observation is chosen. The aspect of an invasion of a right (which results more easily from acts than from omissions) is of secondary importance when the contemplated action best ensures the welfare of protégée. This is the – limited and qualified – sense in which acts and omissions are equivalent within a duty-governed relationship.

The 'devaluation' of the difference between acts and omissions within a duty-governed relationship is, moreover, not unidirectional, implying merely that an omission can be 'as bad' as an act. Judged on care morality's terms, conduct that amounts to an 'omission' by a duty-holder can, in fact, be morally *worse* than an action which brings about the same result. Imagine a parent who deliberately withholds food from a child for a long period of time, and in the face of pleas by the child to be fed, until the child wastes away and dies. Would this parent not be morally more abhorrent to us than a parent who killed her child quickly and painlessly, say by a fast-acting poison? What the first parent has done in starving the child to death seems to us to manifest a cruelty and neglect not necessarily manifested in the actions of the second parent.

The general point is that, when a person has a duty of care, one should not willy-nilly equate actions and omissions leading to the same outcome. Within duty-governed relationships, all conduct is subject to the complex moral inquiry of determining what a proper performance of the duty of care requires of the duty-holder in the particular situation with which he is faced. Doing what is best for the protégée will sometimes mean not doing something that could be done; but if that is so, it is not because it is in any sense generally preferable to do nothing rather than something when one is unsure of the potential benefits of different courses of action.

So much for the morality of duty-governed interactions. But what about the interface between this morality and the law? This is the topic addressed next.

---

[48] See esp. Slote, *Care and Empathy*, ch. 3.

IV   The legal recognition of the morality of duty-governed relationships

This section is concerned with the legal recognition of the moral obligations incumbent upon duty-holders in duty-governed relationships. Now, some views addressing the interrelationship between law and morality would have us believe that these two normative systems have no necessary points of connection. Others treat law and morality as a unified set of norms, or at the very least as importantly interconnected.[49] This is not a debate I want to enter at this point, however. I put to one side the question of whether the validity conditions of legal norms include a requirement of conformity with morality. Instead, I treat the proposition that a person should not be legally prohibited from doing what is morally required of her – that is, the harmonisation of a person's moral duties and her legal obligations – as a political–ethical demand to be made of good law. In doing so, I assume that it is possible for a person to find herself in a situation where the conduct she reasonably takes to be required of her as a duty-holder in a duty-governed relationship clashes with what she reasonably takes to be required of her by 'the law'. Whether we think of this tension as real or theorise it away as merely apparent, it has to be resolved. The kind of resolution I am interested in is a 'surface resolution' at the level of legislation and the court-room operation of legal rules and legal doctrine, as opposed to a 'deep resolution' through a theory of the nature of law. In other words, I look at the pragmatic strategies deployed by English criminal law to resolve a perceived conflict between law and morality for the agent.

Even so, the first question is: why *should* the criminal law attempt such a resolution? My answer to this question, in section A, relies on the theoretical case that has been made for a necessary connection of sorts between morality and – specifically – the *criminal* law. In section B, I then investigate the extent to which care morality's obligations are, in fact, recognised in the application of legal rules. Finding that the criminal law falls short of a 'wholesale recognition' of a duty-holder's moral obligations, section C looks at what may stand in the way of a fuller incorporation.

---

[49] See Martin Detmold, *The Unity of Law and Morality* (London: Routledge & Kegan Paul, 1984); Matthew Kramer, *Where Law and Morality Meet* (Oxford University Press, 2006); Nigel Simmonds, *Law as a Moral Idea* (Oxford University Press, 2007).

A   Why do it at all?

There is good reason to accept some form of wrongfulness constraint when criminalising behaviour. As Andrew Simester and Andreas von Hirsch say, 'the criminal law is distinctive because of its moral voice . . . Conduct is deemed through its criminalisation to be, and is subsequently punished as, *wrongful* behaviour that warrants blame.'[50] This, they argue:

> generates a truth constraint: when labelling conduct as wrongful, and when labelling those it convicts as culpable wrongdoers, the state should get it right . . . People have . . . a moral right not to be censured falsely as criminals, a right that is violated when one is convicted and punished as a criminal without having perpetrated culpable wrongdoing.[51]

At its most basic, acceptance of the wrongfulness constraint means that no one should be criminalised for behaviour that is morally obligatory or (where this is the weaker concept) morally right. Debate is focused mainly on the extent to which the state may, by way of prohibition, encroach upon the wide range of conduct that is morally permitted or morally neutral and hence not pre-legally morally wrong, as well as the extent to which the fact of legislative prohibition changes the moral landscape so that what was previously morally neutral is now morally wrong to do.[52] But there seems to be agreement among writers that the law's morally transformative force is not strong enough for legal commands or authorisations to turn conduct which is morally seriously wrong into conduct that is morally permissible, or, vice versa, to turn conduct that is morally required by the moral entitlements of other persons into conduct that it would be morally wrong to perform. In other words, if the fact of legislation affects the moral 'balance of reasons' at all, it can tip the balance only in cases which are pre-legally fairly near the neutrality line (i.e., only slight wrongs, or only weakly permitted actions). But the law cannot turn a serious pre-legal moral wrong into something that is morally right to do. If the law were to permit me to kill my neighbour's child, this fact would hardly make it morally right for me to do so. And if the law were to prohibit me from feeding my neighbour's

---

[50] A. P. Simester and Andreas von Hirsch, *Crimes, Harms, and Wrongs: On the Principles of Criminalisation* (Oxford: Hart, 2011), p. 19.

[51] Simester and von Hirsch, *Crimes, Harms, and Wrongs*, pp. 19–20.

[52] For discussion, see Simester and von Hirsch, *Crimes, Harms, and Wrongs*, pp. 24–9.

starving child, then this law could hardly make it morally wrong for me to do so.[53]

In the present context, the wrongfulness constraint generates an interpretive assumption: that the law should, where possible, be interpreted so as not to force a person to commit a moral wrong and so as not to prohibit a person from doing what is morally right. This was, in fact, acknowledged by Hoffmann LJ in *Bland* when he insisted that:

> This is not an area in which any difference can be allowed to exist between what is legal and what is morally right. The decision of the court should be able to carry conviction with the ordinary person as being based not merely on legal precedent but also upon acceptable ethical values.[54]

The analysis of the moral character of the doctor–patient relationship developed in the previous section provides the basis for asking whether the law as it stands is sufficiently responsive to the moral demands generated by that relationship – interpreting the law where possible so that the moral and legal duties are aligned.

B   Traces of care morality in the criminal law

As I pointed out in section III, although doing what is best for the protégée sometimes means not doing something that could be done, this is not because it is in any sense generally preferable to do nothing rather than something when one is unsure of the potential benefits of different courses of action. Within a duty-governed relationship, there cannot be a 'default preference' for non-intervention over intervention. But neither does the duty, in empowering and obligating the duty-holder to intervene, automatically override any prohibition that might stand in the way of the required intervention. All one can say in general terms is that the principles which govern the resolution of direct conflicts between what the duty would have the duty-holder do and what the law generally prohibits people from doing, must have due regard to the morality that applies within such relationships.

There are two main options for the approach the law could follow. Deference to the duty-holder's view – an option one might call 'externalisation', because it operates through conferring upon the duty-holder a

---

[53] I explore these questions more fully in my paper on 'The Wrongfulness Constraint in Criminalisation', *Criminal Law & Philosophy*, doi:10.1007/s11572-012-9186-521.

[54] [1993] AC 789, at p. 825.

degree of immunity before the law. And incorporation, that is, allowing the moral obligation to affect the application of the relevant legal rules.

The 'deference option' has received strong support from the judiciary at times. Lord Browne-Wilkinson endorsed something like it in *Bland* when he reasoned thus:

> Different doctors may take different views both on strictly medical issues and the broader ethical issues which the question raises ... In cases where there is no strictly medical point in continuing care, if a doctor holds the view that the patient is entitled to stay alive, whatever the quality of such life, he can quite reasonably reach the view that the continuation of intrusive care, being the only way of preserving such life, is in the patient's best interests. But, in the same circumstances another doctor who sees no merit in perpetuating a life of which the patient is unaware can equally reasonably reach the view that the continuation of invasive treatment is not for the patient's benefit ... [The courts'] only concern will be to be satisfied that the doctor's decision to discontinue is in accordance with a respectable body of medical opinion and that it is reasonable.[55]

The existence of an ineradicable remainder of personal discretion for the duty-holder in determining what his duty of care morally requires him to do is translated into the law as an instance of legal discretion. The legal finding that something is 'permitted' rather than 'obligatory' for the duty-holder to do, is the reflection, in the law's mirror, of the moral conclusion that conscientious duty-holders in these circumstances may not reach the same conclusion as to what their duty requires them to do. Whenever this is so, the law cannot fault them whatever conclusion it is that they, personally, reach in these circumstances.

This deference of the law to professional ethics and opinion is not, however, absolute. The point may be reached where the reasonableness of the doctor's conclusion and the fact that a respectable body of professional opinion supports her choice, does not help her in law. This final frontier is reached when the course of conduct judged to be in the patient's best interests amounts to active euthanasia. Lord Goff admitted that 'it can be asked why, if the doctor, by discontinuing treatment, is entitled in consequence to let his patient die, it should not be lawful to put him out of his misery straight away, in a more humane manner, by a lethal injection, rather than let him linger on in pain until he dies'.[56] The answer is simply and unsatisfactorily that, 'whereas the law considers

---

[55] [1993] AC 789, at p. 884.   [56] [1993] AC 789, at p. 865.

that discontinuance of life support may be consistent with the doctor's duty to care for his patient, it does not, for reasons of policy, consider that it forms any part of his duty to give his patient a lethal injection to put him out of his agony'.[57]

Another example of the recognition of care morality within the criminal law is what has sometimes been called 'the treatment of good intentions'.[58] This covers situations such as the administration of strong pain-killing drugs which also hasten death, where an outcome foreseen as certain by the person administering the drug (the speeding up of death) is, notwithstanding the notion of 'foresight of certainty' as showing an intention in the secondary sense,[59] not treated as an outcome which the agent 'intends' to bring about. *Mens rea*-based explanations for this exception are unsatisfactory. It is unconvincing to say that foresight with certainty is a form of intention unless what you intend (= want to bring about) in the primary sense is actually good. The primary or direct intention, which is directed towards a good outcome or a legitimate aim, cannot make a secondary or oblique intention, which arises with the realisation of a consequence as virtually certain, disappear. Both intentions are simultaneously present, and one of them is a criminal intent.

It is just as unsatisfactory to try to base this exception on the doctrine of double effect, if this is seen as allowing us to ignore the presence of an unlawful 'secondary' intention to hasten a person's death that exists alongside the benevolent 'primary' intention to relieve pain. This still leaves us at a loss as to why we should be allowed to discount the unlawful secondary intention in these circumstances. Yet the outcome is so obviously the right one that we have to find an explanation for it.

The explanation we seek lies, quite simply, in the presence of the doctor's duty of care which exhorts him to relieve the patient's suffering. It is this duty which counterbalances and ultimately overrides certain prohibitions of actions. The reason the 'good' intention matters is not that it is 'there', nor that it negates the bad one. The reason it matters is that it is directed towards doing what is called for by the specific situation in the context of the duty-governed relationship. What the law

---

[57] [1993] AC 789, at p. 866.
[58] Andrew Ashworth, 'Criminal Liability in a Medical Context: The Treatment of Good Intentions', in A. P. Simester and A. T. H. Smith, *Harm and Culpability* (Oxford: Clarendon Press, 1996), p. 176.
[59] Cf. *Woollin* [1998] 3 WLR 382.

recognises in these instances is a permission-generating dimension of the legal duty of care. Hart and Honoré see this clearly when they conclude that because a doctor has a duty to relieve a patient's suffering 'it is permissible for him, when the patient is doomed to die shortly, to administer pain-killing drugs with his consent even if they shorten life', adding that: 'It would not follow that it would be permissible, as opposed to understandable, for someone without such a duty to do the same.'[60]

However, the law's recognition of care morality is not complete. It is limited by what the law treats as its primary distinction between acts and omissions. This, then, is the main point of tension for the law's recognition of the moral requirements of a duty of care.

Our traditional understanding of duty-governed situations in the criminal law obscures a fundamental feature of duty-governed relationships. As lawyers, we tend to think of duties as 'duties to act' in particular ways, rather than as duties to 'pursue particular objectives'. Our concept of a duty is act-based, not aim-based. This leads us to assume that, where there is a conflict between what the duty would have the duty-holder do and what the law generally prohibits people from doing, the most an analysis of a particular fact-situation can yield is 'no duty to act' in the way the law might otherwise require. What we arrive at is a 'cancellation of the duty' and thus a state of affairs in which ordinary restrictions on active conduct remain fully intact.

This traditional conception of the relationship between duties and independent restrictions to act is misguided. It presumes that these independent prohibitions are external to the duty, whereas they are in fact governed by the duty just like every other aspect of the situation. Within a duty-governed relationship, the fact that an action is generally prohibited is not determinative of the extent of the duty. The duty does not cease when it encounters a pertinent general prohibition. That a particular act would generally be against the law does not in and of itself establish that performance of the act cannot be required by an aim-based duty. An act may be required in specific situations in order to achieve the given aim at the same time as it is generally prohibited. When this is the case, a separate determination is necessary of whether the duty provides sufficient legal grounds for the particular act in question to make the performance of the action lawful notwithstanding the general prohibition. A conflict of duties can therefore arise not only where two

---

[60] H. L. A. Hart and Tony Honoré, *Causation in the Law*, 2nd edn (Oxford University Press, 1985), p. 344.

incompatible duties to act pull the agent in different, incompatible directions, but also where an agent's duty to act clashes with a general legal prohibition on performing the act which the duty requires. Whether the duty to act outweighs the prohibition or vice versa is a question that cannot be answered in general and in the abstract in favour of the prohibition, as the cessation view of duty would have it. Doing so would fail to take the existence of a conflict of duties seriously.

Within a duty-governed relationship, the role played by the act–omission distinction will not be the one that it has outside such a context, which is to remove the need to justify a failure to act by someone who is under *no* such duty. Its residual function within that relationship is more like its function in general moral argument: it can help us grasp the moral quality of an action in its fullness, and may sometimes (but not always) help us to conclude that the least invasive course of action is, in the circumstances, best.

The hardest cases are those where the conflict between the moral duty and the legal prohibition persists under current law: can one have a legal duty to do that which it is generally prohibited to do? This situation must be recognised and legally resolved under a conflicts of duties paradigm. Where one duty clearly outweighs the other, the course of action indicated by the weightier duty must be taken. Where neither duty clearly outweighs the other, we should carefully examine whether we have sufficient moral reason in the circumstances to give preference to non-intervention over intervention or whether we should simply leave the matter to the duty-holder's choice.

C   The limits of recognition

The distinct legal nature of duty-governed relationships means that the policing of choices made by duty-holders within these relationships cannot be premised on a complete takeover by lawyers of figuring out what the duty requires. This determination is first and foremost for the duty-holder to make. The contours of the particular duty of care in play (parental, professional in different professional contexts) can provide important guidance as to what considerations are proper or improper for the duty-holder to have regard to. But the complexity of the task and the fact that this task is, to start with, specifically allocated to the duty-holder and is for him to perform, mean that the regime of control exercised through the courts must reflect that reality appropriately.

However, a legal system committed to recognising care morality in the application of its legal rules faces a basic difficulty. 'Care morality' has an inner logic that makes it difficult to translate its requirements into legal regimes. Law's 'public morality' of rights-based relations is structurally closer to a 'stranger morality', which reduces the moral complexity of situations to 'you respect my rights and I respect yours'. This complicates the law's project of responding to the different ranges of wrongs within duty-governed relationships. Outside them, rights violations are the paradigm wrongs, but within them, the paradigm wrongs are failures of care and attention, 'letting the other person down', neglect born of indifference, etc. The law's mode of regulation cannot simply swallow 'care morality' whole. Its structure is such that it cannot be incorporated fully in rule-based guidance – which is, inevitably, the form of guidance law must give.

The choice is therefore between limited recognition in the shaping of specific rules, or abdication of legal control through creating a space of non-regulated empowerment. Where the former route is chosen, something of the richness of care morality will be lost in translation.

To speak of the power-conferring and the permission-generating aspects of care morality, as I have done, is already to distort its content in the process of translating its standards and requirements from the moral world into the legal domain. For if a duty-holder effectively comes across as exercising her power, when she 'pulls rank' on her protégée, she will be morally judged to fail to live up to the requirements of care morality even though her decision may be binding on the protégée and may in substance be perfectly correct. Perhaps this illustrates that care morality is a scale morality, leaving room for degrees of attainment, which means that there is scope for much moral failing that cannot be translated into a breach of legal rules.

But even if care morality and its demands can only be imperfectly translated into legal norms, the law – and especially, the criminal law – must strive to do so even at the cost of some compromise to legal certainty and to the internal requirements of rule-based governance. This is so because of the law's commitment to the 'wrongfulness constraint' – the need to abstain from imposing criminal responsibility on those whose actions were not morally wrong. It is for this reason that 'care morality' finds at least partial space and incomplete reflection in the criminal law in concepts such as 'parental authority' and in the width of necessity based on 'best interests'.

Moreover, even where the recognition of care morality encounters limitations on the level of legal obligation, the demands of care morality provide powerful reasons for mitigation of sentence. A conflict of duties is real, not merely imaginary, when two obligation-generating regimes which apply concurrently to an agent demand compliance. The moral regime of care morality clashes with the legal regime of strict prohibition. It is not obvious that, from a moral point of view, the legal prohibition releases the agent from the need to justify compliance with the law as a moral decision, or that he can always achieve full moral justification by showing that the legal rule (rightly) demands compliance from him. To conflict in the relevant sense, one duty may be moral and the other legal and not immoral.

V   Conclusion

My focus in this chapter has been on the proper role of a duty of care in the criminal law: to uncover its multiple functions, trace its methodo-logical implications and reinstate its centrality for the resolution of the substantive issue that needs deciding. The law is incoherent in insisting that *Bland*'s case should be resolved through the act–omission paradigm while recognising the persistence of the duty of care. This is so because the transformation of the moral situation in a duty-governed relation-ship is more profound than a simple overriding of the act–omission distinction. Within a duty-governed relationship, prohibitions from interference lose their absolute character. The boundaries between duty-holder and protégée are drawn differently to the boundaries between strangers. One can thus have a moral duty to do that which would – between strangers – be wrong to do. Put differently: a duty of care can, in principle, generate permissions or justifications for certain interferences with the protégée's rights. Once this possibility is appre-ciated it is obvious that a fuller argument is needed to sustain the conclusion that treatment must be withdrawn. It simply does not follow from the fact that a stranger or outsider would violate a general prohib-ition against interfering with the rights of the affected person that some-one who stands in a duty-governed relationship towards that person is likewise prevented from interfering.

One implication of my argument is that it is time for the courts to move away from the 'PVS patient exceptionalism' that has developed after *Bland*. The condition of these patients is not such that it leads to a cessation of the duty of care. Only death can bring that about. Hence, the decision to discontinue feeding with a view to letting the insensate patient wither away from lack of nourishment must be motivated and defended as an appropriate implementation of the duty of care. The duty of care remains activated and must positively enable the doctor to defend this choice. Such active justification cannot be circumvented by pointing out that the withdrawal or non-continuation of treatment may be classified as an omission rather than as an act.

Interestingly, Glanville Williams objected to the view that there is no moral difference between a positive act and an omission with the same outcome, even where a duty can be established. He was most concerned with the practical consequences of adopting the contrary position which was argued for by Andrew Ashworth in a well-known article.[61] In response to Ashworth's proposal to treat any omission by a duty-holder that could have averted a given outcome as legally equivalent to an act bringing about that same outcome, Williams memorably stated:

> If there is no fundamental moral distinction between killing and letting die (in breach of duty), it is a fact that has been missed by members of the medical profession, who see a great difference between the two. Whereas killing your patient is absolutely taboo, according to the present law and official medical ethics, letting your patient die is qualifiedly permissible, namely when the patient is dying and there is no point in continuing his agony.[62]

Williams' support for what he called 'the conventional view on omissions liability', which waits for a clear legislative signal before it treats an omission by someone with a duty to act as legally equivalent to the active commission of an offence, was focused on what he perceived to be the absence of *legal* (rather than moral) equivalence between acts and omissions. But I think he might agree with me that morality is the starting point. After all, he defended the 'conventional view of criminal omissions' partly because he thought that to endorse Ashworth's proposal would be to 'bargain away the discretion now allowed to doctors under the omissions doctrine' – a discretion which, for Williams, allows them to sometimes withdraw life-maintaining treatments even though they are not (without legislative intervention) allowed to directly cause a desired death. The point I make in this chapter is that the moral case

---

[61] Andrew Ashworth, 'The Scope of Criminal Liability for Omissions', *Law Quarterly Review*, 105 (1989), 424.

[62] Glanville Williams, 'Criminal Omissions: The Conventional View', *Law Quarterly Review*, 107 (1991), 86.

for that discretion cannot be founded on the act–omission distinction as such. It is grounded in the flexibility required by the duty-holder in a duty-governed relationship to live up to her moral obligations within that relationship – no matter how her conduct is liable to be described in terms of acts and omissions.

14

Professing criminal law

A. T. H. SMITH

This celebration of Glanville Williams' contribution to the world of criminal law scholarship presents an occasion upon which to reflect not only on that contribution,[1] but also upon wider considerations of what professors of the criminal law (the subject broadly conceived)[2] have done and can do in carrying out their professorial duties.[3] The rather limited purpose of this chapter is to alert younger academics, in particular, to the extent to which they become increasingly free to define themselves by what they choose to do as their careers progress. Glanville's was a career that exemplified many dimensions of what is possible, and he excelled in many of them. A survey of his career also affords an opportunity to draw attention to a corollary, namely, that there are certain activities to which academic criminal lawyers are by and large unable to aspire, and in particular the practice of the discipline that they profess.

A principal attraction for those who pursue academic law as a career path is that they are relatively free to make of it what they will. There is no paradigm – we cannot be prescriptive as to what professors of the criminal law should or even might do. Instead, there is a menu of

---

[1] This chapter owes a considerable debt to Peter Glazebrook's description and evaluation of Glanville Williams' life and career: 'Glanville Llewelyn Williams 1911–1997', *Proceedings of the British Academy*, 115 (2002), 411, reprinted in Chapter 1 above. This documented achievement is supplemented in places by personal reminiscence. I hope that I will not be regarded as trespassing upon my readers' patience in so doing.

[2] Glanville Williams' own scholarly range extended to doctrinal criminal law, its theory, evidence and procedure. For the latter, see in particular *The Proof of Guilt: A Study of the English Criminal Trial* (London: Stevens, 1955). Much of his scholarly output in article form was devoted to criminal procedure.

[3] For a recent study of the history of the development of the academic legal role in the United Kingdom, see Fiona Cownie and Raymond Cocks, *A Great and Noble Occupation: The History of the Society of Legal Scholars* (Oxford: Hart, 2009).

possibilities from which scholars are relatively free to choose, within the boundaries dictated by individual aptitudes and the institutional circumstances in which they find (or to which they steer) themselves as careers develop. As a minimum, the modern university-based academic is expected to engage in research[4] and teaching in about equal measure, with the remainder of her or his time devoted to 'administration' or general contribution. Apart from this, there is much more that the academic could do outside the lecture halls and corridors, and Glanville participated in many, perhaps most, of the available options.

He did so, having first established his reputation as a legal scholar of the highest rank, initially in aspects of private law (and in particular the law of obligations)[5] and in public law.[6] He then switched his attentions to the criminal law, which (as far as the world of scholarship in England and Wales was concerned) he utterly dominated for the rest of his life. His impact upon the subject, captured in the remarks of his longstanding friend Lord Edmund-Davies in his introduction to the *Festschrift* presented to Glanville upon his retirement in 1978,[7] was astonishing. Lord Edmund-Davies summarises by saying that whereas the pre-Glanville criminal law was regarded 'with a substantial degree of superciliousness', Glanville 'has been an outstanding member of the small band[8] who have completely transformed the status of criminal law as a subject for academic study'.

For most ordinary human beings, that would have been a sufficient contribution to the world of scholarship. But Glanville was

---

[4] There is nowadays perhaps an emphasis on 'research' reflected in evaluation exercises to which universities are subjected. Funding organisations such as the British Academy now make possible extended periods of reflection of the kind required for research. But the tributes to funding agencies, especially American ones referred to in Glanville Williams' writings, make it plain that support was available for scholars of promise.

[5] *Joint Obligations, A Treatise on Joint and Joint and Several Liability in Contract, Quasi-contract and Trusts* (London: Butterworth, 1949) and *Joint Torts and Contributory Negligence; A Study of Concurrent Fault in Great Britain, Ireland and the Common Law Dominions* (London: Stevens, 1951).

[6] He wrote *Crown Proceedings, An Account of Civil Proceedings by and Against the Crown as Affected by the Crown Proceedings Act, 1947* (London: Stevens, 1948), for example, while holding the Chair of Public Law at the London School of Economics.

[7] P. R. Glazebrook (ed.), *Reshaping the Criminal Law: Essays in Honour of Glanville Williams* (London: Sweet & Maxwell, 1978), p. vii.

[8] It is not entirely clear who this 'small band' would have included, but Sir John Smith (and his co-author Brian Hogan) would probably have been within his contemplation.

extraordinary, and he did so much more than that. He was in addition above all a reformer.[9]

I   The state of English criminal law scholarship in 1953

Glanville's claim to pre-eminence in the criminal law sphere must be judged against the background of criminal law scholarship at the time when he first directed his attention to it, culminating in the publication of the first edition of *Criminal Law: The General Part* in 1953,[10] the work that did so much to establish his reputation.

There was a formidable background tradition of writing about the criminal law, as found in the institutional writers such as Coke's[11] *Institutes*, written in the seventeenth century, and in Hale's[12] and Hawkin's *Pleas of the Crown*,[13] Foster's *Crown Law*,[14] written in the next century, and Blackstone's *Commentaries on the Laws of England*,[15] followed a bit later by East's *Pleas of the Crown*,[16] and later again by Holdsworth's *History of English Law*.[17] The only student text available in the time of the institutional writers was that of Giles',[18] which covered both criminal and civil cases. Whatever insights they might have provided into the history of the criminal law, they had been well and truly overtaken by the growing mass of case law that confronted Glanville

---

[9] The *Festschrift* in his honour, *ibid.*, was subtitled *Reshaping the Criminal Law* in acknowledgement of this. This labelling is entirely consistent with the priorities that Glanville identified to me when I first met him in 1972, namely, his work with the Criminal Law Revision Committee and the Law Commission took precedence over anything other than the requirements of his Chair.

[10] (London: Stevens, 1953), hereinafter *CLGP*.

[11] *The Third Part of the Institutes of the Laws of England: Concerning High Treason, and Other Pleas of the Crown, and Criminall Cases* (London: printed by M. Flesher, for W. Lee and D. Pakeman, 1648).

[12] Matthew Hale, *Historia Placitorum Coronae: The History of the Pleas of the Crown* (London: printed for F. Gyles, T. Woodward and C. Davis, 1736).

[13] William Hawkins, *A Treatise of the Pleas of the Crown*, 2nd edn (London: printed by E. and R. Nutt, and R. Gosling, 1724).

[14] Michael Foster, *Crown Law* (London: printed by W. Strahan and M. Woodfall, 1776).

[15] William Blackstone, *Commentaries on the Laws of England*, vol. IV (Dublin: printed for John Exshaw *et al.*, 1769).

[16] Edward Hyde East, *A Treatise of the Pleas of the Crown* (London: printed by A. Strahan, for J. Butterworth, 1803).

[17] (London: Methuen, 1922).

[18] Jacob Giles, *The Student's Companion: or, the reason of the laws of England* (London: printed by E. and R. Nutt, and R. Gosling, 1725). I am indebted to the editor for this reference.

when he contemplated his task. The same can be said, really, of James Fitzjames Stephen's[19] works[20] which formed the background to that author's prodigious efforts in the field of codification. They gave a wonderfully panoramic view of the background, but were dated when Glanville began. Radzinowicz's four-volume series, *A History of English Criminal Law and its Administration from 1750*,[21] was a modern version of some of Stephen's work, but only volume 1 had been published by the time of the second edition of *The General Part*. The leading practitioners' bible was then *Archbold's Criminal Pleading, Evidence and Practice*.[22]

As far as the study of the criminal law in the universities was concerned, the pickings seem rather thin.[23] In Cambridge, the Regius Professor of Civil Law E. C. Clarke had published a slim volume consisting of his lectures in the latter part of the nineteenth century,[24] but they appear to have had no lasting impact. There were also some occasional volumes dedicated to the examination of select parts of the law, such as R. S. Wright's *The Law of Criminal Conspiracies and Agreements*,[25] D. A. Stroud's *Mens Rea, Or Imputability Under the Law of England*[26] and D. Harrison's *Conspiracy as a Crime and as a Tort in English Law*.[27] Sir Rupert Cross at Oxford, altogether better known for his great work on the law of evidence, came to print rather later with a more overarching conspectus, but his title, *An Introduction to Criminal Law*,[28] gives a clear indication as to his work's aspirations and scope. Also current at the time was J. W. C. Turner's edition of Kenny's

[19] See K. J. M. Smith, *James Fitzjames Stephen, Portrait of a Victorian Rationalist* (Cambridge University Press, 1988); James Coliaco, *James Fitzjames Stephen and the Crisis of Victorian Thought* (New York: St. Martin's Press, 1983) for accounts of Stephen and his works.

[20] *General View of the Criminal Law of England* (London: Macmillan, 1863); *A Digest of the Criminal Law* (London: Macmillan, 1877); *A History of the Criminal Law of England*, 3 vols (London: Macmillan, 1883).

[21] (London: Stevens, 1948–86).

[22] 32nd edn (London: Sweet & Maxwell, 1951), which Glanville had reviewed in *Modern Law Review*, 14 (1951), 233. Volumes are produced annually, and the work is now available on-line. Since 1991 it has been augmented by Blackstone's *Criminal Practice* (Oxford University Press), also published annually and on-line.

[23] I am conscious in making this judgment that the study of law in the universities generally was waking itself from a long slumber.

[24] *An Analysis of Criminal Liability* (Cambridge University Press, 1880), p. 111.

[25] (London: Butterworth, 1873), p. 88. R. S. (later Lord) Wright was identified as being 'Of the Inner Temple, Barrister at Law and Fellow of Oriel College, Oxford'.

[26] (London, Sweet & Maxwell, 1914).   [27] (London: Sweet & Maxwell, 1924).

[28] The first edition had been published in 1948 in London by Butterworth, and the third published in 1953, the same year as the first edition of *CLGP*.

Outlines of Criminal Law,[29] which was just that – an outline intended primarily for teaching purposes. There was, in addition, and also edited by J. W. C. Turner,[30] the two-volume *Russell on Crime.*[31] Although purportedly written with a student audience in mind, its length was such that it seems far too detailed for that purpose. The 12th edition, published in 1964, was the last. In Cambridge, J. W. C. Turner and Arthur Armitage produced a casebook on criminal law,[32] but this was manifestly intended to be a teaching aid rather than a serious contribution to a deeper form of scholarship.

In short, there was no book that was

> concerned to search out the general principles that apply to more than one crime ... By bringing together the authorities on such concepts as knowledge, intent to defraud, and claim of right, the root principles are thrown into relief, and the attention of the practitioner is directed to the relevant authorities that may be decided under different statutes from the one with which he is immediately concerned.[33]

For the first time, then, a book was being written at a level of principle with practitioners rather than students in mind. The non-student nature of the audience contemplated is important, since it is somewhat less necessary to identify a definite structure or taxonomy in a treatise than it is with a student text.

Glanville had intended that his work would be followed 'with a companion volume on specific crimes'.[34] By the time he invited me to collaborate with him on one such volume in 1973, the project had grown in ambition to three companion volumes, on offences against the person, the state and property.[35] Glanville's dedication to his work on reforming the law, and his decision to publish the new work, *A Textbook*

---

[29] 1st edn (Cambridge University Press, 1902), which was described by Kenny himself in the preface as 'another elementary manual'.

[30] Glanville makes some complimentary remarks about the contribution of Turner in his *CLGP* (p. 111 n. 19), though he does so largely as a preliminary to taking issue with what he had to say. Turner also wrote, with L. Radzinowicz, *The Modern Approach to Criminal Law* (London: Macmillan, 1945).

[31] 12th edn (London: Stevens, 1964).

[32] *Cases on Criminal Law*, 1st edn (Cambridge University Press, 1953).

[33] *CLGP*, p. v.   [34] *Ibid.*

[35] The publishers had intended that this would replace *Russell on Crime.* I was invited to take my pick as to which volume I preferred, and I chose property offences, which was eventually published as *Property Offences: The Protection of Property through the Criminal Law* (London: Sweet & Maxwell, 1994) to which Glanville contributed a generous prefatory note.

of Criminal Law,[36] meant that this daunting agenda proved to be too much even for his prodigious energies.

Quite apart from the attention paid to the criminal law in his texts and treatises, regard should also be had to Glanville's contributions to the subject through the periodical literature. The treatment of the criminal law in the leading periodical publications such as the *Law Quarterly Review*, the *Cambridge Law Journal* and the *Modern Law Review* before he turned his attention to the criminal law was sparse. Glanville is also credited with having a considerable input into the founding of the *Criminal Law Review*, first published in 1954 – his was the first article,[37] although he was never a member of its editorial board, which was established in 1959.

The 1953 edition of *The General Part* was, then, a new departure in the discussion of the criminal law.[38] Where did the idea of 'the General Part' actually come from? It was only partly codified in Stephen's Code. Glanville says in the preface to the first edition that it came from 'the Continent'. 'Continental' criminal law scholarship was relatively inaccessible, certainly to those without knowledge of the German language, and no work emanating from European scholarship is mentioned in the bibliography to *The General Part*.

Glanville may have been influenced by American literature, and by the writings of Jerome Hall[39] in particular, with whose works he was clearly familiar, more than has been generally appreciated. In the 1950s, Glanville spent quite a bit of time at Columbia University and at New York University. The *Sanctity of Life*[40] book was originally prepared as a series of lectures delivered in America, and the second edition of *The General Part* was completed when he was in the United States. His knowledge of the American law seems to have been derived in the first instance from a number of casebooks. He says as much in the preface to the first edition. There is a reference in *The General Part*

[36] (London: Stevens, 1978); 2nd edn, 1983. A third edition has been published by Dr D. Baker (London: Sweet & Maxwell, 2012).
[37] 'Requisites of a Valid Arrest', *Criminal Law Review*, [1954], 6.
[38] At the time of writing the work upon which his reputation was ultimately to be founded, Glanville was the Quain Professor of Jurisprudence in the University of London, at University College. He returned to Cambridge in 1955 as a lecturer, and was successively Reader, Professor of English Law and Rouse Ball Professor of English Law from 1968–1978.
[39] Review of *Theft, Law and Society*, *Journal of the Society of Public Teachers of Law*, 2 (1953) (N.S.), 137.
[40] (London: Faber & Faber, 1958).

'abbreviations'[41] to the first edition of Hall's *Principles of Criminal Law*,[42] which had been published in 1947. That book starts with a discussion of 'criminal law theory' and then goes on to discuss the constitutional context. This was based on work that Hall had done in the 1930s – he gave a paper on the principle of legality and the criminal law at a conference in The Hague in 1937, which displayed a familiarity with the European jurisprudence in the area in German and French.

II   Glanville's influence on writing about the criminal law

It is slightly easier to trace some of the effects that Glanville's writings had on the scholarship to come, starting with Sir John Smith's seminal work, jointly with Brian Hogan, *Criminal Law*,[43] which states in the preface:

> In particular, we would acknowledge our debt, which will be apparent in almost every chapter, to the writings of Dr Glanville Williams.

Subsequently, the search for principle is evident in Andrew Ashworth's *Principles of Criminal Law*,[44] and then in Simester and Sullivan, *Criminal Law: Theory and Doctrine*[45] and in Glanville's own *Textbook of Criminal Law*,[46] a new edition of which has been published in 2012 by Dr Dennis Baker.

III   Reformer

Glanville's input into the law reform process took a number of forms. Probably the principal strategy through which he pursued his reforming efforts was as a committee man via institutional reform agencies, such as

---

[41] The works listed in the 'abbreviations' section of the book are what might now be termed a bibliography. There are sixty such references, of which twenty are American in origin, and four from Commonwealth jurisdictions.

[42] (Indianapolis, IN: Bobbs-Merrill, 1947).

[43] J. C. Smith and Brian Hogan, *Criminal Law* (London: Butterworth, 1965). (Glanville reviewed the book in the *Journal of the Society of Public Teachers of Law*, 9 (1966) (N.S.), 169. The work is now in its 13th edition (2011), edited by David Ormerod.

[44] First published in 1991 by Oxford University Press, the work is now in its 6th edition (2009).

[45] First published in 2000 by Hart, Oxford, now in its 4th edition (2010) with assistance from J. R. Spencer and G. Virgo. Professor Simester has also published a book on New Zealand law, *Principles of Criminal Law*, 3rd edn (Wellington: Thomson/Brookers, 2007) with W. J. Brookbanks.

[46] See above, n. 36.

the Criminal Law Revision Committee[47] and the Law Commission. Lord Edmund-Davies in his introduction to *Reshaping the Criminal Law*[48] says of Glanville and the Criminal Law Revision Committee that he 'had been a member ever since it was established in 1959 and had, indeed, been largely responsible for its inception'.[49] It was this Committee whose report was at the base of the Suicide Act 1961. His influence on the reform of the law of theft/larceny is very clear in the Eighth Report[50] and many of the recommendations of the Eleventh Report,[51] which eventually saw the light of day in the Police and Criminal Evidence Act 1984, clearly have their origins in his earlier writings.

Like most academics of his era, he was an advocate of the enactment of a criminal code,[52] which has ultimately proved to be unsuccessful. In particular, the codification of the criminal law, a battle more or less won in the United States through the influence of such titans as Herb Wechsler,[53] has faltered if not foundered in England on the rock of political indifference.[54] The case for a code may be unanswerable. Even the judiciary, who were responsible for scuppering such attempts in the nineteenth century,[55] are now by and large fully behind it. There have been articles in favour by judges as eminent as Lord Bingham when he was Chief Justice[56] and Arden LJ.[57] But politicians in pursuit of glory elsewhere do not feel the need even to answer, never mind act upon, these recommendations.

---

[47] For a potted history, see A. T. H. Smith, in P. Cane and J. Conaghan (eds), *The New Oxford Companion to Law* (Oxford University Press, 2008), p. 274.

[48] Glazebrook, *Reshaping the Criminal Law*.   [49] *Ibid.*, at p. vii.

[50] *Theft and Related Offences* (1966), Cmnd. 2977. See Sir John Smith, 'The Sad Fate of the Theft Act 1968', in W. Swadling and G. Jones (eds), *The Search for Principle: Essays in Honour of Lord Goff* (Oxford University Press, 2000).

[51] *Evidence (General)* (1972), Cmnd. 4991.

[52] In *The Reform of the Law* (1951), prepared by members of the Haldane Society, but edited by Glanville, there is a section on codification (pp. 15–21) and a long section on the state of the criminal law (pp. 154–202).

[53] See Michael Moore, 'The specialness of the general part of the criminal law', Chapter 4, above.

[54] In 2008, the Law Commission announced that it had abandoned the codification project in favour of specific reform projects: *Tenth Programme of Law Reform*, Law Com. No. 311 (2008).

[55] In particular, there was opposition from Cockburn LCJ; see R. Cross, 'The Making of English Criminal Law', *Criminal Law Review*, [1978], 652, 657.

[56] 'A Criminal Code: Must We Wait for Ever?' *Criminal Law Review*, [1988], 694.

[57] 'Criminal Law at the Crossroads: The Impact of the Human Rights Act from the Law Commission's Perspective, and the Need for a Criminal Code', *Criminal Law Review*, [1999], 439.

One of Glanville's abiding characteristics was that he was utterly indefatigable in pursuit of his chosen causes, one example of which can be illustrated by his campaign over the law governing attempting the impossible, which I recount largely because I had something of a ringside seat. Famously, Glanville took the view that there was no such phenomenon as an impossible attempt. All attempts were, by definition, failures, and in that sense impossible and it made no sense to seek to draw a distinction between so-called 'legal impossibility' and 'factual impossibility' as his most famous opponent, Sir John Smith, sought to do. Sir John's version had been accepted by the House of Lords in *Haughton* v. *Smith*,[58] enthusiastically championed by Lord Hailsham, in particular. The Criminal Attempts Bill, as drafted at the behest of the Law Commission, made no such distinction – impossibility was henceforth no longer to be regarded as any answer to the charge of attempt. But when a bill was introduced into Parliament, it had been changed. Some anonymous figure in the Home Office had, without any word of public explanation, reintroduced a distinction. Glanville was furious – we know that, because he wrote an article in the *New Law Journal*[59] saying so. Then, very unusually, when the Criminal Attempts Bill was being deliberated at Committee stage in Parliament, he went to Parliament to discuss with the relevant Committee, in the company of Sir John Smith who, although he had been an opponent on the issue, agreed to wave the white flag, conceding that he could not devise a verbal formula that would capture the distinction that he had sought to draw. So the Act as passed reflected the position adopted by the Law Commission – no defence of impossibility.

That was the background to the decision of the House of Lords in *Anderton* v. *Ryan*[60] in which the House of Lords came to the conclusion that there was a distinction between factual and legal impossibility after all. That really set him off, and he composed a coruscating response – eventually published in the *Cambridge Law Journal*.

It was not very long before the issue arose again in *Shivpuri*.[61] The House of Lords decided to reverse its own previous decision, admitting that it had been wrong – using the power under the 1966 Practice

---

[58] [1975] AC 476.
[59] Glanville Williams, 'The Governments Proposals on Criminal Attempts', *New Law Journal*, 131 (1981), 80, 104, 128. The second part of the article in particular is one of the most ferocious attacks on a government department that I can recall seeing in print.
[60] [1985] AC 560.   [61] [1987] AC 1.

Statement to do so. Glanville's part in shaping the court's decision is acknowledged by Lord Bridge, whose judgment had the approval of all the other members of the House.

> I cannot conclude this opinion without disclosing that I have had the advantage, since the conclusion of the argument in this appeal, of reading an article by Professor Glanville Williams entitled 'The Lords and Impossible Attempts, or *Quis Custodiet Ipsos Custodes?*' [1986] 45 CLJ 33. The language in which he criticises the decision in *Anderton* v. *Ryan* is not conspicuous for its moderation, but it would be foolish, on that account, not to recognise the force of the criticism and churlish not to acknowledge the assistance I have derived from it.

If Lord Bridge thought that the published version of the article was intemperate, it is just as well that he did not see an earlier draft. It is my fond hope that, somewhere in my jumbled papers, I still have the original draft of that article. Had the then editor of the *Cambridge Law Journal* had the temerity to publish it uncensored, both he and Glanville could easily have found themselves answering a charge of contempt of court.[62]

Although a determined crusader, Glanville appears never to have sought the pulpit[63] of an editorship from which to conduct his campaigns. Instead, he waged war through letters to *The Times*, in the pages of the *Criminal Law Review*,[64] which was a very good vehicle for much of this advocacy, since it was produced monthly and read by practitioners (and civil servants in the Home Office as well as by academics), and by publications in the weekly *New Law Journal*.

Glanville's insistence on the central importance of improving the law not infrequently led to his being something of a campaigner.[65] He was President of the Abortion Law Reform Association, and a Vice-President

---

[62] As a footnote to that episode, I can report that Glanville told me that he had sent to the members of the House of Lords the bowdlerised version of the article to assist them in their deliberations. That was the version to which Lord Bridge referred in *Shivpuri*. But Lord Hailsham, whom Glanville regarded as one of the villains in the whole affair replied, thanking Glanville for his efforts, and promising to read the article *after* he had delivered his speech.

[63] I do not use the word with any pejorative connotations. The editorship of a journal such as the *Criminal Law Review* by tradition requires an editorial preface. That particular publication has been blessed with a series of remarkable editors: Andrew Ashworth (1975–1998); Ian Dennis (1998–2011); and latterly (2012–) David Ormerod. Sir John Smith's case commentaries constitute a remarkable and important contribution to criminal law scholarship by any measure of reckoning.

[64] In the period between 1954 and his last article in the *Review* in 1991, he published seventy articles in that periodical.

[65] Glazebrook, Chapter 1, above, uses the word 'polemicist'.

of the Voluntary Euthanasia Society. Peter Glazebrook points out that he refused the presidency of the latter at the persuasion of his wife,[66] who wished to spare him from the immense burdens that such an office would hold. There are here, I believe, lessons for those who contemplate participation in the major issues of the day by way of public advocacy and debate. Particularly where the field is already populated with well-resourced and very vocal pressure groups, the amount of time that can be consumed in engagement with one's critics and detractors is enormous, and may be regarded as a distraction from the central academic role. Participants might be obliged to counter suggestions that they are some-how abusing their position in the academy or at any rate trespassing into areas beyond their competence.[67] Against this, it can be argued that the academic has an obligation to participate in this way. It might even be argued that members of universities are under some sort of obligation to engage in this sort of advocacy. A high point of this perspective is to be found in the New Zealand Education Act 1989, section 162 of which actually provides that it is a characteristic of universities that they are expected to act as 'critic and conscience of society'. I am not sure that this aspiration is one to which I personally am able to rise, at least not on a regular basis.

As far as being a campaigner for many controversial causes in favour of a more relaxed law governing abortion and euthanasia is concerned, one cannot be disqualified simply because one happens to have a pro-fessional interest in the subject, but, equally, one has to be careful not to pretend to a level of expertise that is not given to others in the debate, let alone a monopoly as to the truth.

It strikes me that the would-be criminal law reformer in the United Kingdom has a much harder task in 2012 than was formerly the case. In the last twenty years, the criminal justice process has become the playground of competing political ideologies, none of them much interested in criminal law principle or theory. The prospects for reforming the law, when the prime movers in the political process (politicians, their political advisers and civil servants) will not listen are bleak. Contribution to law reform is one of the most worthwhile activities in which an academic can engage, but it can have considerable costs in terms of time and energy that might more profitably be directed elsewhere. Even contributing to the debates set in motion by agencies such as the Law Commission is not without price. 'Consultation fatigue' sets in when there is a welter of discussion papers, white papers and

---

[66] *Ibid.*   [67] See, e.g., the concluding paragraph of Chapter 11 by John Keown, above.

reports, and the academic has to choose with some care the extent to which participation is possible.

IV Expounder and explainer

Another function that the professor may choose to undertake is that of expounder and explainer, without necessarily having reform as a primary concern. I associate this outlook with George Fletcher, in particular,[68] and in this country with Sir John Smith[69] and such successors as Andrew Ashworth,[70] and Simester and Sullivan.[71] The role is to explain what is the law, and why it is in its current state. This sort of approach will frequently give rise, it is true, to the identification of anomalies and inconsistencies that call out for rectification and amendment, but such scholarship does not have reform as its principal aim. The *CLGP* falls at this point on what might be thought of as a spectrum, being principally a work of exposition, with calls for the reform of the law sprinkled throughout the work.

I am not sure, though, that he was interested in theory (as opposed to principle), and certainly not for its own sake – he was too much the utilitarian for that. For example, he did not think that the distinction between justification and excuse was of any real significance, sharing Stephen's view that because nothing seemed in practice to turn on it in the sense that if a defence availed, it did not much matter whether it was to be characterised as a justification or an excuse, and it was not for him an interesting area of further study.[72] The publication of George Fletcher's *Rethinking* forced him to have another look at this, but ultimately he appears to have been unconvinced.[73]

---

[68] George P. Fletcher, *Rethinking Criminal Law* (Boston, MA: Little, Brown, 1978).

[69] In particular, in his case notes for the *Criminal Law Review*, his book with Brian Hogan, *Criminal Law*, and his work on *The Law of Theft* (Oxford University Press, 1968), now authored by their successor David Ormerod.

[70] With his work, *Principles of Criminal Law* (Oxford University Press, 2009).

[71] *Criminal Law: Theory and Doctrine* (Oxford: Hart, 2010).

[72] I was privileged to hold a joint undergraduate seminar series with him in the late 1970s in Cambridge. I was never able to persuade him that the justification–excuse distinction was one that was an important explanatory framework. Joshua Dressler's chapter, 'Reflections on *Dudley and Stephens* and Killing the Innocent: Taking a Wrong Conceptual Path', Chapter 6, above, clarifies the questions with which we are confronted.

[73] Glanville Williams, 'The Theory of Excuses', *Criminal Law Review*, [1982], 732. See also P. Robinson, Chapter 5, above.

V   Teacher and educator

People outside the academy would be surprised, perhaps, by the fact that I have not before this mentioned the professorial role as educator and teacher. I had virtually no first-hand experience of Glanville in this role (at the undergraduate level), although I did attend some of his lectures. It was in the course of seeking his permission to do so that he confided to me that he did not regard himself as being a particularly good lecturer. I have no way of determining whether this was an accurate self-assessment. If true, it could well have been that in some ways his mind was almost too quicksilver – he could see problems and answers that the rest of us could only glimpse. That was true even of his academic colleagues, who regularly foregathered to discuss the criminal law questions of the day.

His slightly cavalier approach to the undertaking of supervising research (he once told me that he did not really believe in doctorates, largely, I believe, because so many languished on library shelves rather than seeing the printer's ink) would no doubt be regarded with considerable misgivings now that the doctoral path is seen as a form of research training. There was no attempt on his part to groom a series of acolytes, although many of his former students (the Australian Colin Howard, Hearn Professor of Law, University of Melbourne 1965–1990, and serving as dean of law from 1978 to 1983; the Canadian Martin Friedland, James M. Tory Professor of Law Emeritus, University of Toronto; and Stanley de Smith, Downing Professor of the Laws of England 1970–1974, whose *Judicial Review of Administrative Act*[74] began life as a PhD at the London School of Economics) were supervised by Glanville before going on to reach the heights of legal scholarship.

VI   Administrator

One professorial role that the academic criminal lawyer, like any other member of a modern law faculty, might be expected to undertake is that of administration, both within one's own university and nationally.[75]

---

[74] (London: Stevens, 1st edn, 1959; 2nd edn, 1968; 3rd edn, 1973).

[75] One role that Glanville fulfilled with his usual gusto was to act as the President of the Society of Public Teachers of Law (as it then was – now the Society of Legal Scholars). He was instrumental in setting up the subject sections to promote the discussion of legal issues at the annual conferences. See Cownie and Cocks, *A Great and Noble Occupation*, pp. 152–3.

Most modern faculties are run with the help of committees that give advice upon such matters as resource management, law library liaison, promotions and academic appointments, and so forth. Taking on the head of school/faculty role is a major step up in terms of commitment in this process. Historically, this has required the individual to undertake the role and, in consequence, to rein back for a period (usually about three years) from activities such as research, on a kind of rotation basis. Bill Elliott at Newcastle[76] and Edward Griew at Leicester were examples of this. Glanville did a turn as Chairman of the Faculty at Cambridge. Sir John Smith did it very successfully for many years at Nottingham. Sir Arthur Armitage, having been Vice-Chancellor of Cambridge and President of Queens' College, then became Vice-Chancellor of Manchester and Sir David Williams became the first full-time Vice-Chancellor of Cambridge.

A question arises as to whether the holding of these increasingly substantial posts is any longer compatible with serious scholarship, given the changing expectations of management within modern universities. James Hathaway, who was for a short time Dean and Professor of Law in the University of Melbourne, in a brief but provocative paper,[77] posed the question thus to a meeting of the Association of Law Deans:

> The question I pose is therefore whether even well-intentioned, administratively attuned, and prepared-to-play-a-supporting-role scholars are best positioned to serve as modern law deans. Or has the nature of the law school enterprise evolved to a point where our continued attachment to the scholar-as-dean paradigm is in truth largely anachronistic, even if romantically appealing?

The answer that I would give to this question[78] is that it is in truth becoming increasingly difficult. Matters such as institutional fundraising and the managing of increasingly large budgets require time, energy and concentration on a sustained basis, so that making time to keep abreast of developments in one's subjects, never mind finding the time to reflect

---

[76] Author of D. W. Elliott and J. C. Wood, *A Casebook on Criminal Law* (London: Sweet & Maxwell, 1963) now in its 10th edition. Bill was a founder member of the Editorial Board of the *Criminal Law Review* in 1959, and remained a member until his death in January 2004.

[77] 'The Dean as Drudge', available at: www.ialsnet.org/meetings/role/papers/HathawayJames(Australia).pdf, accessed 23 May 2012.

[78] I write as one who is something of a recidivist Dean, having occupied the role (although not necessarily by that title) in the universities of Reading and Cambridge and now Victoria University, Wellington, New Zealand.

upon what one has read becomes increasingly problematic. Furthermore, the demands of a decanal diary are such that it becomes increasingly difficult to undertake lecturing and other forms of teaching within a regular programme, which takes away the stimulus to think in structured ways about recent developments. Research supervision at postgraduate level is certainly a much more easily accommodated possibility – that is, in my experience, frequently a source of ideas for further investigation and thought – but the ancient enemy too easily prevails.

VII Legal practice

Perhaps the only area of the legal life in which Glanville did not actively participate was that of practitioner/advocate.[79] In the field of criminal law, not many academics do, at least not in the United Kingdom. It is, I would say, more or less impossible to combine legal practice in criminal law with a serious academic career. Many young academics start in the hope that it will be possible to combine a career in academia and in legal practice. Some Americans appear to be able to do this – and I have in mind in particular the astonishing career of Professor Alan Dershowitz,[80] who rivals even Glanville in his productivity. But it is very difficult in practice to do this in the United Kingdom, principally because one is generally at the mercy of a timetable that is beyond one's control. Even in the sphere of appellate advocacy, which one might have expected to be more amenable to academic input, it is very difficult for a person who is not full-time at the Bar to make an impression in the criminal law sphere.

The situation is not at all like, for example, international law, where many scholars are advocates too, frequently proceeding from there to the bench. Lord McNair,[81] was a doyen of this group, but he was joined by

---

[79] Glanville was qualified at the Bar, and practised for a while from King's Bench Walk, and he subsequently became an Honorary Bencher of the Middle Temple.

[80] Felix Frankfurter Professor of Law at Harvard University, his website, www.alander-showitz.com, accessed 23 May 2012, lists no fewer than twenty-seven books (two of them being novels). The site also notes that over the course of his thirty-five-year career as a lawyer, Dershowitz has won more than 100 cases – a remarkable record for a part-time litigator who handles primarily criminal appeals.

[81] Lord McNair (1885–1975) had an astonishing career. Appointed to the Whewell Chair of International Law in Cambridge at the age of fifty, he became Vice-Chancellor of the University of Liverpool two years later, returning to Cambridge as Professor of Comparative Law. He then became a judge of the International Court of Justice (1946), President from 1952 to 1955, and President of the European Court of Human Rights, Strasbourg (1959–1965).

his successor in the Whewell Chair of International Law at Cambridge, Sir Hersch Lauterpacht,[82] Sir Robert Jennings[83] and Sir Christopher Greenwood.[84] Professor James Crawford (Cambridge), and Professors Ian Brownlie and Vaughan Lowe (Oxford) are other distinguished scholar practitioners. Nor is this phenomenon confined to the United Kingdom. Sir Kenneth Keith from New Zealand took a similar route, having been Dean at Victoria University, Wellington before being called to the Court of Appeal, to the Supreme Court and ultimately to the International Court of Justice. It is always invidious to produce such lists, I know, and I dare say that readers will have many names that could and should have been added, but this roll call does show what is possible in some subject areas. I suspect that there are some other areas of practice in which it is possible to combine the two,[85] but the criminal law is not one of them.

Nor is the situation like that which prevails in many continental jurisdictions, where it is common for professors to hold positions as members (sometimes very senior members) of the judiciary.[86] In the United Kingdom, it is possible for academics to sit, part-time, in the Crown Court as Recorders, but rare for them to go much further.

VIII   Concluding remarks

A final question arises, for me at least, as to what made Glanville such an extraordinarily good legal scholar? There were several components to this. He wrote with an extraordinary facility and fluency, made all the more potent when his publishers, Sweet & Maxwell, decided that his productivity would be enhanced by giving him a computer. Since at that time (1982) we were collaborators, I too decided to take the plunge – he was the first person to introduce me to the computer and its possibilities.[87]

---

[82] The one having written a charming book about the other: E. Lauterpacht, *The Life of Hersch Lauterpacht* (Cambridge University Press, 2010).

[83] 1982–1995; President, 1991–1994.

[84] Since 2008 a judge of the International Court of Justice. Immediately prior to that he had practised at the Bar and was a professor at the London School of Economics.

[85] Chancery and commercial law being obvious examples, their efforts being rather less visible than those just cited. Professors Sir Roy Goode, Queen Mary College and latterly Oxford, and Rob Merkin, Southampton University, are species of this phenomenon.

[86] See J. Bell, *Judiciaries Within Europe* (Cambridge University Press, 2006).

[87] I was then at the University of Durham and recall successfully applying for a grant from an agency responsible for introducing computers throughout the tertiary education

He had, in addition, a phenomenal memory. In an age when information is increasingly accessible at the click of an 'enter' button on iPad or iPhone, this faculty might appear to be of decreasing relevance or importance. My own view is that a good memory is a great asset in academic as in other walks of life. In Glanville's case, his recall was by no means confined to matters legal. He had great ability to remember and deploy information from his literary and scientific readings. Furthermore, he could see links between the different 'branches' of the law, and was not constrained by the legal categorisation that teachers of the law (and writers about it) feel forced to adopt. He was possessed of an unbelievable work ethic, and was intellectually indefatigable.[88] When all of these characteristics and abilities were united in one person, they produced the cleverest, most intellectually charismatic and able academic lawyer that I have ever had the good luck to meet.

sector, with a view to considering its application to law. This eventually gave rise to the establishment of a Centre for Law and Computing at Durham in 1988.

[88] He once told me that his wife forbade him to work too late in to the evenings, or to get up too early.

INDEX

best interests tests 300
  failure of 301–2
Betty case 242
bind-over powers/orders 45–6, 48
  imprisonment as enforcement of 50, 65–7
  reform of 46–7, 50–2, 63, 64, 66, 67–8
  Williams' criticism of x, 45, 49–50, 53, 63, 66, 67
Bingham, Lord 238, 239, 300
blame 179, 180–1, 191, 195–6, 201
  and culpability 181–3, 198–9, 202–3
Bland case 296–7, 299–301, 319, 320
  interpretations of judgment 298–9, 301–5, 325
Blum, Lawrence 311
Bodkin Adams case 286–7
du Bois-Pedain, Antje xiii
'Book Review of Sanford H. Kadish: *Encyclopedia of Crime and Justice*' (article, Williams) 38–9
Bosco v. *Serhant* 241
Bourne case 283–4
Bradley, F. H. 103
breach of the peace 47–8, 49
  jurisprudence on 53–7
  and unlawful violence 53–7
Bridge, Lord 336–7
Brongersma case 291–2
Brooke LJ 277, 284
Browne-Wilkinson, Lord 320
Butler-Sloss LJ 300

Cane, Peter 73, 84, 87
capacity
  diminished 115–16
  theories of culpability based on 183–5
    criticism of 185–6
  to refuse 210–11
    and sufficient understanding 212–13
care, duty of 297, 305–6, 325
  and duty to preserve life 298, 303–4
  See also conflicts of duties
  and good intentions 321–2

morality of 297, 305, 311–12
  in doctor–patient relationships 312–16
  legal recognition of 297–8, 323–5
  and persistent vegetative state 303–25
Carrier's case 27
Cases on Criminal Law (Turner and Armitage) 332
causation 87–8, 94
  argument in euthanasia cases 287
  theory of secondary liability 238–44
Causation in the Law (Hart and Honoré) 37
Chabot case 291
character-based theories of culpability 193–4
  criticism of 194–9
  integration with choice-based theories 199–201
children
  euthanasia on 267
  evidence given by 18
  teenagers, emotional vulnerability of 214
choice theory
  culpability based on 185–9
    criticism of 196–7
    and inadvertent negligence 190–3
    integration with character-based theories 199–201
  and excuse defences 144, 187–8
Clarke, E. C. 331
codes of conduct, and adjudication 118
codification of criminal law 335
Coleridge, Lord 131–4, 139, 144–5, 278–9
comparative law 43, 44
competence, of patients 314–15
complicity
  criminal liability of 97–9
  and doctrines of imputation 115
  in homicide 231, 246
    jurisprudence on 241–4
  See also joint enterprise liability; secondary liability
The Concept of Law (Hart) 7

9 781107 536241